BERTRAND LOUIS CONWAY

CW01044125

CATHOLIC FAITH

Q&A

NIHIL SINE DEO

Autor: **Bertrand Louis Conway**
Editor: **Francesco Tosi**

Editio Princeps: *The Question-Box answers, Replies to questions received on missions to non-catholics, The Catholic Book Exchange, New York, 1903.*

ISBN edizione cartacea: 9798603862187

PREFACE.

THE Apostolate to the Non-Catholics of
our country, so dear to the heart of Father
Hecker, has proved itself a movement
blessed by God in the thousands of converts it has won to the true Church. Within the past ten years it has been success-
fully inaugurated by the regular and secular clergy in over sixty dioceses of the
United States, and its future is' assured because of the special commendation of Pope
Leo XIII. and the American Hierarchy.

Although no man can blind himself to the
fact that we are living in a period of wide-
spread indifferentism and unbelief, still the
hearty welcome given to the Paulist Fathers
everywhere in the missions to non-Catholics goes to evidence the intense longing
of thousands of earnest souls for the truth
of God. The many outside the fold are
like travellers lost in a forest at night, per-
plexed, worried, anxious, on the alert for a

divine guide to lead them out of the labyrinth of their doubting. What better field for the Church than in this our beloved country, where the multitudes require but the kindly presentation of the Church's claims, and the heartful prayers of the Catholic people, to answer God's call to believe?

The Question Box is the most interesting feature of these missions to non-Catholics. At the door of the church a box is placed, and into it non-Catholics are cordially invited to deposit their difficulties and objections. These are answered the following evening. In this way the lecturer learns the mental troubles of his particular audience, and his fair, kindly answering interests the most listless and disarms the most prejudiced. The Agnostic finds his doubts vanish; the Protestant his prejudices disappear; and the Catholic his faith strengthened. Frequently the unlearning of one lie, or the answering of one difficulty, removes the veil that hid the beauty of the Church from some good soul, and he becomes "obedient to the heavenly vision."

This book answers in a brief and popular manner the most important questions actually received by the author during the past five years of missionary activity in all parts of the United States from Boston to Denver. Its object is to interest fair-minded inquirers in the further study of the Church's claims, by removing many of their false notions regarding her. We hope that many of the clean of heart approaching this study in the humble, docile spirit of the child, and asking not " How can these things be ? " but simply " Has God revealed these truths ? " will find their prayer for light answered by the Holy Spirit of Truth. May He guide them back to the fold of the one True Shepherd !

Faithfully yrs. in X°.

James Card. Gibbons

Archbp. of Baltimore

FEAST OF THE CONVERSION OF ST. PAUL,
BALTIMORE.

THE QUESTION BOX.

THE EXISTENCE OF GOD.

How do you prove to a certainty the existence of God? Cannot a man be moral without belief in God? Is not virtue its own reward?

The most common proof, and perhaps the oldest argument, is the argument from design ("The heavens show forth the glory of God, and the firmament declareth the work of His hands."—Ps. xviii. 1); namely, that the harmony and order of the universe point to an Intelligent and Infinite Designer, God. The chronometer with every particle of its mechanism moving in such perfect harmony as to declare the time of day to a second; the automatic machines in our large factories, which do the work of thousands of men silently from morning until night under the influence of steam or electricity, evidence a skilled human intelligence that designed them. So likewise this vast universe of ours, with its thousands of complex, interlacing laws, all manifesting a wondrous intelligent adaptation of means to ends, points to a Supreme Intelligence that designed them all.

The heavens with its myriads of stars revolving through space without the slightest interference one with the other; this earth with its quick rush through space, of which we are unconscious; the constant succession of the seasons, the beauty of the structure of the tiniest fern, the laws of instinct in the brute creation, the special adaptation of the various organs and senses of the human body, all declare an Intelligent Lawmaker by whose wisdom all has been established.

Scientific men have in our day of unbelief endeavored to destroy the force of this argument; but their attempt has failed, for science is merely furnishing new data for its defence. Says Professor Huxley ("Evolution and Ethics," page 58, Appleton, 1894) : "If the belief in a God is essential to morality, physical science has no more to say against the probability of that doctrine than the most ordinary experience has. And it effectually closes the mouths of those who pretend to refute it by objections drawn from merely physical data."

Some have said that this harmony is due to mere physical causes, and that matter must necessarily obey the laws of nature. But who but God established these laws? To say that nature did, is to make nature intelligent, or to call God by another name. Again, with some the theory of evolution has in some way wea ened the force of this argument. And yet, as Romanes declared (*Nineteenth Century*, June, 1888), all that evolution has accomplished "is to throw back the question of design from the facts immediately observed to the causes subsequently discovered. And there the question must be left by science, to be taken up by philosophy." As the evidence of design points to a Designer, so evolution points to an Intelligence who is the origin of the universal law of progress.

Again, the fact that all nations, civilized and barbarian alike, have believed in the existence of a Supreme Being admits of but one explanation, viz., that the human mind, by the principle of causality, can prove that God does exist. So plain is this that the Psalmist and the Apostle do not hesitate to call those who deny this truth inexcusable and foolish (Ps. lii. 1 ; Rom. i. 20–23), and the Catholic Church voices their teaching in the Vatican Council (Const. Dei Filius, ch. xi.), "declaring that God, the beginning and end of all things, may be known with certainty by the natural light of human reason, by means of created things." (Fox, "Religion and Morality," Part I., ch. ii ; Tylor, "Primitive Culture" ; Quatrefages, "The Human Species" ; Lang, "The Making of Religion.")

One of the strongest and most convincing proofs, however, is the moral argument. In every man, no matter how low he may be in the scale of civilization, there is a conviction of the essential difference between good and evil, and the obligation to do good and avoid evil. No matter how much men may differ as to what is right and what is wrong, all feel that in doing evil (as murder, adultery, theft, calumny) they are going directly against an inward monitor called conscience, which voices the commands of the eternal moral order, and speaks in the name of a Supreme Moral Lawgiver, God.

Men have obeyed this law although it meant the denial of self, and went counter to all their inclinations and desires, for it carried with it the sanction of reward and punishment hereafter. The literature, law, and institutions of all peoples are based on the existence of this moral order, which points clearly to an Eternal Lawgiver who is the origin and foundation thereof.

The unbelievers of our day have attempted in vain to frame theories of morality independent of religion. Is utility to be the basis of morality? Then all those who are a burden to the state, the sick, the aged, the convicts, should not be allowed to live. Is happiness the basis of morality? Then marital infidelity is moral, when both husband and wife agree to be unfaithful. Is virtue its own reward? Experience proves that often virtue walks in rags and poverty, while vice drives by in a coach and four. Is the benefit to posterity sufficient? Not one man in a million would be influenced by that motive.

No, the only basis of morality is the existence of God, the great Lawgiver, who has written His law on the heart of man (Rom. ii. 15), and given him the light of reason to find out the rest of the moral law that He has revealed. "Morality," writes Liddon ("Some Elements of Religion," p. 18), "severed from religious motive, is like a branch cut from a tree; it may here and there, from accidental causes, retain its greenness for awhile, but its chance of vigorous life is a very slender one. Nor is it possible to popularize a real morality, a morality that shall deal with motives as well as with acts, without unveiling to the eye of the soul something more personal than an abstract law." (Fox, "Religion and Morality"; Ward, "Witnesses to the Unseen"; Newman, "Grammar of Assent," ch. v.; Schanz, "Apology," vol. i.; Card. Gibbons, "Our Christian Heritage," chaps. i., ii., iii.; Ronayne, "God, Knowable and Known"; Driscoll, "God.")

Do not some travellers declare that there are tribes without any belief in God?

Many indeed have so declared (Lubbock,

"Origin of Civilization"), only to be corrected by later and more exact investigators, who have shown that the mistake arose from a too superficial study of the religion in question, an ignorance of the peculiar idioms of a language, a false inference whereby tribes with false and crude notions of the Deity were thought absolutely to deny His existence. (Flint, "Antitheistic Theories," p. 525; Tylor, "Primitive Culture," vol. i. ch. xi.; De Harlez, "World's Parliament of Religions," vol. ii. p. 613.)

Is not conscience a sufficient guide for a man, without his believing in God? I know many unbelievers who live better lives than some Christians.

No; for conscience, although it is reason telling us in a particular instance the good to be done and the evil to be avoided, would be powerless to command men unless it voiced the eternal law and spoke with the authority of God. If we were to divorce religion from morality, and allow reason, subject as it is to public opinion, caprice, passion, prejudice, to speak in its own name, the whole basis and sanction of the moral order would at once disappear, and the essential distinction between right and wrong would soon be lost.

Concerning the good lives of unbelievers, Balfour writes: "Biologists tell us of parasites which live, and can only live, within the bodies of animals more highly organized than they. . . . So it is with those persons who claim to show, by their example, that naturalism is practically consistent with the maintenance of ethical ideals with which naturalism has no natural affinity. Their spiritual life is parasitic; it is sheltered by convictions which belong, not to them but to the society of which they form a part; it is nourished by processes in which they take no share. And when those convictions decay, and those processes come to an end, the alien life which they have maintained can scarce be expected to outlast them '' ('' Foundations of Belief,'' pp. 82, 83).

DIVINE PROVIDENCE.

How is it that a good and just God allows the wicked to prosper in the world, while the good are afflicted with every misery?

As a matter of fact prosperity is by no means the special prerogative of the wicked, and misery the universal lot of the good. Many good souls are gifted by God with health, wealth, social position, and other blessings, while the wicked frequently receive their punishment in this life in the form of remorse, poverty, disease, disgrace, imprisonment, and death.

We must also not forget that in the midst of great adversity the virtuous poor frequently possess a happy home, true friends, the consolations of religion, and the joy of a good conscience, which more than compensate for their lack of worldly goods.

Granted, however, that in many an instance the wicked prosper and the good are afflicted. That does not prove God unjust or evil, but proves rather the existence of an after life, where an infinitely just God will right all the injustice of this. This life is a time of trial, during which man must prove himself worthy of eternal happiness. The reward comes only after our work is done,—at the hour of death. The sufferings, therefore, of the good in this life. ought to be regarded as part of the punishment due to their sins and as a chance of merit, while the prosperity of the wicked ought to be looked upon as the reward here for the good they have wrought. "Woe to you that are rich, for you have your consolation" (Luke vi. 24). "For I reckon that the sufferings of this time are not worthy to be compared with the glory to come" (Rom. viii. 18).

MORAL AND PHYSICAL EVIL.

If God is infinitely good, why does so much evil exist in the world? Why does not God, who is all powerful, destroy evil? Christians must choose between either horn of this dilemma: if God cannot prevent evil, He is not omnipotent. If God will not, He is not infinitely good.

The difficulty of reconciling the existence of evil with the providence of God has been felt from the beginning. Christianity does not pretend to answer the problem fully, but declares it the height of folly for men to deny the many and overwhelming proofs that reason gives us of God's infinite goodness and love, simply because in our ignorance we cannot explain the complete working out of the divine plan.

The Christian is not disconcerted by the existence of physical evils, for he knows they are the consequence of original sin. If Adam had been faithful, the race would have been free therefrom. The Christian realizes also that much of the poverty, sickness, and misery in the world is directly traceable to the actual sins of men. Is it reasonable to blame God for the poverty of the tenement-house dweller, when often we know that it is due to the drunkenness and improvidence of an unworthy father of a family? Is it reasonable to blame God for the diseased children who are the fruit of immoral parents? God, indeed, could, in His omnipotence, prevent nature's laws from acting in these cases; but no one can prove that *He is bound* to perform a miracle.

The Christian, again, knows that physical evil is often in reality a positive favor and blessing of God to the individual, and always, though we in our ignorance may not perceive it, has some good purpose in God's universal plan. That frequently a bed of pain has brought a great sinner back after many years to his God, the priest who works among the people can testify. How often the loss of worldly goods has stripped a man of his pride, avarice, and lust, because he began for the first time to realize the uncertainty of material prosperity and the fact of his utter dependence on God. God can bring good out of evil, as we see in the case of Joseph in the Old Law, or in the great mystery of the redemption—the death of Jesus Christ at the hands of those He came to save. Even if we at times cannot see the good, our reason tells us it must be there.

But the innocent suffer so much! Granted, but again Christianity teaches that this life is not the all; that physical evils give us a chance to acquire the virtues of humility and patience, to satisfy in union with Christ for our sins, and to merit through Christ for God's kingdom. They are a constant reminder that "we have not here a lasting city, but we seek one that is to come" (Heb. xiii. 14); "for that which is at present momentary and light of our tribulation, worketh for us above measure exceedingly an eternal weight of glory" (II. Cor. iv. 17).

With regard to moral evil, the Catholic Church teaches that God in no way wills sin. On the contrary every page of Scripture witnesses how greatly He detests it, and how severely He punishes it. Any sect which made God the author of evil, was by the very fact stamped as an irrational and immoral parody of Christianity.

Does God cease to be infinitely good because the creatures He made with free will to obey His law, and endowed with the grace necessary to fulfil their destiny, refuse knowingly and deliberately to observe that law, and reject God's proffered help? God is perfect justice, and will take into account every possible factor that might palliate the sins of men, such as the example of wicked parents, birth in the slums, inherited tendencies of evil, lack of religious education, temperament, and the like; but the worst of men realizes that he is free to do the right and avoid the wrong. Can he rightly blame God, if he freely choose evil with its consequences here and hereafter?

Why, then, did God make us free? is the further objection of the unbeliever. We grant that God could have created a world free from all evil; that He could by constant miracle have preserved man from all sin without interfering with His free will. But as a matter of fact He has not done so, and no one can say that He was bound so to do.

He made us free because He wished to be freely served by His creatures; because He knew He could restore the disturbed moral order by the sanction of His eternal punishment of the sinner; because He knew how to draw good out of evil.

We must in the last analysis, therefore, say that the existence of moral evil is a great mystery, but that its existence is in no way referable to God, but to the sins of our first parents and the actual sins of men. The great remedy of evil is Jesus Christ's atonement on the cross and the grace of God which comes therefrom, especially in the Mass and the Sacraments established by the Saviour.

Take, if you dare, the alternative: There is no God. Does that do away with the fact of moral evil? Or the alternative: God is infinitely bad. Does the addition of such badness to the sum of moral evil help the case? (*American Catholic Quarterly*, 1889, p. 140).

THE IMMORTALITY OF THE SOUL.

How do you prove that the soul is immortal ? May not the soul perish with the body, and death end all ?

Independently even of the clear witness of revelation in both the Old Testament and the New, reason plainly postulates the immortality of the soul.

(1) Everywhere and at all times have men believed firmly in an after life. No matter what false and superstitious notions might prevail among savage tribes, or what philosophical doctrines might be held by the more cultured, the respect shown for the bodies of the dead, the religious rites and practices connected with their burial, the conviction of a reward or punishment hereafter for good and evil done in this life, all clearly point to a universal belief in immortality, planted in man's reason by God, who made us for Himself.

(2) Many, like Rousseau, have considered the evident inequality and injustice of this life one of the strongest proofs of a life to come. The virtuous and innocent poor often suffer greatly, while the dishonest and unjust rich travel about in luxury and comfort. Suffering, sorrow, disease, poverty, are by no means apportioned according to a man's guilt or innocence.

Life, therefore, is a meaningless, insoluble problem, and pessimism the only philosophy, unless we postulate a future life, in which an infinitely just God will make good the injustice and inequality of this, rendering just judgment to each according to his works.

(3) Again, the great craving of man's intellect for truth, and his intense longing for happiness, both of which are never satisfied in this life, point to God, the Eternal Truth, Goodness, and Beauty, who can alone make man perfectly happy hereafter. Man may follow after riches, pleasures, place, science; he may seek and attain a certain amount of knowledge and happiness here; but the sense of life's incompleteness and its vanity soon dawn upon him, and he realizes the word of St. Augustine : '' Thou hast made us for Thyself, O God, and our hearts are not at rest until they rest in Thee.''

(4) Conscience, by its commandment to do the right and avoid the wrong, and its reward of peace for good done and its punishment of remorse for evil, points clearly to God, who in the life to come will eternally reward the good and punish the wicked.

Indeed, if there be no future life, why should an intelligent man give heed to the dictate of conscience when it warns or threatens ? What difference would there be between right and wrong? Why worry about the law, if there will be no punishment for the law-breaker? If this life is all, why preach patience to the poor, justice to the rich, purity to the sensual, humility to the proud? No wonder that anarchy to-day seeks to gain its end by murder; it is the logical outcome of unbelief in the soul's immortality.

(5) The soul does not perish with the body, because it is not a material, but a simple, spiritual substance, containing in itself no element of destruction or disintegration. Although united to the body, the soul's life is independent of the body, and is not subject to the laws that govern matter. Any text book of philosophy may be consulted on this argument. (*Cf.* Maher's " Psychology," Stonyhurst series; J. S. Vaughan, "Immortality of the Soul"; Driscoll, "The Soul," ch. xi.; *American Catholic Quarterly*, 1877, pp. 123, 347).

Why was any revelation needed? Could not man get along by his own unaided reason ?

A study of the nations before the coming of the Saviour will show the failure of the unaided reason to tell man of his duties toward self, his neighbor, and God. We find the prophets Jeremias, Ezechiel, and Nahum protesting against the impure rites of Moloch and Baal. The blood of human sacrifice flowed in Phœnicia, Tyre, Chanaan, Carthage, Athens, and Rome. The worship of idols was carried on with the most impure orgies, as we may read on nearly every page of the early church writers. Fable and myth were the basis of gross idolatry, and thieving, treacherous, and adulterous gods were held up to the imitation of the people. Superstition affected all classes, so that the trade of soothsayer, augur, and magician was actually a sacred priesthood. Scepticism reigned among the cultured and the philosophers, who still kept up the public worship in the temples the better to control the people. Even Plato recommends the exposure to death of weakly children, advocates community of wives, upholds slavery, and tolerates the worst forms of immorality. Cicero tells us that nothing was too absurd for a philosopher's creed, and that, together with their ignorance, uncertainty, and contradictions on the most elemental questions of reason—*i. e.*, the existence and nature of God, the immortality of the soul, etc.—they led lives of the greatest immorality. In our own day the same holds good. Reason alone cannot teach men, for the modern pantheistic philosopher in one moment exalts man to the divinity, while in the next the materialist places him on a level with the brute beast.

At the time of Christ, the world felt the need

of a teacher who could teach with authority the truths of God to all men. Without divine revelation the truths of dogma and morals could never be known fully, and indeed some of them would have remained a puzzle and an enigma until the end. Men had to be taught by God His truth, His commandments, His pure worship, the malice of sin, the need of atonement and of pardon, the means of reaching the God who made us, the salvation of God in Christ Jesus.

Christ was the answer of the world's longing for a divine, infallible teacher of God's truth. His Church is the continuation of that divine, infallible teaching until the second coming of the Christ. (Hettinger (Bowden), " Revealed Religion," ch. ii.; Schanz, "A Christian Apology," vol. ii. ch. viii.; Gibbons, "Our Christian Heritage," *passim.*)

Is not religion a question of education and environment rather than of intellectual conviction ?

I readily grant that many are Catholics, Protestants, or unbelievers because their parents were so before them, or because of their early education. But the Catholic Church teaches that faith is an act of the intellect based on rational motives of credibility that will stand any test, needing only a good will on the part of the individual, and the grace of God, which is never refused to those who ask it, to enable a man to counteract the false teachings of his education or environment. The nature of faith can be seen from its official definition at the Vatican Council, Sess. III. ch. iii. : " Seeing that man wholly dependeth upon God as his Creator and Lord, and seeing that created reason is entirely subject to the uncreated truth, we are bound to submit by faith our intellect and will to God the Revealer. But this faith, which is the beginning of man's salvation, the Church confesseth to be a supernatural virtue, whereby, with the help of God's grace, we believe what He revealeth, not because we perceive its intrinsic truth by the natural light of our reason, but on account of the authority of God the Revealer, who can neither deceive nor be deceived."

If one's education and environment happen to be in accord with divine truth, so much the better. But if as the years roll by a man realizes the poverty of the partial gospel he possesses, or the nothingness of a despairing unbelief, he is bound in conscience and in loyalty to truth to search earnestly for the revelation of God to man.

Is not religion a mere question of feeling or emotion ? I have noticed at revivals that the amount of religion seemed to be in proportion to the excitement caused.

Not at all. You must not judge Christianity by the excesses of those who have lost the pure gospel. The Catholic Church protests most strongly against a religion of mere subjective feeling, which at revival meetings, under stress of great nervous excitement, makes the emotions take the place of rational conviction. There is nothing in the Scriptures to warrant an absolute certainty of salvation. On the contrary they declare that "No man knoweth whether he be worthy of love or hatred" (Eccles. ix. 1), and warn us "to work out our salvation with fear and trembling" (Phil. ii. 12). The Catholic Church, while cultivating rational religious emotion, safeguards her children against all emotional delusion, by declaring faith an act of the intellect guided by an upright will, and helped by God's grace; and conversion possible only by a heartfelt sorrow for sin committed, and confession of the same to the Ambassador of Christ (II. Cor. v. 20), with a firm promise to offend no more. A Catholic knows there is no danger of deception, because he believes in the authority of God, voiced to him by the living, infallible witness of Christ's mouthpiece, the Church of God.

INDIFFERENTISM.

Are not all religions good?

Is not one religion as good as another?

Why is it necessary to accept any creed? Will not my hereafter be secure if I live a good, honest life according to my conscience?

What difference does it make what religion a man professes, provided he lives up to it?

Will God ask me hereafter what creed I professed, or rather, what kind of a life I have lived?

These questions all voice the most popular religion of the twentieth century: the religion of Indifferentism. It is practically the creed of nine out of ten in the outside churches to-day, which have almost completely lost the old-time orthodoxy of the sixteenth century. It is the inevitable reaction from the first false principle of Protestantism: the formula, "Faith alone without works will save," has now become, in the hands of· the descendants of Luther, " Works alone without faith will save." Men have wearied of the many dissensions of the sects, with their denial of one pope and their creating of many, and have carried the second principle of Protestantism, private judgment, to its logical conclusion by utterly denying the right to be taught by any man, which first clothes itself under the quasi-respectable

garb of Indifferentism prior to going the full
way of unbelief.

Indifferentism is the most subtle enemy of the
true faith, much harder to combat than the
bitter bigotry of the old-fashioned Protestant.
The latter, once disabused of his false ideas of
the Church and his inherited prejudices, is open
to conviction. But the Indifferentist who declares God is indifferent to truth simply because
he himself is so, and who boasts of a religion
free from obligations and restraint, is hardly
apt to consider the claims of a definite dogmatic religion which requires absolute faith
and enforces its laws under penalty of damnation.

Is it not strange, however, that the very man
who worries night and day over some business
difficulties, or who sacrifices health and comfort
in his search for money, political preferment,
the interests of science and the like, should on
the other hand be totally indifferent to his
eternal welfare? How can any serious-minded
man neglect to consider the claims of God and
his immortal soul?

The assertion that "one religion is as good
as another" is evidently a self-contradiction.
It is a first principle of reason that two contradictory statements cannot both be true. If one
is true, the other is undoubtedly false. Either
there are many Gods or one God; either Jesus

Christ is the Son of God or He is not; either
Mohammed is a prophet or an impostor; divorce
is either lawful or not; either Jesus Christ is
present in the Blessed Sacrament or He is not.
To declare that therefore Protestantism, Mohammedanism, Polytheism, Catholicism are
equally true, is therefore to deny objective
truth altogether. On this theory a man ought
to change his religion as he changes his clothes
—according to his environment. He ought to
be a Catholic in Italy, a Protestant in Sweden,
a Mohammedan in Turkey, a Jew in Judea, a
Brahmin in India, and a Parsee in Persia.

The God of Indifferentism is, moreover, not
a God to be adored by rational men; God is
the essential, absolute, and eternal truth. Of
necessity He must hate error and wickedness.
To assert, therefore, that God does not care
what men believe, that He is indifferent whether
they believe truth or falsehood, consider good
evil or evil good, accept His revelation or reject it at will, is nothing short of blasphemy.
A man indifferent to truth—a liar, in other
words—cannot have the respect of his fellows.
A God indifferent to truth is a self-contradiction. No wonder, then, that men who form so
low a conception of the Deity should end in
denying Him altogether. Indifferentism is unbelief in disguise.

But is not " goodness " the one thing essential? Why worry about creeds, dogmas, or formulas of belief? Undoubtedly goodness is absolutely necessary; but the Indifferentist forgets that faith is a virtue essential to salvation; that a firm, unhesitating belief in the doctrines revealed by God is the very foundation-stone of supernatural goodness. A creed is merely the concrete expression of revealed truth. A good man must accept God's word, once he knows it; a good man must seek to discover what God has said, once he doubts regarding his own religious faith. Faith is part of a good life; it is the first step on the road to God's Kingdom; it is the entrance virtue to the supernatural life. If it were not necessary the Son of God could not enforce it upon us all under penalty of damnation, as He did when He said to the Apostles, "He that believeth not shall be condemned (damned)" (Mark xvi. 16). If it were a matter of option the Apostle could not have written, "Without faith it is impossible to please God" Heb. xi. 6).

The Indifferentist tends to an easy, vague, varying sort of goodness, which reason and revelation both emphatically declare to be evil. He calls good whatever falls in with his own inclinations. He is not good according to the divine standard, which is the only kind of goodness that avails for salvation.

There is no record of the doctrine of Indifferentism in the Scriptures; there is no trace of it in all Christian history. Jesus Christ told His Apostles (Matt. xxviii. 19, 20) to preach to all men the doctrines that He had commanded them to teach: "Going, teach ye all nations: teaching them to observe all things whatsoever I have commanded you." His was a definite, clear gospel, that the Apostles were to guard faithfully with their life-blood and hand down to their successors until the end of the world. Useless indeed would have been their preaching, suffering, and death, a mockery the death of millions of martyrs, a stupendous bit of folly the sacrifices of converts from the first day of Christianity, if it were true that it made no difference what a man believed.

Why does St. Paul insist so much on the unity of faith, "one Lord, one Faith, one Baptism" (Eph. iv. 5), and so bitterly denounce the Judaizers of his time for attempting to force the obsolete customs of the Old Law upon the early Christians, if it matters nothing? "There are some that trouble you and would pervert the gospel of Christ. But though we, or an angel from heaven, preach a gospel to you besides that which we have preached to you, let him be anathema" (Gal. i. 7, 8; *cf.* I. Tim. vi. 20; II. Tim. i. 14; II. Thess. ii. 14).

So from the beginning, the Popes, as the

great confirmers of the faith of the wavering
brethren (Luke xxii. 32), have always denounced error and heresy, and council after
council of Christian bishops, from the Council
of Jerusalem in the first century to the Council of the Vatican in the nineteenth, have ut-
tered their protest against any corruption of
the faith of Christ, giving the lie direct to the
false and destructive creed of modern Indifferentism.

It is, therefore, the first duty of a rational
man to love truth, and to embrace it at the
cost of any sacrifice. It is the mark of a
coward and a fool to shirk one's responsibility to the light that God vouchsafes to every
intellect that He has fashioned after His own.
We despise a man who has no convictions
or principles; he is not to be trusted. God
despises a man without religious convictions,
or firm principles of faith. He says Himself
to the Indifferentist: "I would thou wert
cold or hot. But because thou art lukewarm,
and neither cold nor hot, I will begin to vomit
thee out of my mouth" (Apoc. iii. 15, 16).
We despise a "trimmer"; can God love the
Indifferentist?

Practically also we find that the man who
says first, "It does not make any difference
what a man believes," is tempted to adopt
its logical conclusion, and say "It does not

make any difference what a man does." His morality is built on the shifting sands of opinion, fancy, human respect, and therefore will hardly stand the strain of sorrow, disgrace, difficulty, or temptation. If religion is mere opinion, a man realizes that all certainty of doctrine or morals is impossible, and therefore some form of unbelief is the inevitable result. (MacLaughlin, "Is one Religion as Good as Another?")

Does not the Bible declare that "God is not a respecter of persons" and that "He who feareth Him, and worketh justice is acceptable to Him"? (Acts x. 34, 35). Is it not sufficient, therefore, for a man to be good and charitable, as this pagan centurion was, without bothering about creeds?

This text is frequently on the lips of men who from force of tradition still quote Bible texts, although they are unwilling to follow the Scripture teaching in every point. To quote the words of St. Peter without the context, and thus make God's word witness to the doctrine of indifferentism, is anything but reasonable.

The text evidently means that the gospel of Jesus Christ is not limited to the Jews, but is for all peoples, and that His grace also is given to all men without exception. Again, that a man living according to the light vouchsafed him, fearing God and doing good as far as he possibly can under the grace of God, although ignorant of the true gospel, is acceptable to God. The instant such a one discovers the true religion, he will embrace it at once without question, as Cornelius did, no matter what the cost.

Why does the God of truth permit so many false religions in the world ? In view of the multitude of religions in the world, and the diversities of sects among Christians, is not the attitude of a sceptic perfectly reasonable ? All religions claim to be right, and yet all cannot be. What, then, is a man to do, for he has not time to study all ?

We readily admit that the existence of so many false religions is a great evil, and that its explanation will ever remain difficult and mysterious. But because finite man has not been admitted into the secrets of the Infinite God, must he thereby deny His all-ruling providence ? By no means. The true manner of arguing is thus set forth by Balmes : " The evil exists, it is true; but that Providence also exists, is no less certain ; apparently these are two things which cannot coexist; but as you know for certain they do exist, this apparent contradiction is not sufficient to make you deny their existence. What you should do, is to seek a means of removing this contradiction; and in case you cannot possibly discover one, attribute this impossibility to your own inability" (" Letters to a Sceptic," II. p. 24, W. B. Kelly, Dublin, 1875).

This is our way of acting in every-day life when we come across some fact, vouched for by unimpeachable testimony, which appears to contradict our previous knowledge. "I do not see how it can be so," a man says, with regard to some of the facts of hypnotism, "but it undoubtedly is so. My ignorance of the explanation does not render the facts any the less true."

The only solution to the mystery lies in the Catholic dogma of original sin, with its countless train of evils all down the course of history.

Practically, however, this fact should not make a man a sceptic or an infidel. The man of science is spurred on to study and investigate, so that the working hypotheses now held by the scientist in general may be stepping-stones for him to true facts and principles. If a man, therefore, is without faith in Christ, he surely ought not to rest content with his ignorance of the truth of God. His reason will tell him that God exists; that God is good and true and loving; that God has spoken. A man that studies conscientiously, and prays with humility for the truth, will, through God's help, find out what God has said, and which religion is the true one. He is not bound to study them all, any more than a scientist has to worry over the exploded theories of the ancients. ·

Surely the first demand upon one's study is that Church which has taught infallibly for 1900 years the pure gospel of Jesus Christ, witnessing to Him even through countless storms of persecution, thriving on the blood of many martyrs, fulfilling the prophecies of the old law, proving herself by miracles, winning the intellect of men by the sublimity of her dogma, conquering the heart by the holiness of her morality—the Church Catholic, the great defender of the rights of God and the rights of man.

MYSTERIES.

What scientific proof is there of the divinity of the Christian religion?

The facts of science can be proved and tested, but what proof can you show of things invisible and incomprehensible? I am willing to accept only what can be clearly demonstrated.

This common objection of the modern unbeliever is about as reasonable as the denial of the existence of South Africa to-day, or of George Washington a hundred and fifty years ago, simply because these facts were not capable of scientific demonstration, but rested merely on the authority of others. Although indeed the testimony of others may at times be false and misleading, because the witness may be deceived or a deceiver, still no one can reasonably reject altogether the principle of human evidence as a criterion of truth, any more than he would reject ocular testimony because a particular individual was short-sighted, cross-eyed, or color-blind.

Indeed, the very man who boasts of accepting nothing unless he can personally prove it to his own satisfaction, is daily giving the lie to his pet theory. Most of his knowledge depends not on personal investigation, but on the authority of others. No progress would be possible in any science or art unless a man started with the data gathered by his predecessors. Will a historian of universal history be able to read all the original documents? Will a chemist find time to test every experiment of his forbears? Will a lawyer manage to study every case in the reports, a geographer visit every country, a physician experiment with every drug, before he accepts anything as true? Life is too short and facts too many to allow of this. And yet some of these men reject the idea of authority in religion. Is it not the way that most men must learn anything whatever?

How frequently it happens that the same man who swallows without question the human, fallible, hesitating, and changing authority of an anti-Christian dogmatist, will refuse the authority of God, voiced in a certain, unchanging, infallible and divine authority. Is not this unreasonable, to say the least? "If we receive the testimony of men, the testimony of God is greater" (I. John v. 9).

A thinking man, therefore, realizing that he is exercising faith every day in his business, intellectual, and social life, will not demand of Christianity a method of proof impossible in the nature of things, but will reasonably investigate the reliability of the authority that voices to him the truths of God. He asks not experimental proof for the divine truths that are over and above reason, but simply : Is there evidence from authority that Christ is the Son of God, and His religion divine ? He will disabuse himself of every prejudice, and study with humility and earnestness the various evidences of Christianity ; the argument from miracles and prophecy, the absolute perfection of Jesus Christ, His resurrection from the dead, His sublime, unique teachings, the marvellous spread and continuance of His Church despite every obstacle, the testimony of the martyrs, the lives of the saints of God, the transformation of the world effected by Christianity, etc. Only those who come with the humility and docility of little children will learn the mysteries of God. " Unless you be converted, and become as little children, you shall not enter into the kingdom of heaven " (Matt. xviii. 3).

Should not a man be perfectly impartial in the study of Christianity, and not be carried away by a wish to believe?

If by impartiality you mean a mere abstract interest in the matter of religion, being perfectly indifferent whether the issue be faith or agnosticism, I answer that such impartiality would be fatal to all deep, earnest study. While, on the one hand, a rational mind ought not to be carried away by the superstitious enthusiasm of revival religion, he must, however, realize that he cannot face the religious problem as he would a theme in geometry, for it is fraught with knowledge of the greatest possible personal importance to himself,—it concerns his happiness here and hereafter.

The existence of God, our origin and destiny, the fact of eternal punishment, or the divinity of Christ, must be viewed in their practical bearing. There must be a desire to know, a wish to believe these stupendous truths, if belief in them is rational, and an earnest resolution to do one's utmost to see whether they are true or not.

This supposes a will to believe, which does not blind one's mind to the evidences of Christianity by substituting, as some think, the emotions for the intellect, but on the contrary makes the rational seeker after truth more alert to know, and more careful in his search.

For a full treatment of this difficulty read "The Wish to Believe," by Wilfred Ward; London, Kegan Paul, 1885.

I cannot accept Christianity, because it deals with incomprehensible mysteries. My reason tells me not to accept anything that I do not comprehend.

Must not a man blind himself perfectly, before he accept such dogmas as the Trinity, the Divinity of Christ, Transubstantiation, etc.?

Do not these so-called truths evidently go counter to my reason?

It is strange that so many to-day, in the name of reason and science, refuse to accept the mysteries of faith. One would imagine that mystery or the incomprehensible was peculiar to religion, yet a moment's reflection will convince us that we are surrounded by mystery. In the order of nature the scientist finds it impossible to explain the simplest phenomena of light, heat, force, electricity. Science may tell of facts: that this earth of ours travels through space at the rate of a thousand miles a minute; that the sun, which weighs 300,000 times as much, is suspended,

one knows not how, in an element subtler than
air; that the planets and the stars move in
certain paths, so well defined that their position
can be foretold a century hence if need be;
that given certain conditions of light, heat,
and moisture, the little seed will develop into
a mighty tree, etc.; but to explain them, it can
do no more than coin words which but veil the
ignorance of their framers. "I know," said
Newton, "the laws of attraction; but if you
ask me what attraction is, I really cannot tell."
(J. S. Vaughan, "Faith and Folly," chap.
i.; Hettinger, "Revealed Religion," edited by
H. S. Bowden, ch. i.)

How foolish to hope adequately to comprehend all the truths of God. Can the finite
mind of man grasp the infinite? As well say
that the unlettered miner, who slaves from morn
till night in the bowels of the earth, can follow
the theme of a Beethoven symphony, or appreciate a canto of Dante's "Inferno." What
indeed is a revelation that reveals nothing?
What is a religion all of whose truths are within the compass of reason? If indeed in religion the element of mystery were done away
with, our rationalist objector would instantly
point in triumph to its human origin.

The true rationalist does not first ask, "How
can this be true?" but "Has God spoken?
Can we know with real certainty all that He

has said?" He knows that if God has given
a message unto men, there must needs be difficulties and mysteries, for these abound even
in the works of God (Eccles. viii. 17). None
of the mysteries of Christianity go counter to
reason. St. Thomas says: "Although the
doctrines of faith surpass the truths of human
understanding, there can be no opposition between them. Both proceed from God in their
respective orders of grace and nature. And
the doctrines of faith become as indubitable,
through the evidence of the divine authority
revealing them, as the primary truths of reason do through their self-evident testimony
("Cont. Gent." i. 7).

Reason having once ascertained the fact of
revelation, tells us the obligation to accept
God's word without question. It is the height
of unreason to dogmatize about unproved
scientific hypotheses, which demand a mere
blind acceptance of mysterious data, more incomprehensible than any Christian dogma, and
in the same breath to question "the greater
testimony of God" (I. John v. 9; Bishop
Ricards, "Catholic Christianity and Modern Unbelief," ch. ii.)

The unbeliever who sincerely wishes to know
the truths of God must approach the study of
Christianity with the docile and humble spirit
of a child, ready to accept all the teaching of

the Master, the Son of God, no matter how mysterious or incomprehensible it may appear. "Unless you become as little children, you shall not enter into the kingdom of heaven" (Matt. xviii. 3).

The mysteries of Christianity rest merely on private interpretation of the Scriptures, a very variable quantity. Why then demand my assent to them?

Our objector grasps the fact that Protestantism, with its fundamental principle of private judgment, cannot afford a satisfactory basis for belief in the mysteries of Christianity. This is evidenced practically in the denials to-day of such fundamental dogmas as the divinity of Christ, the Trinity, eternal punishment, etc., which are made frequently from the pulpit, and by the pen of Christian ministers with "liberal" views.

The mysteries of Christianity, on Catholic principles, come to us on the divine authority of the Catholic Church, which voices infallibly the teaching of the Master, Jesus Christ. She advises the unbeliever to divest himself of all prejudice, and to ask in a humble, prayerful spirit: "Has God taught these truths to the world? Is there a divine teacher in the world to-day that guarantees to me absolute certainty of all His teaching?"

THE TRINITY.

I cannot believe an absurd contradiction in terms. In your dogma of the Trinity you declare that one is three and three are one. My reason tells me of a personal God, and that is all.

The dogma of the Trinity, although one of the most profound mysteries of Christianity, does not involve the contradiction you assert. The teaching of the Catholic Church is that there is *one divine nature*, and in that divine nature there are *three persons*. As therefore the words one and three refer to two essentially distinct things, *nature* and *person*, there can be no question of any absurd or contradictory statement of doctrine.

The dogma is thus set forth by the Athanasian Creed: " This is the Catholic faith : that we worship one God in Trinity, and Trinity in Unity, neither confounding the persons nor dividing the substance. For there is one person of the Father, another of the Son, and another of the Holy Ghost; but the Godhead of the Father, of the Son, and of the Holy Ghost, is all one, the glory equal, the majesty coeternal. . . . The Father is made of none, neither created nor begotten ; the Son is of the Father alone, not made nor created, but begotten ; the Holy Ghost is of the Father

od the father means Cosmic
" " Son " the spirituality that come
.. man when he conquers

and of the Son, neither made, nor created, nor begotten, but proceeding.''

Undoubtedly your reason would never find out such a mystery, which even when known by revelation, is still utterly beyond the comprehension of man. Catholics believe it on the word of the Son of God, evidenced to them with infallible certainty by the divine, infallible teacher appointed by the Saviour—the Catholic Church.

CHRISTIAN FAITH.

I would give worlds to believe, but cannot. Will God condemn me for something I cannot help ?

God, who is infinitely just, will condemn only those who knowingly and deliberately commit grievous sin and die unrepentant.

If, as you say, you cannot at present believe, I assure you that this condition of mind is only temporary. Your duty is plain.

Do not expect to be able to grasp everything in Christianity, for God's revelation cannot be adequately known by any human intellect. Do not look for mathematical evidence for the truths of faith, but study carefully the Christian evidences with a view to obtaining a good working certainty that excludes all doubting. Do not be dismayed by

difficulties, remembering, as Cardinal Newman well said, that ten thousand difficulties
do not make one doubt. Do not rationalize,
asking, with Nicodemus: "*How* can these
things be done?" (John iii. 9) ; or the unbelieving Jews at Capharnaum: "*How* can this
Man give us His flesh to eat?" (John vi. 53) ;
but rather: "Is this Jesus who teaches regeneration and the Real Presence indeed God
revealing His divine truth to men?" Remember that although your reason must demand sufficient proof of a revelation before
accepting it, it is not the standard of revealed
truth. Ask God's pardon for all your sins,
for wickedness blurs the spiritual vision of
many an unbeliever; as St. Paul teaches:
"The sensual man perceiveth not these things
that are of the spirit of God, for it is foolishness to him, and he cannot understand, because it is spiritually examined" (I. Cor. ii.
14). It is frequently a short step from the
confiteor to the *credo ;* from the act of sorrow
to the act of faith. Earnest, heartfelt prayer
will be answered infallibly, if we come to God
with the humble and docile spirit of the child.
"If any man will do the will of Him, he shall
know of the doctrine, whether it be of God"
(John vii. 17). "If you ask the Father anything in My Name, He will give it you"
(John xvi. 23).

MIRACLES.

How are miracles possible when the laws of nature are fixed and unchangeable? Is not a miracle a violation of the laws of nature?

It is indeed true that nature works according to fixed laws; but these laws are not, like the truths of mathematics, intrinsically and absolutely necessary. Experience tells us that, as a rule, they are unchanging, but neither reason nor experience asserts that the omnipotent, free God, cannot intervene at will to prevent their operation. God in creating the world did not subject Himself to the laws of His creation. A miracle, however, does not destroy any law or even suspend its working, but merely in a particular instance supposes the intervention of God to prevent a certain law from having its ordinary effect. There is no danger of the laws of nature being overthrown, or science disturbed in the least; for miracles are rare occurrences, which simply emphasize the more the ordinary course of nature. Were it not for the uniformity of nature's laws, one never could be certain of a miracle.

Is it not strange that one should grant that man can interfere with the working of laws, *v. g.*, overcome the law of gravitation by hold-

ing a stone in his hand, and yet deny that
the infinitely free God can act above and beyond the laws of His own framing? (Schanz,
"A Christian Apology," vol. i. ch. x.)

**Do not miracles argue a change in an un-
changeable God?**

Not at all. The ordinary action of the laws
of nature as well as the divine interference
therewith, evidenced in miracles, were alike
foreseen and willed by God for all eternity.
There is no past and future with Him. He is
the Eternally Present.

Human intelligence can suspend and control
the forces of nature to its own temporal advantage. Why then insist that the Creator
of the world must be entirely subject to the
laws He Himself has framed?

**Perhaps what you style a miracle may be due
to some unknown law of nature. You must admit that as yet we do not know all her secrets.**

A little reflection will convince a man that
a knowledge of all the laws of nature is not
necessary to determine whether a particular
fact be miraculous or not. Medical science
may make great strides within the next century, but no new medicine will ever be able
to call the dead to life. Hypnotic suggestion
may effect some wonderful new cures, but it

never will give sight to a man without eyes. A new Edison may make some new discoveries more marvellous than his, yet no inventor will ever be able to calm the winds and waves at a word or to pass through a closed door.

If, then, we have good evidence of an effect beyond the power of any creature, as, for instance, the feeding of five thousand men with five loaves, the very uniformity of the laws of science forbids us to deny the miracle in virtue of some unknown law. It is merely a question of evidence.

Granting miracles are possible, how, taking into account the general unreliability of human testimony, can any particular one be proved?

If the miracles of the Gospel were wrought before a body of scientists, well and good; but how trust the evidence of ignorant Galilean peasants?

To deny the possibility of proving a miracle because testimony is sometimes unreliable, is about as sensible as denying all historical facts whatsoever because some historians may have been deceivers or deceived. A miracle is a question of evidence, and being a phenomenon that falls under the senses, it can be known with the same certainty as any other fact,—by trustworthy evidence. An ignorant peasant could testify as well as the most cultured pharisee or modern scientist to the fact that, first, Lazarus was dead and his body corrupt, and that afterwards at the words of Christ, "Lazarus, come forth" (John xi. 43), he instantly came to life.

A body of scientists might themselves be poor witnesses, especially if they would not divest themselves of the rationalistic prejudice which denies that miracles are possible. But it requires no scientific acquirements whatever, but the mere use of one's eyes, to testify to the instant cure of a man born blind, a leper cleansed of his leprosy, and the like.

Do not all religions claim their miracles? What special proving power, therefore, have the miracles of Christ? Did not Simon Magus, Apollonius of Tyana, Buddha, Mohammed, claim to work miracles? What of the Christian Scientists and Dowieites of our own day?

It is true that every false religion has put forth this claim, but these false wonders no more disprove the existence of true miracles than a counterfeit coin disproves the existence of a good original.

On the contrary, they prove the universal acceptance of miracles as a test of divine truth.

A little study of the miracles wrought by the Saviour will bring out in clear contrast the difference between the true and the false.

As regards the question of fact, many of the pagan miracles were based on poetic legends related centuries after their occurrence, *v. g.*, the myths of Greece and Rome, the miracles of Buddha, etc.; while the miracles of Christ are attested by authentic contemporaneous documents. Again, the alleged wonders or false religions are absurd, ridiculous, and meaningless, being evidently framed to show the great power of their author: *v. g.*, the five hundred white lions, and the dragon-harnessed chariot of Buddha; the walking statues, or flights through the air of Simon Magus; the moon-dividing of Mohammed. The miracles of Christ, on the contrary, are never extravagant or foolish, but consist of wonderful cures and manifestations of divine power, to which He could appeal as proof of His divine mission: "Though you will not believe me, believe the works; that you may know and believe that the Father is in me, and I in the Father" (John x. 38).

The perfect spotlessness of the life of Christ is warrant for belief in these words. On no other hypothesis can the miracles of Christ be explained, save as works requiring divine power; whereas the alleged wonders in the false religions of Buddhism, Brahminism, Greek and Roman paganism, or in modern spiritism, theosophy, Christian Science, and

Dowieism, can be traced either to fraud, hallu-
cination, hypnotic suggestion, or diabolism.
(Jaugey, "Dict. Apol.," 2088, 2116; Newman, "Essay on Miracles," i. sec. 3).

THE GOSPELS.

**Your account of Christ rests on the four gos-
pels. How are we sure to-day that they are
genuine history? They may have been written
long after the events they record; or, again,
what guarantee is there that we have the original statement of Christianity after so many
years?**

It is impossible for us to discuss in a few
words the genuinity or authenticity of the four
gospels. No clear-headed man, however, can
in conscience reject them after he has carefully
studied the question. We merely outline some
of the chief arguments.

1st. The four gospels are quoted verbatim or
in paraphrase by writers of the first three centuries, viz.: Pope Clement of Rome (96 A. D.),
the Doctrine of the Twelve Apostles (80–120),
the Epistle of Barnabas (120–130), Ignatius,
martyr (105–117), Polycarp (168), Papias
(125), Justin (160), Tatian (170), The Mura-
torian Fragment (190–210), Irenæus (177),

Tertullian (199), Clement of Alexandria (192), Origen (230), etc.

2d. The early enemies of Christianity—the Jew, the heretic, and the pagan—although they ridiculed and perverted the gospels, never dreamt of denying their genuinity, for they realized the utter impossibility of so futile an argument gaining credence.

3d. Another witness is the number of apocryphal gospels written by heretics to spread their false doctrines, or by the orthodox as pious forgeries to complete the gospel narrative. Their very existence testifies to the four gospels, as a counterfeit coin evidences the existence of a true original.

4th. The very fact that the four gospels were universally accepted in the fourth century by the Fathers—men tenacious of tradition and haters of every novelty of doctrine—points conclusively to their genuineness. Considering, too, their great love and reverence of the Scriptures, no writer, no matter how clever, could foist a new gospel on them, [any more than a history of the Revolution written to-day could pass current with the American people as a document of the eighteenth century.

5th. There was likewise no danger of the gospels undergoing any substantial change. The gospels were known and read in all the churches, copies and versions were being continually made, the early teachers of Christianity quoted them frequently from their pulpits and in their writings ; any change would instantly be met by a mighty protest from both pastors and people, as we see in the case of the heretical and Jewish perversions of the Sacred Scriptures.

6th. Some unbelievers have accused the gospel writers of ignorance, superstition, fanaticism, and even deliberate fraud, the better to controvert their testimony. But an earnest, sincere student of the gospels will find, on the contrary, that they were men of truth who related what they themselves had seen and heard (I. John i. 1–3 ; II. Pet. i. 6); they told of miracles performed and doctrines preached publicly before unbelievers (John xviii. 20, 21), which none dared gainsay ; they had no possible motive for deception, for they went counter to the current Jewish and pagan ideas and knew that they would meet persecution and death ; they won many converts and helped in the foundation of a religion which stands unique in the world by its sublime doctrine of faith and morality. No explanation will account for the fact save that they were true speakers sent by God.

THE DIVINITY OF CHRIST.

Is it not incredible that God should become man?

What proofs are there that Jesus Christ was the Son of God?

May not the texts in which Christ speaks of unity with the Father imply only the moral unity of an adopted sonship?

Cannot a man reverence Jesus as the highest and most perfect type of the race without acknowledging Him to be divine? I believe that men should strive more to live Christ's life than to discuss the dogma of His divinity.

" We need to appreciate that the doctrine of the Incarnation is not a hard one to accept. There is no revolt in the natural mind against the thought of God becoming man. It is not a thought which arouses aversion in us. Indeed, we give it welcome. That man should be raised to a participation in the divine nature is a difficult thing to *understand*, if the word is meant to imply a full and clear comprehension. But the human race or any part of it has never felt it to be incredible. . . . The dignity of man suggests the possibility of the Incarnation ; the aspirations of man suggest its probability ; the degradation of man cries out for it, and implores its immediate gift " (Elliott, " Life of Christ," Epilogue, pp. i.–vii.)

The divinity of Christ is the foundation-doctrine of the Christian religion. Deny Him as the Son of God, and at once the whole fabric of revelation falls to pieces; confess Him to be divine, and the logical mind grasps at once the necessity of a divine, infallible teacher in the world to-day, speaking in His name and with His authority.

The arguments for the divinity of Christ are:

1st. Throughout the four gospels Christ clearly asserts His divinity.

He claims perfect equality with the Father—the Jehovah of the Jews—in absolute oneness of essence ("I and the Father are one."—John x. 30), in parity of working power (" My Father worketh until now, and I work."—John v. 17; " What things soever the Father doth, these the Son also doth in like manner."—v. 19), in eternal Being (" Before Abraham was made, I am."—John viii. 58), in the equal right to the homage of mankind (" That all may honor the Son as they honor the Father."—John v. 23; *cf.* xiv. 1, 13; xv. 10; Matt. x. 37).

It is evident that our Lord, in John x. 30, spoke of His absolute, essential oneness with the Father because He " was addressing earnest monotheists, keenly alive to the essential

distinction between the life of the Creator and
the life of the creature, and religiously jealous
of the divine prerogatives. The Jews did not
understand Christ's claim to be one with the
Father in any moral, spiritual, or mystical
sense. Christ did not encourage them so to
understand it. The motive of their indigna-
tion ("we stone Thee for blasphemy, because
that Thou, being a man, maketh Thyself
God."—John x. 33) was not disowned by Him.
They believed Him to mean that He was Himself a divine Person; and He never repudiated that construction of His language" (Liddon, "The Divinity of our Lord," Lecture iv.
pp. 188–189).

Again, the Jews evidently understood our
Saviour to claim a right to break the Sabbath as the Lord of the Sabbath, the equal
of Jehovah who had prescribed the law, and
for that reason they "sought the more to kill
Him, because He said God was His Father,
making Himself equal to God" (John v. 18).
A third time they stoned Him as a blas-
phemer (John viii. 59), when He claimed to
be the "I am who am" of Israel (Exod. iii.
14), the eternal "Now."

Every one who studies the life of Christ
must admit that He was sincere (John vi. 26;
xiii. 38; xviii. 37), unselfish (John v. 30;
vi. 38; x. 11; Matt. xxvi. 39), and humble

(Luke viii. 51; Matt. ix. 30; Mark viii. 11; Matt. xi. 29). But "is He, if He be not God, really *humble?* Can Jesus bid us to believe in Him (John xiv. 1), love Him, obey Him (John xv. 10), live by Him (John vi. 58), live for Him (Matt. xvi. 24); can He thus claim to be the universal Teacher (Matt. xxviii. 20) and the universal Judge (Matt. xxv. 31–41), the Way, the Truth, the Life of humanity (John xiv. 6), if He be indeed only man?
. . . If Jesus Christ be not God, is He really *unselfish?* He bids men make Himself the centre of their affections and their thoughts (John xiv. 6, 14; xi. 25; xiv. 1; vi. 29; v. 23; viii. 42; xv. 23; xiv. 15, etc.); and when God does this, He is but recalling man to that which is man's proper duty, to the true direction and law of man's being. But deny Christ's divinity, and what will you say of the disinterestedness of His perpetual self-assertion?
. . . If Jesus Christ is not God, can we even say that He is *sincere?* For if He is not God, where does He make any adequate repudiation of a construction of His words so utterly derogatory to the great Creator, so necessarily abhorrent to a good man's thought?
. . . Would not a purely human Christ have anticipated the burning words of the indignant Apostle at the gate of Lystra?" (Acts xiv. 14; Liddon, *ibid.*, pp. 195–203).

There can be no doubt that the Sanhedrin condemned our Lord to death because He claimed to be divine. Their words to Pilate were: "We have a law; and according to the law (Lev. xxiv. 16; Deut. xiii. 5) He ought to die, because He made Himself the Son of God" (John xix. 7). The high-priest put the question plainly to our Lord: "Art Thou the Christ, the Son of the blessed God? And Jesus said to him, I am" (Mark xiv. 61, 62; *cf*. Matt. xxvi. 64). This open claim of being the Son of God in a real, true sense was styled blasphemy, and sealed the death-sentence of Jesus Christ.

2d. The Apostles clearly teach that Jesus is God.

St. Peter, when questioned by Christ on this very point, declares explicitly "Thou art Christ, the Son of the Living God" (Matt. xvi. 16), and our Lord in answer blesses him for his profession of faith, and declares it inspired by His Heavenly Father. "Blessed art thou, Simon Bar Jona, because flesh and blood hath not revealed it to thee, but My Father who is in heaven" (*cf*. John vi. 70; I. Pet. i. 2; iv. 2; II. Pet. i. 1).

The unbelieving *St. Thomas*, convinced by the fact of the resurrection, is forced to cry out "My Lord and my God" (John xx. 28). *St. John* wrote his whole gospel that men "may believe that Jesus is the Christ the Son of God" (John xx. 31), and in his opening chapter he declares Jesus the only begotten Son of God, eternal and consubstantial with His Father (John i. 1–14; *cf.* I. John iv. 15; v. 20). *St. Paul* writes clearly of Christ: "Who being in the form of God, thought it not robbery to be equal with God" (Phil. ii. 6), and in many other passages speaks of Him as the eternal Son of God, the Creator of all things, etc. (Col. i. 15, 16; Rom. ix. 5; viii. 32; Heb. i. 1–14).

This public unanimous preaching of Christ's divinity by the Apostles can be explained on no other hypothesis than the positive revelation of Jesus Christ their Master.

3d. The miracles which Jesus wrought in His own name and by His own power prove Him to be God.

When Jesus found that His testimony was gainsaid, He frequently appealed to the miracles He wrought as setting the seal of the divine approval upon His teachings, and His claim of equality with the Father (Matt. xi. 4, 5; John v. 36; x. 38; xiv. 12). His life is one series of miracles. He stills the storm with a word (Mark iv. 39), He walks upon the sea (Matt. xiv. 25), He feeds the multitudes with a few loaves and fishes (John vi. 10), He changes water into wine (John ii. 9), He drives out demons from the possessed (Mark i. 25; iii. 11; v. 8, etc.), He heals the blind, the deaf, the dumb, the leper, and the paralytic (Mark ix. 25; viii. 1–5; Luke v. 24), He raises the dead to life (Matt. ix. 25; Luke vii. 15; John xi. 44). He is transfigured before the Apostles (Mark ix. 3), He rises from the dead, converses with the disciples for forty days, and then ascends on high to His heavenly Father (Matt. xxviii.; Acts i. 9, etc.)

The saints and prophets work miracles also, but they always do so in the name of God or Christ Jesus. He alone performs them of Himself: ".I will, be thou made clean" (Matt. viii. 3); "Do you believe that I can do this unto you?" (Matt. ix. 28; *cf.* Luke vii. 14; John xi. 44; Matt. viii. 5–13, etc.)

The unbelievers of our day have striven to give us a life of Jesus, while utterly denying the historical reality of the miracles recorded of Him. But "to expel miracles from the life of Jesus is to destroy the identity of tne Christ of the Gospels; it is to substitute a new Christ for the Christ of Christendom: . . . these (rationalistic) commentators do not affect to take the history as it has come down to us. As the Gospel narratives stand, they present a block of difficulties to Humanitarian theories; and these difficulties can only be removed by mutilations of the narrative so wholesale and radical as to destroy their substantial interest, besides rendering the retention of the fragments which may be retained a purely arbitrary procedure.''

In a word, miracles are so interwoven with the life of Christ, and so prominent a feature of His daily teaching, that the '' moral integrity of our Lord's character is dependent, whether we will or not, upon the reality of His miracles '' (Liddon, *ibid.*, pp. 161–163).

5th. Pascal considered the prophetical argument the strongest proof of Christ's divinity (Pascal's '' Thoughts,'' p. 128). Even among the pagan nations there was a general expectation of a new revelation and a new teacher from on high. The Old Testament in a series of prophecies extending over thousands of years announces all the details of the life of Christ. God promises a redeemer to Adam (Gen. iii. 15). He is to be of the stock of Abraham (Gen. xii. 13), Isaac (xxvi. 4), Jacob (Gen. xxviii. 14; Num. xxiv. 17), of the tribe of Juda (Gen. xlviii. 8–10; *cf.* Heb. vii. 14), and of the family of David (Isa. ix. 7; ii. 1–7; *cf.* Rom. i. 3; II. Tim. ii. 8).

Moses declares that He will be a great prophet (Deut. xviii. 15), Isaias foretells His birth of a virgin mother (vii. 14) and His power of miracles (xxxv. 4–6), Malachias tells of His precursor (iii. 1; *cf.* Luke i. 76; iii. 2),

Micheas marks the place and Daniel the time
of His coming (Mich. v. 2, 3; *cf.* Matt. ii. 1;
Luke ii. 4; Dan. ix. 24–27), Isaias declares
Him the prince of peace (ix. 6; *cf.* Luke ii.
14; John xiv. 27), foretells the place of His
preaching (ix. 1. 2; *cf.* Matt. iv. 15), and says
He will make a new covenant for the gentiles
(ii. 4; *cf.* Luke i. 3; Matt. xvi. 28; xxviii.
19; Mark xvi. 15); the Psalms (xxi. and
lxviii.), Isaias (liii.), and Zacharias (xi. 12)
tell the minutest details of His passion and
death. (Maas, "Christ in Type and Prophecy.")

5th. Christ's own power of prophecy proves
Him God.

He foretells His own death and resurrection (Matt. xii. 40; xvii. 21–22; xxvii. 63;
xx. 17–19; Luke xiii. 32; John ii. 19), the
treachery of Judas (John xiii. 26), the denial
of Peter and the manner of His death (Matt.
xxvi. 34; John xxi. 18–22), the destruction of
Jerusalem (Matt. xxiv.), the dispersion of the
Jews (Luke xxi. 24), and the spread of His
Church (John x. 16; Matt. xiii. 31).

6th. One of the most striking proofs of
Christ's divinity is His absolute sinlessness.
He proposes the highest standard of sanctity
possible: "Be you therefore perfect, as also
your heavenly Father is perfect" (Matt. v.
48); and instead of insisting on His own per-

sonal unworthiness, as He must needs have
done were He only a great prophet like Isaias
(" I am a man of unclean lips," Isa. vi. 5), He,
on the contrary, challenges His enemies to find
in Him the slightest sin : " which of you shall
convince Me of sin ? " (John viii. 46), and
declares that He always does His Father's will,
" for I do always the things that please Him "
(John viii. 29 ; Bougaud, " The Divinity of
Jesus Christ," ch. iv.; Liddon, *l. c.*, p. 165–
168).

7th. The sublime teachings of the Saviour,
together with the wonderful spread of His
Church by the simplest methods against the
mightiest enemies, the transformation of the
world from the lust, pride, cruelty, and idolatry of paganism to the Christian purity, humility, gentleness, love of God and the brethren
for God's sake, prove that the Worker of this
change was not human but divine.

8th. " If Christ be not divine, actually God,
then the supreme Ruler of men's souls has
failed both in His messenger and His message,
and failed fatally. Christ was sent to eradicate idolatry, which had proven to be the
deepest seated evil of humanity, and to establish impregnably the very opposite, the knowledge and worship of the true God. The light-
est belief in Divine Providence identifies its
rulings in this sense with Christ and His mis-

sion, and they resulted in universal Christ-worship. . . . If Christ be not God, He is the author of the most obstinate idolatry ever known. No teaching so awfully authoritative as His, no life so irresistibly attractive, no death so solemn and so triumphant. Has the only result been idolatry?" (Elliott, "Life of Christ," Epilogue, xv. xvii.)

Men cannot remain indifferent to this doctrine, for it is fraught with mighty consequences here and hereafter. This world takes on another aspect to the man who knows that God has deigned to honor it by living here for a time, and to exalt human nature by making it His very. own. You cannot do away with Christ's divinity and pretend to follow out His teaching. If He be only man, His power to command is subject to the caprice of every individual. If He is God, then it follows naturally that His doctrines must be believed under penalty of damnation (Mark xvi. 16), and His commandments obeyed under penalty of hell. Logically, also, there must be in the world to-day a teacher of His gospel, divine as He was divine, infallible as He was infallible, voicing His gospel to all men unto the end (Matt. xxviii. 20; Acts i. 8); an authority of which He said: "He that heareth you heareth Me" (Luke x. 16; Fouard, "Life of Christ"; Didon, "Life of Christ"; Lacordaire, "Conferences on Jesus Christ"; Nicolas, "The Divinity of Christ"; Freppel, "Discourses on the Divinity of Christ.")

If Christ performed the miracles recorded in the New Testament, why then did the Jews put Him to death?

This difficulty is thus answered by Father Lambert:

"The argument of this question is, that because the Jews put Christ to death, they did not believe in His miracles as recorded in the Gospels. But this conclusion is false. The Jews believed that God had forbidden them to abandon the law of Moses, even if a prophet performing miracles required them to do so. From the time of Christ down to the present the Jews have always and uniformly believed in the reality of the miracles of Christ. If you do not believe this, consult their Talmuds.

"Well, then, you will ask, if they admitted the fact of His miracles, why did they not accept Him as the Messias? While they admitted the miracles, they did not believe that they proved Him to be the Messias. Their prophets had performed miracles under the Mosaic law. They had even raised the dead. The Jews in the time of Christ could not understand how miracles could be worked to abrogate that law. Fixed habits and prejudices,

then, caused them to reject the *evidence* of His
miracles, while they admitted the *fact* of them.
They attributed them to Beelzebub.

"Again, they believe that the promised Son
of David was to be a great temporal prince,
that He was to free the Jewish people, and
establish a great Jewish empire, restore the
Jewish nobility, and raise the Aaronic priesthood to its ancient pre-eminence and glory.
His preaching and humble life gave no encouragement to these hopes, and they refused to
believe in Him as the promised Messias, even
while they admitted His miracles. And they
put Him to death as they had put to death their
acknowledged prophets" (Lambert, "Notes on
Ingersoll," chap. xvi. pp. 140–141).

THE INCARNATION AND REDEMPTION.

**What does the Catholic Church teach concern-
ing the Incarnation ?**

The Catholic Church teaches that Jesus
Christ is both God and man—the eternal, only
begotten Son of the Eternal Father, who became flesh and dwelt among us (John i. 14).

In Jesus Christ there are two natures, the
divine and the human, perfectly distinct from
each other, and yet forming but one divine personality. The Athanasian Creed declares that

Jesus is "God of the substance of the Father, born before all ages, and man of the substance of His mother, born in time. Perfect God and perfect man, subsisting of a rational soul and human body. Equal to the Father, according to His divinity ; less than the Father, according to His humanity. . . . One not by the changing of the divinity into flesh, but by the assumption of the humanity unto God. One not by the confounding of substance, but by the unity of person. For as the rational soul and the body is one man, so God and man is one Christ."

"Just as one may point out a man, and say of him, 'This is my brother' or 'my friend,' so we can say of 'Jesus Christ, 'This is the Eternal God, Creator of heaven and earth, my Master, my Judge, my everlasting Hope. . . . His humanity is no fiction. His body is a real true body, born of Mary, ever Virgin, pierced on the Cross, sitting now at the right hand of God. . . . He has a human soul, united to His flesh like our souls are to our flesh. . . . The two natures were each the nature of one and the same Person; and what each nature did the Person did ; what each nature was the Person was.

"God was made man, and was man. A man was God. . . . It was not the humanity which created all things, it was not the

Godhead which was nailed to the cross; but the Person to whom both belonged did the one and suffered the other, and the Person was Jesus Christ" (Bishop Hedley, "Our Divine Saviour and other Discourses," Sermon I.)

What is the Catholic doctrine of the redemption?

The Church has defined that "Christ is the mediating cause of salvation, inasmuch as through His death, as a sin-offering, He has merited our salvation, and making satisfaction for us to God, has blotted out sin. In other words, His merits and satisfaction, as being those of our Representative and Mediator, have obtained for us salvation from God." . . . "The Council of Trent several times insists upon the merits of the Mediator: *e. g.*, by the merit of the one Mediator original sin is taken away (Sess. V. can. iii.) ; the meriting cause of our justification is Christ, who for us made satisfaction to God, the Father" (Sess. VI. ch. vii.) (Wilhelm-Scannell, "A Manual of Catholic Theology," vol. ii. p. 183; *cf. ibid.*, p. 181–207; Oxenham, "The Atonement.")

Why should God punish His innocent Son for the guilt of men?

"In the economy of salvation the sinner is

bound to give personal satisfaction; if he does not, his lot is damnation. Christ was not punished instead of the sinner, nor against His own will as sinners are punished; by the holiest of free acts He bore the penalties of sin in order to merit for the sinner a means of satisfying which lay beyond human power. His vicarious satisfaction is not the transfer of punishment from the unjust to the just, but the transfer of the merits of the just to the unjust" (Wilhelm–Scannell, "A Manual of Catholic Theology," vol. ii. p. 188.)

THE BIBLE.

Is not the Bible an all-sufficient guide to the truths taught by the Saviour?

Is it not better to trust an infallible, divine book for the gospel teaching, than the mere traditions of men?

I will accept none of your teachings unless you give me Bible proof. Where in the Bible do you find, etc.

Is not the meaning of the Bible evident to any Christian who reads it devoutly?

The Reformers of the sixteenth century declared that the Bible only, understood according to an individual's private judgment, was the complete source and organ of revealed truth for man's salvation. They had denied the divine, infallible authority established by Jesus Christ, and so, in words at least, endeavored to substitute an authority equally divine and infallible.

Catholics, on the contrary, hold with St. Paul, that "faith cometh" not by reading, but "by hearing" (Rom. x. 17); that the gospel of Christ is to be learned from a divine, infallible living voice—the Catholic Church, which guarantees to every one not merely the unwritten word, but also the unwritten teaching of divine tradition (II. Thess. ii. 13, 14).

Let us not mistake the point at issue. Many write and talk as if there were question of the dignity or sacred character of the Bible ; as if, forsooth, Protestantism had for the first time given it its due place of honor.

But history is the witness how well the Catholic Church has ever defended the integrity, historical value, canonicity, and inspiration of the Scriptures, and their helpfulness and worth to the Christian people. The real question is: Is the Bible and the Bible alone the way to find out the gospel of Christ?

The Catholic answers this question in a decided negative; for, 1st. If this fundamental principle of Protestantism were true, the Bible should record it somewhere. On the contrary, there is not one text in the Old Testament or the New which declares any such principle.

2d. Let us ask whether Protestantism has been consistent? As a matter of fact, how many Protestants have learned the doctrines of Christ by independent Bible-reading? Indeed, from the very beginning, in the endeavor to save themselves from the inevitable destruction that follows every protest against divine truth, they have gone directly counter to their first principle, and have trusted to human creeds, confessions, catechisms, teachings from the pulpit and lessons in the Bible class. Each denomination has drawn up its own interpretation of the Bible, emphasizing some texts and utterly ignoring others, and has made the acceptance of this human, fallible interpretation a condition of church-membership.

3d. It is only by the divine authority of the Catholic Church that Christians know that the Scripture is the Word of God, and what books certainly belong to the Bible.

The Bible was not written in English. How can a Protestant of to-day—learned or ignorant —know whether his version is a correct translation, or a human travesty of God's word?

The Bible nowhere points out the number of books on the canon, and critical arguments can never afford the divine certainty that rational men demand before believing with divine faith.

The Protestant starts with the unproved assumption that the Bible is the inspired word of God.   How, we ask, independently of a divine authority outside the Bible, can any one prove the internal, supernatural fact of divine inspiration?

In a word, the Bible is not its own witness. It is like a will without a signature or probate. Especially in our own day, when the modern Higher Criticism has made sad havoc with the old Protestant estimate of the Bible.   Deny the Church's infallible witness, and lo! the Bible is reduced to the level of mere Oriental literature, full of errors and utterly devoid of divine inspiration.   The Catholic Church alone guarantees infallibly the authenticity of the Latin Vulgate, the contents of the Canon, and the inspiration of all the seventy-two books of Holy Writ.

The Catholic Church gives the world the Bible, so that St. Augustine could rightly say in the fifth century: "I would not believe the gospel unless moved thereto by the authority of the Church" ("Contra Epis. Fund.")

4th.   The Bible does not pretend to be a formulary of belief, as is a creed or catechism. There is nowhere in the New Testament a clear, methodical statement of the teachings of Christ.   It was never intended as such.

The Epistles of St. Paul, for instance, were written as occasion arose to different local Churches, to settle disputes about dogma, to insist on certain Christian principles of morality, to protest against pagan philosophy and pagan crimes, and to warn the first converts against Judaizers.

The Bible was never intended to take the place of the living, infallible teacher, the Church, but was written to explain or to insist upon a doctrine already preached.

How indeed could a dead and speechless book, that cannot be cross-questioned to settle doubts or decide controversies, be the exclusive and all-sufficient teacher of God's revelation.

5th. The very nature of the Bible ought to prove to any thinking man the impossibility of its being the one safe method to find out what the Saviour taught. It is not a simple, clear-as-crystal volume that a little child may understand, although it ought to be so on Protestant principles. Luther declared that any one could understand the Bible—as long as his own interpretation was unquestioned (Wittenb. Opera, vol. ii. p. 474, A.D. 1539), but once his authority was set aside by his own followers, the Bible became a most difficult book ! (Walch, vol. v., 1652, 472, xiv. 1360; De Wette, iii. 61; Tischr. ii. c. 5, § 46;

J. Verres, "Luther: An Historical Portrait," p. iii., *et seq.*)

St. Peter speaks of the difficulties one meets with, especially in the epistles of St. Paul, "in which are certain things hard to be understood ; which the unlearned and unstable wrest, as they do also the other scriptures, to their own destruction " (II. Pet. iii. 16).

Again, the Acts of the Apostles testify to the obscurity of that passage in Isaias (liii. 7, 8) which the eunuch of Queen Candace could not understand until Philip assured him that it referred to the Passion of Jesus Christ, the Son of God : "Thinkest thou that thou understandest what thou readest? Who said : And how can I, unless some man show me ? " (Acts viii. 30, 31).

Indeed, when one reflects for a moment what the Bible is—a number of sublime, mysterious books, written thousands of years ago by men of a different civilization and tongue ; and especially when one knows that it deals with God's revelation of doctrine and morals to His people, he must needs expect to find "things hard to be understood."

Many questions face the reader of the New Testament, and demand a divine authoritative answer, if men are to know with certainty the gospel of Christ. Is this a counsel or a commandment? (John xiii. 14.) Is this passage literal or figurative? (John vi.; Matt. xxvi. 26.) Has an apostolic priesthood the pardoning power? (John xx. 23.) Is Christ the Son of God? (John xiv. 28), etc.

If the Scriptures were so clear, why then did the principle of private interpretation bring forth so many denominations, each claiming to know the true meaning of God's word?

If Jesus had promised the wonderful gift of divine insight to every individual, as some have arbitrarily pretended, well and good. But there is not the slightest evidence of any such promise. On the contrary, the contradictions of the various human societies in the world to-day absolutely point to their origin,—man's private and fallible opinion, and not to the infallible guidance of the Holy Spirit of Truth.

The Bible is not so much printer's ink and paper; not the ignorance, errors, and prejudices of men read into the Old or New Testament; not a babel of discordant opinions as to what Christ our Lord meant; but the one divine, infallible voice of God to his people, known with divine, infallible certainty to every creature by the divine interpreter and custodian of Holy Writ—the one Church of Jesus Christ.

6th. Is it not strange that if Christianity were to be learned from the Bible only, that Christ Himself never wrote a line, nor ever commanded His Apostles to write. Only five of the twelve did write; for their divine commission was not to write, but to preach and teach the gospel (Matt. xxviii. 19; Mark xvi. 15; Luke x. 16; Acts i. 8). They wrote merely to confirm their teaching, never giving the slightest intimation that Christianity was to rest solely on a Bible foundation.

7th. Historically, we are certain that the Bible has never been the way to find out Christ.

For just as the Jewish religion existed before the Old Testament, so the Christian religion existed before a line of the New Testament was written. The Church came first and not the Bible, and there is not the slightest evidence to show the substitution, in later times, of a dead book for the living voice of Christ's Church.

8th. Again, it has ever been practically impossible for men, generally, to find out Christ from the Bible only. In the first days of Christianity the poverty and illiteracy of the primitive Christians (I. Cor. i. 26–28), the continued pagan persecutions, the rarity of manuscripts, the doubts existing about the canon until the end of the fourth century, the spread of apocryphal and heretical versions,—prove to evidence that they learned, as Christ and His Apostles declared all Christians must learn, not from a book they did not possess, not from a book they could not read, but from the voice of a divine, infallible teaching authority.

Indeed, it is as futile to speak of "Bible Christians" in the days of primitive Christianity, when men died for Christ by the thousands, as to speak of the Emperor Nero or Decius travelling about in a Pullman palace car, their families going down the Appian Way in an automobile, their generals using smokeless powder, Maxim guns, or Mauser bullets. or their ministers reading telegraphic despatches from all parts of the Empire. Let us not picture the Roman Christian of the third century with a ninety-eight-cent edition of the Protestant Bible.

What, again, of the millions of Christians all down the centuries who possessed no copies of the Scriptures, or who could not read them, or understand them, if they did? What of the illiterates of our own day?—when, as W. S. Lilly says, "the average man is as well fitted to interpret the Bible as he is to lecture on the Hegelian philosophy, or to settle fine points of Hindu law."

9th. Finally, if the Bible were the only way to find out Christ, individual Bible reading should of itself have tended to maintain and spread Christianity. Surely candid men must admit that it has not done so.

"The divisions of modern sects afford a strong argument," writes Palmer (Protestant), "for the necessity of submission to the judgment of the universal Church; for surely it is impossible that Christ could have designed His disciples to break into a hundred different sects contending with each other on every doctrine of religion. It is impossible, I say, that this system of endless division can be Christian. It cannot but be the result of some deep rooted, some universal error, some radically false principle, which is common to all these sects. And what principle do they hold in common except the right of each individual to oppose his judgment to that of all the Church? The principle, then, must be utterly false and unfounded" ("The Church," vol. ii. p. 85).

Luther bears witness to the destructive character of his principle of private judgment in his own day: "This one will not hear of baptism, that one denies the sacrament, another puts a world between this and the last day; some teach that Christ is not God; some say this, some say that; there are about as many sects and creeds as there are heads. No yokel is so rude but when he has dreams and fancies he thinks himself inspired by the Holy Ghost, and must be a prophet" (De Wette, vol. iii. p. 61).

Catholics of the sixteenth century prophesied

the result, and any student of twentieth century Protestantism will acknowledge they were right. Men have appealed to the Bible to justify every denial of Christian teaching, until in our own day the descendants of Luther are either indifferentists, or utter unbelievers. The orthodox Protestant to-day finds himself powerless before the onslaught of the modern destructive rationalistic Higher ·Criticism, and is inevitably drifting either toward Rome or Rationalism.

You teach that we must find out the teachings of Jesus from the Church. Did He not say: " Search the Scriptures, for in them ye think ye have eternal life, and they are they which testify of me " ? (John v. 39).

These words of our Lord by no means imply an obligation on all men to read the Bible in order to find out His teaching. He was speaking to the unbelieving doctors of the law, whom neither His words nor works had convinced. They were well versed in the Old Testament—not a word of the New Testament was written—and held it as the word of God. Christ tells them, therefore, to read carefully those passages of the Old Testament that testify of Him as the promised Messias. Thus Catholics say to Protestants to-day: Read carefully those passages of the New Testament that declare the Catholic Church the divine, infallible teacher of Christ's revelation.

The argument of Protestants from this text, if clearly understood, is evidently unsound. It runs thus : Christ told the Jews to search the Old Testament for proofs of His Messianic mission. Therefore, the New Testament is to be searched in order to find out all He taught! This is logic with a vengeance.

Did not the Bible praise the Bereans for their study of the Bible (Acts xvii. 11), "searched the Scriptures daily, whether those things were so " ?

" This earnest toil of the Bereans was evidently one of verification, not one of construction. They did not think to find the truth by reading Scripture without note or comment, and building up each for himself a system of faith, morals, and worship. They went to the Scriptures full of what they had just heard. They searched diligently to see whether matters really stood as St. Paul had represented them in his sermon, whether he had quoted the Scriptures correctly, and whether the interpretation he had given was a plausible, a probable, a convincing one " (Bridgett, " The Ritual of the New Testament," p. 13).

DIVINE TRADITION.

By what right do you teach doctrines not found in the Bible? Does not this put the Church above the word of God? Did not Christ rebuke the Pharisees for "teaching doctrines and commandments of men" (Matt. xv. 9) and "making void the word of God by your own tradition"? (Mark vii. 13).

Because the origin of our faith is not the Bible alone, but the Church which gives us both the written and the unwritten word. St. Paul speaks of "traditions learned by word and by epistle" (II. Thess. ii. 14). Christ rebuked the Pharisees for setting up their own views, viz., regarding the Sabbath, as part of the divine revelation. Still the Jews held by divine tradition many truths that were not set forth in the Scriptures, *v. g.*, the canon and inspiration of the Old Testament.

So in the New Law, Catholics believe some things not in the Scriptures, although wholly in accord with them, because of the infallible witness of the Church as to their divine or apostolic origin. Why do Protestants accept the Scriptures as inspired? Why do they honor the first day of the week instead of the seventh? Why do they baptize children? Contrary to their principles, they must look outside the Bible to the voice of tradition, which is not human, but divine, because guaranteed by the divine, infallible witness of the Catholic Church.

Why are there more books in your Bible than in ours? Why do Catholics consider the Apocrypha as Scripture? Why don't all Christians have the same number of books in their Bible?

Catholics are infallibly certain that all the books of their Bible are inspired, because of the divine, infallible witness of the Church of Jesus Christ, voiced by the Councils of Trent (1545–65) and the Vatican (1869–70). Protestants, lacking this divine, infallible teacher, can never be certain what books form the canon of Holy Scripture.

The Hebrew canon of the Palestinian Jews differed from that of the Greek Septuagint of the Alexandrian Jews, which contained in addition the books of Tobias, Judith, Wisdom, Ecclesiasticus, Baruch, I. and II. Machabees. With regard to the New Testament, the early Christians greatly doubted as to the canonicity of the Epistle to the Hebrews, II. Peter, II. and III. John, St. James, St. Jude, and the Apocalypse.

Other books, now reckoned by the Catholic Church as apocrypha, were read in the early Christian churches, and deemed by many a part of Holy Writ; *v. g.*, the Epistle of Barnabas, the Shepherd of Hermas, the Epistles of Clement.

Amid this great doubt and uncertainty regarding the sacred canon, the Catholic has the only way of attaining certainty—the infallible voice of the divine authority established by Christ. The Protestant, on the other hand, is totally at loss, for he has no standard of judging. So, inconsistently, he rejects the seven doubtful books of the Old Testament, and accepts the seven doubtful books of the New. Is this reasonable?

Remember, too, that the Council of Trent merely repeated the same list of canonical books enumerated as early as the fourth century in the Council of Hippo (A.D. 393) and the two Councils of Carthage (A.D. 397 and 419).

Is it not strange that if the Septuagint version enumerated books not belonging to the canon, Christ and His Apostles should have continually cited it? For some 300 out of the 350 quotations from the Old Testament found in the New are taken from the Greek of this version, which contained all the books of the Catholic Bible of to-day.

In the sixteenth century Luther, on the Protestant principle of private judgment, rejected the Epistle of St. James as "a straw-epistle," and said of the Apocalypse : "I find many things defective in this book, which make

me consider it neither Apostolic nor prophetic"
(Introduction to the New Testament of 1522;
cf. J. Verres, "Luther," p. 113).

To-day the rationalistic descendants of Luther claim the same right of private judgment
to reject not merely one or seven books, but the
entire canon of the Old and New Testament,
denying its divine inspiration, and put the
Bible on the level of mere Oriental literature.
Protestantism has no rational, certain argument
whereby to defend its canon. ("Canon of the
New Testament," *Dublin Review*, Oct., 1893;
T. Mullen, "Canon of the Old Testament";
Gigot, "General Introduction to Holy Scripture"; Loisy, "Histoire du Canon de l'Ancien
Testament"; Loisy, "Histoire du Canon de
Nouveau Testament"; Vigoroux, "Diction-
naire de la Bible.")

**What do Catholics mean by the inspiration of
the Scriptures? Must Catholics believe that
God inspired every word?**

"Biblical inspiration may be described as a
divine and positive influence exerted upon
certain men for the purpose of transmitting
truth to others, and in such a manner that the
books composed by the sacred writers have
God for their author" (Gigot, "Biblical Lectures," p. 351).

Catholics believe that "the books of the Old

and the New Testament are to be received as sacred and canonical, in their integrity, and with all their parts, as they are enumerated in the decrees of the said Council (Trent), and are contained in the ancient Latin edition of the Vulgate, . . . because, having been written by the inspiration of the Holy Ghost, they have God for their author" (Vatican, Sess. III. ch. ii.) The Bible is, therefore, inspired not merely because it *contains the Word of God*, but because it is in a true sense *the Word of God*.

As regards God's share in the production of the Scriptures, Cardinal Manning writes: "Inspiration, in the special and technical sense, includes the three following operations of the Holy Ghost upon the sacred writers: (1) the impulse to put in writing the matter which God wills they should record; (2) the suggestion of the matter to be written, whether by revelation of truths not previously known, or only by the promptings of those things which were within the writer's knowledge; (3) the assistance which excludes liability to error in writing all things, whatever may be suggested to them by the Spirit of God, to be written" ("The Temporal Mission of the Holy Ghost," p. 161).

As regards man's share in the production of Holy Writ, Catholics believe that, "though

acting, as co-agents under God's special influence, the inspired writers are no mere pas-
sive instruments, but bear themselves under
the divine action as truly intelligent, active,
and free agents " (Gigot, "General Introduction to the Holy Scriptures," p. 546). The
sacred writers may have been unaware of the
fact of their inspiration, they may commit to
writing what they already know from personal
knowledge, pre-existing documents, eye-wit-
nesses, and other aids (Luke i. 3; John xix.
35; II. Mach. ii. 27) ; their literary style and
wording may be their own (II. Mach. xv.
39, 40); hence verbal variances between inspired writers (Matt. v. 3 ; Luke vi. 20; Matt.
xxvi. 26; Luke xxii. 19 ; Mark xiv. 22, and
I. Cor. xi. 23). The dictation, therefore, of
each word—verbal inspiration—is by no means
essential to a true notion of inspiration
(Schanz, "A Christian Apology," vol. i. ch.
xiii.)

**How do you know what are the inspired books
of Scripture ?**

By the divine, infallible testimony of the true
Church of God, which is the only completely
adequate and rational ground for a divine faith
in all the Sacred Scriptures. "As the inspiration of the sacred books is a divine operation not necessarily known even to the mind

that is acted upon by the Holy Spirit, it necessarily follows that the testimony of God Himself is required to make men perfectly sure of its existence; but this divine testimony comes to their knowledge, and is the absolute ground of their faith, only by the voice of that infallible and living Church which He has commanded us to hear" (Gigot, "Biblical Lectures," p. 368; Wiseman, "Doctrines and Practices of the Catholic Church," Lecture II.)

Protestants, rejecting the divine| authority of the living voice of God's Church, generally fall back upon intrinsic proofs for inspiration, namely, the superhuman structure and contents of the sacred books, their inspiring and elevating character, their organic unity, their moral effect upon the earnest reader, and the like. Other Protestants, realizing the inadequacy of these merely internal criteria, appeal to the authority of Christ and the Apostles; but they fail to see that our Lord's testimony, given previous to the writing of the book,— which he nowhere directed to be written or even named or suggested,—cannot be made to apply to the New Testament; and that although an argument may be deduced from the fact that a book was written by an Apostle, still such reasoning will not apply to all the books of the New Testament; for instance, the

Acts, the Gospels of St. Mark and St. Luke,
etc. (Gigot, *ibid.*, pp. 355–368).

No wonder, then, that Protestantism with its
vague and varying views regarding inspiration,
its narrowing of inspiration to certain parts of
the Bible, its admission of error in the sacred
writings, its inadequate proofs for the fact of
inspiration and the right of a book to be on the
canon, is powerless to resist the attacks of the
rationalistic Higher Criticism, which endeavors
to strip the Word of God of its divine character. Many lovers of the Bible have come
to recognize the Catholic Church as its only
adequate and rational defender. No matter
what difficulties may be raised by the unbeliever against the inspiration of the Scriptures,
Catholics can always ground their certain faith
in them on the infallible authority of God's
Church. It is the old argument of St. Augustine : " I would not believe the Gospel, unless
the authority of the Church moved me thereto." (Gigot, "General Introduction to the
Scriptures,"; Breen, "Introduction to the
Study of Holy Scripture.")

Why does the Catholic Church withhold the
Bible from the laity?

Why are Catholics forbidden to read the Bible?

Why are not Catholics allowed to read the
Protestant Bible?

Did not the Scriptures practically perish in the dark ages owing to the disregard of the clergy for the pure word of God?

Was not Luther the first to translate the Bible into the language of the people?

It is a calumny arising from ignorance or malice to declare the Catholic Church was ever an enemy to the devout reading of the Word of God.

In the Middle Ages the monks and nuns copied out the Bible word for word from Genesis to the Apocalypse, the clergy preached from it continually, lectured on it in their schools and universities, and often prepared from its pages special prayer-books for the people. " There is a good deal of popular misapprehension about the way in which the Bible was regarded in the Middle Ages," writes Dr. Cutts (Protestant; "Turning Points of English History," p. 200). Some people think that it was very little read, even by the clergy ; whereas the fact is that the sermons of the mediæval preachers are more full of Scriptural quotations and allusions than any sermons in these days; and the writers on other subjects are so full of Scriptural allusion that it is evident their minds were saturated with Scriptural diction. We have the authority of Sir Thomas More ("Dial." iii. 14) for saying that "the whole Bible was, long before Wyclif's days, by virtuous and well-learned men translated into the English tongue, and by good and goodly people with devotion and soberness well and reverently ·read.''

Dean Maitland (Protestant) shows clearly˜the reverence of the Middle Ages for God's holy Book (''The Dark Ages,'' pp. 208–241), and answering the calumnies of certain anti-Catholic controversialists, says: '' I do not recollect any instance in which it is recorded that the Scriptures, or any part of them, were treated with indignity, or with less than profound respect.''

'' The notion that the people in the Middle Ages,'' writes another fair-minded Protestant, '' did not read their Bibles . . . is not simply a mistake ; it is one of the most ludicrous and grotesque blunders '' (*Church Quarterly Review*, Oct., 1879).

Another strange bit of old-time controversy is the pretended discovery by Luther of the hitherto unknown Bible, at Erfurth, in 1503, and his first giving it to the people in the vernacular in 1534.. This calumny, resting on the authority of D'Aubigné, in his unscholarly history of the Reformation, has been given the lie direct by honest Protestants like Dean Maitland (''The Dark Ages,'' pp. 475–6, 506–514).

What are the facts ? '' Before the first

Protestant version was sent forth into the
world there appeared 84 printed editions of
Holy Writ in the ancient languages; 62 in
Hebrew, of which 12 were of the Old Testament entire, and 50 of selected portions; and
22 in Greek, of which 3 were of the Old
Testament, 12 of the New Testament, and
7 of separate portions' of the Scriptures. In
the Latin, which occupied a special position as being the universal language of
the educated men of the time, there were
published 343 editions, of which 148 were
of the entire Bible, 62 of the New Testament,
and 133 of separate books of the inspired
writings.

"In the modern languages . . . there
were issued 198 editions, of which 104 were
of the entire Bible, comprising 20 in Italian,
26 in French, 19 in Flemish, 2 in Spanish, 6 in
Bohemian, 1 in Sclavonic, and 30 in German,
and 94 of single portions of Holy Writ, consisting chiefly of copies of the New Testament
and the Psalms. In all, including the Poly-
glot printed at the cost of Cardinal Ximenes,
626 editions of the Bible and portions of the
Bible, of which 198 were in the languages of
the laity, had issued from the press with the
sanction and at the instance of the Church,
in countries where she reigned supreme, before
Luther's German version of the Bible appeared

in 1534 " (Gigot, " Biblical Lectures," pp. 311, 312).

The Catholic Church has never prohibited the reading of the Bible in the original texts, or in the approved Latin Vulgate version.

The Jews and heretics in the early Church, the Albigenses in the thirteenth century, the Wyclifites in the fifteenth, the Protestants of the sixteenth sought to defend their errors by perverting the sacred text.

Naturally, therefore, as its guardian and interpreter, the Catholic Church, out of zeal for the pure word of God, was in duty bound to warn her children against human travesties thereof in the vernacular. The local and universal laws against Bible reading in the vernacular except with proper safeguards— *v.g.*, the synod of Toulouse (1229 A.D.), of Tarragona (1233 A.D.), of Oxford (1408 A.D.), the rules of the Index (1574 A.D., 1897 A.D.), the laws of Benedict XIV. (1757 A.D.), Pius VIII. (1829), etc., are evident proofs of her love of Holy Scriptures. The same principle guides the state in passing her laws against counterfeiters. Would you say our country is opposed to the use of good money because she does not permit unlimited counterfeiting?

A study of the English Protestant versions— Tyndale's New Testament, Cranmer's Great Bible (1539 A.D.), the Bishop's Bible (1568

A.D.), the Authorized Version (1611), and the Revised Version (1881)—will show a record of grave omissions, additions, and changes in the sacred text.

Consider, for example, the changes in the King James version which affect some of the essential doctrines of Christianity; *v.g.*, the priesthood (Acts xiv. 23; xv. 2; Tit. i. 5; I. Tim. v. 17, 19; James v. 14), the episcopate (Acts xx. 28), and the fact that it omits seven entire books of the Old Testament, and parts of Daniel and Esther.

The inaccuracy of Luther's German translation was pointed out by his Catholic contemporary Emser, and Bunsen says there are at least 3,000 faulty translations (Verres, "Luther," p. 111; Audin's "Life of Luther," vol. ii.) Indeed, Luther never scrupled to change the text, if the change would enable him to Lutheranize St. Paul; *v.g.*, Rom. iii. 20, 28, where he changes the sense entirely by adding the words *only* and *alone*.

The Catholic Church, therefore, encourages the reading of translations of the Bible in the vernacular provided they bear the imprimatur of the bishop, and are edited with explanatory notes. On the title-page of many English Catholic Bibles one may read the letter of Pius VI. to the Archbishop of Florence (April, 1778):

"At a time that a vast number of bad books, which grossly attack the Catholic religion, are circulated even among the unlearned, to the great destruction of souls, you judge exceedingly well that the faithful should be excited to the reading of the Holy Scriptures; for these are the most abundant sources, which ought to be left open to every one, to draw from them purity of morals and of doctrine, to eradicate the errors which are so widely disseminated in these corrupt times."

Pius VII. wrote in the same strain to the English vicars-apostolic "to encourage their people to read the Holy Scriptures; for nothing can be more useful, more consoling, and more animating, because they serve to confirm the faith, to support the hope, and to influence the charity of the true Christian."

Leo XIII. said in his late encyclical (1893) on the Bible : "The solicitude of the apostolic office naturally urges, and even compels us, not only to desire that this great source of Catholic revelation should be made safely and abundantly accessible to the flock of Jesus Christ, but also not to suffer any attempt to defile or corrupt it."

Indeed, on December 3, 1898, Pope Leo granted an indulgence to all Catholics who will spend fifteen minutes a day in the devout reading of the Gospels of Jesus Christ.

Why did the monks chain the Bible in the Middle Ages?

To save it from thieves. · Why do people chain a cup to the town-pump, or a city directory to a desk in a drug store? This is readily understood when one considers how valuable a copy of the Scriptures was in those days, owing to the fact that they were copied out word for word by the monks. Whole libraries were chained in this way, both in England and on the Continent. What great ignorance of history is shown by those who imagine that "the chained Bible" implied that the Bible was only accessible to a few monks, who were under orders from the Pope to keep it from the people as far as possible! How prejudice will read into facts its own false inferences!

Why are Catholics opposed to the reading of the Bible in public schools?

One good reason is because the Protestant version used in the public schools is a faulty translation of the Word of God, and leaves out a number of books in the Old Testament. Moreover, Catholics object to its being read, and often commented on, by men and women of every creed and no creed, who often know little or nothing of its meaning, and even regard it at times as a mere human book.

CREATION IN SIX DAYS.

Must Catholics believe that the world was created in six days?

Not at all. The Catholic Church has decided nothing dogmatically about the Mosaic cosmogony, so that Catholics are allowed the greatest liberty in interpreting the meaning of the six days.

The purpose of the writer of Genesis is to declare the great fact of the creation of the world, and to lead the Jews to honor the Sabbath day (Exod. xxxi. 16). The chief theories regarding the six days are:

1st. The *allegorical* theory of St. Augustine ("De Gen. ad Lit.," iv. v. 26) and St. Thomas ("De Pot.," q. 2, a. 4), that the whole act of creation occupied but an instant of time.

2d. The *literal* theory of days of twenty-four hours each, which is now generally rejected (Veith, Bosizio).

3d. The *periodic* theory that the "days" are indefinitely long epochs, which allow for all the data required by geology and paleontology (Hettinger, Holzammer, Pianciani).

4th. The *revelation* theory that the days are so many visions vouchsafed Moses by God, with no reference to time whatsoever (Von Hummelauer).

5th. The *idealistic* theory, which regards the

whole account of the creation of the world as a hymn in which various portions of creation are commemorated on the days of the week. (Bishop Clifford, pp. 280–343, G. P. Putnam & Sons, 1870; G. Molloy, "Geology and Revelation"; Bishop Clifford, *Dublin Review*, April, 1883; Mgr. Meignan, "Le Monde et l'Homme primitif"; Arduin, "Le Religion en face de la Science"; Vigouroux, "Manuel Biblique," vol. i.)

Who was Cain's wife? (Gen. iv. 17). If Adam, Eve, Cain, and Abel were the only people in the world, where did Cain get his wife?

Cain most probably married his own sister, or his niece. Cain and Abel had many brothers and sisters, as we learn from Gen. v. 4: "And the days of Adam after he begot Seth were eight hundred years. And· he begot sons and daughters." This query, which is met with universally on the non-Catholic missions, arises from one of two difficulties: 1st, the morality of an apparently incestuous marriage; or, 2d, the denial of the unity of the race.

With regard to the first, St. Augustine answers this very question nearly fifteen centuries ago: "As, therefore, the human race, subsequently to the first marriage of the man who was made of dust, and his wife who was made out of his side, required the union of male and female, in order that it might multiply; and. as there were no human beings except those who had been born of these two, men took their sisters for wives; an act which was as certainly dictated by necessity in these ancient days, as afterwards it was condemned by the prohibitions of religion " ("The City of God," book xv. ch. xvi.)

The moral principles involved are plain to any student of Catholic ethics. Some actions are so intrinsically evil and opposed to the natural law, that no power, not even God, can permit them for any reason whatsoever— *v.g.*, blasphemy, lying, etc. Other actions against nature are evil because of the evil consequences that result, unless God by a special providence intervene to prevent. In this class must be put the marriage of brother and sister. Nature itself vetoes such marriages as utterly subversive of all domestic and social morality. This was felt even by the pagan Roman, although the Egyptians and the Athenians permitted such marriages. No human power—no church—could grant dispensation in such a case, but God the Lord and Creator of all things could permit such marriages in the beginning to propagate the human race, there being no other way to do so save by miraculous intervention.

The second difficulty likewise dates from the

Preadamites of the seventeenth century, who held that Adam was the father of the Jewish people, but not of the pagans. This theory is in direct contradiction to the Scriptures (Gen. ii. 5, 20; iii. 20; Wis. x. 1.; Acts xvii. 26; Rom. v. 12), which expressly declares the race descended from Adam and Eve, especially as set forth in the dogmas of original sin. For a complete discussion of the subject, and answer to the objections brought forward by unbelievers, read Vigouroux, "Manuel Biblique," n. 301; "Les Livres Saints," vol. iii. ch. 5; Guibert, "Origin of Species," ch. v.

In the King James version it is said that Cain went into the land of Nod and there knew his wife; but this is spurious Scripture.

THE AGE OF THE HUMAN RACE.

Must Catholics believe that the human race dates from the year 4004 B. C.? Does not modern science give the lie direct to the Biblical chronology with regard to the antiquity of man?

By no means. Catholics are perfectly free to form their own opinion upon this question, which has never been defined by the Church.

The Abbé Moigno writes ("Splendeurs de la Foi," ii. p. 612) : "The exact date of the creation of man, of his first appearance upon the

earth, remains entirely uncertain or unknown ;
but there would be some rashness in carrying it
back beyond 8,000 years."

Another distinguished scholar, Abbé Hamard
("La Science et l'Apologétique Chrétienne," p.
31), says: "That it is necessary to adopt the
chronology of the Septuagint, as affording us
notably more time, we are convinced ; but we
fail to see any reason for carrying this chronology beyond the 8,000 or 10,000 years which it
affords us as a maximum."

Father Zahm, after a careful discussion of the
question in four articles of the *American Catholic Quarterly* (1893, pp. 225-248, 562-588, 719-
734 ; 1894, pp. 260-272), thus sums up : "The
evidence we have examined regarding the age
of our race proves one thing, and proves it most
conclusively ; and that is, that the question we
have been discussing is far from being definitely
answered by Scripture or science, and according
to present indications it seems improbable that
we shall ever have a certain answer regarding
this much controverted topic. The testimony
of astronomy does not, as such, make either for
or against the Biblical chronology, because
astronomy as a science was not cultivated until
some thousands of years after the advent of man
on the earth. The testimony of history, and
especially the history which takes us back
farthest—the history of Egypt, Assyria, Chal-

dea, and Babylonia—admirably corroborates the testimony of the Bible concerning the antiquity of man. The sciences of linguistics, ethnology, and physiology have discovered nothing that is incompatible with the acceptance of the chronology of Scripture as understood by our most competent apologists. The statements of geology and prehistoric archæology are so vague and conflicting and extravagant that nothing definite can be gathered from them beyond the apparently indisputable fact that the age of our species is greater than the advocates of the Hebrew and Samaritan texts of the Bible have been wont to admit. It may, however, be asserted positively that no certain geologic or archæologic evidence so far adduced is irreconcilable with archæology that we are warranted in deducing from the known facts and geological records of the Book of Books." (*American Catholic Quarterly*, vol. xix. pp. 269, 270; Sir J. W. Dawson, "Modern Science in Bible Lands"; Vigouroux, "Manuel Biblique," vol. i.; "Les Livres Saints," vol. iii.)

VICIOUS CIRCLE.

You Catholics prove the Church by the Bible, and then, reversing the process, prove the Bible by the Church. Is not this reasoning in a circle ?

If we proved the divine authority of the Church from the inspired Scriptures, and then proved the inspiration of the Scriptures from the divine authority of the Church, we should indeed be faulty in our logic. But such is not the Catholic position, as fair-minded Protestants like Palmer readily grant ("The Church," vol. ii. p. 63).

The average Protestant does not seem to realize that the historical character of the New Testament is totally separate from the fact of its inspiration. He assumes without proof that the Bible is God's word, although the unbeliever will tell him that is to be proved absolutely, before a man can back an argument with a Bible text.

The Catholic carefully distinguishes between the historical value of the New Testament, which is a matter of evidence, and the divine inspiration, which demands a divine witness. The Catholic proves by mere critical arguments —just as he would prove a book of Cæsar or Tacitus—that the New Testament Scriptures are genuine and authentic documents of the first century, which relate how Jesus Christ, who claimed and proved Himself to be the Son of God, established in the world a divine, authoritative, and infallible teacher, to teach His gospel and pardon sin in His name until the end of the world. Having proved this by reason, the Catholic accepts without question the divine, infallible teaching of this representative of Christ, the Catholic Church, on matters of faith and morality; among these teachings is the divine, internal fact of Bible inspiration, which could never be known by textual criticism, human traditions, or prayerful study of the Word of God.

In a word, therefore, the Church is proved on the historical authority of the New Testament; but the historical value of the New Testament is not proved by the Church; therefore there is no fallacy in our reasoning.

Indeed, all Catholics know that their Church was well established, and that her claims were acknowledged by thousands of Christians—converts from Judaism and paganism—before a single line of the New Testament was written, and that many martyrs died before the books of the New Testament were gathered together, once for all, at the close of the fourth century.

The Church could be proved, then, without the Bible; so likewise to-day, if there were no Bible in the world, she would bear witness to

Christ by her unity, holiness, catholicity, and apostolicity (Wiseman, "Doctrines of the Church," Lecture III., p. 62, *et seq.*)

THE CHURCH.

What are the conditions of entrance into the Catholic Church?

Must a convert to your Church be baptized again, and confess the sins of a lifetime?

The Catholic Church, in accordance with the teaching of the Scriptures, requires of all adults who seek admittance into her one true fold the repentance of all past sin, the detestation of all past error, and the firm, certain belief in all the doctrines taught by Christ. "He that believeth and is baptized shall be saved" (Mark xvi. 16); "Do penance and be baptized" (Acts ii. 38).

If a convert is absolutely sure of his baptism, he cannot be rebaptized, but is bound to confess all grievous sins committed after baptism. If a Protestant is uncertain about his former baptism—a frequent case in our day of lax Christian views and practice—he is baptized conditionally, with the form: "*If thou art not baptized*, I baptize thee in the name of the Father, and of the Son, and of the Holy Ghost." The sacrament of penance is also given conditionally, so that a convert is certain of the forgiveness of sins through one sacrament or the other.

A convert is obliged to study carefully the doctrines of the catechism, so that he may have an accurate knowledge of Catholic teaching, and be able intelligently to take the oath of the profession of faith : " With a sincere heart, therefore, and with unfeigned faith, I detest and abjure every error, heresy, and sect, opposed to the said Holy, Catholic, and Apostolic Roman Church. So help me God, and these His holy Gospels, which I touch with my hand."

Should not a person live and die in the Church of their baptism, especially if they have sworn to do so ?

I have met a number of Lutherans in the Northwest who told me that they had taken an oath to die Lutherans. Such an oath to worship Christ in a false Christianity, which He as the God of truth necessarily condemns, is not binding, once a person discovers that the Catholic Church is the only Church possessing the entire gospel of the Saviour. He must abandon his heresy and schism once he discovers them, else salvation is impossible.

Such a one does not hate his own parents and other relations, as some simple souls are taught to believe, but rather loves them the more, and prays until death for their conversion. Naturally he will be anxious for them, knowing that possibly they may be sinfully resisting the grace of God which would bring them into the true fold. How strangely intolerant are some parents, who contrary to that first principle of their Protestantism—private judgment—persecute with bitter hatred their own flesh and blood who, obedient to conscience and to God's grace, embrace the religion of their forefathers, in the old Church of Jesus Christ. Error is never consistent.

"The religion of my parents is good enough for me," say some. If you were born in poverty, would you think the condition of your parents precluded all notion of your bettering your condition? So, in like manner, once convinced of the poverty of the partial gospel you possess, as a rational man you are bound to embrace "the unsearchable riches" of the true gospel of Christ (Eph. iii. 8).

Is it true that Catholics are bound to hate Protestants? I read in your profession of faith that every convert must take the following oath on the Gospels: "With a sincere heart, therefore, and with unfeigned faith, I detest and abjure every error, heresy, and sect opposed to the said Holy, Catholic, and Apostolic Roman Church."

It is not true. The universal love of our fellow-men, no matter what their race, color, or religion, is the strict commandment of Christ: "Thou shalt love thy neighbor as thyself" (Matt. xix. 19). And the beloved disciple, St. John, teaches: "If any man say, I love God, and hateth his brother, he is a liar. For he that loveth not his brother, whom he seeth, how can he love God, whom he seeth not" (I. John iv. 20).

The words of the profession of faith are objective, and imply that, as followers of Christ in the one divine society which has ever kept His gospel pure and uncorrupted, we detest, even as He and His Apostles did (Matt. vii. 15; xii. 25, 30; xvi. 16; xviii. 17; Rom. xvi. 17; I. Cor. i. 10; Gal. i. 9; Eph. iv. 4; Heb. xiii. 7-9, etc.), all heresy which is a denial of God's truth, and schism, which is a withdrawal from the one fold of the Good Shepherd (John x. 16). They in no way refer to the individuals belonging to false religions or spurious Christianities, who, through the sins of their ancestors and ignorance of the true gospel, are separated from the Church of the living God.

My mother—a good soul and a sincere Protestant—assures me that it will break her heart if I become a Catholic. I believe all the teachings of your Church, but find it hard to pain one so dear to me.

A very practical difficulty, and one that has been given me scores of times by timid, doubting souls.

The true follower of Christ dare not hesitate to obey His teaching once it is known, for to be false to one's conscience is to instantly imperil one's eternal salvation.

Our Lord speaks of this opposition of relatives, but declares that He and His teaching must come first:

" For I come to set a man at variance against his father, and the daughter against her mother. . . . He that loveth father or mother more than Me, is not worthy of Me" (Matt x. 35, 37).

No true parent can find fault with a child who is loyal to conscience and to truth; no true parent can desire a child to commit grievous sin by deliberately refusing to do what he knows to be the will of God.

The Catholic Church interprets the fourth commandment, "Honor thy father and thy mother," to imply obedience in all that is good and lawful. If a parent command or advise something contrary to God's law, a child is bound to disobey, on the apostolic principle: "We ought to obey God rather than men" (Acts v. 29).

VISIBILITY.

What do Catholics mean by the Church?

Did not Jesus declare that His kingdom was only to exist in the heart of man? " The kingdom of God is within you " (Luke xvii. 21).

Should not the bond of fellowship in Christ be merely internal?

"By the Church on earth, Catholics understand the visible community of believers, founded by Christ, in which by means of an enduring apostleship, established by Him, and appointed to conduct all nations, in the course of ages, back to God, the works wrought by Him during His earthly life, for the redemption and sanctification of mankind, are, under the guidance of His Spirit, continued to the end of the world " (Möhler, " Symbolism," ch. v. pp. xxxvi. 253).

All the figures and parables used by our Saviour and the Apostles to designate the Church declare it to be a visible organism. It is called a kingdom (Matt. iv. 23; xiii. 24), a field (Matt. xiii. 24), a grain of mustard-seed that becometh a tree (Matt. xiii. 31, 32), a flock (Acts xx. 28), a city seated on a mountain (Matt. v. 14), a body (I. Cor. xii. 13), the body of Christ (I. Cor. xii. 27; Eph. i. 22, 23).

The very fact of the Incarnation—the Word

becoming flesh to speak, teach, work, suffer, and die as man—ought to lead any thinking man to believe that the perpetuation of the Incarnation must needs be through a visible medium which, like Christ, would be both human and divine.

Christ was not merely a teacher of doctrine, but an organizer of a society. He chooses twelve men under the leadership of Simon Peter, gives them power to teach all nations in His name, and declares those condemned who will not hearken. Our Lord could not command us to hear the Church (Matt. xviii. 17; Mark xvi. 16), unless it were a visible society that could be recognized by all.

Undoubtedly the Church is a spiritual and supernatural society, and the externals of its government, hierarchy, preaching, and sacraments have no other purpose than the invisible cleansing of men's hearts from sin, and the invisible enlightenment of men's minds of error; but, as Cardinal Newman declared, "the Church is not a secret society." Its doctrines, laws, and worship can be known clearly and definitely at all times and in all places.

The true follower of Christ, therefore, is the man living in the faith and love of Christ Jesus, which is infallibly guaranteed and given him by the visible Church established by the Son of God.

The text in question is not to the point. The Pharisees, who expected the Messias to come with kingly power, asked Jesus, when the kingdom of God should come? He rebuked them, and declared the kingdom of God had already come, and was being preached by Him to the Jews.

INFALLIBILITY.

How are we in the twentieth century to find out with certainty all that the Saviour taught?

How can you arrogantly claim that your Church is infallible?

The Catholic says, with St. Paul: "Faith cometh by hearing" (Rom. x. 17). The only way for all men to find out all Christ's teachings with certainty is to listen to the living voice of a divine, infallible teacher: the Catholic Church. The Catholic believes that, together with the written word of God, there is a divine tradition of gospel truth—both of which are safeguarded and interpreted by a divine, infallible authority instituted by Christ.

If we study well the Scriptures, merely as genuine historical documents, we find that the Saviour selected certain of His disciples to be the teachers of His revelation, and that He invested them with His own divine power and authority. He sent them to preach His gospel to the whole world, He commanded men to believe them under penalty of damnation, He promised to guarantee all they taught by His own abiding presence, and to preserve them from error by the abiding of the Holy Ghost, the Spirit of Truth.

"And He chose twelve of them, whom also He named Apostles" (Luke vi. 13).

"All power is given to Me in heaven and in earth. Going therefore, teach ye all nations. . . . Teaching them to observe all things whatsoever I have commanded you; and behold I am with you all days, even to the consummation of the world " (Matt. xxviii. 18–20).

"Go ye into the whole world, and preach the gospel to every creature. He that believeth and is baptized, shall be saved; but he that believeth not, shall be condemned " (Mark xvi. 15, 16).

"As the Father hath sent Me, I also send you " (John xx. 21).

" He that heareth you, heareth Me; and he that despiseth you, despiseth Me; and he that despiseth Me, despiseth Him that sent Me" (Luke x. 16).

"And if he will not hear the Church, let him be to thee as the heathen and publican " (Matt. xviii. 17).

"But you shall receive the power of the

Holy Ghost coming upon you, and you shall be witnesses unto Me in Jerusalem, and in all Judea, and Samaria, and even to the uttermost part of the earth " (Acts i. 8).

"And I will ask the Father, and He shall give you another Paraclete, that He may abide with you for ever, the Spirit of truth. . . . He shall abide with you, and shall be in you" (John xiv. 16, 17).

"But the Paraclete, the Holy Ghost, whom the Father will send in My name, He will teach you all things, and bring all things to your mind, whatsoever I shall have said to you" (John xiv. 26).

It is evident from these words of the Saviour that the gospel is not to be limited to a book, but learned from living teachers whose doctrine and government are identical with His, authoritative, infallible, and divine.

If we turn to the writings of the Apostles, we see that they expressly claim the authority of divine infallible teachers of God's revelation, and demand absolute obedience under penalty of damnation (Mark xvi. 16). All other teachers are to be avoided, as teaching false doctrine.

"How then shall they call on Him, in whom they have not believed? Or how shall they believe Him, of whom they have not heard? And how shall they hear without a preacher?

And how shall they preach unless they are
sent? . . . Faith then cometh by hearing; and hearing by the word of Christ"
(Rom. x. 14, 17).

"By whom [Jesus Christ] we have received
grace and Apostleship for obedience to the faith,
in all nations, for His name" (Rom. i. 5).

"To us God hath revealed by His Spirit.
. . . Now we have received not the spirit
of this world but the Spirit that is of God;
that we may know the things that are given
us from God, which things also we speak" (I.
Cor. ii. 10, 12, 13).

"We have the mind of Christ" (I. Cor.
ii. 16).

"We are God's coadjutors" (I. Cor. iii..9).

"Let a man so account of us as of the ministers of Christ, and the dispensers of the mysteries of God" (I. Cor. iv. 1).

"[God] hath given to us the ministry of
reconciliation. . . . For Christ, therefore,
we are ambassadors, God as it were exhorting
by us" (II. Cor. v. 18–20).

"Sound doctrine, which is according to the
gospel of the glory of the blessed God, which
hath been committed to my trust" (I. Tim.
i. 10, 11).

"There are some that trouble you, and
would pervert the gospel of Christ. But
though we, or an angel from heaven, preach

a gospel to you besides that which we have preached to you, let him be anathema. . . . The gospel which was preached by me is not according to man. For neither did I receive it of man, nor did I learn it, but by the revelation of Jesus Christ " (Gal. i. 7–11).

" We are of God. He that knoweth God, heareth us. He that is not of God, heareth us not. By this we know the spirit of truth, and the spirit of error " (I. John iv. 6).

" When you had received of us the word of the hearing of God, you received it not as the word of men, but, as it is indeed, the word of God " (I. Thess. ii. 13).

Nothing is plainer, therefore, in the Scriptures than the appointment by Jesus Christ of a divine, infallible teaching body which was to preach His entire gospel to the world. There is never a word commanding His doctrine to be written ; His gospel is to be preached by the Apostles, and hearkened to by the faithful, as if He Himself were speaking.

Was this divine economy to end with the death of the Apostles? No ; Jesus Christ plainly tells us that His gospel should be taught until the end by a perpetual series of successors of the Apostolic teaching body.

He promised to be with them all days (Matt. xxviii. 20), and to send the Holy Spirit to abide with them for ever to teach them all things (John xiv. 16, 26); He gives them a mission to the whole world (Matt. xxviii. 19); to every creature (Mark xvi. 15). They personally were not to remain upon earth until the end, and so Christ's words evidently refer to a perpetual Apostolic succession to witness His gospel for ever.

We read, accordingly, in St. Paul's epistles how the Apostles ordained teachers, and commanded them in turn to ordain others who would faithfully guard the deposit of faith, and hand down to succeeding generations until the end every doctrine that had been taught by Jesus Christ.

"For this cause I left thee in Crete, that thou shouldst set in order the things that are wanting, and shouldst ordain priests in every city, as I also appointed thee" (Tit. i. 5).

"Stir up the grace of God which is in thee by the imposition of my hands" (II. Tim. i. 6).

"O Timothy, keep that which is committed to thy trust, avoiding the profane novelties of words, and oppositions of knowledge falsely so called" (I. Tim. vi. 20).

"Hold the form of sound words, which thou hast heard of me in faith, and in the love which is Christ Jesus. Keep the good thing committed to thy trust by the Holy Ghost, who dwelleth in us" (II. Tim. i. 13, 14).

"The things which thou hast heard of me by many witnesses, the same commend to faithful men, who shall be fit to teach others also" (II. Tim. ii. 2).

"Therefore, brethren, stand fast; and hold the traditions which you have learned, whether by word or by our epistle" (II. Thess. ii. 14).

"And He gave some apostles, and some prophets, and other some evangelists, and other some pastors and doctors, for the perfecting of the saints, for the work of the ministry, for the edifying of the body of Christ (*i.e.*, the Church) until we all meet in the unity of faith" (Eph. iv. 11).

Thus we see clearly that the only certain way for all men to learn the gospel of Christ is from the living voice of an infallible Church, "the pillar and ground of the truth" (I. Tim. iii. 15). Such is the teaching of Scripture; such the constant voice of tradition from the beginning.

Thus, Origen wrote in the third century: "Many think they believe what Christ taught, and some of these differ from others. . . . All should profess that doctrine which came down from the Apostles, and now continues in the Church; that alone is truth which in nothing differs from what is thus delivered" (Præf. Lib. i. Periarchon). And St. Augustine in the fifth century: "Do thou run to the tabernacle of God. Hold fast to the Catholic Church; do not depart from the rule of truth, and thou shalt be protected in the tabernacle from the contradiction of tongues" (Enar. iii. in Ps. 30).

Reason and revelation both demand that the teacher of Christ's doctrine and morality should speak with no uncertain voice. A church which disclaims infallibility must sooner or later be powerless to teach men the revelation of God. "Any supernatural religion," says the Protestant writer, Mallock, "that renounces its claim to this [absolute infallibility], it is clear can profess to be a semi-revelation only. It is a hybrid thing, partly natural and partly supernatural, and it thus practically has all the qualities of a religion that is *wholly natural*. In so far as it professes to be revealed, it of course professes to be infallible; but if the revealed part be in the first place hard to distinguish, and in the second place hard to understand; if it may mean many things, and many of those things contradictory, it might just as well have been never made at all. To make it in any sense an infallible revelation, or in other words a revelation at all, *to us*, we need a power to interpret the testament that shall have equal authority with that testament itself" ("Is Life Worth Living?" ch. xi. p. 267 *et seq.*, Putnam, 1879).

Indeed, once you grant that God has made a revelation to the world through Jesus Christ His Son, you must also grant that if all men are "to come to the knowledge of the truth" (I. Tim. ii. 4), and to believe under the penalty of damnation (Mark xvi. 16), God must necessarily guarantee with absolute infallible certainty the doctrines of salvation. He cannot allow His followers to be led astray by false prophets (Mark xiii. 21) and lying teachers (II. Pet. ii. 1), who preach a new gospel opposed to His (Gal. i. 8).

Is not Protestantism to-day, with its vagueness, contradictions, uncertainty, lack of unity in government and doctrine, constant variations, its inability to command and teach, its denial of the fundamental dogmas of Christianity, its downward tendency toward indifferentism and unbelief, a standing argument of the necessity of an infallible teacher? Disclaiming infallibility, it cannot demand the assent of any rational man.

Catholicism, with its perfect Catholic unity of government and doctrine, its definiteness, certainty, permanence amid changes of time and place and people, its divine power of teaching and commanding under penalty of hell, its absolute uncompromising condemnation of indifferentism and infidelity in every form, stands unique and alone as the divine, infallible, one,

holy, Catholic, and Apostolic society established
by the Christ. (MacLaughlin, "The Divine
Plan of the Church"; Bagshawe, "The
Church"; Cox, "The Pillar and Ground of
the Truth"; Lyons, "Christianity and Infallibility"; Möhler, "Symbolism," ch. v.;
Schanz, "A Christian Apology," vol. iii.;
Newman, "Essay on Development," p. 75 *et
seq.;* Duke, "King, Prophet, and Priest.")

Is not your doctrine of Infallibility opposed
to liberty of thought?

Is not a Catholic hampered in his search after
truth by his blind, degrading obedience to the
claims of an infallible Church?

The doctrine of infallibility is opposed to the
false liberty of thinking error, but not to the
true liberty of thinking the truth. This objection is based on the false notion that unre-
stricted liberty of thought is a good thing, and
that every man has a right to think just as he
pleases. The Catholic Church maintains, however, that no one has a right to believe what is
false, any more than he has a right to do what
is evil. Christ plainly tells us that error and
sin imply not the liberty but the slavery of the
intellect and will. "You shall know the *truth*,
and the truth shall make you free" (John viii.
32); "Whosoever committeth sin, is the servant of sin" (*ibid.* 34).

Universal liberty of thought is impossible, for every principle and fact of reason or revelation that we acquire must necessarily restrict our liberty of thinking the opposite. Once we clearly grasp any truth, we are bound by the law of our reason to accept it. No intelligent man to-day would consider himself free to deny the fact of wireless telegraphy, the existence of bacteria, or X rays, the phenomena of hypnotism, or the earth's movement around the sun. No man of sense, even if he had never travelled beyond his own little village, would question the testimony of others regarding the existence of London, Pekin, or Calcutta. Speculation is useless, and opinions are absurd, when we are face to face with undoubted facts. A man full of prejudice, ignorance, and error may think himself free to believe many calumnies against the Catholic Church. He may believe that Catholics adore the saints and worship their images, sell indulgences, pay money for confession, and the like. He may believe that they teach that the end justifies the means, that it is lawful to lie to heretics, that the Pope can do no wrong. But surely he is not to be congratulated for this freedom of believing what is not so. Such liberty of thought is not a blessing, but a curse, to be done away with as soon as possible by a knowledge of the truth.

We can readily see how non-Catholics, whose

religion disclaims infallibility and rests on the
shifting sands of private judgment, should
quarrel with any certain teaching in religion.
They cannot agree among themselves about
the most fundamental doctrines of Christianity,
and their belief resting on mere opinion, logically is uncertain, hesitating, and questioning.
The result with those who carry matters to
their logical conclusion is scepticism, indiffer-
ence, and unbelief.

The Catholic, however, believing in a Church
authority which, like Christ, is divine and infallible, speaking in His name and with His
authority, gladly welcomes the revelation of
God she voices, with a certain, unhesitating
assent. The Church to him is Christ speaking : '' He that heareth you, heareth Me ''
(Luke x. 16), and therefore he knows she cannot deceive nor be deceived. A Catholic, therefore, would no more question the doctrine
of auricular confession, transubstantiation, the
Trinity, eternal punishment, than a mathema-
tician would the fact that two sides of a tri-
angle are greater than the third.

The submission of the Catholic to the Church
is not '' a blind, degrading obedience '' to a
mere human authority, but the assent of faith
to a divine authority, which he can prove pro-
claims to the world all the teachings of the
Saviour. He *knows by reason* that God hath

spoken; he *believes by faith* all that God has said, because He is the Infinite Truth. "If we receive the testimony of men, the testimony of God is greater" (I. John v. 9).

The Catholic is not hampered in his search for truth, any more than the scientist is hampered by any ascertained principle or fact of science. Indeed, the certainty of revealed truth gives him a greater confidence and freedom in the pursuit of new truths. Many things are left open to speculation, outside the domain of defined dogma. With an infallible guide, he calmly views the progress of science, carefully distinguishing opinion from principle, hypothesis from fact, and does not change his doctrines to meet the shifting views of unproven scientific theories.

Infallibility, therefore, is the corrective of ignorance and error, and the foe to uncertainty about the dogmas revealed by God. As Cardinal Newman wrote: "It is a supply for a need, and it does not go beyond the need. Its object is, and its effect also, not to enfeeble the freedom or vigor of human thought, but to resist and control its extravagance" ("Apologia," p. 253, Longmans, Green & Co., 1897).

And the Protestant writer Mallock: "It [the doctrine of infallibility] is not a fetter only; it is a support also; and those who cling to it can venture fearlessly, as explorers, into cur-

rents of speculation that would sweep away
altogether men who did but trust to their own
powers of swimming '' ('' Is Life Worth Living?'' ch. xii. p. 310).

**Is not your Church a spiritual despotism in
which men must surrender their private judgment in religion to men like themselves?**

If the Church were a mere human authority
that undertook to give its own views of Christ's
teachings, like Luther, Calvin, Wesley, Fox,
Socinus, Mrs. Eddy, Dowie, a rational thinker
might indeed call it a spiritual despotism when
it attempted in the slightest degree to command
in matters of faith or morals.

But the Catholic Church is a divine teacher,
commissioned by the Almighty Son of God to
teach all nations till the end of time in His
name and with His authority, and guaranteed
as ''the pillar and ground of the truth '' by
His abiding presence and the Holy Spirit's
(Matt. xxviii. 18-20.; Mark xvi. 15, 16; John
xiv. 16; xvi. 13; Luke x. 16; I. Tim. iii. 15,
etc.) There can, therefore, be no question of
any intellectual or moral slavery for a man to
submit to her authority, which is God's. '' He
that heareth you heareth me '' (Luke x. 16).

'' It is not the Church that established spiritual despotism; it is she who saves us from it.
Spiritual despotism is that which subjects us,

in spiritual matters, to a human authority, whether our own or that of others,—for our own is as human as another's,—and the only redemption from it is having in spiritual matters a divine authority. Protestants themselves acknowledge this when they call out for the pure word of God. The Church teaches by divine authority; in submitting to her we submit to God, and are freed from all human authority. She teaches infallibly; therefore, in believing what she teaches, we believe the truth, which frees us from falsehood and error, to which all men without an infallible guide are subject, and submission to which is the elemental principle of all spiritual despotism. Her authority admitted excludes all other authority, and therefore frees us from heresiarchs and sects, the very embodiment of spiritual despotism in its most odious form " (O. A. Brownson's Works, vol. x. p. 128).

Indeed, what is the fundamental reason to-day of the downwafd trend of Protestantism toward infidelity? Is it not the fact that intelligent men are beginning more and more to realize the slavery of being subject to a sect's human and fallible version of Christianity? How many Protestants to-day, for example, hold to the original doctrine of Luther or of Calvin! Very many even deny the essential dogmas Christ taught, viz.: the Trinity, the

Divinity of Christ, eternal punishment, and the like. A pretty conclusive argument this that either there is in the world to-day a teacher divine, infallible, and authoritative even as Christ, namely, the Catholic Church, or no man living can be certain that he possesses the complete gospel the Saviour taught.

Does not your Church substitute her authority for reason ?

By no means. She undoubtedly demands the acceptance of her divine authority, for faith is essentially the acceptance of truth on the authority of God. She does not, however, ask men to accept her claims blindly, but desires them first of all to convince themselves by their reason of the fact of God's revelation and its content, and then before obeying her to be morally certain that she is, as she claims, the divine authoritative, infallible teacher of God upon earth. What can be more reasonable ?

Far from denying the rights of reason, she condemned in Reformation times those who asserted that the fall rendered man unable to attain to any truth without revelation (Trent, Sess. VI., can. 4–6), and in our own day she condemns the unbeliever who denies the power of reason to demonstrate the existence of God.

Many a convert, who has found peace after

many years of seeking, can voice the following words of Father Hecker : " It was one of the happiest moments of our life, when we discovered for the first time that it was not required of us to abandon our reason or drown it in a false excitement to be a religious man. That to become a Catholic, so far from being contrary to reason, was a supreme act of reason " ("Questions of the Soul, p. 286; *cf.* " Aspirations of Nature," xxiii. xxiv.)

Did not Martin Luther, in his bold protest against an usurped authority, stand for the rights of the individual reason ?

One might think so from the vague and erroneous assertions of certain non-Catholic writers and speakers, but no student of his works would dare to claim him as a champion of reason. On the contrary, no one could possibly underrate it more.

He declared that " its activity is always evil and godless," that it is useless as a guide to the truth of God : " The Christian revelation rejects clearly all flesh and blood—that is, what is human, and all human reason, since these certainly are not able to lead us to Christ." In fact, he held that "reason goes straight against belief. We ought, therefore, to let reason slide. Reason must be killed and buried in faith. You say reason is a light to faith, that

it should enlighten faith where it shall go.
Yes, in my judgment reason sheds light, like a
piece of dirt in a lantern " (Quoted by Hecker,
"Aspirations of Nature," xvii. pp. 116, 117,
119. *Cf.* Mohler's "Symbolism ").

How different the Catholic teaching, which
holds that original sin did not destroy any of
man's natural faculties, but left his reason and
his free will essentially unimpaired. With the
Catholic, reason "is the most distinguished
gift of Heaven " (Pius IX., Letter to the Aus-
trian Bishops, 1856). It is the guide to faith
whereby a man can prove beforehand certain
fundamental dogmas, such as the existence of
God, the spirituality of the soul, and free will,
and the fact that God has made a revelation to
men. Otherwise faith would be an irrational
act and not a "reasonable service " (Rom. xii.
1 ; see "Aspirations of Nature," ch. xxiii.
xxiv.)

**How can you put the laws of your Church on
the same level as the Commandments of Sinai,
and say that any one who disobeys them merits
damnation ?**

Because the Catholic Church is not a mere
human institution founded by men, who imposed laws and creeds of their own devising,
but a divine, infallible society founded by
Jesus Christ to teach and command in His

name and with His authority until the end of
time. To believe her teaching is to believe
Christ ; to obey her commands is to obey
Christ ; to despise her is to despise Christ.

" As the Father hath sent Me, I also send
you " (John xx. 21).

"All power is given to Me in heaven and in
earth. Going, therefore, teach ye all nations "
(Matt. xxviii. 19).

" And if he will not hear the Church, let
him be to thee as the heathen and publican "
(Matt. xviii. 17).

" He that despiseth you, despiseth Me "
(Luke x. 16).

" Whatsoever you shall bind upon earth
shall be bound also in heaven " (Matt. xviii.
18).

Any one, therefore, who knows that the
Catholic Church is God's only Church, and
refuses to obey her, is guilty of grievous sin
before God. To eat meat on Friday, to stay
away from Mass on Sunday, or to fail to receive the sacraments at Easter time—if done
deliberately and in malice—are direct insults
to Jesus Christ whose representative the Church
is, and therefore deprive the sinner of God's
friendship.

**I believe that a Christian can personally fol-
low Christ without spiritual rulers, popes or**

bishops, to dictate by creeds, rites, and laws what men must think and do to be saved.

You do not, then, believe in the Christianity of Jesus Christ, as witnessed to in the New Testament.

The Saviour selected twelve Apostles (Matt. x. 1), sent them to preach the gospel to the whole world (Matt. xxviii. 19), to administer the seven sacraments (Matt. xxviii. 19; John xx. 23; I. Cor. xi. 23-29; Acts viii. 14-17; James v. 14, 15; I. Tim. iv. 14; Matt. xix. 6), to make laws and to govern (Matt. xviii. 18; Acts xx. 28), with and under the chief Apostle, St. Peter (Matt. xvi. 18; Luke xxii. 32; John xxi. 15-17). St. Paul speaks clearly of men who have divine power to rule, to teach, and to command the Christian people. "And he gave some apostles, and some prophets, and other some evangelists, and other some pastors and doctors, for the perfecting of the saints, for the work of the ministry, for the edifying of the Body of Christ [the Church], until we all meet into the unity of faith" (Eph. iv. 11-13; *cf.* I. Cor. xii. 28, 29).

Creeds are verbal, concrete expressions of the truths revealed by God, and guaranteed to the world by the divine, infallible witness of the Church guided by the Holy Spirit (John xiv. 26). Rites or sacraments are not merely human or ecclesiastical ceremonies, but outward signs of the grace of God instituted by Christ, to convey to us the fruits of His death upon the cross. Laws are necessary to a visible society like the Church, that it might not degenerate into anarchy of doctrine and government.

If, as you pretend, the claims of your Church are so strong, why is it that so many intelligent non-Catholics fail to see their force ?

There are many reasons to account for this. *Prejudice* is a great obstacle to faith. Many from childhood have been taught by parents, teachers, ministers, and books that the Catholic Church is the enemy of reason, science, and progress, the falsifier of Scripture and of history, the home of corruption, superstition, and intolerance. Indeed, many a convert has told me that he would as soon have thought of considering the claims of Mohammedanism as those of Catholicity, so much did he despise it.

The easy, modern dogma of *Indifferentism* likewise keeps many from the truth. Many men are wearied of the uncertainty and contradictions of Protestant Christianity, and yet, untrue to reason and conscience, they shrink from earnest and sincere search after the revelation of God, vainly striving to satisfy the claims of conscience by the plea that it makes no difference what a man believes, provided he lead a pretty good life, and is kind to his family and his friends.

Above all, the *Sins* of pride, worldliness, sensuality, and avarice bandage men's eyes to the light of God's truth. "The sensual man," says St. Paul, "perceiveth not those things that are of the spirit of God; for it is foolishness to him, and he cannot understand" (I. Cor. ii. 14). A man's unbelief, or sometimes his denomination, sits lightly upon him, enforcing few obligations beyond those of external propriety and good form, not interfering in the slightest with his private religious opinions, however erroneous, or with his cherished habits of sin. It is hard, indeed, for such to consider the claims of a Church that teaches with the authority of God a certain body of definite dogmas; that prescribes in His name certain hard religious duties, as confession, obligatory church attendance, fasting and abstinence; that denounces strongly divorce and all immorality in the marriage state.

Other unfaithful ones dread *the Consequences of Conversion,* viz.: the bitter opposition of relatives, the loss of friends, the injury to one's business prospects, the social ostracism, and the hostile voice of public opinion in a town or city where Catholics are looked down upon as poor and ignorant.

We remind our questioner, however, of the

many thousands of the best and most intelligent men and women in Protestantism and unbelief who are coming back every year to the Church their forefathers left some four hundred years ago. ' Nothing but the absolute satisfaction given by the Church to every demand of mind and will and heart could make these courageous souls conquer the many difficulties that lie in a convert's path. With a mind alert to know God's truth, with a will to embrace it wherever found, with a heart repenting of past sin and full of the childlike spirit the Master spoke of as essential, the return is easy for every earnest soul.

Is not the whole tendency of the Catholic Church to hinder the direct relationship of man with God ?

On the contrary, its sole aim is to bring the individual souls of men into immediate union with God, through Jesus Christ. ·

While Protestantism leaves men subject to every vagary of private judgment with regard to Christ's teachings, so that millions in their doubting and uncertainty are led to unbelief, the Catholic Church, as a divine, infallible, ·authoritative teacher, teaching in the name of the Son of God, guarantees to the world an absolute certainty of all the truths of God.

Protestantism, again, with its partial or total

denial of Christianity as a sacramental religion, deprives men of the great helps to that union with God that Christ gave the world, and which all Christians enjoyed until the Reformation. How many non-Catholics to-day regard Baptism as a mere ceremony! The Catholic Church declares it the divinely appointed way of entrance into the kingdom of God, and of oneness with Christ through cleansing from sin. How many non-Catholics who believe in baptismal regeneration, and yet know of no sacrament for the forgiveness of sins committed after baptism, and are anxious, and wonder whether or not their souls are free from stain! The Catholic Church in the sacrament of penance guarantees the sinner real certainty of pardon; if he but repent and promise amendment, he is again united with God in the friendship of God's grace.

Protestantism again, with its cold and barren eating of bread and drinking of wine in memory of Christ, must yield to that wonderful, sublime doctrine of the Catholic Church, which declares that there is no closer union possible of the soul and its God than that of Holy Communion, for as Christ Jesus Himself promised: "He that eateth My flesh, and drinketh My blood, abideth in Me and I in him" (John vi. 57).

The Blessed Virgin and the other saints of

God, loved by every Catholic because manifestly the friends of Christ, do not prevent our direct access to Him, but rather help it, for they know how much we need Him. With the Mother of God they say to us: "Whatsoever He shall say to you, do ye" (John ii. 5), or with St. Paul: "Be ye followers of me, as I also am of Christ" (I. Cor. xi. 1).

The Catholic priesthood does not at will frame doctrines which the people must accept, nor does' it interpret capriciously the moral code and force the conscience of the individual through the confessional; but it preaches the doctrines of the deposit of the faith, and interprets the law of Christ according to the Christian principle handed down from the beginning. The priest no more interferes with a man's relationship with God than our ambassador to England hinders that country's relations with ours.

Does not the Catholic Church insist rather on an outward conformity with her teachings than on fidelity to conscience?

Did not the Reformation do away for ever with a morality based on an obedience to a priesthood, and substitute one founded on the sacred character of the individual conscience?

On the contrary, the Catholic Church has always maintained the inviolability of the indi-

vidual conscience. The only reason of her existence is to teach men their individual responsibility to the truths taught by Christ, that,
following out a rightly instructed conscience,
they might enjoy God's presence for ever. She
teaches that conscience is ever the interpreter
of the moral law to the individual; it must
needs be obeyed, for its power to command rises
from its being the voice of God. Pope Innocent III. taught plainly: " Whatever is done
contrary to conscience leads to hell " (Decret.
Lib. II. tit. 13, c. 13). And St. Thomas:
"Therefore it must be said, that every [sin-
cere] conscience, whether it be right or inculpably erroneous, whether it regards things in
themselves evil or indifferent, is obligatory, so
that he who acts against conscience sins "
(Quodlibet, q. iii. a. 27).

The Church does not put herself in the place
of conscience; neither does the priesthood.
The infallible teaching authority of the Church,
declaring with certainty the morality of Christ's
gospel, gives firmness and strength to the moral
judgment of the individual, who without it
would be left to build on the shifting sands of
private judgment. The Catholic priest does
not shoulder the individual conscience, and
weaken character by enforcing a stupid obedience; but rather strives in every way to edu-
cate the conscience of the people according to

the teaching of Christ, so that they may better know the truth and do the right.

Catholics, indeed, obey the laws of their Church, because they know she has a divine right to command. Does obedience to the laws of the state militate against the individual conscience? Why, then, should obedience to Christian law?

The Reformation produced indeed an exaggerated individualism, which by declaring every man equally competent to find out the doctrines of the Saviour from his own private reading of the Scriptures, has led millions to the utter denial of Christ and His doctrines of faith and morality.

INDEFECTIBILITY.

Is it not a notorious fact that the Church of Rome flagrantly erred? How, then, can you call it the Church of Christ?

Although it is a commonplace of Protestant controversy to state that the Church fell into error any time from the fourth to the sixteenth century, and that it was resurrected in all its pristine purity by the Reformation, such statement has never been proved. Indeed, it would give the lie direct to the promises of Christ: "Thou art Peter, and upon this rock I will build My Church, and the gates of hell shall not prevail against it '' (Matt. xvi. 18). '' Behold I am with you all days, even to the consummation of the world '' (Matt. xxviii. 20). '' I will ask the Father, and He shall give you another Paraclete, that he may abide with you for ever '' (John xiv. 16).

True, indeed, in certain times and places her unfaithful children have grown lax in discipline, weak in religious fervor, and through heresy and immorality defections have occurred ; still, Christ's divine words are the guarantee that in her constitution and her doctrines she can never cease to exist as the kingdom of God on earth.

Suppose, for example, that the Church could fail. Instantly her power to teach men would cease, for one could readily refuse obedience on the plea that the Church had already failed, or that her Founder was a mere man without divine authority to teach. Christ, therefore, either established a Church that could not err, or He never established any teaching authority at all.

Will you not admit that a reformation was needed in the sixteenth century ?

We will readily grant that a reformation in the lives of many unworthy churchmen of the day was imperatively needed, and that unless many Catholics of the period had been living most corrupt lives, they would never have abandoned the Church of Jesus Christ. The Catholic's loss of faith is ever traceable to the breaking of the Ten Commandments. The Church felt this keenly herself, and reformed many abuses at the Council of Trent, 1545-1563.

But once grant that the Church is a divine institution founded by Jesus Christ, the Son of God, to teach and save men for all time; once grant that He promised to build it secure for ever against all attacks of hell, and to guarantee its perpetuity by His own abiding presence and that of the Holy Spirit (Matt. xxviii. 19, 20; Matt. xvi. 18; John xiv. 16), and the right of separation can in no way be justified.

As long as our country remains a country it will ever have the power to reform by law the abuses inevitable to any government among men. If, for example, a city became full of corrupt officials, we would not be justified in trying to destroy it, but would strive at the next election to put the proper men in power. So the Church, in like manner, has within herself the power to remedy any abuses that may arise. You do not cure a man of cancer by chopping off his head.

A so-called reformation which denied the constitution of the Church, the doctrines of Christ, and the manner of Christian worship—Holy Mass, handed down from the beginning—was not of God.

St. Paul put it plainly : " Though we, or an angel from heaven, preach a gospel beside that which we have preached to you, let him be anathema " (Gal. i. 8).

The very lives of the Reformers ; the immoral, destructive, unchristian doctrines they taught—*v. g.*, private interpretation of the Scriptures, justification by faith alone, total· depravity, the slave will, God the author of evil, the denial of the sacramental system—are proof positive that the Reformation was inevitably a tendency toward utter unbelief.

Whence again, Catholics ask, the right of Luther, Calvin, etc., to teach? What were ' their credentials? "How shall they preach, unless they be sent?" (Rom. x. 15).

No wonder, then, that the Reformers themselves admitted that their Reformation did not reform, but on the contrary led to intellectual, social, moral, and religious deterioration. This is amply shown in a work drawn exclusively from Protestant sources, "The Reformation, its Interior Development and its Effects," by Döllinger, Ratisbon, 1846–8. (*Cf.* article in *Dublin Review*, September, 1848.)

Did not Savonarola, in the fifteenth century, attempt to- do what Luther did in the sixteenth ? Was not Savonarola the precursor of Luther ?

" Savonarola's life, teaching, and creed were

the very antithesis of the life, teaching, and creed of the Reformers of the sixteenth age. They left the cloister for the world; he left the world for the cloister, and was ever true to his vows. They began by self-deformation, on their own admission; he by self-reformation, on the evidence of friend and foe. They dragged down public morality, on their own showing; he raised it to the highest perfection. They aimed at reforming creed and doctrine; he reformed morals and men, upholding always doctrine and creed. They denied what he taught: the necessity of good works, the need of the sacraments as channels of grace, transubstantiation, rites and ceremonies, loyalty to Peter's See, and devotion to the Mother of God. How, then, can he be their 'leader,' their 'harbinger,' who condemns and anathematizes them all?" (J. Procter, "Savonarola and the Reformation," Catholic Truth Society publications).

UNITY.

Is there not a vast difference between the faith of a learned and an ignorant Catholic?

Both believe the same, inasmuch as both believe on the authority of God revealing, as witnessed to infallibly by a divine, authoritative teacher, speaking in the name of Jesus Christ—the Catholic Church.

The trained theologian may know more facts, have a better grasp of principles, and be better able to defend Catholic doctrine than the average Catholic; still, the self-same dogmas must be believed by both under penalty of damnation.

You claim to have always taught the same doctrine ? Why, I remember myself two new teachings of your Church, the Immaculate Conception and the Infallibility of the Pope.

Can the Catholic Church impose as many new creeds as she pleases ? Are not all the doctrines of Christianity contained in the Apostles' Creed ?

The Catholic Church maintains that after the death of St. John there has been no objective increase in the deposit of faith, although there is a progress and a development in our understanding of it. She declares that no new revelation shall ever supersede the revelation of Jesus Christ, and that no additional teaching can ever be taught.

Jesus Christ plainly taught that all truths were manifested to the Apostles by Himself and the Holy Spirit (John xvi. 12, 13; xiv. 26), and His commission to them is to preach "all that He had commanded " (Matt. xxviii. 20). St. Paul declares the impossibility of any new teaching being of Christ : " Though we, or an angel from heaven, preach a gospel to you besides that which we have preached to you, let him be anathema " (Gal. i. 8). He warns Timothy to guard the deposit of faith (I. Tim. vi. 20), and in his Epistle to the Hebrews he clearly teaches the perpetual, unchanging character of the new dispensation (Heb. viii. 7, 13 ; xii. 27, 28 ; vii. 11, *et seq*) So in the Catholic Church, novelty or newness of doctrine has ever been regarded as the sign of error.

Thus the Vatican Council : " For the Holy Spirit was *not promised* to the successors of Peter, that by His revelation they might make known *new doctrine*, but that by His assistance they might inviolably keep and faithfully expound the revelation or deposit of faith delivered through the Apostles " (Sess. IV. ch. iv.)

What, then, is meant by the definition of new dogmas—as, for example, the Immaculate Conception (1854), and the Infallibility of the Pope (1870) ? Definition is not the making of new beliefs, but the infallible declaration that such belief is a part of the original deposit of the faith handed down from the Apostles. Before such declaration the dogma existed, although it was not explicitly believed by all Christians. After the definition, it must be believed by all Christians because of the infallible witness to its truth by the living voice of God's Church.

If a Protestant call the doctrine of infallibility an addition to the faith because only defined in late years, on the same principle he ought logically to call the doctrines of the divinity of Christ (defined in A.D. 325) and the divinity of the Holy Ghost (defined in A.D. 381) new doctrines.

There is, however, a development of dogma in the Catholic Church, although no teaching of new dogmas. Vincent of Lerins (A.D. 431) wrote: "Is there, then, no progress of religion in the Church of Christ? Surely there is; and very great progress. . . . But it is truly a *progress* in the faith, and not a change. It is of the nature of progress that the particular thing should itself be amplified, but of change that something should be turned from one thing into another" (Common. xxiii.) Development, therefore, means the increase of knowledge on the part of Christians regarding the doctrines of Christ. There is hardly a dogma of the Christian revelation that has not been brought out into clearer light and minuter detail under the strain of controversy or the attacks of heresy. The early heresies concerning the Trinity and the Incarnation brought out more clearly the fact that God was one nature in three divine Persons; that the Son was consubstantial to the Father; that the Holy Ghost proceeded from the Father and the Son; that in Jesus Christ the divine and the human natures were united in one divine personality; that the Blessed Virgin was the Mother of God, etc. The new teachings of the Reformation caused the explicit teachings of the Church concerning Justification, the Sacraments, Indulgences, the veneration of the Saints, the existence of Purgatory, etc.

How illogical indeed for some men, like the Anglicans, to admit the right of the Church in the first five centuries to define dogmas and deny it to her afterwards, when Christ promised to be always with His Church as the infallible guarantee of her true teaching (Matt. xxviii. 20).

Not all but only the chief doctrines of Christianity are explicitly contained in the Apostles' Creed, although all are implicitly comprised in the article "I believe in the Catholic Church." The Church has the right to make new creeds to safeguard her doctrine against new heresies; but a new creed does not imply new dogmas, but merely new and fuller explanations of the deposit of faith handed down from the beginning. (Newman, "Development of Christian Doctrine"; Oxenham, "The Catholic

Doctrine of the Atonement," Introd.; Livius,
"The Blessed Virgin in the Fathers," pp. 1–
33, Introd.; Gibbons, "The Faith of Our Fathers," ch. ii. p. 30–35.)

**Has not your Church, in striving to maintain
an impossible uniformity of belief, ever been the
enemy of natural science ?**

**How do you reconcile the teachings of your
Church with the teachings of modern science ?**

The Catholic Church is not nor can she be
the enemy of science. The truths of natural
science cannot contradict the truths of revelation, for the same God is the author of both.
Any apparent conflict, therefore, between
science and religion arises from the fact that
theologians have put forth their own views for
the doctrines of the Church, or scientists have
either been ignorant of the Church's teaching
or put forth unproved hypotheses for undoubted
truths. On this subject the Vatican Council
says (Sess. III. ch. iv., On Faith and Reason) :
"But although faith is above reason, there can
never be any real discrepancy between faith
and reason, since the same God who reveals
mysteries and infuses faith has bestowed the
light of reason on the human mind ; and God
cannot deny Himself, nor can truth ever contradict truth. The false appearance of such a
contradiction is mainly due, either to the dog-

mas of faith not having been understood and expounded according to the mind of the Church, or to the inventions of opinion having been taken for the verdicts of reason. We define, therefore, that every assertion contrary to a truth of enlightened faith is utterly false."

The Catholic Church has no direct mission to teach the truths of astronomy, biology, or geology; her mission is to teach and defend the revelation of God. Yet she claims the right to proscribe all false scientific systems which are opposed to the deposit of faith. The true scientist, as a rule, is the most modest of men, never claiming absolute assent to what he knows is merely a working hypothesis for the advance of science. But the popularizers of science, who reach the people through the magazines and the lecture platform, are often the most dogmatic of men, demanding acceptance by all of hypotheses they themselves are incompetent to demonstrate, and declaiming against Christianity for refusing to swallow wholesale their theories of a day. So the Vatican Council continues: "The Church, which together with the Apostolic office of teaching, has received a charge to guard the deposit of faith, derives from God the right and the duty of proscribing false science, lest any should be deceived by philosophy and vain fallacy " (Col. ii. 8).

If men in the name of science, although without its warrant, deny the existence of God and the unity of the human race, or maintain the evolution of man, body and soul, from the monkey, the infallible Church of God in the name of truth denounces them as false teachers. But if, for example, men declare the six days of Genesis to be long epochs, and not days of twenty-four hours each, the Church has no quarrel with them. They have contradicted none of her dogmas.

As a matter of fact, the Church has rendered great services to science, as we can see from the fact that the great universities of Italy, France, England, and Spain were founded before the Reformation. Indeed, even in the seventeenth century the great majority of scientists belonged to the secular and regular clergy. (Vaughan, ''Science and Religion''; Zahm, ''Science and Religion''; Zahm, ''Bible, Science, and Faith''; Ronayne, ''Religion and Science''; Wiseman, ''Science and Revealed Religion''; Brennan, ''What Catholics have done for Science''; Molloy, ''Geology and Revelation.'')

Are not all Christians agreed on essentials? Why, then, worry about petty details of doctrine or ritual?

The Catholic notion of divine faith is the

acceptance of all God's truth on His divine authority. To reject one doctrine the Son of God taught is to give Him the lie. He did not say to His Apostles : " Teach all nations what you deem essential and fundamental," but "teach ALL things whatsoever I have commanded you."

If a friend were to relate to you an event he had witnessed in another city, and you accepted only what you deemed essential of his account, you would evidently consider him guilty of habitual lying or exaggeration. If he were a true speaker, every word must be believed. So with God, revealing His truth to men. The man of faith accepts all that God has spoken, once convinced of the fact of a revelation.

The distinction of fundamental and non-fundamental doctrines, invented by Jurieu ("Le Vrai Système de l'Église," p. 166) to cover in some way the evident lack of unity in Protestantism, is without warrant in reason or Scripture, and is useless, practically, for no agreement has ever been reached as to what doctrines are really fundamental.

God is the Absolute Truth. How could He, then, declare it made no difference whether one denomination of Christians believed in the Trinity or another denied it? Whether one believed Jesus Christ to be God, and another that

He was only man ? Whether one believed in
the Real Presence of the Eucharist, and another that the Lord's supper meant mere bread
and wine ? One of each of these contradictory
statements must be false. It is not a mere question of petty detail, but of the essential unity of
faith for which Christ prayed, "that they all
may be one, as Thou, Father, in Me and I in
Thee, that they also may be one in Us ; that
the world may believe that Thou hast sent
Me " (John xvii. 21).

The Apostles always insist upon unity of
belief in all Christ's doctrines, and the sins of
schism and heresy are classed with drunkenness, fornication, and murder (Gal. v. 20, 21).
" I beseech you, brethren, . . . that you
all speak the same thing, and that there be no
schism among you " (I. Cor. i. 10); " One
Lord, one faith, one. baptism " (Eph. iv. 5) ;
" For we being many, are one head, one body "
(I. Cor. x. 17) ; " If any one preach to you a
gospel besides that which you have received,
let him be anathema " (Gal. i. 9) ; " I beseech
you to mark them who make dissensions and
offences contrary to the doctrine which you
have learned, and to avoid them " (Rom. xvi.
17) ; " If any man come to you, and bring not
this doctrine, receive him not into the house "
(II. John i. 10).

Indeed, the very existence of the different

sects of Protestantism proves their differences essential. If not, what was their reason of being? To-day, perhaps, these differences are not so clearly marked, for indifferentism and unbelief have played sad havoc with the old doctrines, and ministers meet in synods to revise their worn-out, human creeds.

St. Augustine in the fifth century answered this objection with regard to the Donatists of his day: "Both of us have baptism; in that we are united. We have the same gospel; in this we are also united. They celebrate with us the feasts of martyrs; in this we also agree. . . . But *they are not with us in all things.* They are not with us in their schism, they are not with us in their heresy. And by reason of those few things in which they are not with us, the many things on which they are with us avail them nothing" ("On the Unity of the Church," ch. iii.)

Are there not divisions and sects in the Catholic Church—i. e., Jesuits, Dominicans, etc.— who teach different doctrines? How, then, do you claim unity?

No, the religious orders in the Catholic Church are not like the denominations of Protestantism, sects with creeds of their own devising. They have arisen from time to time to answer some great need of religion, which demanded the example of a certain virtue, like the poverty of the Franciscan, or the obedience of the Jesuit, or a special work to be done in charity, education, missions to the pagan, the ransom of captives, and the like. Every order holds exactly the same beliefs; their only differences are in matters of opinion, in which every Catholic is left perfectly free. A vast difference between this and the denial of dogmas of faith, whereof all the Protestant sects can plead guilty. Cardinal Newman says on this point: "Augustinians, Dominicans, Franciscans, Jesuits, and Carmelites have indeed their respective homes and schools; but they have, in spite of all that, a common school and a common home in their Mother's bosom; . . . but Protestants can but agree to differ. Quarrels, stopping short of divisions, do but prove the strength of the principle of combination; they are the token, not of the languor but of the vigor of its life. . . . The doctrines of faith are the common basis of the combatants, the ground on which they contend, their ultimate authority, and their arbitrating rule" ("Diff. of Anglicans," vol. i. Lect. x. p. 261).

Is not the bond of charity sufficient (John xiii. 34, 35), without insisting on dogmas and creeds?

The love of the brethren is indeed the corollary of the one great commandment, the love of God. But Christians cannot be united in the true love of Jesus Christ, the teacher of the revelation of God, unless they accept His each and every teaching. "Without faith it is impossible to please God" (Heb. xi. 6); "He· that believeth not shall be condemned" (Mark xvi. 16). St. Paul bases love on the unity of faith : "Careful to keep the unity of the Spirit in the bond of peace. One body and one Spirit; as you are called in one hope of your calling. One Lord, one faith, one baptism" (Eph. iv. 3, 6). "Be of one mind, having the same charity, being of one accord, agreeing in sentiment" (Phil. ii. 2).

It is ridiculous to claim unity for your Church. Were there not three Popes at one time?—i.e., during the Great Western Schism, A.D. 1378–1417.

The great Schism of the West was by no means destructive of the unity of the Church, for no one during it ever denied the Papal supremacy. ' On the contrary, all admitted the supreme authority of the legitimate Pope if they could only be certain which one had the lawful succession. It was a controversy not about dogma, but about persons. It seems most probable that Urban VI. was validly elected, for during three months the cardinals

privately and officially acknowledged him as
Pope. If so, he and his successors, Boniface
IX., Innocent VII., and Gregory XII., were
legitimate Pontiffs, and preserved the Church
in unity, although many who did not recognize them were excusable because of their
good faith.

HOLINESS.

**Why do you claim to be a holy Church, when
you must admit that many leaders in your
Church—popes, bishops, and priests—have been
corrupt and wicked men? Christ said: " By their
fruits you shall know them " (Matt. vii. 16).**

We readily admit that there have been a few
wicked Popes, like Stephen VII. (A.D. 896),
Benedict IX. (A.D. 1032), and Alexander VI.
(A.D. 1480), out of a long line of 258 illustrious
pontiffs, many of whom lived lives of heroic
sanctity, and even died for the faith of
Christ. There was a Judas among the twelve
Apostles. Many cardinals, bishops, and prelates in high places have also been guilty
of grave moral disorders. Worldliness, pride,
avarice, lust, and drunkenness have characterized some pastors of God's people, as the
history of every ex-priest from the Reformers
down to the latest scandal in the daily news-
paper clearly shows.

Still, to any logical mind, all outcry against
unworthy leaders or people in the Church is of
no value or force whatsoever, unless it can be
proved that their unworthiness is directly traceable to the doctrines, worship, devotions, laws,
or institutions of the Catholic Church. We
do not judge the merits of an apple-tree from
the rotten apples that lie in profusion upon
the ground beneath it, but rather by the ripe
fruit on the bough. So the Church of God
is not to be judged by the wicked who refuse
to obey her laws or follow her teachings, but
by the countless good souls who show forth
her sanctity by their faithful following of
Christ. And, indeed, every one with the
slightest knowledge of history must admit that
the Papacy, the episcopate, and the priesthood have been the greatest factors for the
moral and religious well-being of Christianity from the beginning. The Catholic Church
can proudly point to Popes like Leo the Great,
Gregory the Great, Gregory VII., Innocent
III., Pius V., and Leo XIII.; and to Bishops like Athanasius, Basil, Cyprian, Ambrose, Augustine, Patrick, Fisher, Fénelon,
Newman, Manning, Hughes, Neumann, and
Baraga. The Catholic people by their universal
love and reverence for their priests testify to the
world their high standard of virtue and sanctity. "It appears to be the testimony of

history," writes Dean Maitland, "that the monks and the clergy were in all times and places better than other people" (Preface to the "Dark Ages," p. 8).

Is not your Church the only Church that does not demand moral character as a qualification for membership?

Why is it that you allow drunkards, rum-sellers, and boodlers to be members of your Church in good standing? Are they in the fellowship? Why are there so many wicked, poor, and ignorant in your Church?

An habitual drunkard, a saloon-keeper whose saloon is a proximate occasion of sin to himself or others, a thief who is enjoying stolen property which he does not intend to restore— these are not members in good standing, for no unrepentant sinner is allowed to receive the sacraments in the Catholic Church. She, however, does not pretend to be a social club for the *élite*, the outwardly respectable or the well-to-do, for, like Christ, she is universal, with a message for sinner and saint, rich and poor, cultured and ignorant.

Christ came for sinners: "For the Son of Man is come to save that which was lost" (Matt. xviii. 11). "I am not come to call the just, but sinners" (Matt. ix. 13). He loved the poor and the ignorant, and John the Baptist was told to recognize "the preaching of the Gospel to the poor" (Matt. xi. 5) as one of the signs of His Messiasship. So the Church, Christ's representative, never abandons the sinner, but, like another Christ, goes after the lost sheep that she may win them back to the fold. Her priesthood, her Mass, her sacraments, her devotions, her missions— all are for the sinner. She is the Church also of the poor, for at our altars all are equal—"all are one in Christ Jesus" (Gal. iii. 28).

I remember meeting a Unitarian minister from Vermont in Boston, last June, who told me that he was about to resign his ministry, because his efforts to reach out to the poor of his city had been met by the decided protest of the rich members of his fashionable congregation. The Church of God knows no such distinction. How false the notion of the Reformation, that the Church of the living God ought to be composed merely of the elect. Such is not the teaching of Christ, as we learn from the parables of the cockle and the wheat (Matt. xiii. 24–30), the net of good and bad fish (xiii. 47), the flock of sheep and goats (xxv. 32), the house containing vessels of honor and vessels of dishonor (II. Tim. ii. 20). So shall it be until the harvest come, until the final eternal separation at the day of Judgment.

Are there not many illustrious men and women to be found in our several churches, and good souls by the thousands striving their best to follow the Lord Jesus? Why is it that you Catholics claim exclusively to be "a holy Church"?

Yes, undoubtedly, many outside the body of the Catholic Church, and even among the pagans, have been remarkable for their natural virtues; and often they had supernatural faith, hope, and charity, which they possessed in virtue of their union with the soul of God's Church. But the holiness of these individuals of the several churches is not due to the sect to which they belong, but to the Catholic Church, many of whose teachings and principles their sect still retains. Their errors and schism of themselves are destructive, and lead millions of their followers into indifferentism and unbelief. To say nothing of the immoral heresies of early and mediæval church history, the principles distinctively Protestant (thank goodness that many Protestants are better than their principles!) do not make for holiness of life.

The Lutheran doctrine of *justification by faith alone* is essentially immoral, and has, in union with the other demoralizing principle of private judgment in matters of faith, led logically to the reaction of the common Protestant creed of to-day, indifferentism or *justification by works alone*, which is only a step removed from outright unbelief.

The most logical system of the Reformation, Calvinism, by making God the author of sin, utterly destroyed the very basis of morality. No wonder that men to-day are striving to revise their original sixteenth century creed.

The Reformation also deprived men of many divine aids to holiness. The Mass, which applies the merits of Christ's atonement to the individual soul, was abolished ; the priesthood with its apostolic mission to preach, and its celibacy that insured a greater devotion for the people's service, was done away with ; the seven sacraments, which sanctified the whole life of the Christian from his birth to the grave, were denied for the most part, and false views held and lax practice followed in regard to the two (Baptism and the Lord's Supper) they retained ; the greatest bulwark against wickedness the world ever knew, confession, was set at naught; the precepts of fasting and abstinence, which tend so much to the eminently Christian virtues of mortification and self-denial, were rendered obsolete ; the love and veneration of the Blessed Virgin and the saints of God was strangely enough turned to hatred, and men deprived of their wonderful examples of every Christian virtue ;

the counsels of the Saviour—poverty, chastity, and obedience—were forgotten, and the ideal of the religious life lost; the beautiful symbolism of the Church, which had fostered so much the spirit of devotion by giving it outer expression, fell before the vandalism of these so-called reformers; in a word, Protestantism with its denial of many of the doctrines of the gospel, and its discarding of most of the means of grace, cannot claim to be that "glorious Church, not having spot or wrinkle, or any such thing, but that it should be holy, and without blemish " (Eph. v. 27).

The Catholic Church claims exclusively the mark of holiness, because her Founder is the Lord Jesus Christ, and because she alone has kept inviolate every dogma and every commandment and counsel that He taught. She has kept from the beginning all the means of grace and sanctity wherewith Christ endowed her—the Mass, the seven sacraments, and prayer. She holds up to her children the example of the Saviour, and His perfect followers, the saints; she urges the sinner to repent, promising him the mercy and love of God in the sacraments of penance and the Eucharist; she encourages them to read the Scriptures and other devout books, like the " Imitation of Christ," and to listen as frequently as possible to the Word of God; her laws of fasting, abstinence, attendance at Sunday Mass, and yearly confession and communion, help wonderfully to encourage the spirit of devotion and self-denial. Only in her fold are the Gospel Counsels followed by thousands of devout souls, whose zeal and charity are written large in the history of Christian civilization. A great multitude of saints belong to her—men and women of every race and country, who lived lives of heroic sanctity and proved by their miracles to be blessed by God.

Why is it that the Catholic nations, like Italy and Spain, are less prosperous and progressive than Protestant nations, like England, Germany, and the United States?

Why is it the Catholic nations are so much inferior to the Protestant in the scale of civilization?

It seems to many Protestants that one of the most conclusive arguments against the Catholic Church is the present material prosperity of certain Protestant nations. I do not believe that lectures are ever given to non-Catholics in our country without this objection being presented in some form or other. And yet it is the old pagan difficulty answered in the fifth century by St. Augustine; it is the pagan scoff of the apostate Emperor Julian.

Jesus Christ never made wealth or material

greatness a mark of His true Church. On the contrary, from His words a student of the Scriptures would draw a totally different conclusion. He declares that no man can serve God and Mammon (Matt. vi. 24), and denounces riches as one of the greatest obstacles to the Kingdom of Heaven: "Woe to you that are rich; for you have your consolation" (Luke vi. 24); "It is easier for a camel to pass through the eye of a needle, than for a rich man to enter into the kingdom of heaven" (Matt. xix. 24); "My kingdom is not of this world" (John xviii. 36); "What doth it profit a man if he gain the whole world, and suffer the loss of his own soul?" (Matt. xvi. 26).

The falsity of the argument of national prosperity as a mark of the divine favor is at once shown, when we observe in the course of history, pagan, Catholic, and Protestant nations alike standing out pre-eminently in worldly greatness. Must we blasphemously declare that the unchangeable God of truth approves of different religions in turn, no matter what irrational or immoral doctrines they hold? Egypt, Assyria, Greece, Rome—all were once mighty and prosperous nations. Were the Jews under the slavery of Pharao, or the early Christians who worshipped in the underground catacombs of Rome, professors of a false religion because at the time not blessed with worldly goods?

Again, the criterion works both ways. Was the Catholic Church true when Spain ruled the world at the beginning of the sixteenth century, and false when she to-day no longer claims a place among the first powers of Europe? Was the Protestantism of Holland true in the seventeenth century, when she did the carrying trade of Europe, and false now in the period of her decline?

If we apply the argument to an individual, we can at once grasp its inanity. Mr. A. of New York is worth some hundreds of millions of dollars; therefore he is the best man in the United States! We may find some of our millionaires good Christian men, but we do not find that as a class the very wealthy necessarily stand forth as pre-eminent in the Christian virtues of self-denial, humility, meekness, purity, honesty, and the like.

There are many factors that go towards making a country wealthy and prosperous; but they are due rather to natural resources, the energy, intelligence and economy, and often thievery, of individuals—rather than to religion.

The instituting of a comparison between Catholicity and Protestantism as a civilizing force is a most difficult undertaking, for there are many factors to be considered. A man must have a perfect grasp of what is meant by the term civilization; he must consider it in its various aspects, economic, social, political, moral, and religious; he must take into account all the influences that favor or retard it, viz.: climatic and racial conditions; he must take a period when Catholicity or Protestantism is still a living, vital force, and know well the proportion of Catholics, Protestants, and infidels in a country; he must appreciate well the fact that nations, like individuals, have their time of birth, growth, and decay. Men may speak of the United States as a Protestant country; and yet if one were to count the church-going Christians, the Catholic Church could readily claim half the number. There are undoubtedly more indifferentists than Protestants in these United States. According to our questioner's logic, our national prosperity then is due to our infidelity, and not to the country's natural wealth, and the sturdiness of the American character.

However, Catholics are glad to challenge any comparison when it comes to morality and religion. In this regard we strongly commend to our non-Catholic friends the chapters on education, pauperism, crime, drunkenness, suicide, illegitimacy, prostitution, divorce, etc., in that interesting volume of Father Alfred

Young, "Catholic and Protestant Countries Compared," Catholic Book Exchange, New York, 1898. We are perfectly willing that the statistics on these matters should be carefully considered. (Read also Balmes, "Catholicity and Protestantism Compared"; J. S. Vaughan, "Faith and Folly," pp. 432–466; Ricards, "Catholic Christianity and Modern Unbelief," ch. xiv. p. 277; Spalding, "Essays," p. 156; Schanz, "A Christian Apology," vol. iii. ch. xv.; "The Church and Civilization.")

Does not your Church teach that it is lawful to lie to Protestants?

How can we "heretics" believe any statement you may make, when one of your fundamental teachings, as set forth in the Council of Constance, declares that "Faith need not be kept with heretics"? Was not the safe-conduct granted by this council to John Huss violated on this very principle?

The Catholic Church never taught that it was lawful to lie or break faith with any one. She has always considered lying as intrinsically evil, according to the eighth commandment: "Thou shalt not bear false witness against thy neighbor." An honest inquirer after truth has merely to read the words of the decree (cited by Alzog, "Universal Church History,"

vol. iii. p. 964) to recognize the utter dis-
honesty of the above accusation. This false
principle was preached and acted on by Protestants in Ireland after the treaty of Limerick
in 1691.

This calumny has been refuted time and
time again, as by Lethmathius in 1544, Copus
in 1581, Campion in 1585, Molanus in 1611, Ros-
weidt and Sweert in 1608, 1609, 1611, Becanus
in 1612, Marquez in 1645, etc. (*cf.* Hergenröther,
" Church and State," Essay xvi.; Jungmann,
" Church History," vi. p. 339 ; Hefele, " History of the Councils," vol. vii. p. 767, cited
in the Catholic University Bulletin, July, 1896,
pp. 380, 381).

The Council of Constance never granted a
safe-conduct to John Huss. The Emperor Sigismund did, but his letter was merely a pass-
port commending Huss to all the officials of
the empire in order to assure him protection
from violence on his way to the Council. It
by no means protected him from the due course
of the law of the empire, which in the fifteenth
century regarded heresy as a civil offence punishable by death. This is evident from the
safe-conduct itself, the address of the Bohemian nobles of the council, and the letter of
Sigismund to the King of Aragon on this very
point (Alzog, " Church Hist.," vol. iii. pp.
952-967).

What is the attitude of your Church on the temperance question ?

How can you explain the fact that so large a proportion of liquor dealers are regular attendants of your Church, in good standing ? Are they not responsible for most of the sin and misery of the present time? They are not on the books of any Protestant Church.

The Catholic Church regards intemperance as a great vice, which carries in its train many other sins, such as anger, blasphemy, neglect of Mass and the sacraments, murder, lust, theft. Catholics realize that the drink evil is the fruitful cause of pauperism, insanity, disease, death, corruption in citizenship, and the destruction of home life.

The Church declares temperance, or moderation in the use of drink, binding upon all under penalty of sin. She declares total abstinence binding upon all who find in drink the proximate occasion of sin, as is the case with the habitual drunkard. She counsels total abstinence to all for four reasons: first, As a protest against a public abuse in our country; second, As an example to the weaker brethren (Rom. xiv. 21) ; third, As a practice of self-denial; fourth, As a reparation for the sins committed by the drunkard.

The mind of the Church can be seen from the words of the Bishops of the United States in

the Second Council of Baltimore, 1866, No. 470 :
"Since the very worst scandals owe their origin to excess in drink, we exhort pastors, and
we implore them for the love of Jesus Christ,
to devote all their energies to the extirpation
of the vice of intemperance. To that end we
deem worthy of praise the zeal of those who,
the better to guard against excess, pledge
themselves to total abstinence "; No. 469 :
" Let pastors frequently warn their flocks to
shun saloons, and let them repel from the Sacraments liquor-dealers who encourage the
abuses of drink, especially on Sunday."

The Third Council of Baltimore, held in
1884, declares, No. 263 : "We admonish
Catholics engaged in the sale of intoxicating
liquors to consider seriously how many and
how great are the dangers and the occasions
of sin which their business, though not in itself illicit, is surrounded. Let them, if possible, choose some more honorable way of
making a living. And if they find it impossible to quit it, then let them strive with all their
might to remove the occasions of sin from themselves and from others. Let them not sell
drink either to minors, or to those who they
foresee will go to excess. Let them keep
their saloons closed on the Lord's day. Let
them at no time permit on their premises blasphemy, cursing, or obscene language. But if

through their action, or with their co-operation, religion is dishonored and men are led to ruin, let them remember that there is an Avenger in heaven, who will certainly demand of them a terrible retribution.''

A Catholic saloon-keeper, whose saloon is evidently an occasion of sin to others, is not a Catholic in good standing. For although he may attend Sunday Mass, he cannot approach the sacraments of penance and the Eucharist until he promise amendment. Membership with us, however, does not mean enrollment on the church's books, but is a right God-given in the sacrament of baptism. No matter how low a man may have fallen, the Church is always ready, like Christ, to go after the lost sheep of the house of Israel. Public excommunication is a penalty she rarely employs.

Do the Jesuits teach that a good end justifies a bad means ?

No ; although this calumny is repeated time and time again despite its frequent refutation. It is evident that those who make this charge are ignorant of the very first principles of Catholic ethics, unless we are to ascribe their false statements to downright malice. The teaching of Catholic theology is plain : If a man perform a good action for a bad purpose, or a bad action for a good purpose, his conduct in both instances is immoral. Conduct, to be good, always presupposes two conditions: first, that conscience declare the act good in itself; and second, that it declare the intention good with which it is performed. Thus, Clement VII. did not grant a divorce to Henry VIII., even though its granting might have saved England to the Church, for divorce is contrary to the law of Christ; or again, the Catholic Church absolutely forbids craniotomy, even though a physician might declare it the saving of a mother's life. We challenge, therefore, our objector to bring forward one passage from any approved theologian—Jesuit or not—who maintains that a good end justifies a bad means.

We hold, on the contrary, that this was a principle of Martin Luther. He with other Reformers allowed the Landgrave of Hesse to have two wives, the better to be continent, and again urged him to deny publicly that Margaret von Sala was his real wife, to avoid scandal. Here plainly we find polygamy and lying justified; and the principle set forth that it is lawful to do evil that good may come. (Verres, "Life of Luther," ch. xxi. pp. 312 *et seq.*)

Frequently in this country and abroad the Jesuits and Catholic laymen have offered thousands of dollars to the Protestant who could produce one Jesuit author who had given utterance to this false teaching. The challenge has never been accepted save to the discomfiture of the challenger, as in one instance of its acceptance at the University of Heidelburg in 1872. Littledale's statement in the "Encyclopædia Britannica," vol. xiii. p. 661, is a malicious calumny, as any one can see by consulting any Jesuit theologian (*American Catholic Quarterly*, 1888, p. 119).

MENTAL RESERVATION.

How can Catholics ever be trusted in view of your doctrine of mental reservations?

Does the Catholic Church teach absolute truthfulness in all things, small and great?

The essence of a lie consists in saying the contrary of what is thought, and every lie necessarily implies the will to deceive. The unanimous teaching of Catholic theologians from and before the time of St. Augustine has been that a lie is intrinsically and absolutely evil, as opposed to the very nature of man and society. No reason can ever justify it.

A mental reservation, or restriction, is the limitation of an affirmative or negative. If not verbally expressed, it can be either known by the circumstances or else it is purely mental. A purely mental reservation being equivalent to a lie, is never lawful. Reservation not purely mental—that is, equivocation—is in general forbidden, because language is intended to express thoughts, not to hide them. It is, however, allowed for a just cause, in virtue of the principle of morals, that we can lawfully perform an act having two effects, the one good and the other evil, whenever the good effect is paramount to the bad. Thus, a servant could say to a visitor whom her mistress did not want to receive, "Not at home," or a priest or any professional man when asked a secret could answer, "I do not know"; in both instances the limiting of the negation can be gathered from the circumstances. Surely the Catholic teaching is much more strict than that of Protestant writers and theologians, such as Melancthon, Bodin, Gentilis, Grotius, Pufendorf, Heineccius, Cocceius, Jeremy Taylor, Johnson, Paley, and others, who permit lying when the person addressed has no right to the truth. Are we, then, to distrust Protestants in view of this lax teaching?

No sensible man can deny the lawfulness of mental reservations once he understands our teaching. It is witnessed to in the Gospels. Our Lord said that He would not go up to the Holy City on the feast-day, not wishing to go there publicly with His disciples, but afterwards in secret (John vii. 8, 10); He said again that He knew not the day of the judgment, implying that He was not at liberty to disclose it (Mark xiii. 32).

Why are Catholics so superstitious?

I know Catholics who think a scapular will save them from drowning, a miraculous medal in a house will prevent it from burning, the swallowing of a picture-stamp will cure a person better than medicines, etc. Is this not superstition?

Is it sinful to consult fortune-tellers?

Do Catholics believe in dreams?

Catholics regard superstition as undoubtedly a sin against the first commandment, and therefore on principle are less apt to be superstitious than the average Protestant or infidel.

Superstition consists in ascribing to certain things or happenings a power they do not possess, naturally or supernaturally.

It is superstition to consider Friday an unlucky day, to regard thirteen at table as prophetical of evil, to carry about with one a lucky coin, to read dream books to interpret the future, to consult fortune-tellers, palmists, and other charlatans, and the like.

It is not superstition in Catholics to wear medals, crosses, or scapulars blessed by the Church of God (I. Tim. iv. 5), thereby calling to mind Christ Jesus, His Mother, and the saints; but if one were to attribute to these sacred articles powers they do not possess, then he is guilty of superstition.

" We clutch eagerly," writes Father Tyrrell, "at a miraculous medal, a girdle, an infallible prayer, a scapular, a novena, a pledge, a vow— all helps, in their way, all excellent if used rightly as stimulants to greater exertion; but if adopted as substitutes for labor, for the eternally necessary and indispensable means, then, no longer helps, but most hurtful superstitions" ("External Religion," pp. 89–90).

Pagan peoples, lacking the knowledge of the one true God, are naturally superstitious, attributing wonderful power to idols of wood and stone, wearing amulets to protect themselves against disease and death, invoking spirits by magical formulæ, etc. In our own day, the pagan augurs, astrologers, and medicine men have their counterpart in the modern superstitions born of a decadent Protestantism, spiritism, Christian Science, theosophy, palmistry, and the like. Unbelief, craving for the truth of God it does not possess, naturally finds satisfaction in various superstitious beliefs and practices.

What do you think of the "Monita Secreta" of the Jesuits?

The " Monita Secreta " is a deliberate, calumnious forgery, published for the first time in 1612 at Cracovia, Poland, and probably written by the apostate Jesuit, Jerome Zaorowski. It was condemned by the Congregation of the Index at Rome in 1616 as an impudent forgery, and conclusively proved to be so by the Jesuit Fathers Gretser (A. D. 1617) and Huylenbrowcq (A. D. 1713). It has been edited many times by the enemies of the Jesuits—1662, 1669, 1702, 1719, 1761—although many opponents of the Church, like Paulus and Huber, grant that it is not authentic. It is on a par with the false encyclicals published by the A. P. A. in the United States some ten years since, and accepted by the stupid and ignorant as genuine. Error is naturally driven to defend itself by calumny and lying.

CATHOLICITY.

Why do Catholics make exclusive claim to the title of Catholic? We Protestants claim the name in like manner, for we say in the Apostles' Creed: "I believe in the Catholic, i.e., Christian Church."

Are not Protestants everywhere in the world to-day spreading the gospel of the Christ?

Who are the more numerous to-day, Catholics or Protestants?

Jesus Christ, the Son of God, was a catholic, or universal, teacher of the divine revelation. His gospel was not merely for the Jews of Palestine in the first century, but for all times and places. The Church that represents Him, therefore, must also be a catholic, or universal, teacher of divine revelation. She must bear upon her brow the stamp of universality, and by her extension in time and place ever stand forth pre-eminently as the one unchanging faith the Saviour taught. This is shown plainly in the Scriptures. (1) She is catholic in *time :* "Behold I am with you all days even to the consummation of the world " (Matt. xxviii. 20); "The gates of hell shall not prevail against it " (Matt. xvi. 18). (2) She is catholic *territorially :* "Teach ye all nations " (Matt. xxviii. 19) ; "Go ye into the whole world, and preach the gospel to every creature " (Mark xvi. 15; Gen. xii. 3; xxvi. 4; xxviii. 14 ; Ps. ii. 8; xxi. 28 ; lxxi. 8; Isa. ii. 2 ; xlix. 6 ; Mal. i. 11 ; Acts i. 8 ; Rom. i. 5 ; I. Tim. ii. 4–6). (3) She is catholic in *unity of all doctrine :* "Teaching them to observe all things whatsoever I have commanded you " (Matt. xxviii. 20).

Catholicity as a distinctive mark of the Church of Christ does not mean that she must exist in every country of the world at once, but that she have within her the germ of growth and development, which in the course of the

centuries no human power can ever success-
fully retard. She must ever be a missionary
Church, and though by heresy and schism
many may go forth from her (I. John ii. 19),
she will as a matter of fact be far more numerous than any, and stand forth with so universal
a unity of government, doctrine, and the means
of grace as to witness to her unique claim
of teacher of the complete gospel of Jesus
Christ.

Protestantism can never claim the title of
Catholic, for it is built on the disintegrating
principle of private judgment, every man discussing at will the meaning of a mysterious Bible,
of which he possesses no certain interpretation.
The germ of error, discord, contradiction, and
denial is within the bosom of Protestantism, and
therefore its tendency is neither to maintain
Christianity nor to spread it in the universal
unity which it should possess. Again, Protestantism is not Catholic in *time*, for it did not
dawn upon the world until the sixteenth century, and we need more than the mere word of
men of the stamp of Luther, Calvin, Henry
VIII., or Knox to bridge the chasm that divides
them from the beginning. The denominations
are known by the name of their founders, who,
without any commission, assumed to have
unearthed a forgotten gospel; they are over
1,500 years too late to be in any sense Catholic.

Nor is it Catholic *territorially*, for, strange
enough, for over two hundred years it
manifested no missionary spirit whatsoever,
but, identified with the princes upon whose
favor it flourished and grew, it kept within national and local lines, caring nothing
for the pagan in distant lands. And in our
day, when Protestantism has reached out its
hand to the pagan, its success has been
ridiculously small, as its own ministers testify, despite the expenditure of many millions,
and the distribution of countless copies of
the Bible (Marshall's "Christian Missions";
Canon Taylor, *Fortnightly Review*, Oct., 1888;
Dublin Review, Jan., 1889; *Nineteenth Century*,
July, 1888).

Nor is it Catholic in matters of *doctrine*, for
the various denominations deny many doctrines
of Christ's gospel. Each voices a different
interpretation of His teaching, and allows,
even within the limits of one sect, all manner
of doctrine, from the denial of such elementary
Christian teachings as the Trinity and the Incarnation to the holding of all the doctrines
of the Catholic Church minus Papal infallibility. Since the Reformation the tendency has
ever been towards infidelity, and the average
Protestant to-day indignantly repudiates the
teachings of Luther or Calvin, and frequently
is an indifferentist in matters of belief.

On the other hand, the Catholic Church is Catholic *in time*, for she goes back to the beginning, and no man can trace any other origin for her than Jesus Christ and His Apostles.

She is Catholic *territorially*, for there is nothing local in her constitution. She is just as much at home in a republic as in a monarchy; she has her message for the cultured American or the barbarian of mid-Africa; she ministers to the multi-millionnaire and then to the poor of the tenement-house; she speaks to the greatest saint and to the most degraded sinner. Like Christ, she is for all men, for all places. A striking illustration of her universal jurisdiction was the Vatican Council in 1870.

She is Catholic in *doctrine*, for although growing and developing as Providence guides her, making new definitions of old doctrines as new errors arise to confuse the minds of men and render clearer statements necessary—she is ever the same unchanging Church, guarding infallibly the divine deposit of the one gospel of Christ, under the divine guarantee of the abiding presence of Christ (Matt. xxviii. 20) and the Holy Spirit (John xiv. 17).

Catholics are more numerous to-day than Protestants, although in this matter exact statistics are difficult to obtain. I quote some authorities cited by Tanquery ("Synopsis Theol. Dog.," vol. i. pp. 419, 420):

	Catholics.	Protestants.	Greeks.
O. Werner (Cath.), Orbis Terrarum Catholicus, .	230,000,000	215,000,000	
The Bible Atlas (Prot.), . . .	172,000,000	208,000,000	
Behm & Wagner (Prot.) (Schaff, Erzog, Encyc., p. 2058), . . .	215,938,500	130,329,000	84,007,000
Tablet (Oct. 17, 1885), ...	275,000,000		
Groffier (Cath.?), Planisphere des Religions, ...	212,100,000	123,800,000	83,810,000

Why do you deny us Episcopalians the title of Catholic? We claim to be Anglo-Catholics, not Roman Catholics.

Is not the Established Church of England one and the same with the Church that existed in England prior to the Reformation?

Did not the early English Church deny the supreme jurisdiction of the Roman See?

Catholics deny that Episcopalians have any claim whatsoever to the title of Catholic, for at the time of the Reformation they broke away from the centre of Catholic unity; denied the Papal Supremacy, always recognized by their forefathers, to acknowledge the spiritual supremacy of the sovereign; denied many fundamental Catholic doctrines; abolished the ancient Catholic discipline; proscribed utterly the Catholic liturgy, and in a word became Protestants of the Protestants.

It is not difficult to prove that the Church of England prior to the Reformation was in union with all Christendom, Roman Catholic in government, doctrine, and ritual, and that it underwent an essential change in all of these when it became by law established under the Tudor sovereigns.

The spiritual supremacy of the Pope was never denied in England until the time of Henry VIII. It is undoubted history that the Archbishops of Canterbury, the Primates of the English Church, were not recognized until their appointment had been confirmed by the Pope; at their consecration and investiture with the pallium, which the Pope sent as a symbol of their jurisdiction (Protestant Bishop Stubbs, "Constitutional History," vol. iii. p. 305), they swore "to defend the Roman Papacy against all men, to obey the commands of the Holy See with their whole strength, and to cause them to be obeyed by others" (Rymer's "Fœdera," vol. vi. p. 80, ed. 1741). In their letters they continually call themselves the "Legates of the Apostolic See" and declare "their service and obedience" to the Roman Pontiff (Letter of Archbishop Chicheley to Martin V., 1426 A.D.; Haddan and Stubbs, "Ecc. Councils," iii. 448, 541).

The English Bishops before the Reformation were never recognized without the Pope's confirmation, and as a rule were directly appointed by him. The oath at their consecration ran as follows: "I will be faithful and obedient to Blessed Peter and the Roman Church, and to my Lord the Pope N——, so help me God and these God's holy Gospels." Again, all important cases of trial were referred by the Bishops to Rome as the Supreme Court of Appeal (Stubbs, "Const. Hist.," vol. iii. p. 315), and its jurisdiction continually recognized by the appeals of various kings regarding episcopal appointments, by their applying for dispensations (Edward the Confessor in favor of Westminster, Henry VII. to be freed from his Crusade promise, Henry VII. to marry within the prohibited degrees), the acceptance of papal excommunications and interdicts, the receiving of Papal legates, the presence of English Bishops in councils called by the Pope, etc. Sixty-eight Archbishops succeeded St. Augustine in the See of Canterbury, each one of whom received the pallium from Rome. We know full well that there were many protests to Rome against the appointment of foreigners to

English benefices, the demands of money made by the Papal court, and the interference of some Popes in the civil affairs of England. But while questioning some of the feudal rights of the Pope, the English kings and people never for an instant questioned his spiritual supremacy. They held with the Venerable Bede (Hist., lib. ii. c. i.) that "the Pope (Gregory) was invested with the first, *i.e.*, supreme pontificate in the whole world, and was set over the Churches converted to the true faith, making our nation, till then given up to idols, the Church of Christ."

From the sixth to the sixteenth century the Catholic Church in England flourished and grew, as every other part of Christendom, in union with Rome. Under Henry VIII., for the first time in her history, did England deny the supremacy of the Pope, and cut itself off from the body of Christendom. This monarch, having tried for a long time to persuade Pope Clement VII. to annul his marriage with Queen Catherine that he might marry his mistress, Anne Boleyn, determined to take the law in his own hands, and constitute himself supreme by act of Parliament. "By the Act of Supremacy, authority in all matters ecclesiastical was vested solely in the Crown. The courts spiritual became as thoroughly the King's courts as the temporal courts at Westminster. The statute ordered (1534) that the King ' shall be taken, accepted, and reputed the only supreme head on earth of the Church of England, and shall have and enjoy, annexed and united to the Imperial Crown of this realm, as well the title and state thereof as all the honors, jurisdictions, authorities, immunities, profits, and commodities to the said dignity belonging, with full power to visit, repress, redress, reform, and amend all such errors, heresies, abuses, contempts, and enormities, which by any manner of *spiritual authority* or *jurisdiction* might or may lawfully be reformed ' " (Green's " History of the English People," vol. ii. book v. p. 159, Harper's edition).

By this act the national Church of England came into existence, and the Tudor sovereigns and their parliaments became the origin of church jurisdiction and the arbiters of church doctrine and ritual. The idea of the Church as a kingdom, independent, sovereign, catholic, and supernatural was for ever lost, and a religious body under the government of the sovereign came into existence dependent, national, and natural. It had no living voice, for it had ceased to be the divine institution of Jesus Christ. This essential change in government placed the Church of England in unmistakable schism, and forfeited at once the title of this state establishment to the term Catholic. Men like Sir Thomas More, the Chancellor of England, and Henry's preceptor, Bishop Fisher of Rochester, recognized this at once, and died on the scaffold, rather than, as More said in his famous defence, "to conform my conscience to the counsel of one kingdom against the general consent of all Christendom."

Under Edward VI., who claimed the same supremacy, another step was made towards the Protestantization of the Church of England, by the change in doctrine and ritual evidenced by the Book of Common Prayer (1548), the forty-two articles (1553), the new catechism, and the book of homilies, all of which were markedly Protestant in tone (Green, *ibid.*, pp. 226, 233, 234). All the altars in the churches were removed by order of the Royal Council, and communion tables substituted, the object being expressly stated, "to move the people from the superstitions of the Popish Mass unto the right use of the Lord's Supper." Repealed under Mary, these statutes of the Royal Supremacy were re-enacted under Elizabeth by the Parliament of 1558 (Green, *ibid.*, p. 303). England became Protestant, a new Protestant hierarchy being substituted for the old Catholic Bishops. Elizabeth exacted the oath of supremacy which no Catholic could lawfully take, enforced the Act of Uniformity in a public worship which no Catholic could conscientiously attend, and made (1563) thirty-nine of the Calvinistic articles drawn up under Edward VI. the standard of faith of the English Protestant clergy (Green, *ibid.*, p. 343).

Strange, therefore, that to-day many High-Churchmen in England and in this country repudiate Protestantism and the Reformation, and, ignoring the facts of history and the anti-Catholic denials of the teaching authority of the Church, transubstantiation, the Mass, the seven sacraments, purgatory, devotion to the Blessed Virgin and the saints, etc., claim the name of Catholic. But their claim is merely based on the frail foundation of Protestant private judgment, and is denied by the majority of their brethren, the other denominations of Protestantism, the Greek schismatics, and the Catholic Church. Imagine a governor of one of these United States denying the presidency of Mr. Roosevelt, and setting up a constitution directly opposed to the fundamental principles and ideals of the American Republic, and yet withal claiming to be a vital part thereof, and you have an idea of the imaginary theory of a minority of the Church of England, which, denying the primacy of the Pope, and setting up a doctrinal constitution directly opposed to the fundamental teachings of the universal Church, is still declared to be a part of the Catholic Church.

How, indeed, after three hundred years of insistence on their Protestantism, and the enactment of penal laws of the severest kind against Catholic doctrine and practice, can any member of the Established Church of England who subscribes to the Thirty-nine Articles which evidence the essential Protestantism of their framers, claim with any show of probability the title of Catholic? The very oath that remains in the coronation service of the English sovereign, "to defend the reformed religion," is proof conclusive against any such claim.

In the United States, moreover, the official title of the Episcopalians is "the Protestant Episcopal Church of America," despite many protests of High-Churchmen in synod after synod (Catholic Truth Society publications).

When was the word Catholic first used? When Protestant?

Does not the word Roman localize your Church and plainly deny it as the Catholic Church? Is not Roman-Catholic a contradiction in terms?

The Church of Christ has been called Catholic as early as the beginning of the second century or the end of the first. St. Ignatius Martyr in his letter to the people of Smyrna (n. 8) says: "Where the bishop is, there let the multitude of believers be; even as where Jesus Christ is, there is the Catholic Church."

It has ever since been the name of the Church founded by Jesus Christ, and although for thousands of years others have endeavored to usurp the name, they have done so despite the protest of the Catholic Church, and even of the great majority of their own members, as, for instance, the High-Church Episcopalians of our day. St. Augustine wrote in the fifth century: "The name itself of the Catholic Church keeps me—a name which, in the midst of so many heresies, this Church alone has, not without cause, so held possession of as that, though all heretics would fain have themselves called Catholics, yet to the inquiry of any stranger, 'Where is the Assembly of the Catholic Church held?' no heretic would dare point out his own basilica or house" (Contra Ep. Manich. Fund., n. 5).

The name *Protestant* is derived from the protest of the Lutheran princes of Germany against the principles of liberty and toleration set forth as a basis of agreement by the Catholic princes at the Diet of Spires in 1529. These articles maintained liberty of worship, and at the same time deprived the Protestants of their power to plunder and persecute Catholics. To this they would not agree. No wonder, therefore, that the mild Melancthon styled this protest "a terrible deed" ("Eine Schreckliche That"), for it cost Germany a civil war, in which she lost over half her population. And yet men say that the Reformation stood for liberty.

The term Roman Catholic is by no means a contradiction in terms, as some have erroneously declared, but simply affirms that the Vicar of Jesus Christ, the Bishop of Rome, is the chief Bishop and head of the whole Church, and only those under his jurisdiction are within the one true fold of the Saviour. No one is a Catholic who is not a Roman Catholic. The terms are identical and interchangeable. The adjective Roman merely accentuates the fact of the vital character of Christianity, having a local government on earth, whose head is the Bishop of Rome.

Why do Catholics take offence at the words Romish or Romanist?

Because the name of their Church is "The Catholic Church," or "The Roman Catholic Church," and the words *Romish* and *Romanist* are used by her enemies in an insulting sense. In the same way an Italian would object to the word "dago," or a German to the word "Dutchman." The standard dictionary says of these words: "*Romish*—Used by Protestants, and generally indicating disesteem." "*Romanist*—A term used chiefly by those whose views are adverse to that Church."

In what does the Greek Church differ from the Catholic Church? Was not the Greek Church the first Church?

In points of doctrine the Greek Church denies the primacy and infallibility of the Pope, the procession of the Holy Spirit from the Father and the Son, the Immaculate Conception, and allows divorce in case of adultery. There are also some differences of discipline, *v. g.*, the use of leavened bread in the Eucharist, the permission of priests to marry. The Greek Church, therefore, is guilty of both heresy and schism.

Until the middle of the ninth century the Greek Church was in communion with the Roman Pontiff. The natural antipathy of the Greeks to the Latins, the many differences in ecclesiastical discipline, the close alliance of the Papacy and the Empire of the West, and Constantinople's jealousy of the power of the Roman See, prepared the way for the schism of the ninth century.

It began in A.D. 858, when the Greek Emperor, Michael the Drunkard, at the instigation of his profligate uncle, Bardas, banished Ignatius, the patriarch of Constantinople, and intruded the layman Photius in his place. Bardas had been angered by the patriarch's protest against his incest and impiety, and his public refusal of Holy Communion; the Emperor was displeased because Ignatius refused to give the veil to the unwilling Theodora, the Emperor's mother, and her daughters.

The consecration of Photius was uncanonical, because Ignatius still remained the lawful patriarch; and the consecrator, Gregory of Syracuse, was at the time under sentence of deposition and excommunication. Everything possible was done to secure the approbation of Pope Nicholas I., as, for example, an embassy to Rome, the bribery of the Papal legates sent to Constantinople, lying letters, forged decrees, and the like. But after a thorough investigation, the Pope declared Ignatius the rightful patriarch, and deposed Photius as a usurper (A.D. 863).

Photius, however, through the influence of the Emperor, retained his power, and in 867 convoked a synod of his own at Constantinople, which pretended to anathematize and depose the Pope. Twenty-two venal bishops signed the decrees, and to give some dignity to the proceedings Photius forged scores of other names. Soon after Photius wrote a letter to the Eastern bishops, denouncing the Latins, and broaching the heresy regarding the procession of the Holy Spirit.

The Emperor Basil, who succeeded Michael, for political reasons deposed Photius and reinstated Ignatius, besides asking the Pope to annul the decrees of the schismatic synod held by Photius. Hadrian II. (867–872) finally brought about the union of Greeks and Latins at the Eighth General Council of Constantinople, A.D. 869.

In 878 Photius again usurped the patriarchate, and, although excommunicated in turn by Pope John VIII., Marinus I., and Hadrian III., he retained his power until the accession of the Emperor Leo VI. (886), who banished him. From the death of Photius (891) until 1054 the patriarchs of Constantinople remained in communion with the Holy See, although the relations were never cordial.

The final break occurred under the Emperor Michael Cerularius (A.D. 1043–1059), who, after refusing to submit, was solemnly excommunicated by the Papal legates sent to Constantinople by Leo IX. (A.D. 1054). Although there have been several attempts at reunion (Fourth Lateran Council, A.D. 1215; Lyons, 1274–1280; Florence, 1439), the schism has continued to this day. Once separated from Rome, the Greek Church became, like the Church of England, subject to the state, and the tool of the imperial power (Alzog, "Church History," vol. ii. pp. 449-466).

APOSTOLICITY.

Why do you deny us Protestants the claim of Apostolicity ? We claim that your Church was a corruption of the Apostolic Church and that Luther restored it to its primitive purity.

Is not the true successor of the Apostles that preacher of the Gospel who inherits the Apostolic spirit, and who works for the good of men as the Apostles did ?

Do not we Protestants stand for the true Apostolic preaching ?

The Catholic Church denies that the Protestant denominations are Apostolic, for they are new teachers of new doctrines, who without the slightest shadow of proof assert that the promises of Christ have been of no avail to preserve His Church from the corruption of error. The Reformers of the sixteenth century, indeed, claimed a special mission to overthrow the existing government of the Church by denying the universal jurisdiction of the Pope; they also claimed light from above to interpret the Bible at will to find out what the Saviour taught, independently of the divine authority He established. But to claim is one thing; to prove a claim another. Insane asylums are full of people who claim to be Napoleon, Alexander the Great, Leo XIII., and the like. The Reformers produced no evidence in support of their new mission save their own private opinion. They were self-credited ambassadors without authority, who gave no evidence by miracle or holiness of life that they were sent of God. "He that entereth not by the door into the sheepfold, but climbeth up another way, the same is a thief and a robber" (John x. 1 ; I. Tim. i. 6, 7 ; II. Tim. iii. 1–5).

The true Apostolic succession demands more than mere natural love of the brethren. An Apostolic church must have Apostolic doctrine, orders, and authority. The Bible gives us unmistakable evidence of a Church built on the Apostles, and continuing one and the same for ever without even the possibility of failure.

Christ Himself chose the twelve Apostles, and made them, with Peter as their head (Matt. xvi. 18 ; Luke xxii. 31–32 ; John xxi. 15–17), the foundation of His Church. "You have not chosen Me, but I have chosen you " (John xv. 16 ; Matt. iv. 18–22 ; Mark iii. 13, 14 ; Luke vi. 13–16 ; John vi. 71 ; Eph. ii. 19, 20).

He gives to the Apostles a divine commission to preach His doctrine and pardon sin in His name and with His authority for all times and for all places, guaranteeing their faithfulness by the perpetual guidance of Himself and the Holy Spirit (Matt. xxviii. 18–20 ; Matt.

xviii. 17 ; Mark xvi. 15, 16 ; Luke x. 16 ; John xx. 21–23 ; John xiv. 26 ; John xvi. 13).

The Apostles continually claim to be divinely commissioned ministers and ambassadors of God (Rom. i. 5; x. 14, 15; I. Cor. iv. 1; I. Cor. xii. 28 ; II. Cor. ii. 17 ; v. 19, 20 ; vi. 4 ; I. Thess. ii. 3, 4, 13 ; Eph. iv. 11, 12; Col. i. 25; Heb. v. 4; I. Tim. ii. 7; I. John iv. 6). They are most strong in their denunciation of those who dared teach a new gospel, because they realized it must needs be man-made, and therefore false (Gal. i. 8 ; Heb. xiii. 9). They know nothing of a Church that will become corrupt, for they had heard Christ's words which speak clearly of a perpetual Church (Matt. xxviii. 20; John xiv. 16). Consequently we find them ordaining successors to carry on their work of preaching and pardoning, whom they commanded to hold fast to every doctrine of the gospel, and in turn transmit it pure and undefiled to faithful and capable men (Acts xiv. 22 ; II. Tim. ii. 2 ; i. 6; Tit. i. 5). It is plain, therefore, to one who studies these texts of Scripture carefully, that the whole work of Christ Jesus as Teacher, Ruler, and Sanctifier of men is to be carried on for ever by the Apostolic body, and those divinely associated to that Apostolic body by the fact of orders received and jurisdiction given. If, for example, a body of twelve men receive from the owner of a large farm of five thousand acres the contract to gather in his entire harvest, they receive also as a matter of fact the right to hire as many others as are necessary in order to fulfil their contract. But no outsider can rightly cut a swathe or bind a single sheaf of that harvest, unless he receive authority so to do from one of the twelve, or some sub-contractor who acts in their name and with their authority. If he attempt it he will be treated as a trespasser.

So with the Lord of the harvest, Christ Jesus (Luke x. 1–12). He has given over the harvest of all nations to twelve men (Matt. xxviii. 18–20; Mark xvi. 15, 16), and they, to carry out that divine commission, must necessarily choose others to carry on the work after their death. So we find them, immediately after the death of Judas, selecting Matthias in his place (Acts i. 26). Only those appointed by the Apostles, or their associates, have any right to labor in the harvest of souls. "He that entereth not by the door into the sheepfold, but climbeth up another way, the same is a thief and a robber" (John x. 1).

As for the Reformation dogmas of Protestantism being identical with the early preaching of the gospel, many Protestants themselves to-day repudiate the teaching of the Reformers entirely. Much of the modern unbelief comes of the realization of the fact, that if the Reformers had a right to give the world a new Christianity, others also have the same right to call themselves Christians while stripping Christianity of all its supernatural character. A study of the Fathers, or of the catacomb inscriptions, will prove every Catholic doctrine and practice, and completely refute the Protestant denial of the visible Church, the apostolic ministry, the efficacy of the sacraments, the true notion of faith and good works, etc. "So much must the Protestant grant," writes Cardinal Newman, "that if such a system as he would now introduce ever existed in earlier times, it has been clean swept away as if by a deluge, suddenly, silently, and without memorial; by a deluge coming in a night, and utterly soaking, rotting, tearing up, and hurrying off every vestige of what is found in the Church before cock-crowing" ("Historical Sketches," vol. i. p. 418).

What right has your Roman branch of the Universal Church to lord it over the Greek and Anglican branches?

We ask in reply: What is the Church of England? What are its doctrines? What its history? What its witness to-day? What its authority? And we find three parties among Episcopalians, all claiming to represent her truly. The High-Church party with its Church idea minus the Pope; the Low-Church party Protestant of the Protestants, with the Bible only, and horrified at the thought of any movement Romeward; the Broad-Church party, repudiating both the prayer-book and the Thirty-nine Articles, and standing for liberal, rationalistic Christianity with the Unitarian and the Universalist. Which is the Church of England?

The High-Church party evolved the Branch theory—*i.e.*, the Roman, Greek, and Anglican branches form one universal Church; but it is a theory unknown till the last century, and therefore over eighteen centuries too late.

We can readily understand what is meant by the Roman Catholic Church with its perfect unity of Apostolic doctrine, of episcopal government under one infallible head, the Pope, who can teach authoritatively and bear infallible witness to the doctrines of Christ. We can understand what is meant by the Church of England as an organization, or corporate body, dependent upon the state in its origin and continuance. But we can form no conception of this imaginary three-branch church of whose existence nine-tenths of its members are ignorant. We cannot grasp the notion of a union of men holding doctrines and principles fundamentally opposed despite their earnest protest. For all Catholics, Greeks, and Protestants, with the majority of Episcopalians themselves, deny the existence of any such body.

If a union were possible between churches that affirm and deny the most essential doctrines of Christianity, it would follow that the Church had ceased entirely to perform her chief office as the infallible teacher, witness, and guardian of Christ's revelation; the abiding presence of Christ (Matt xxviii. 20) and the Holy Spirit (John xiv. 16, 17, 26) have failed to keep her pure from the taint of false doctrine, and the gates of hell have prevailed, contrary to Christ's promise (Matt. xvi. 18).

The branch theory, therefore, gives us a church in name only. What indeed is a church that cannot speak authoritatively and declare the true doctrine of the Saviour? What is a church divided against itself, teaching one thing in London, another in St. Petersburg, and another in Rome. "Every city or house divided against itself shall not stand" (Matt. xii. 25).

The Catholic Church does indeed regard the Greeks and Anglicans as dead branches, cut off from the centre of unity; national churches only, whose fulness of ecclesiastical power rests in the person of the King or the Czar. She does not lord it over them, but rather regrets their heresy and schism, and prays earnestly for their return to the faith of their forefathers. (Bagshawe, "The Church"; MacLaughlin, "The Divine Plan of the Church.")

We Anglicans claim Apostolic succession from the present bishops back to the Apostle Paul, who first brought Christianity to Britain. Why, then, do you dispute our claim?

Because there is not the slightest evidence for the claim. As for St. Paul's preaching in Britain, no proof whatsoever is forthcoming. We deny the claim of Apostolic succession made by some members of the Church of England and the Protestant Episcopal Church of America, because, in the first place, we consider their priests and bishops to be mere laymen for lack of valid orders. But even granting that their orders were valid, the fact of their being cut off from the centre of unity, the See of Rome, which has ever been the test and guarantee of the true Apostolic succession, is proof positive against them. "How shall they preach unless they be sent?" we ask with St. Paul (Rom. x. 15). Whence came the mission of the Anglican bishops to teach? Not from the Pope, whom they repudiated; not from the Catholic bishops, who in Elizabeth's time denounced them as spurious; not from the crown, for it could not give what it did not itself possess.

No, the Church of England is a modern church dating from the decree of Parliament that made Henry VIII. the head of the church in spirituals as well as temporals, and all attempts to prove it the same church in government, doctrine, and ritual with the Church of the Apostles in England before the Reformation provoke a smile with all outsiders, and are pronounced futile by the majority of their own communion.

Why do you class us Episcopalians with other Protestant denominations when we resemble your Church so closely in many respects?

Because the Church of England and its sister in this country, the Protestant Episcopal Church of America, have for their basic principle the private judgment of the individual, and not the voice of the living, infallible Church. At the outset of the Tractarian movement indeed, about seventy years ago, some notion existed that a bishop as the successor of the Apostles had a right to teach authoritatively; but the constant contests between ministers and bishops with different views concerning doctrine and practice have finally destroyed all notion of authority whatsoever. And so in our day an Episcopalian bishop may ordain a man against the indignant protests of the clergymen of his diocese, while, on the other hand, a ritualistic minister may defiantly hold doctrines his bishop considers false, or go through with a so-called "mass" that his bishop regards as idolatrous. And worse still, a High-Church bishop may be forced to tolerate within his diocese men whose views are so broad that they deny with impunity the dogmas of the Trinity and the Divinity of Christ.

The mere outward semblance, therefore, of ritual, or the mere holding of dogmas as matters of opinion, does not constitute identity with the Catholic Church; although, undoubtedly, the hand of God is thus visible directing many sincere souls to consider the one great question : Is there on earth a divine, infallible teacher which voices authoritatively all the gospel of the Saviour ?

THE CHARGE OF INTOLERANCE.

Do you believe that sincere Protestants will be damned ?

Where do good Protestants go after death ?

Does the Roman Church claim the monopoly of salvation ?

Do you believe that all Catholics go to heaven, and all Protestants to hell ?

Do you honestly think all pagans are doomed to eternal hell fire ?

Does not your catechism teach that "outside of the Church there is no salvation"? Is this not an intolerable doctrine?

The Catholic Church teaches that no one goes to hell, unless he has freely and deliberately turned his back on God, and died guilty of mortal sin. The axiom, "Outside of the Church there is no salvation," is a technical expression, to be understood only in the sense that Catholic theologians have ever put upon it. A non-Catholic once said to me: "You cannot explain that away, for the words are too plain. They admit of but one meaning, viz.: the wholesale damnation of all that are not members of your Church." And yet, on further questioning, he admitted that a constitutional lawyer ought to be the authority on the meaning of a clause in the Constitution rather than an ignorant voter who could not explain why he was a Republican rather than a Democrat. According to his argument, the axiom of English law, "The king can do no wrong," would imply that King Edward VII. was confirmed in grace, rather than the fact of his not being amenable to any court in England.

The Catholic Church has always believed that men outside of her fold might live in error, and still be saved; that men outside of her visible organization through invincible ignorance might still be in the soul of the Church, by a true spiritual communion of faith and charity; that every anathema or condemnation by the Church relates to error itself or false principles contrary to the gospel of Jesus Christ, and does not concern the interior guilt of men or women in error; that no Catholic has a right to judge the guilt of any individual.

Pius IX., writing on this matter, says: "Far be it from us to dare set bounds to the boundless mercy of God; far be it from us to desire to search into the depths of the hidden counsels and judgments of God, an abyss that the mind of man cannot explore. . . . We must hold as of faith, that out of the Apostolic Roman Church there is no salvation; that she is the only ark of safety, and whosoever is not in her perishes in the deluge; we must also, on the other hand, recognize with certainty that those who are in invincible ignorance of the true religion are not guilty for this in the eye of the Lord. And who will presume to mark out the limits of this ignorance according to the character and diversity of peoples, countries, minds, and the rest?" (Allocution, Dec. 9, 1854). And again he writes: "It is known to us and to you that those who are in invincible ignorance of our most holy religion, but who observe carefully the natural law and the precepts graven by God upon the hearts of all men, and who being disposed to obey God lead an honest and upright life, may, aided by the light of divine grace, attain to eternal life ; for God, who sees clearly, searches and knows the heart, the disposition, the thoughts and intentions of each, in his supreme mercy and goodness by no means permits that any one suffer eternal punishment who has not of his own free will fallen into sin " (Encyclical to the Italian Bishops, August 10, 1863).

We see, therefore, that the plain teaching of the Catholic Church is " He who is outside the one visible Church of Christ by his own fault cannot be saved." Thus, a man convinced that the Catholic Church is the one Kingdom of God established on earth for the salvation of men, and yet refusing to belong to her communion because it means loss of social or political position, of money, of friends, rebels wilfully against his conscience, gravely insults Christ, and is guilty of grievous sin. Again, a man who gravely doubts about his own belief and refuses to study the Catholic claim, sins against the light.

How absurd to think that we believe all Catholics are to be saved by the very fact of their being Catholics, when the Council of Trent teaches expressly against Luther that no

one can ever be absolutely certain of salvation
(Sess. vi., de Just., can. 15).

With regard to pagans, it is the teaching
of the Church that God sincerely wills all men
to be saved, and that He gives sufficient grace
to all men, pagan or Christian, for salvation.
It follows, therefore, logically, no pagan is lost
except by his own fault.   It is an old axiom of
the schools, " God will not refuse His grace to
any man that does the best he can " (what
lies in his power) (Du Blanchy, "Extra
Ecclesiam non est salus "; Hergenröther,
" Church and State," vol. ii. xvii. par. 3).

Intelligent non-Catholics recognize clearly
the true sense of this formula, and the boundless charity and hatred of intolerance that
marks the spirit of the Catholic Church.   Mallock writes : " There is no point, probably, connected with this question, about which the
general world is so misinformed and ignorant
as the sober but boundless charity of what is
called the anathematizing Church.   So little
indeed is this charity understood generally,
that to assert it seems a startling paradox.
.   .   .   It is the simple statement of a fact.
Never was there a religious body, except the
Roman, that laid the intense stress she does on
all her dogmatic teachings, and had yet the
justice that comes of sympathy for those that
cannot receive them.   .   .   .   The holy and

humble men of heart who do not know her, or who in good faith reject her, she commits with confidence to God's uncovenanted mercies; and these she knows are infinite. . . . Her anathemas are on none but those who reject her with their eyes open, by tampering with a conviction that she really is the truth. These are condemned, not for not seeing that the teacher is true, but because, having really seen this, they continue to close their eyes to it. They will not obey when they know they ought to obey " (" Is Life Worth Living ? " ch. xi. 283–285). A Catholic could not state the doctrine more clearly.

If I can be saved outside the Catholic Church, what is the use of my joining it ?

One might as well ask : If I can swim across the Hudson River, why should I pay three cents to ride in a ferry-boat?

Jesus Christ was a divine teacher, who commanded us to believe all His teaching under penalty of damnation, and a divine organizer who commanded us to join His society, the Catholic Church. " He that believeth not shall be condemned " (Mark xvi. 16) ; " Teaching all things " (Matt. xxviii. 20); " If he will not hear the Church, let him be to thee as the heathen or publican " (Matt. xviii. 17). The Catholic Church alone preaches the entire gos-

pel, and in her inner and outer life is the
ordinary way of salvation God gave to men.
As a non-Catholic, therefore, you are, even
if inculpably outside the Church, deprived
of much of God's revelation, and many of
His helps for salvation; *v. g.*, Penance, the
Eucharist, the Sacrifice of the Mass.

Again, if God's grace urge you to join His
true Church, and you hesitate about studying
her claims because you dread the opposition
of relatives and friends, the anxiety and worry
of protracted study, the loss of political or
social position, the burden of new obligations
—like obligatory Sunday Mass or confession—
there is no possibility of your salvation, because you are false to conscience. How many
a doubting soul, utterly unable to swear on
the Gospel that their sect is the' one true
Church of Christ, and unwilling to die for
that belief, yet refuses to do away with his
doubts by study and prayer. We cannot remain indifferent to our eternal welfare without
forfeiting the friendship of God.

Would you as a Catholic priest like to have
the members of your Church take in a series of
lectures by a Protestant on. Protestant doctrines,
where the lecturer would insist that his Church
is the only true one?

If you are broad-minded and liberal enough to

invite us Protestants to come to your services, why in your bigotry and intolerance deny Catholics the liberty to come to ours?

For what reason does a priest forbid Catholics to attend non-Catholic churches? Should not an honest person study both sides?

Protestants are invited by us to listen to the explanation of Catholic doctrine and the answers to their difficulties, because we know that they can attend without violating any principle of their Protestantism, which is a religion of fallible, private opinion. Disclaiming infallibility, a logical Protestant must necessarily be in the attitude of a seeker after truth. He usually says "that one church is as good as another" because he lacks the divine witness to the unique Christianity Jesus founded. He is often a doubter, who questions at times whether or not the old historical Church may be right. Was the Reformation a step towards Christ or in the direction of infidelity and indifferentism? Is the Bible its own witness? Will faith alone save a man? Are those stories about the Church of Rome true or false? Is this her real teaching or a parody thereof? Are these her moral principles, or has she repudiated them as calumnies of her enemies? Is confession of sin an institution of Christ? Does the Saviour really dwell with His people? With thousands who have not yet denied the Christ there is an eagerness to know the message of the Catholic Church, as the large attendance at these lectures to non-Catholics in every part of our country abundantly proves.

On the other hand, the Catholic, resting not on the varying, contradictory human and fallible views of men, but on the uniform, certain, divine, infallible witness of Christ's Church, is possessed of an absolute divine certainty that his Church alone has the true religion Jesus Christ gave the world.

A logical Protestant must ever be in the state of chronic doubt; a Catholic never has the slightest doubt.

A logical Protestant is ever a seeker after truth; a Catholic has found it, and therefore is under no necessity of further search.

Catholics, therefore, could not without violating the essential principles of Christianity take part in religious services they know to be false, or consider doctrines they know on divine authority to be contrary to the gospel of Christ.

St. Paul told the early Christians that it was sinful to participate in the sacrifices of paganism (I. Cor. x. 21); the same Apostolic Church forbids to-day co-operation in any erroneous religion as displeasing to the God of truth.

Practically, the Catholic Church, having a uniform faith, can satisfactorily explain her teaching to the world; but Protestantism, divided hopelessly, would find it impossible to explain what she protests against. Imagine, for instance, the Episcopal Church attempting to give a series of lectures explanatory of her teachings, and the three lecturers are severally High-Church, Low-Church, and Broad. Each man would deny in turn what the other held was the gospel of Christ.

It is not a question of liberality or broad-mindedness, for Catholics maintain that no man can without sin deny the doctrines of the Saviour. To countenance the preaching of a false gospel is practical denial of the Christ; to take part in a false worship is to sinfully declare all worship equally pleasing to God. True, our spirit is one of kindliness to all and hatred toward none, and utterly devoid of that bigotry which implies an irrational belief in a doctrine one cannot prove, together with the hatred of all others who believe differently. Catholics hate none who profess a false religion, but rather compassionate them and pray for them.

But one's good will is never shown by the sacrifice of principle; one's kindliness is never manifested by declaring that essential differences do not exist. We cannot be "liberal" with the doctrine. of the Saviour, for it is God's truth. You would not call the man liberal who was lavishly spending his employer's money.

As for studying both sides, a Protestant is bound to do so; for, like the scientist in face of an unproved hypothesis, he cannot be infallibly sure that his theory is right. A Catholic has no other need to study than the scientist with proved and tested facts is obliged to go over the ground of his predecessors. His faith rests on God's authority, not on man's, and therefore he cannot be deceived.

Why do you forbid Catholics to attend Spiritistic seances ?

Can a Catholic be a medium?

Why is the Catholic Church opposed to Spiritism ?

A short summary of the facts and teaching of Spiritism will at once explain the attitude of the Catholic Church. Spiritism, or the systematic communication with spirits that claim to be departed souls, is merely a new form of pagan necromancy, anathematized by the law of Moses (Exod. xxii. 18; Lev. xix. 26; Deut. xviii. 10; I. Kings xxviii. 9). In its modern dress, it dates from the spirit revelations of the Fox family at Hydesville, New York, in 1848. Within a few years Spiritism counted some ten million adherents in this country alone. The fact of its rapid progress showed the evident weakening in faith of the various Protestant denominations that fed it. Its doctrines, learned from spirit manifestations, are given us in detail by leading spiritists like Wallace, Kardec (Rivail), Crookes, Home, Tuttle, and others.

It claims to be a *religion*, although it gives no worship to God, and substitutes in His stead a great crowd of spirits of every grade of intellect and morality. Its external worship is the feverish excitement of the uncanny séance, and its priests chiefly women "mediums," who, under stress of hypnotic influence or diabolic possession, bring about many strange phenomena, such as table-rapping, the writing of the planchette, oral and written spirit communications, the reading of secret thoughts, the diagnosis of diseases, the speaking of unknown tongues, the prophesying of future events, the describing distant happenings.

Undoubtedly some of the so-called facts of Spiritism may be ascribed to fraud, for time and time again mediums have figured in the police courts ; others can be explained by mere natural causes, such as hypnotic influence, or some hitherto unexplored natural force in man (Dr. J. Wieser, S.J., of Innsbrück, "Spiritism and Christianity "). But over and above this there are facts which seem to have overwhelming testimony in their favor, and which point to diabolic agency.

Spiritism pretends to be the final perfection of Christianity, although it denies its every dogma, and declares that Jesus Christ is not the Son of God, but merely one of the highest spirits.

Its history has been marked with the greatest immorality, as the Mountain Cave, the Kiantone Movement, the Sacred Order of Unionists, and the Order of the Patriarchs amply prove. Some have argued that this was merely an abuse, but we say that Spiritism is essentially anti-moral. It has no worship of God, and no eternal sanction of reward and punishment to safeguard morality. It declares that human existence is merely a time of trial for spirits until they reach the final perfection which is the destiny of all. Surely such a teaching is not calculated to curb the evil passions of men's hearts.

Rightly, then, does the Church warn her children against this irreligious and immoral superstition, which often seems to evidence the power of Satan; and forbid them not only to become mediums, but even to attend the Spiritistic séances. (" Is Spiritism a Development of Christianity ? " *Amer. Cath. Quart.*, vol. viii. p. 153 ; "Modern Spiritism versus Christianity," *ibid.*, vol. vii. p. 208.)

In what way does Christian Science conflict with the teachings of the Catholic Church ?

Can a Catholic be treated by Christian Scientists merely for health, provided he or she do not believe in their teachings ?

Can you in the face of such overwhelming evidence deny the many cures wrought by Christian Scientists ?

The Catholic Church regards Christian Science, with its denial of a personal God distinct from the universe, the divinity of Jesus Christ, and every Christian dogma, as an essentially pagan system. Discovered in 1866 by Mrs. Eddy, of Boston, it was given to the world in 1875 as "the final revelation of the absolute principle of scientific being and of healing," in her work "Science and Health, with Key to the Scriptures" (Joseph Armstrong, Boston, ed. 1901).

Christian Science is a very striking example of that inevitable tendency toward unbelief that characterizes the Protestant principle of private interpretation ; for while pretending, with many another false prophet (Mark xiii. 22), that the Bible is her "sole teacher, guide, and text-book" (pp. viii. 4, 20), Mrs. Eddy perverts its meaning at every step ; and while

quoting its words she gives them, without
any warrant whatsoever, a meaning which will
agree with her irrational mingling of Ideal-
ism, Manicheism, and Pantheism. The Divinity of Christ is absolutely denied, and His
divine gospel becomes a mere system of metaphysical healing (pp. 32, 346, 363, 478, 574,
etc.) After reading Mrs. Eddy's book from
cover to cover, one wonders how any rational
man or woman could ever believe without the
shadow of proof in a pretended prophet, claiming absolute obedience, who cures by the mere
reading of a book, or by absent treatment,
functional and organic diseases (pp. 135, 71,
443, 43). Much of the book is unintelligible;
and therefore its author tells us that we may not
hope to fathom its meaning. Such phrases as
these are indeed incomprehensible: "There is
no physical science. Matter is nothing but mortal belief. Man is the compound idea of God.
Gender is a quality, a characteristic of mind,
not matter. Electricity is not a vital fluid,
but the least material form of illusive consciousness—a material mindlessness" (pp. 21,
19, 471, etc.)

Here are a few specimens of the new logic:
"If drugs are part of God's creation, then
drugs cannot be poisonous. If we live after
death and are immortal, we must have lived
before birth. If soul sinned, it would be

mortal. You say a boil is painful; but that is impossible, for matter without mind is not painful" (pp. 50, 427, 464, 47).

Mrs. Eddy refuses to be called a *pantheist*, but her own words convict her, if words mean anything: "There can be but one Mind, because there is but one God. In one sense God is identical with nature. Soul or spirit signifies deity and nothing else. There is no finite soul or spirit. There is but one mind or intelligence. God, Spirit, being all, nothing is matter. Science reveals nothing in spirit out of which to create matter. All is mind, and mind is God. Soul is God, unchangeable, eternal" (pp. 465, 13, 462, 112, 7, 174).

She holds the old Manichean doctrine that the material world is evil, and that therefore God is not its Creator: "To regard God as the creator of matter is not only to make Him responsible for all disasters, physical and moral, but to announce Him as their source" (pp. 13; *cf.* 546, 174, 8).

She renders religion impossible by denying a personal God distinct from the universe, the existence of soul in body, free will, sin, etc.: "The great mistake of mortals is to suppose that man is both matter and spirit. Soul or spirit signifies deity and nothing else. Willpower is but an illusion of belief—the delusion of sin" (pp. 112, 462, 486, 100, 468).

She denies every fundamental dogma of
Christianity, *v.g.*, the Trinity, the divinity of
Jesus Christ, the fact of original and actual sin,
the redemption, the existence of a divine society to preach the gospel, the sacramental
system, the necessity of faith, grace, prayer,
fasting, the resurrection of the body, the last
judgment, angels, devils, eternal punishment.

" The theory of three persons in one God,
i.e., a personal Trinity, or tri-unity, suggests
heathen gods. Jesus was the highest human
concept of a perfect man. He was not divine,
but a mere healer of the sick; the legend of
the serpent, a myth, a dream narrative; sin is
a delusion. That God's wrath should be visited
upon His beloved Son is divinely unnatural.
Such a theory is man-made. Christianity as
Jesus taught it was not a creed. The true
science of God and man is no more supernatural than is the science of numbers. Our
Lord's first article of faith was healing. Our
Baptism is a purification from all error. Our
Eucharist is a spiritual communion with the
one God. Faith is the acceptance of Christian
Science. The 'new man' of Scripture is a
Christian Scientist. Audible prayer can never
do the works of divine understanding ; prayer
is unnecessary, as the ALL has already decreed
what is good for us. Fasting is a senseless
belief; the belief that material bodies return

to dust hereafter to rise up spiritual bodies is
incorrect. No final judgment awaits mortals.
Angels are . . . not messengers but mes-
sages of the true idea of divinity. Evil or
devil is not mind, is not truth, but error. Hell
is mortal belief, error, remorse, hatred '' (pp.
152, 508, 478, 32, 523, 519, 154, 100, 416, 468,
238, 327, 29, 492, 467, 5, 39, 340, 484, 196, 310,
187, 195, 465, etc.)

Her denial of the evidence of the senses, the
reality of matter, the facts gained by medical
science and surgery, the utter lack of coherency
and system in her many contradictory statements prove her system to be as unscientific
as it is irreligious and anti-Christian. '' What
we term the five physical senses are simply beliefs of mortal mind. When an accident happens . . . declare you are not hurt, and
you will find the ensuing good effects to be in
exact proportion to your disbelief in physics
and your fidelity to God. The corporeal senses
are the only sources of evil and error. Christian Science explains all cause and effect as
mental not physical. There is no physical
science. One disease is no more real than another. All disease is cured by mind. Belief is
all that ever enables a drug to cure mortal ail-
ments. What is termed disease does not exist.
Science can heal the sick who are absent from
their healer. Where there are fewer doctors

and less thought is given to sanitary subjects, there will be better constitutions and less disease " (pp. 170, 365, 485, 7, 21, 69, 67, 81, 71).

How account for the growth of Christian Science? Its followers are recruited for the most part from the ranks of those indifferentist or unbelieving Protestants who, ignorant of the first principles of Christianity, are the ready victims of any new teaching. Again, this new phase of modern unbelief allows the unthinking mind to call itself Christian, while at the same time it does not demand the acceptance of the doctrines or moral principles the Saviour taught. Furthermore, like errors of other times, it appeals to the suffering multitude who long for some panacea of disease, and care little for the method of the cure. Witness in our country the following gained by such evident impostors as Dowie, Schlatter, and the millions spent annually in the fees of quacks. The financial side of the movement is another factor in its growth, for it provides an easy way of practising medicine.

How account for its so-called cures? I recall two cures of the Christian Science kind—one of a pretended operation in a large city hospital, which completely cured a woman of an internal (imaginary) disease of many months standing ; another of a woman bedridden for years, who during the panic induced by a fire in her house recovered the use of her limbs by the mere exercise of will-power long dormant. So, frequently physicians have treated their wealthy hypochondriac patients on a harmless diet of bread-pills and water, and daily discussed without a smile the marked progress caused by their wonderful prescription.

The many cures, especially in the nervous diseases of women, wrought abroad in our generation by hypnotic suggestion at the hands of the scientific graduates of the schools of Nancy and Paris, have made us realize more than ever before the influence of the mind and the imagination over bodily disease (Le Hypnotism Franc-Coconnier). Christian Science has adopted this child of modern therapeutics, and dressing it up in the clothes of unchristian and unscientific principles, endeavors by dint of vigorous and oracular assertion to win for it the reverence of its credulous following. We can safely challenge any of these modern curists to bring forward one authentic case—proved by affidavits of reputable Catholic, Protestant, Jewish, and infidel physicians—in which the mind of a metaphysical healer has set a broken arm or leg, healed a cancer or a tumor, or effected the cure of any organic disease. As for healing the deaf, the dumb, the blind, the lame, lepers—only Jesus Christ, the Son of God, and the saints of the old law and the new, have worked such miracles.

Indeed, we deem those who suffer the sick under their care to die for the want of proper medical attendance to be guilty of criminal neglect, and if in their ignorance and superstition they do not realize their sin, the law of the state should, in the interests of society, see to it that those dependent on such fanatics be publicly provided for, just as the Society for the Prevention of Cruelty looks after children maltreated by their parents.

No Catholic is warranted in having recourse to Christian Science healers for the cure of bodily disease, because it is grievous sin to encourage charlatanism or superstition in any form; and even if a real cure were certain, Catholics know they cannot deny Jesus Christ or His divine teachings for any temporal benefit whatsoever. It is not allowed to do evil that good may come.

The Catholic Church teaches clearly the efficacy of prayer, but forbids her children to neglect the ordinary means at their disposal for the cure of disease, doctor's skill and medicines, as irrational and sinful. Miracles are exceptional things, and not the ordinary law of God's providence. She quotes the words of Holy Writ: "Honor the physician for the need thou hast of him; for the Most High hath created him. . . . The skill of the physician shall lift up his head, and in the sight of great men he shall be praised. The Most High hath created medicines out of the earth, and a wise man will not abhor them. . . . My son, in thy sickness neglect not thyself, but pray to the Lord, and He shall heal thee" (Ecclus. xxxviii. 1–10).

She declares infallibly that Jesus Christ came to teach men the truth of God and to save them from sin, and that He sent His apostles to preach and pardon in His Name until the end of the world. Christian Science, which denies His divinity and His gospel, is to her a superstition against the first commandment of God.

What is your opinion of theosophy?

Theosophy is a modern pantheistic illusion borrowed from the East, and popularized for the West, chiefly by Madame Blavatsky and Colonel Olcott. It regards the universe as a manifestation of the Great Eternal Reality, the human soul as an emanation thereof. Man is composed of seven parts, four of which are *perishable* (personality)—the physical body, the principle of life, the astral or invisible body, and the animal soul,—and *three eternal* (individuality)—the Great Reality, the spiritual soul, and the understanding.

At death, however, the animal soul may still remain in a disembodied state, and entering into other persons act as a medium of communication. A Mahatma—that is, one who has become perfectly independent of the faculties of sense—can project his astral body to any distance, and communicate through the astral senses to the members of the mystic brotherhood, detect things invisible to ordinary eyes, read the thoughts of absent persons, etc. The world is governed by an inexorable fatality or law of retribution, called Karma. Good is necessarily rewarded, evil necessarily punished. Forgiveness, of sin is impossible. Man, if wicked, sinks lower and lower, until he reaches the goal of complete annihilation ; if good, he is by successive reincarnations finally absorbed into the one Eternal Reality (Nirvana), losing his personality, although, strangely enough, not his individuality.

This teaching is a queer mixture of Brahmin and Buddhist pantheism and atheism, and contradicts the elemental notions of Christianity by its denial of a personal God, of the possibility of forgiveness of sin, of the fact of probation in this life, of future eternal reward and punishment, of the individually responsible sinner. Its wonders are to be ascribed either to fraud, self-delusion, or to diabolical agencies.

Does not your Church claim the right to imprison, torture, and kill heretics ?

Does not the Catholic Church sanction persecution?

No; the Catholic Church declares it sinful to force people to join her communion, or to punish for heresy or false religion those outside her fold. With Tertullian ("Ad Scapulas"), she declares that "It is assuredly no part of religion to compel religion—to which free will and not force should lead us." Conversion is a matter of persuasion, and forced conversion simply means hypocrisy. With St. Paul she declares: "What have I to do with judging them that are outside? Them who are outside God will judge" (I. Cor. v. 12, 13). As to inflicting bodily penalties, according to canon law any one who takes part in the shedding of blood becomes by the very fact irregular, or incapable of receiving or exercising Holy Orders.

We regret that Catholic rulers, Catholic ecclesiastics, and Catholic people have often as a matter of fact persecuted. We denounce as strongly as Protestants do the dragonnades of Louis XIV., the enforced conversions of the Moors and Jews in Spain, the cruelty and the excesses that often attended the punishment by the state of heresy, which used to be regarded as a political crime.

Those were times of severity and cruelty. Thank God they have passed away for ever.

(J. Rickaby, "Persecution," Catholic Truth Society publications, vol. xxxvi.)

"I heartily pray," writes Cardinal Gibbons, "that religious intolerance may never take root in our favored land. May the only king to force our conscience be the King of kings; may the only prison erected among us for the sin of unbelief or misbelief be the prison of a troubled conscience; and may our only motive for embracing truth be not the fear of man, but the love of truth and of God" ("Faith of Our Fathers," p. 297).

By what right did Catholic sovereigns persecute men for their opinions?

No Catholic government ever persecuted a man for a mere private opinion, but for the public teaching and spread of opinions which were thought destructive of society. So to-day, every government in the world claims the right to punish men for certain crimes, no matter what the plea of private opinion. In a court of law, an anarchist might plead conscientious motives for the murder of King Humbert or President McKinley, a socialist might justify his stealing by his theory of the injustice of private ownership, a bigamist might plead that he was a Mormon, a publisher of indecent literature that he was merely exercising a private right—yet the law would not recognize any of these pleas, else society would be powerless to protect itself against any form of vice.

Catholic rulers regarded heresy as destructive of the social order, and against the law of Christendom which made it a political crime, and while we denounce those monarchs who endeavored to force religion on unbelievers at the point of the sword, as Charlemagne, Louis XIV., or Philip II., contrary to the principle of the Catholic Church, we cannot, on the other hand, blame them for punishing those whom they considered enemies of the state. This becomes more plain when we study the immoral, irreligious, and anti-social principles of the Albigenses, the Hussites, and the Wyclifites.

Is it not due to Luther, Calvin, Knox, and the other great Reformers that to-day men are no longer imprisoned, tortured, or burned for their religion?

Would not Catholics persecute Protestants to-day, if they had the power?

No; for the Reformers in every country where they obtained power, Germany, England, Scotland, Denmark, Sweden, the Netherlands, preached and practised the most bitter intolerance. Luther held that the Anabaptists ought to be burned, declared all measures lawful against Catholics, and invoked the civil power against Carlstadt and the Zwinglians. In Saxony blasphemy was punished with death, and heresy with banishment. The Calvinists were equally bitter. Calvin burned Servetus for denying the Trinity, and wrote a book in defence of the right of persecution. Bucer and Melancthon congratulated him on his action, and also wrote to the same purpose.

In England the history of the penal laws of Henry VIII., Elizabeth, Edward VI., James I., Charles I., Cromwell, Charles II. is a history of fines, imprisonment, banishment, torture, and death for the practice of the Catholic religion (Cardinal Moran, "Historical Sketch of the Persecutions suffered by the Catholics of Ireland"; *Dublin Review*, Jan., 1882; W. S. Lilly, *Dublin Review*, July, 1891; Hallam, "Constitutional History of England," vol. iii. pp. 359, 381, *et seq.;* Gerard, "The Condition of Catholics under James I."; D. Murphy, S.J., "Cromwell in Ireland"; "Records of the English Catholics under the Penal Laws, from the archives of the See of Westminster"). Cranmer advocated persecution, and burned many Protestants at the stake before openly professing Protestantism himself. Ranke and Hume both call Elizabeth's High Commission a Protestant inquisition. We find the English Parliament of James I. urging persecution as "necessary to advance the glory of God," while the Scotch Parliament in 1560 decreed death to all Catholics. Archbishop Usher declared: " To give any toleration to Papists is a grievous sin " (Neale, " History of the Puritans," vol. ii. p. 469); John Wesley at the time of the Gordon riots, 1780, wrote: " They (Catholics) are not to be tolerated by any government, Protestant, Mohammedan, or pagan " (Canon Flanagan, "History of the Church in England," vol. i. p. 380; W. J. Amherst, S.J., " History of Catholic Emancipation ") ; John Knox, who deemed persecution a holy and a sacred duty, strongly urged the English people to kill Queen Mary and all her priests with her (Milner, Letter XLIX., " The End of Controversy ").

There is therefore not the slightest evidence to show that the Reformation ever upheld, in doctrine or practice, the toleration that exists everywhere to-day by force of circumstances. Religious toleration is a practical necessity, unless men wish to live in a state of chronic war and discord; the common good demands it. It is wrong, however, to base it on the principle of indifferentism which declares that certainty in religious matters is impossible, and that one religion is as good as another.

Let me quote an unbiased non-Catholic witness on this question, W. Lecky, in his "Rationalism in Europe," vol. ii. pp. 57–61:

"But what shall we say of a church (Protestant) that was but a thing of yesterday; a church that had as yet no service to show, no claims upon the gratitude of mankind; a church that was by profession the creature of private judgment, and was in reality generated by the intrigues of a corrupt court, which nevertheless suppressed by force worship that multitudes deemed necessary for their salvation, and by all her organs, and with all her energies, persecuted those who clung to the religion of their fathers? What shall we say of a religion which comprised at most but a fourth part of the Christian world, and which the first explosion of private judgment had shivered into countless sects, which was nevertheless so pervaded by the spirit of dogmatism that each of these sects asserted its distinctive doctrines with the same confidence, and persecuted with the same unhesitating virulence, as the Church which was venerable with the homage of more than twelve centuries? . . . Persecution among the early Protestants was a distinct and definite doctrine, digested into elaborate treatises, and enforced against the most inoffensive as against the most formidable sects. It was the doctrine of the palmiest days of Protestantism. It was taught by those who are justly esteemed the greatest of its leaders."

There is not the slightest reason to suspect

that Catholics would persecute to-day if they had the power. The Church claims no coercive authority over those outside her fold. She considers faith an act not only of the intellect, but of the will, which ought to be perfectly free when there is question of God's truth. Once the pure gospel of Christ has been lost by men, nothing but a willingness to believe and a conviction of the intellect can by God's grace give it back. When Lord Baltimore started the Catholic colony of Maryland, he decreed that "no person within the province professing to believe in Jesus Christ shall be anyways troubled, molested, or discountenanced, for his or her religion, or in the free exercise thereof." Protestants, persecuted in Virginia, sought refuge in the Catholic province of Maryland. Does not this compare favorably with the conduct of the Puritans who, on the accession of Cromwell, disfranchised the Catholics of the province, with the laws of New England which put Quakers to death, or the intolerance of other colonies that legislated against Catholics? (Bancroft, "History of the U. S.," vol i. p. 233, *et seq.;* Hergenröther, "Church and State," vol. ii. xvi. par. 15 ; Backus, "History of the Baptists in New England," vol. i. 290 ; Yorke, "Yorke-Wendte Controversy," pp. 182-205.)

Was not the Spanish Inquisition one of the most inhuman institutions the world has ever known, with its imprisonment, torture, and burning of heretics for conscientious belief ?

The Spanish Inquisition was no more cruel than the Genevan Inquisition of Calvin, the Court of High Commission of Elizabeth (Hume, History, ch. xii.; Neale, " History of the Puritans," vol. i. p. 10), or the penal laws against Catholics in England, Scotland, Ireland, Holland, Sweden, Denmark, and Germany. Is it fair to speak continually of this tribunal, indifferent to statistics, oblivious of comparison with Protestant belief and practice in the sixteenth century, ignoring the spirit of the age which everywhere regarded heresy as a crime punishable by the state, and cared little for severe punishments which no nation to-day would tolerate for an instant? Is not this to excite the passions and prejudices of the ignorant?

The Spanish Inquisition was established in 1478 by Ferdinand and Isabella to punish the apostate Jews of Spain, who were openly professing Christianity for gain and preferment, while secretly practising Judaism and favoring the Moors. These Maranos, through their wealth and intermarriage with noble families, were deemed a menace to the unity of the kingdom.

After the conquest of Granada many of the Moors also became Christians, not out of conviction but for personal gain, and uniting with the Jews, were greatly feared by the government. Popular hatred of the Jews, for real or supposed crimes commonly attributed to them, added to the bitterness with which apostates were sought after and punished according to the law. The Inquisition, however, did not force Christianity on those who did not believe, but prosecuted those who professed a Christianity they inwardly rejected. Under Philip II. the Inquisition, besides preventing the introduction of Protestantism into Spain, also saved it from the religious wars of France and Germany. Finally, at the close of the eighteenth century, its aim was chiefly directed against the introduction of French infidelity into Spain. It was finally abolished in 1830.

We must put ourselves in the place of the Catholic people of the time. Heresy was a crime that the state considered worse than treason, and punished with death. Catholic rulers, knowing that the introduction of a false religion inevitably carried with it religious war and social disturbance, naturally, out of zeal for the Church they loved and solicitude for the kingdom they ruled, would prevent this to the utmost of their power. Was not the Church in possession for centuries? Was it

not the duty of a Christian prince to safeguard
his people from false teaching?

One would think that the Reformers held
different views on this matter. On what principles could a new religion founded on the
individual's private interpretation of the Scriptures, and disclaiming infallibility, persecute
another which demanded the same liberty of
denial? And yet, as Rousseau declared, "The
Reformation was intolerant from its cradle,
and its authors universal persecutors" ("Let-
tres de la Mont"). A Protestant historian,
Hallam ("Literature of Europe," vol. ii. ch.
ii.), bears the same testimony : "Persecution
for religious heterodoxy, in all its degrees, was
in the sixteenth century the *principle* as well
as the *practice* of every church. It was held
inconsistent with the sovereignty of the magistrate to permit any religion but his own, inconsistent with his duty to suffer any but the
true." And again : "Persecution is the deadly
original sin of the reformed churches, which
cools every honest man's zeal for their cause,
in proportion as his reading becomes more ex-
tensive" ("Const. Hist.," vol. i. ch. ii.)

Why, then, is there so much said of the
Spanish Inquisition? Has it peculiar horrors,
or are its practices merely a reflex of the manners of the age? Men speak of the number of
its victims. They forget that the authority in

this matter is a Spanish priest, Llorente, who was false to both Church and country, and wrote his history after his banishment from Spain. Moreover he declares that he burned nearly all the official reports. What would any fair-minded man say of a historian who, when asked to substantiate certain statistics, would calmly declare that he had burned the original documents? In the England of the period (1598) Sir James Stephen reckons "800 executions a year in the forty English counties" ("History of the English Criminal Law," vol. i. p. 467).

Is it fair to pass over in silence the many Catholics who suffered the death penalty for their faith in England and Ireland under Henry VIII., Elizabeth, James I., Charles I., Cromwell, and Charles II.? (Card. Moran, "Historical Sketch of the Persecutions in Ireland"; *Dublin Review*, Jan., 1882; July, 1891).

Others complain of the severity of the punishment by fire, the use of torture to extract confession, the terrible dungeons in which the accused were confined, the unjust mode of procedure, etc. We simply challenge comparison with any other country where Protestantism was dominant.

Thousands were burnt at the stake for witchcraft in England, Scotland, and Germany, others for heresy in England and Switzerland.

("Chambers's Encyclopedia"; Charles W. Upham, "Salem Witchcraft.") Boiling to death, half-hanging, disembowelling and quartering were common penalties under Henry VIII. and Elizabeth. Why, the death penalty was awarded to a theft above twelve pence by the English law of the time! (1577). (Rye, "England as seen by Foreigners in the days of Elizabeth," p. 269.)

The use of torture was common in nearly all the European states until the close of the eighteenth century. It was used frequently by Elizabeth against Catholics, even though it was contrary to the common law. Hallam writes ("Constitutional History," vol. i. p. 200) : "The rack seldom stood idle in the Tower for all the latter part of Elizabeth's reign." In this matter, therefore, the Inquisition merely shared one of the errors of the time.

The dungeons of the Tower in which Catholic priests were imprisoned for the mere saying of Mass were far worse than the Inquisition prisons, being "dark cells below the high-water mark, infested with rats and vermin" (Jardine (Protestant), "Reading on the Use of Torture in England").

The mode of trial was far more just than the English law, which concealed from the accused not only the names of his accusers but the charges also until he appeared in court;

and which denied him both the use of witnesses and advocate, while the Inquisition allowed both (see James Stephen, *ibid.*, p. 350).

Undoubtedly there were many abuses incident to the tyrannical use of the royal power. But who will deny that the same objection holds good of the Tudor and Stuart sovereigns of Protestant England? We must not forget that the Inquisition was in great part a political institution, as Protestant writers like Ranke (German), Guizot (French), and Creighton (English) admit, to render secure the stability of the Spanish throne. Time and time again we find the Popes—Leo X., Paul III., Paul IV., Sixtus IV.—protesting against the arbitrary conduct of the Spanish kings in using the Inquisition.

Place yourself, therefore, at the viewpoint of the sixteenth century; study the principles and practices of the age. Choose between Isabella, Ferdinand, and Philip II., and Elizabeth, Henry VIII., and Cromwell.

Robespierre and his associates in the French Revolution, while deluging France in the blood of her best and noblest men and women, hypocritically declaimed against the cruelty of the Inquisition in Spain. (*American Catholic Quarterly*, vol. i. p. 254, vol. xii. p. 69; *Dublin Review*, June, 1850, Jan., 1867; De Maistre, "Letters on the Spanish Inquisi-

tion " ; Balmes, " Protestantism and Catholicity Compared "'; Smith, " The Spanish Inquisition," Catholic Truth Society publications ; Hefele, " History of Cardinal Ximenes,"
chs. xviii. xix.)

What excuse is there for the cruelty of Innocent III., who ordered Simon de Montfort to persecute the Albigenses ?

The real cause of the crusade against the
Albigenses was their immoral and irreligious
doctrines, whereby they were a menace to the
social order then existing, which was founded
on the principles of the Christian faith. They
held that there were two Christs, and that the
bad Christ suffered on the cross ; rejected the
Blessed Eucharist ; disowned the Old Testament, its law and its God ; denied the resurrection of the body ; declared oaths unlawful ;
condemned marriage ; called the begetting of
children a crime. Not content with preaching
these doctrines everywhere, and causing social
disturbance thereby, they destroyed churches
and monasteries, murdered priests, and spared
neither orphans, age nor sex, as we learn from
the Third Council of Lateran in 1179.

We ought not to blame Pope Innocent III.
for taking severe measures, because one hundred years of preaching and persuasion had
utterly failed, and these disturbers were be-

coming stronger every year. Imagine in our own country, to-day, that in a certain State thousands of fanatics began to deny, theoretically and practically, the lawfulness of oaths, the dignity of marriage, and destroyed hundreds of churches, massacring all that opposed their teaching. Suppose that the governor of the State was powerless to handle them because of their number. Would you blame President Roosevelt for sending United States troops against them? Do you blame the Allied Powers for uniting to secure in China the protection of Christians against the atrocities of the Boxers? We do not apologize for the terrible cruelties of the campaign against the Albigenses. Those were cruel times. But, as Sheridan rightly said: "War is hell."

Did not your Church order the massacre of thousands of inoffensive French Huguenots on St. Bartholomew's day (Aug. 24, 1572), and the Pope chant a Te Deum for it in Rome?

How could an infallible Pope authorize and approve the massacre of 100,000 inoffensive French Protestants whose only offence was their refusal to obey the Church of Rome?

Religion had nothing whatever to do with the massacre of St. Bartholomew. It was inspired out of purely political motives by the unscrupulous, irreligious Catherine de Medici, who urged it on her son Charles IX., either to forestall a real plot against the life of the king, or to anticipate the threatened Huguenot vengeance on account of the attempted assassination of Admiral Coligny on August 22.

The court of France, anxious to right itself before the world, declared by Parliament, August 26, that in carrying out this severe measure it had merely anticipated a plot of Coligny and his associates against the life of the king and princes of the royal family. Margaret of Valois admits the existence of this plot in her memoirs (x. p. 408). Be this as it may, it is just as absurd to accuse Catherine or her weakling son of zeal for religion as it would be to accuse a modern saloonkeeper of zeal for the cause of total abstinence..

It is certainly false that the massacre of the Huguenots was long premeditated, or that the saintly Pius V. knew anything of it (*Civiltà Cattolica*, Set. vi. vol. viii., p. 679; vol. ix. 267, 662 ; vol. x. p. 268; vol. xi. 14).

Gregory XIII. had a Te Deum sung in the Church of St. Mark on September 5 because he believed, on the testimony of the French ambassador Beauville, that a Huguenot plot to murder the king and place the Huguenot Henry Bourbon on the throne had been discovered, and its authors had suffered the penalty of their crime. When he learned the real facts of the case, he expressed his horror at the deed (Brantome, "Vie de M. l'Amiral de Chastillon," viii. p. 190). His joy is no more extraordinary than the congratulations of President. McKinley to the Prince of Wales after he had escaped the assassin's bullet. We must remember that there was no telegraph in those days, to correct the false views sent at first by the king to Rome.

Philip of Spain and Queen Elizabeth both accepted the account of the Huguenot conspiracy (Theiner, "Annales," xlvii.) All remembered the conspiracy of Amboise to seize the person of King Francis II., the assassination of the Duke of Guise under the probable connivance of Coligny (Lingard, "History of England," vol. vii. p. 320), and the constant murders that had marked the history of the Huguenots. There was nothing, therefore, to render the account improbable, so that no one can blame Pope Gregory for accepting the story.

Were the Huguenots inoffensive citizens? No one with the slightest knowledge of the facts could say so. For years they had endeavored, by secret understanding with the enemies of France and by open rebellion, to destroy the Catholic faith and overthrow the government; they had three times started civil war, and although granted after each defeat full amnesty and toleration, they still conspired against the king; they delivered two important cities of France to England, and lastly, these inoffensive, freedom-loving, persecution-hating Calvinists destroyed some fifty cathedrals and five hundred churches, demolished the tombs of Catholic kings and saints, profaned sacred shrines, burned monasteries, murdered priests after torture only comparable to that of the Chinese Boxers, butchered thousands of defenceless men and women, burned and sacked hundreds of towns and villages. Could any sensible man expect Catholics to be quiet in the face of such outrages?

Let us hear Protestant testimony as to the spirit of meekness that characterized French Protestants: "Whatever may be the popular notion respecting the necessary intolerance of the Catholics, it is an indisputable fact that, early in the seventeenth century, they displayed in France a spirit of forbearance and Christian charity to which the Protestants could make no pretence" (Buckle, "History of Civilization," vol. i. ch. viii. p. 518).

"Whoever has read the great Calvinist divines and, above all, whoever has studied their history, must know that in the sixteenth and seventeenth centuries the desire of persecuting their enemies burned as hotly among them as it did among any of the Catholics even in the worst days of Papal dominion" (vol. i. ch. viii. p. 505).

How many were massacred on St. Bartholomew's day? The numbers vary from one thousand to one hundred thousand, though the Calvinists could only succeed in obtaining seven hundred and eighty-six names for insertion in their so-called "Martyrology," published in 1582. A generous number would be two thousand. Even Froude, in his "History of England" (vol. x. ch. xxiii. p. 408), admitted that without exact statistics we should at least divide the extreme number by ten.

Let us ask, in conclusion, is it fair to be for ever and always pointing to this page of history, when Catholics can say with Christ to the accusers, "He that is without sin among you, let him first cast a stone" (John viii. 7).

Is it fair to pass over the frightful massacre at Nîmes on St. Michael's day, 1567, instigated by the Calvinistic preachers, when two hundred and fifty Catholics were mercilessly butchered one by one, and their bodies cast into a deep well? Is it fair to pass over the murder of the clergy in the Corpus Christi procession at Pamier? What, too, of the outrages at Montaubon, Rodez, Orthez, Valence, Troyes, Tours, Bayeux, Grenoble, Poitiers, and Le Mans?

In a word, any one that recalls the seventy-one years of civil war (1557–1628), in which all the evil passions of men were roused to the utmost, the difference of religion fanning the flame, will not be a bit surprised to meet with frightful atrocities on both sides. If during our civil war a regiment of Protestant soldiers should have been guilty of the most shameful outrages in the South, would any one be justified in throwing the blame upon the several denominations to which they belonged?

Remember also that in combating the violence of Protestant zeal, which, not content with toleration, sought totally to extirpate the Catholic faith, and by constant treason at home and abroad to undermine the French monarchy, the Catholics of France were merely acting in self-defence. Surely they had more right to use violence in preserving the faith of centuries, than the Protestants in Germany, England, Sweden to use violence in establishing a new religion. (Rev. Wm. Loughnan, "The Huguenots"; "The Massacre of St. Bartholomew," Catholic Truth Society publications; Hergenröther, "Church and State," xvii. sec. 22; *Amer. Cath. Quarterly*, vol. xix. p. 508; *Dublin Review*, Oct., 1865; Parsons, "Studies in History," vol. iii. p. 393–402.)

Was not the revocation of the Edict of Nantes

one of the most cruel acts known to modern history ?

Suppose for a moment that it was, this personal act of Louis XIV. is no more to be attributed to the Catholic Church than the impure life of the Grand Monarch to the principles of the gospel of Jesus Christ. It is a fact of history that Innocent XI. openly disapproved of his harsh measures against the French Huguenots, and through his nuncio in London requested James II. to intercede with Louis XIV. in their favor (Hergenröther, "Church and State," vol. ii. p. 379, who quotes Macaulay, Lingard, Ranke, Döllinger, etc.)

By the Edict of Nantes, in 1598, Henry IV. granted a number of privileges to the French Huguenots, hoping thereby to put an end to the long series of civil wars that had divided the kingdom. It never effected its purpose. In 1685 Louis XIV., acting on the Protestant principle set forth at Westphalia despite the protests of the Church, "*cujus regio, illius est religio,*" that "the kingdom should follow the religion of the prince," decided to revoke these privileges. These edicts were revocable at the will of the monarch, as Grotius tells us, and the parliament of 1598 had expressly declared that they could be revoked, if a future sovereign should deem it for the public good. We must remember that the Edict not only gave religious toleration but gave the Huguenots political independence, which enabled them to stir up disorder whenever it suited their interests. ("Life of Richelieu," Lodge, of Glasgow, 1896).

It does not concern us to defend the political policy of Louis XIV. The followers of Calvin surely could not find fault with so perfect an imitation of their master, who in Geneva expelled the sect of the Libertines, burned Servetus at the stake, beheaded Gruet, imprisoned Gentile, and upheld in his writings the most drastic and cruel treatment of heretics to be found in all history. Those in glass houses ought not to throw stones.

We are just as ready to denounce the severe method of Louis XIV., especially the dragonnades, as was Innocent XI., the Pope of the time.

Did not the Catholic Queen Mary of England by her persecution of Protestants merit the title of "Bloody Mary"?

She surely does not deserve the title as much as the cruel Protestant Queen Elizabeth. In the last three years of her reign there were undoubtedly bitter persecutions, but the motive was simply political. They were not based on Catholic principles. Men are so apt to forget that the Protestants in her reign strove to dethrone her (Wyatt, "Lady Jane Grey"), made attempts upon her life, prayed publicly for her death, and published many treasonable pamphlets against her. Cranmer and his associates were executed by the laws they had themselves devised under Edward VI. and carried out against the Anabaptists. Any one who knows the utter worthlessness of Cranmer's character, and his burning of the Protestants Lambert, Frith, Allen, Knell, Van Par, and Askew, will surely see a just retribution in his fate (Stone's " Life of Queen Mary ").

Does your doctrine of excommunication and anathema imply a delivering up of a man to eternal perdition ?

No, it is the penalty of exclusion from the Church. Her object, however, is to warn the sinner of the danger he is running of eternal ruin. St. Paul, when he said (Gal. i. 8) " let him be anathema " who preaches another gospel, did not thereby consign to hell men whom he would have died to save, but wished to denounce most strongly the teachers of false doctrine. The Church follows the example of St. Paul in pronouncing her anathemas (*American Cath. Quarterly*, 1887, p. 663).

Is not your claim of forbidding Catholics to read certain books intolerable ?

No ; the right of the Church to prevent her

children reading books that are either immoral
or irreligious, arises from the fact that she is the
divinely appointed teacher and guardian of the
revelation of Jesus Christ. It is her duty to
warn the faithful against evil reading, just as it
is the state's office to prevent the sale of obscene literature or the staging of immoral plays.
It is an Apostolic practice, for we read in the
Acts (xix. 19) of the Ephesians burning their
books of magic after the preaching of St. Paul.
In the same spirit the Council of Nice proscribed the works of Arius, and Leo the Great
the works of the Priscillianists in Spain. Only
those who are totally indifferent to dogmatic
belief, or who have lost all conviction of the
essential difference between good and evil, can
deny this right, so beneficial alike to the individual and society.

Why is your Church opposed to cremation?

On May 19, 1886, a Roman decree forbade
Catholics "to join those societies whose object
it was to spread the practice of cremation, or
to leave orders for the cremation of one's
body or that of another." The reasons for the
Church's opposition are:

1st. Although there is no intrinsic reason
why cremation is unlawful, and no divine precept to bury the dead, still it is contrary to
the universal practice of the Jews under the

Old Law (Gen. xxiii. 4 ; Tob. ii. 7–9) and the Christians under the New.

2d. It is to-day advocated by modern unbelievers, who knowing the Christian respect for the dead arises from the fact of the resurrection, hope by this practical method to undermine the belief in immortality. "Catholics have grave reason to oppose cremation," writes the pantheistic Freemason Ghisleri (*Almanacco dei Liberi Muratori* for 1881) ; "this purification of the dead by means of fire would shake to its foundations Catholic predominance, based on the terror with which it has surrounded death." . . . "Oh rapid transformation ! —in one short hour commingled with the inner being of the great All."

3d. The early Christians buried the dead after the example of Christ as a protest against the pagan denial of the resurrection, and out of respect for the body which had been the dwelling place of God by the reception of the Eucharist.

4th. Cremation to-day is opposed to the whole spirit of the burial service of the Catholic Church, although should cremation be made a compulsory law, as some of its advocates demand, she could easily adapt her prayers and funeral services to this new method.

5th. Medical men and jurists have opposed cremation on the ground that it destroys all evidence of the cause of death, so often needed in criminal cases of poisoning.

6th.- There is no objection to cremation in times of pestilence, or in such cases as the late flood in Galveston, when it is needed for the public good. ("Cremation and Christianity," *Dublin Review*, April, 1890; "The Ethics of Cremation," *The Month*, May, 1875; "Is Cremation Christian Burial?" *ibid.*, 1884.)

Why is your Church so bitterly opposed to the Freemasons, who are often good, charitable members of society?

Why do you forbid Catholics joining the Masons?

Do the Masons date back to the time of King Solomon?

What secret orders are forbidden by your Church in this country?

Why don't the Church condemn all secret organizations?

As early as 1738 Clement XII. excommunicated the Freemasons, and his example has been followed by Benedict XIV. (1751), Pius VII. (1821), Leo XII. (1826), Pius IX. (1869), and Leo XIII. Catholics, therefore, who join this society contrary to the known law of the Church, are guilty of grievous sin, and incur the extreme penalty of excommunication, or exclusion from membership. This deprives the

Mason of the Sacraments, of all share in the public prayers of the Church, and finally of Christian burial. The prohibition of the Church is enough for the Catholic who recognizes her divine right to command, and knows that it is only exercised for the common good of her children. She, the great advocate of charity in all centuries, would undoubtedly not condemn any society of men for its benevolence or love of the brethren, or wantonly legislate to deprive her children of the money and help they might require in the hour of need. The reasons of her condemnation of Masonry are :

1st. Masonry is undoubtedly a sect, with a code of belief, ritual, and ceremonies, standing for mere naturalism in religion and for a morality founded on merely human motives. Frequently the Masons of Europe have claimed Freemasonry as the religion of *nature*, and the Catholic Church therefore, as the *supernatural* religion of Jesus Christ, the Son of God, cannot allow her members to join it. One cannot be a Mason and a Catholic at the same time, any more than he could be both Methodist and Catholic. " The God of Freemasonry is Nature. . . . There is no need of privileged agents making a trade of their pretended mediation " (*Revue Maçonnique*, Sept., 1835); and again : " Freemasonry is progress under every form, in every branch of human activity. It teaches us that there is only one religion, one true and therefore natural religion, the worship of humanity. . . . God is only the product of a generous but erroneous conception of humanity '' (Jan., 1870, p. 539).

2d. It is undoubtedly certain that the Masons have been noted in Italy, France, and other countries for a marked hatred of the Church, which, veiling itself under the name and love of liberty (Liberalism), helped in the spoliation of the Church in 1870, forced the clergy to enter the army, closed many religious houses by excessive taxation, appropriated church revenues, favored civil marriage, secularized education, and in public print and speech repeatedly pledged themselves, as in Naples in 1870, '' to the prompt and radical abolition of Catholicity, and by every means to procure its utter destruction.'' You may say that the American and English Masons are not of this type, and have openly severed all connection with these atheistical Continental Masons. I answer that if Albert Pike's book, '' Morals and Dogma of the Ancient and Accepted Scottish Rite of Freemasonry,'' be authentic, the esoteric doctrine of the higher degrees is essentially anti-Christian and immoral. (C. Coppens, S.J., '' Is Freemasonry anti-Christian ? '' *Amer. Eccl. Review*, Dec., 1899). The Church as a universal society makes laws that have a universal application. Nor is it at all certain that American Masons refuse fellowship to the Masons of Latin Europe and America.

3d. It is also contrary to morality to pledge one's self to absolute secrecy from those who have a right to demand a revelation, especially when death is the penalty attached to disloyalty to that oath—the case with Freemasons.

4th. Practically, Masonry in these United States, by putting all religions on a level, fosters the spirit of indifferentism, which is only unbelief in disguise, and substitutes in the mind of the ignorant the lodge for the church. I have heard scores of Protestant Masons say, on our missions to non-Catholics, "My lodge is church enough for me"; "the only religion I believe in is the doing good to my fellow-man," etc. I have frequently, too, heard their Protestant church-going wives trace their husbands loss of Christian faith to the lodge. Some Protestant denominations have come out strongly against secret societies (The National Association of Chicago), but they lack that universal power to command which only a divine authority like the Catholic Church can exercise.

The condemnation (1895) of the Knights of Pythias, the Oddfellows, and the Sons of Temperance was based on the conviction that these societies were doing harm to the faith of Catholics. Other secret societies have not been included in this condemnation. ("Freemasonry in Latin-America," *Amer. Cath. Quarterly*, vol. xxiii. p. 802 ; "The Laws of the Church and Secret Societies," vol. v. p. 252.)

Why are Catholics opposed to the American system of public schools ?

Because they make no provision for the religious instruction of children, which Catholics consider absolutely necessary.

It is the direct duty of the Catholic Church, as the divine, infallible teacher of the revelation of Jesus Christ ("Teach ye all nations," Matt. xxviii. 19), to safeguard the religious education of each succeeding generation. With her it is vastly more important to know well the doctrines of faith and morals than to be able to work out a problem in geometry, or to know the position of Cape Nome upon the map. An infidel or an indifferentist Protestant may not appreciate the value of a religious education entering into the daily life of a child, but any fair-minded man, no matter what his religious convictions, must admit that Catholics, holding their doctrines as infallible certainties and not as mere opinions, must consider their religion when there is question of the education of their children.

Although the divine commission of the Catholic Church to teach the world directly concerns religious truth, she is essentially bound to offset any danger to faith and morals incident to the prosecution of secular studies. She therefore, on principle, demands whenever possible a good Catholic education for her children, and must needs view with disfavor the principle on which exclusively secular education is based. The Catholic, therefore, objects to the public-school system:

1st. Because he considers the separation of human learning from religion a false principle. The total ignoring, day by day, of the most vital element in education—religion—is not Christian, and must in many cases lead to bad results. Its tendency is to foster the spirit of indifferentism in matters of religion, and to lead the child to believe that Christianity need not enter into its every-day life, but is reserved for Sunday and the Sunday-school. God is often lost sight of; the motive and basis of morality becomes merely natural; there is a general weakening in the grasp of fundamental Christian principles.

2d. It is practically impossible, taking human nature as it is, or considering, for example, the subject matter of a history class, to avoid allusions to religion. A non-Catholic teacher must put forth some views of morality, and Catholics claim that these belong to religion. Even unwittingly, because of his ignorance of Catholic teaching, he may teach doctrines opposed to Catholic principle. Catholics do not want their children to be taught that the Pope sold indulgences, or that Luther was a holy man, and the Reformation a step forward and a blessing.

I remember lately a high-school teacher in Brooklyn giving as a theme '' The Causes and Effects of the Reformation,'' which was treated by Catholic, Protestant, Jewish, and infidel pupils. What manner of teaching can that be which claims no power to teach authoritatively, and simply leaves minds unable to judge for themselves open to confusion and uncertainty?

3d. Again, Catholics realize that children are easily worked upon, and that there is a close personal relation between a strong-minded teacher and an impressionable boy or girl. It is natural that prejudiced Protestantism or blatant infidelity will at times voice its objections against the Catholic Church or against Christianity. Even when this is not done in so many words, the false idea may be conveyed by an insinuation, an interrogation, or a mere shrug of the shoulders.

4th. Catholics, again, object to the double burden laid upon them of supporting both the public and their own parochial schools. They hold that as citizens of the United States they are entitled to have their conscientious difficulties about the purely secular education of their children considered and respected. This country acknowledges its obligation to provide for secular education, and Catholics claim that such provision should so be made that they can avail themselves of it without going against their religious principles. They object to the exclusion of religion from the schools in which their children are taught, and to non-Catholics as teachers of their children.

But you may say that in a country like ours, with a mixed population of various religions, religion cannot be taught by the state. Granted. Catholics do not ask a cent from the state to provide catechisms or Bibles, or to pay for religious instruction. In all fairness, however, they demand that secular training be provided for their children by the state, in such a manner as not to prevent religious teaching by Catholic teachers, as is done in other countries, England, Germany, Austria, Belgium, where the same conditions prevail. The state can see to it that the secular teaching is up to the required standard, so that the public money be well spent. This is a mere matter of justice.

I know very well that many sincere Catholics have attended the public schools, and that the lack of religious instruction was in some degree made up elsewhere. But no one can deny that the general tendency of such education is evil and harmful.

Indeèd, patriotism should protest against the exclusion of religion from the schools. Undoubtedly men are better citizens if they are good Christians. The fear of God is a stronger motive for keeping the law of the land than the fear of the police court.

Furthermore, many Protestant denominations have come gradually to the Catholic way of thinking, and have provided religious schools for their children. (" Catholic Free Schools in the United States," *Amer. Cath. Quarterly*, 1884, p. 713; " Prof. Fisher on Unsectarianism in the Common Schools," *ibid.*, 1889, p. 505; " The Idea of a Parochial School," *ibid.*, 1891, p. 441; " Liberalistic View of the Public School Question," *ibid.*, 1877, p. 1, 240; " Our Parochial System," *ibid.*, 1892, p. 867; " Public School System and Protestantism," *ibid.*, 1886, p. 730; " Religion in Education," *ibid.*, 1891, p. 760.)

THE OCCASIONS OF SIN.

Our Church is opposed entirely to dancing, card-playing, and all theatre-going. Why are your Church laws so lax on these matters?

The principles of the Catholic Church are

clear and explicit with regard to amusements. God delights in seeing his people enjoy themselves in innocent recreation. The Catholic Church declares that it is lawful to see a good, pure play in a decent theatre; that dancing, far from being evil in itself, was often a part of divine worship in the Old Law (II. Kings vi. 14; Judg. xxi. 21 ; Exod. xv. 20); that card-playing around one's fireside or at a public euchre may be quite an innocent means of enjoyment.

But if, on the contrary, the theatre becomes a school of vice by its immoral plays, if dancing excites the passions and means the companionship of the wicked, if card-playing implies the feverish excitement of the gaming table, Christians know at once that in such cases amusements in themselves harmless become the occasions of sin. The Third Plenary Council of Baltimore legislated against dangerous amusements, especially certain kinds of dancing.

The Catholic Church declares that any person, place, or thing that by our natural or acquired weakness leads us to grievous sin, must be avoided under penalty of sin. However, to forbid certain amusements in general merely because if abused they lead some to sin, is peculiarly a Protestant tradition without warrant in reason or in Scripture.

Do Catholics believe that, provided they go to church Sunday morning, they can do what they please the rest of the day?

No! Besides the obligation of attending Mass every Sunday under penalty of grievous sin, Catholics are also forbidden all unnecessary servile work in order to give the needed rest to the body, and in order to devote a certain part of the day to God. Remembering, however, the words of Christ, '' The Sabbath was made for man and not man for the Sabbath '' (Mark ii. 27), the Catholic Church does not prohibit servile work that is absolutely necessary, nor frown down innocent amusements. There is naught of the Pharisee or the Puritan about her.

What Bible authority is there for changing the Sabbath from the seventh to the first day of the week?

Who gave the Pope the authority to change a command of God?

If the Bible is the only guide for the Christian, then the Seventh Day Adventist is right in observing the Saturday with the Jew. But Catholics learn what to believe and do from the divine, infallible authority established by Jesus Christ, the Catholic Church, which in Apostolic times made Sunday the day of rest to honor our Lord's resurrection on that day, and to mark off clearly the Jew from the Christian. St. Justin Martyr (Apol., c. 67) speaks of the early Christians meeting for the holy sacrifice of the Mass on Sunday.

Is it not strange that those who make the Bible their only teacher should inconsistently follow in this matter the tradition of the Church?

Why do Catholics have so many holydays? Did not Paul find fault with the Galatians for this very thing: " Ye observe days, and months, and times, and years "? (Gal. iv. 10).

The Apostle is not finding fault with God, who set aside certain days and seasons as especially sacred, namely, the Sabbath (Exod. xx. 10), the Sabbatical year (Exod. xxiii. 11), the year of Jubilee (Lev. xxvii.), the Passover (Exod. xii. 6), the feast of tabernacles (Lev. xxiii. 34), etc.; but he is writing against the Judaizers who insisted that Christians were still subject to the obsolete Mosaic law. So he says in the preceding verse, " How turn ye again to the weak and beggarly elements, whereunto ye desire again to be in bondage? "

The Catholic Church has her religious festivals to continually remind her people of the great mysteries of Christianity, and to honor our Saviour, His Mother, and the Saints.

It is the same spirit that prompts our country to set apart certain days in honor of her
great events and her illustrious dead, such as
Decoration Day, Fourth of July, Washington's
birthday. Will you tell me that it is right for
an American citizen so to honor Washington
or Lincoln, and wrong for a Catholic to remember the birthdays of the heroes or saints
of Christianity?

ABSTINENCE.

**Why not eat meat on Friday more than on any
other day? Does not St. Paul call this "the
doctrine of devils" (I. Tim. iv. 1–3), and Jesus
say "not that which goeth into the mouth de-
fileth a man"? (Matt. xv. 11).**

**What self-denial is there if one is allowed to
eat all the fish they want?**

Catholics abstain from meat on Friday in
honor of our Saviour's death on that day. St.
Paul refers to the early Manichean heretics,
who absolutely condemned the use of meat,
because they held that all flesh was from an
evil principle. It is true that the mere eating of meat is not sinful, but the deliberate
disobedience to the Church, which stands in
the place of Jesus Christ with a real, divine
power of command, is undoubtedly a grievous
wrong. Those who "eat all the fish they

want " and are gluttonous, may, indeed, fulfil the letter of the law, but not its spirit,
which insists on mortification in imitation of
the Saviour.

FASTING.

Why do Catholics fast ?

Because it is one of the precepts of the
Church. No one at all conversant with Holy
Scripture can object to fasting. We have the
example of Moses (Exod. xxxiv. 18; xxxiv.
28 ; Deut. ix. 9, 18), David (II. Kings xii. 16),
Elias (III. Kings xix. 6), John the Baptist
(Matt. iii. 4), our Saviour Himself (Matt. iv.
2), and the Apostles (Acts xiii. 3 ; xiv. 22).
Christ tells us how to fast (Matt. vi. 16), and
foretells that His people will fast after He has
left them (Matt. ix. 15 ; Mark ii. 20). Time
and time again we find seasons of fasting mentioned in both Old Testament and New (II.
Chron. xx. 3 ; I. Esdras viii. 21 ; II. Esdras
ix. 1; Esther iv. 16 ; Joel ii. 15 ; Jonas iii. 5 ;
Acts xxvii. 9).

The object of fasting is to mortify the flesh
and keep it in subjection to the spirit (I. Cor.
ix. 27; Luke ix. 23; Gal. v. 24). The glut-
ton and the drunkard are never spiritual men.
Fasting conciliates God's mercy and obtains
the pardon of our sins, prepares the soul for

the special grace of the Holy Spirit (Acts xiii.
2, 3 ; xiv. 22), casts out evil spirits (Matt. xvii.
20 ; Mark ix. 28), reminds us of the bride-
groom, Christ Jesus (Matt. ix. 15 ; Mark ii.
20 ; Luke v. 35. *Cf.* Tob. xii. 8 ; Joel ii. 15 ;
Ps. xxxiv. 13 ; Luke ii. 37 ; II. Cor. vi. 5).
Mere fasting in itself is not pleasing to God
(I. Cor. viii. 8), unless we use it as a means
of penance and mortification for Christ's sake.

**Why do Catholics have Ember days, and what
are their significance?**

The Ember days—a corruption of the Latin
quatuor tempora—are three days of fasting at
the beginning of each season, the Wednesday,
Friday, and Saturday after December 13, the
first Sunday in Lent, Pentecost, and September 14.

Originally the ordinations to the priesthood
were held on the Saturdays of Ember week,
and it was deemed fitting that the people
should fast and pray at such times for the
clergy. "Pray ye, therefore, the Lord of the
harvest that He send forth laborers into His
harvest" (Matt. ix. 38) ; so Christ taught His
people to pray for a good, apostolic priesthood.
Fasting before ordination was an Apostolic custom (Acts xiii. 2, 3).

**What is the meaning of the Lenten observance
in your Church?**

The forty days' fast of Lent is a custom of Christian antiquity mentioned by Tertullian (A.D. 99) in his book on fasting, and by Origen (A.D. 230) in his homily on Leviticus, N. 2, in memory of our Lord's fast of forty days before He undertook the work of His three years ministry. St. Jerome in the fourth century speaks of it as an Apostolic tradition: "We fast, the whole world agreeing with us, one Lent, in accordance with the tradition of the Apostles" (41 Letter to Marcella).

Why are women not allowed to be bareheaded in a Catholic Church as well as men ?

Because an Apostolic tradition forbids it (I. Cor. xi. 5-11). "Every woman praying, or prophesying with her head not covered, disgraceth her head, . . . therefore ought the woman to have a power (veil, or covering) over her head, because of the angels. . . . You yourselves judge : doth it become a woman, to pray unto God uncovered ? "

Why do Catholics make the sign of the Cross ?

Because it is an Apostolic devotional practice, and an open profession of their belief in the Trinity, the Divinity of Jesus Christ, and His death upon the Cross for our salvation. Many of the early Church writers speak of it ("Faith of Catholics," vol. iii. p. 422-438). Says Tertullian, in the second century : " In all our travels and movements, in all our coming in and going out, in putting on our clothes and shoes, at the bath, at the table, in lighting our lamps, in lying down and sitting down, whatever employment occupies us, we mark our forehead with the sign of the Cross. For these and such like rules, if thou requirest a law in Scriptures, thou shalt find none; tradition will be pleaded to thee as originating, custom as confirming, and faith as observing them '' ('' De Corona Mil.,'' 3, 4).

We never could understand why Christians should be ashamed of that holy symbol, when St. Paul tells us the mind of the true lover of Christ: ''God forbid that I should glory save in the Cross of our Lord Jesus Christ '' (Gal. vi. 14). A great proof that the reformers were not of Christ was the dishonor they showed to the symbol of man's salvation. It is the same spirit that animated the pagans in China when the test of apostasy was the trampling on the Cross.

SCAPULARS.

Why do Catholics wear the little brown badge, and what its meaning ?

Have not Catholics a superstitious reverence for the Scapulars, which they consider sure charms against all sorts of misfortune ?

If rightly understood, there is no more superstition in a Catholic wearing the scapular than in a soldier wearing his uniform, or a judge of the Supreme Court his gown. As part of the religious habit of the Carmelites and other orders, the scapular is a brown broad piece of cloth with an opening for the head, which hangs down in front and behind almost to the ground. The two pieces of square cloth, joined with two strings, and worn by the people, is a symbol of this.

The wearer of the brown scapular belongs to the confraternity of Our Lady of Mount Carmel, and shares in all the good works and prayers of that order; undertaking to lead a good Christian life, he also professes a special devotion to the Mother of God, and places himself under her special protection.

CEREMONIES.

Why do you Catholics make so much of a show in your churches during divine worship?

Cannot Christians worship God without so much pomp and ceremony? I deem it superstitious.

Why do you have so many silly and meaningless ceremonies?

If the ceremonies do appear silly and meaningless, remember that the trouble is not with

us, but with you who do not understand
their beautiful symbolism or know their ancient Christian origin. Not a word is said,
not a gesture made, not an action performed
in the Catholic Church but has its deep and
beautiful meaning to the initiated. "Judge
not according to the appearance," said the
Lord, "but judge a just judgment" (John
vii. 24).

We could, perhaps, worship God without
ceremony; but only by going contrary to
human nature, the teaching of the Old and
New Testament, and the constant practice of
the Christian people from the very beginning.

Ceremonial is natural to man. We are not
disembodied spirits, but creatures made up of
body and soul. It is a fact that in everything
else we give expression outwardly to what we
know and feel interiorly. Why, then, should
religion be the one exception?

Why should ceremony be the law in things
human, viz., in society, in the court-room, in
the army and navy, [the lodge, and yet be de-
barred in things divine?

We might say to one of our questioners:
"Why do we Americans make so much show
over our love of country?" Why, for instance, when Admiral Dewey came to New
York in October, 1899, fresh with the laurels
of the victory at Manila, did the whole city

clothe itself in bunting, fly the American flag, and our citizens vie with one another to honor him and the other heroes of the Spanish-American War, with processions on land and sea, fireworks, the playing of patriotic airs? A cynic might have remarked: "Why make such a fuss over men that merely did their duty?" The true American answers: "It was to give expression to the feeling of patriotism."

So Catholics, believing with the certainty of faith that Jesus Christ is really present upon the altar, so that our churches are indeed the temples of the living God, wish to give outward expression to their love of Him. Therefore silver, gold, flowers, incense, lighted candles, processions, architecture, sculpture, painting, music—all strive to pay their homage.

If it were silly or superstitious, how then do you account for God's sanction of the minutest detail of the Mosaic ritual? (Exod. xxvi., xxvii., xxviii., Num., Lev.) Our Saviour did not disdain to use certain ceremonies; for instance, in curing the deaf and dumb man: "He put His fingers into his ears, and spitting, He touched his tongue, and looking up to heaven He said, Ephpheta, which is, be thou opened" (Mark vii. 33, 34); in curing the blind man, "He spat on the ground, and made clay of the spittle, and spread the clay upon his eyes"

(John ix. 6) ; prostrating upon the ground in the Garden of Gethsemani (Matt. xxvi. 39) ; invoking a blessing at the Last Supper (Matt. xxvi. 26) ; breathing upon the Apostles (John xx. 22). So in the Apostolic Church we find the sacrament of orders administered by the imposition of hands (I. Tim. iv. 14 ; II. Tim. i. 6), and the sacrament of extreme unction by the anointing of oil (James v. 14).

There would indeed be reason to object if these outward ceremonies did not give expression to internal feelings of reverence and devotion ; if all Catholics were merely like the Pharisees of old, who made " clean the outside of the cup and of the dish, but within were full of rapine and uncleanness " (Matt. xxiii. 25). We readily grant that an individual Catholic may make the sign of the cross or genuflect in church before the Blessed Sacrament mechanically, out of habit, but it is totally gratuitous to suppose that the Catholic people in their outward ceremonial are merely honoring " God with their lips (externally) while their hearts are far from Him " (Isa. xxix. 13).

There are to-day many intelligent non-Catholics who greatly deplore the ignorance and vandalism of the Reformation, which, in doing away with the beautiful symbolism of the Catholic ritual, deprived men of one of the greatest aids to devotion. Indeed, there has been among certain Protestants in our own country and England a complete return to the old ceremonies of the Catholic Church, discarded some four hundred years ago. It is sad, however, to see them borrow only our externals, without having a priesthood for their vestments, a sacrifice for their altar appurtenances, or the real presence of Jesus Christ, to whose honor all the ceremonial and ritual should tend. Strange, too, that frequently the very man who objects to what he calls the formalism of Catholic ceremonial will gladly submit to every detail of the lodge's ritual, whether he be a Mason, Oddfellow, or Pythian. Deprive man of the reality, and sooner or later he will frame for himself a counterfeit, to satisfy in some way the heart's inner craving for outward ceremonial. Error is never consistent. (Bridgett, "The Ritual of the New Testament.")

Why are so many thousands of dollars put into the building of churches where there are thousands of poor people sadly in need of even the necessaries of life? Should not Christ be served in his poor?—*An unbeliever.*

A similar objection was made by the traitor Judas Iscariot, when Mary Magdalen anointed the feet of Jesus with the precious ointment.

"Mary therefore took a pound of ointment of right spikenard, of great price, and anointed the feet of Jesus. . . . Then one of His disciples, Judas Iscariot, . . . said, Why was not this ointment sold for three hundred pence, and given to the poor? Now he said this, not because he cared for the poor, but because he was a thief, and having the purse, carried the things that were put therein." Our Saviour did not find fault with her, however, for He said: "Let her alone, that she may keep it against the day of my burial. For the poor you have always with you, but Me you have not always" (John xii. 3-8).

In the same spirit of love for Jesus Christ the Catholic people to-day, as ever, gladly spend their hard-earned money that their Lord God might have a fitting dwelling place upon earth.

The Jews of the Old Law did not spare gold or precious stones in the Temple of Solomon (II. Paral. iii. iv.), which was merely a figure of the Catholic Church on whose altars Jesus Christ was to be really present—the Emmanuel —God with us.

The Catholic Church has ever been pre-eminently the Church of the poor, the Catholic priest ever their truest friend, as the universal love of the poor for him abundantly proves.

Her principles of justice set forth clearly the duty of capital to provide a just, living wage for the workingman, and charity is written large on the page of her history from the beginning (Leo XIII., ''On the Condition of Labor '').

The money spent in church-building is well spent, for it means a practical, substantial proof of the true faith in Christ and the love for Him and the brethren, which otherwise would disappear before the inroads of our modern paganism. Every Catholic church means a new home where the poor are ever welcome, to be cared for spiritually, and materially if need be, by those who remember Christ's words: ''As long as you did it to one of these my least brethren, you did it to Me'' (Matt. xxv. 40).

I wonder how many dollars our unbelieving friend devotes annually to charity.

DEVOUT PRACTICES.

Why do you burn fragrant spices during your services ?

Incense, according to the Old Testament and the New, is symbolic of prayer. ''Let my prayer, O Lord, be directed as incense in thy sight'' (Ps. cxl. 2). ''And golden vials full of odors, which are the prayers of saints''

(Apoc. v. 8). "Another angel came and stood before the altar, having a golden censer; and there was given him much incense, that he should offer of the prayers of all saints upon the golden altar, which is before the throne of God" (Apoc. viii. 3). The burning of incense before the altar was part of the prescribed ceremonial of the Old Law. "And Aaron shall burn sweet smelling incense upon it (the altar) in the morning" (Exod. xxx. 7; *cf.* xxv. 6 ; xxx. 23 ; Lev. xvi. 13 ; Num. xvi. 46). In the Church of God it is used at High Mass, Vespers, and Benediction of the Most Blessed Sacrament.

Why do Catholics sprinkle themselves on entering the church ? What warranty in the Bible for the use of holy water ? Is not this a superstitious practice ?

Catholics use holy water because they believe that the prayers of the Church in blessing it are efficacious to excite in the well disposed acts of faith, hope, and love in Christ Jesus, and to drive forth the evil one through the exorcisms of those vested with divine authority. St. Paul tells us : " Every creature of God is good, . . . for it is sanctified by the word of God and prayer " (I. Tim. iv. 4, 5).

If it were superstitious, how then do you

account for the miracles wrought at the pool
of Bethsaida? (John v. 2-4). How explain
the use of holy water by God's commandment
in the Old Law?—viz., "Aaron and his son
shall wash their hands and feet in it (a
brazen laver), when they are going into the
tabernacle" (Exod. xxx. 19, 20); "And he
shall take holy water in an earthen vessel"
(Num. v. 17); "Let them be sprinkled with
the water of purification" (Num. viii. 7; *cf.*
Exod. xix. 10-14; Lev. viii. 6; IV. Kings,
v. 10).

Moreover we know that holy water was used
as early as the second century ("Apostolical
Constitution," book viii. ch. 29), and in the
catacombs of Rome (Rock, "Hierurgia," vol.
ii. ch. xiii. p. 258). It is symbolic of the
purity of heart with which Christians ought
to appear before the altar of Jesus Christ.
(Lambing, "Sacramentals of the Church," ch.
viii.; Rock, "Hierurgia," vol. ii. ch. xiii. p.
258.)

Why do you use candles in your Church in the
day-time?

Why are candles used in the sick-room, or
around the body of the dead?

Historically, the use of candles on the altar
during Mass bears witness to the days of persecution, when the early Christians heard Mass

in the darkness of the catacombs under the city of Rome.

Symbolically, they bring before the Catholic people Jesus Christ, "the Light of the World," " the True Light which enlighteneth every man that cometh into this world " (John i. 9, viii. 12), and tell them with the Saviour that their faith should be manifested before men and burn brightly in the performance of good works. " So let your light shine before men, that they may see your good works, and glorify your Father who is in heaven " (Matt. v. 16).

Why do Catholic priests wear such peculiar clothes during services ?

The vestments worn by the priest at Mass mark him a man apart from the world, as in the Old Law: "And these shall be the vestments which they shall make : a rational and an ephod, a tunic and a straight linen garment, a mitre and a girdle. They shall make the holy vestments for thy brother Aaron and his sons, that they may do the office of the priesthood unto me " (Exod. xxviii. 4).

Symbolically, they call to mind some detail of our Lord's Passion, for the Mass daily "shows forth the death of the Lord until He come " (I. Cor. xi. 26). The *amice*, a linen covering of the priest's head and shoulders, is symbolic of the linen scarf placed over our Lord's eyes (Luke xxii. 64) ; the *alb*, the long linen garment of the priest, of the white garment wherewith Herod in mockery clothed Him (Luke xxiii. 11) ; the *cincture and stole*, of the cords with which He was bound (John xviii. 12, 24) ; the *chasuble*, of the purple garment the soldiers gave Him (Mark xv. 17). The different colors of the vestments worn at different seasons of the year and on different feast days are also symbolic—white of innocence, red of martyrdom, purple of penance, green of hope, and black of mourning.

These vestments naturally seem peculiar to the eye of the twentieth century, for they all date back to Roman days—none of them being later-than the eighth century. In the same way the dress of the Oriental to-day is strange to us, as our collars, cuffs, and trousers are extraordinary to him.

Why do Catholics wear medals? Are they not similar to the superstitious amulets of the pagan to prevent disease, ward off danger, etc.?

On the contrary, there is no more superstition in the wearing of a blessed medal, stamped with the impression of our Lord, the Blessed Virgin, or one of the saints, than there is in a boy or girl wearing a locket containing a mother's picture. They are not charms, but reminders of Christ's love for us, or of the perfect sanctity of His saints.

What is an Agnus Dei?

It is a little emblem of blessed wax, enclosed in a silken covering, worn by Catholics to remind them of Jesus Christ, " the Lamb of God, who taketh away the sins of the world " (John i. 29).

Why are ashes placed on the foreheads of Catholics the first day of Lent?

To make us realize the thought of death, the priest repeating the words of God to Adam, "for dust thou art, and into dust thou shalt return " (Gen. iii. 19). Ashes in the Old Law were always symbolic of penance, the characteristic virtue of the season of Lent (Job xlii. 6 ; Jonas iii. 6 ; Isa. lviii. 5, etc.)

Why do you bless palm-branches in your Church a week before Easter?

They tell the Catholic people of Christ's triumphal entry into the Holy City on the first Palm Sunday. " And others cut down boughs from the trees, and strewed them in the way " (Mark xi. 8).

Why do you baptize church bells?

Bells are not baptized, for only rational

creatures are fit subjects for Christ's baptism. They are merely blessed, as are many other inanimate objects, with a special prayer prescribed by the liturgy. The Bible authority for this is I. Tim. iv. 4–5 : "Every creature . . . is sanctified by the word of God and prayer."

What is the meaning of the Forty Hours' Devotion ?

It is a special time of devotion in which the Catholic people gather in great numbers to visit and adore Jesus Christ in the Blessed Sacrament, to attend Mass and receive Holy Communion. The worship of Jesus in the Eucharist is the primary devotion of the Catholic Church, before which all the other devotions pale as the stars at the coming of dawn.

What is the Vesper service in your Church ?

It is a part of the divine office which every priest is bound to say daily for the glory of God and the good of the Universal Church. It is made up of five psalms, which vary according to different feasts (generally Pss. 109–113), a hymn, the Magnificat (Luke i. 46-55), and some prayers. In the convents of the old religious orders the entire office is sung every day (Matins, Lauds, Prime, Tierce, Sext, None, Vespers, and Compline), but because of its great length only Vespers is sung in the Catholic churches of to-day, in accordance with the practice of primitive Christianity: "speaking to yourselves in psalms, and hymns, and spiritual canticles, singing and making melody in your hearts to the Lord" (Eph. v. 19 ; Col. iii. 16).

SAINT PETER IN ROME.

What particle of proof have we that Peter was ever in Rome?

It has been denied, under the stress of controversy, that St. Peter was ever in Rome, and this false statement is still repeated without hesitancy by many who have never studied the question. The best answer to this query is to cite the many fair-minded non-Catholic scholars who admit the fact as beyond all question; viz., Grotius, Cave, Lardner, Whitby, Macknight, Hales, Cludius, Mynster, Schaff, Neander, Steiger, DeWette, Wieseler, Credner, Bleck, Meyer, Hilgenfeld, Renan, Mangold.

"That Peter was at Rome," says Cave, "and held the see there for some time, we fearlessly affirm with the whole multitude of the ancients." ("Scriptorum Eccles. Historia Literaria," vol. i. p. 5, cited by Livius ; "St. Peter, Bishop of Rome," p. 442.)

Dr. Lardner writes : " It is the general, un-contradicted, disinterested testimony of ancient writers in the several parts of the world —Greeks, Latins, Syrians " ("Hist. of the Apost. and Evang.," ch. xviii.; cited by Alnatt, Catholic Truth Society publications).

Pearson declares : " Since it has been handed down from almost the beginning that St. Peter preached the gospel in Rome, and there suffered martyrdom, and since no one has ever affirmed that either Peter or Paul was crowned with martyrdom elsewhere, I think, with full security, faith may be given to this account. (Minor Theological Works, vol. iii. p. 341.)

Whiston, the translator of the works of Josephus, says : " That St. Peter was at Rome is so clear in Christian antiquity that it is a shame for any Protestant to confess that any Protestant ever denied it " (Memoirs, London, 1750).

The universally received interpretation of I. Pet. v. 13, " the Church that is in Babylon saluteth you," declares that Babylon means Rome, from which city St. Peter wrote his Epistle. The " Speaker's Commentary " (Protestant) says : " We find an absolute consensus of ancient interpreters that there Babylon must be understood as equivalent to Rome." (*Cf.* also Bishop Ellicott's Commentary ; cited by Livius, p. 453-454.)

One of the greatest proofs, perhaps, is the fact that although the Protestant scholar Lipsius spent his entire life endeavoring to disprove this evident historical fact, the world of scholars is unmoved by his arguments. (*Cf.* Hilgenfeld's " Zeitschrift," 1877, pp. 486–508.)

What proofs have you for the Roman episcopate of the Apostle Peter ?

To oné eager to study this question I would earnestly recommend Father Livius' book on this subject: "St. Peter, Bishop of Rome " (London : Burns & Oates, 1888), or the little leaflet of the London Catholic Truth Society by C. F. Alnatt.

" Regarded simply as an event of past history, St. Peter's Roman episcopate, like other such events, is a matter of historical evidence. If judged by this test alone, we claim for it a more ample and precise verification than usually obtains for most of those events which learned, impartial criticism has pronounced to be historically true " (Livius, Introd. p. xi.)

1. " The Roman episcopate of St. Peter was never questioned, even by heretics or schismatics, until the thirteenth century. Indeed, until the Reformation it was the universal persuasion of the Christian people that from his see the constitution and authority of the

Church were derived. It is rather puerile to deny such a fact, in view of the demands of controversy " (pp. 4, 193–197).

2. The testimony of the Fathers of the first four centuries—men eminent for their learning and sanctity—is given, p. 11–36.

3. " As everybody well knows, the memory of the holy Apostles Peter and Paul has from the earliest times till now been inseparably associated with many places, buildings, and other material objects in Rome ; amongst these, the dungeons in which they were imprisoned, the chains of St. Peter, the place of his martyrdom, and the tombs of the Apostles have ever been the most celebrated. Moreover, not a few churches in the very earliest times were built in some of the more famous places, where either the Apostles themselves, or their disciples, such as St. Pudens and his family, Aquila and Priscilla, and others, were used to reside. And here, too, we may mention the feast of the chair of St. Peter, as well as the material chair itself of the Apostle, which is preserved in Rome until the present day " (p. 38, 105–187).

4. It is a striking fact that none of the Eastern schismatics who broke away from Rome in the early days ever denied the Roman episcopate of St. Peter, although it would have proved one of the strongest justifications

of their schism (p. 17 *et seq.*, p. 57, pp. 193 *et seq.*, 288, 349 *et seq.*, 378 *et seq.*)

5. The many objections brought forward since the Reformation by non-Catholic controversialists are ably answered by Father Livius, viz., the silence of the Acts and the Epistles of St. Paul (pp. 50–56), the meaning of Babylon in I. Pet. v. 13 (pp. 56–59), the rationalistic theory (pp. 63–65; *cf.* pp. 113, 129, 178–181, 193, 196, 201, 206, 235, 241 *et seq.*, 272–275, 294, 298 *et seq.*, 323, 337 *et seq.*, 390–392, 424, 438 *et seq.*, 445, 459 *et seq.*, 465 *et seq.*, 511–519).

THE PAPAL AUTHORITY.

Is not the ruling power of the Roman Popes a usurpation?

Where does the Bible declare that Jesus appointed a Pope?

What proof does Scripture give that Peter had any authority over the other disciples?

Were not all the Apostles equal?

Did not Jesus give to all the power of binding and loosing (Matt. xviii. 18).

Matt. xvi. 18, 19: "Thou art Peter, and upon this rock I will build my Church, and the gates of hell shall not prevail against it. And I will give to thee the keys of the kingdom of Heaven. And whatsoever thou shalt bind upon earth, it shall be bound also in heaven; and whatsoever thou shalt loose on earth, it shall be loosed also in heaven.''

Luke xxii. 31–32 : '' Simon, Simon, behold Satan hath desired to have you, that he may sift you as wheat. But I have prayed for thee, that thy faith fail not; and thou being once converted, confirm thy brethren.''

John xxi. 15–17 : '' Jesus saith to Simon Peter : Simon, son of John, lovest thou Me more than these? He said to Him : Yea, Lord, Thou knowest that I love Thee. He saith to him : *Feed my lambs.* He saith to him again : Simon, son of John, lovest thou Me? He said to Him : Yea, Lord, thou knowest that I love Thee. He saith to him : *Feed my lambs.* He saith to him the third time : Simon, son of John, lovest thou Me? Peter was grieved because He had said to him the third time : Lovest thou Me? And he said to Him : Lord, thou knowest all things; Thou knowest that I love Thee. He said to him : *Feed my sheep.*''

A careful study of all these words clearly proves that St. Peter held a unique place among the twelve Apostles, and that Jesus Christ made him His vicar and representative on earth.

1. Jesus Christ the Rock (I. Cor. x. 4; Matt. xxi. 42 ; Acts iv. 11 ; Eph. ii. 20–22 ; I.

Pet. ii. 6) promised to make Peter the rock-foundation of the Church in association with Himself (Matt. xvi. 18). The foundation of a building gives it unity, strength, and stability (Matt. vii. 24, 25); so the Church built on Peter is, through him, to be kept for ever strong and united in government and in doctrine.

2. Christ the Key-bearer (Apoc. iii. 7) promises to make Peter Key-bearer in His kingdom; that is, to have complete power and jurisdiction in the Church.

3. In Luke xxii. Christ prays for Peter that his faith ever remain strong and pure to strengthen the faith of the wavering and doubting brethren.

4. Christ the Good Shepherd (John x. 11) plainly gives to Peter His own full power as Shepherd (John xxi. 15).

All the Apostles were commissioned in common to establish the Church, to preach the gospel, to baptize (Matt. xxviii. 19, 20), to forgive sins (John xx. 23), to say Mass (Luke xxii. 19), etc.; but Peter alone was made the Rock, the Key-bearer, the Confirmer of the brethren, and the Shepherd of the flock. This has ever been the witness of Catholic tradition. (See "A Manual of Catholic Theology," vol. ii. p. 316–327; "Faith of Catholics," vol. ii. pp. 1-59).

Indeed, our Lord indicated the pre-eminence

of St. Peter by the promised change of name at their first meeting: "Thou art Simon the son of Jona; thou shalt be called Cephas, which is interpreted Peter" (John i. 42). Throughout the New Testament his name is given first (Matt. x. 2; Mark iii. 16; Luke vi. 14; Acts i. 13); and he is treated as the leader of the twelve (Matt. xvii. 23–26; xxvi. 37–40; Mark v. 37; xvi. 7; Luke v. 2–10; ix. 20, etc.) He presides at the election of Matthias (Acts i. 15); he is the first preacher of the Gospel and the first converter of the gentiles (Acts ii. 14 *et seq.*, x. 9 *et seq.*); he is the first to work miracles (Acts· iii. 6); he condemns the guilty Ananias and Saphira (Acts v. 1–10); the Church prays unceasingly for his release from prison (xii. 1–15); he settles the dispute at the first Council of Jerusalem (xv. 7–12); he is visited by St. Paul (Gal. i. 18, 19, etc.)

The exercise of Papal supremacy, and the strong steady witness to it in the pages of Christian history, may be studied in many volumes which treat this subject at great length. (*Livius*, "St. Peter, Bishop of Rome"; *Allies*, "St. Peter, His Name and His Office," "The See of Peter," "Church and State," "The Throne of the Fisherman"; *Rivington*, "Authority—Dependence," "The Primitive Church and the See of Peter"; *Allnatt*,

"Cathedra Petri"; *Kenrick*, "The Primacy of the Apostolic See"; *Smith*, "Papal Supremacy and Infallibility," Catholic Truth Society publications; *Hettinger*, "The Supremacy of the Apostolic See."

Is it probable that such a power, recognized to-day by the vast majority of the Christian people, is a usurpation? It was in possession at the time of the Reformation, and no valid argument has ever been produced to invalidate the Catholic claim. Is it probable "that many various nations will agree that the head of their religion should be external to themselves? Will the members of these various and zealous nations, who are equal in their episcopal power, allow a brother to arrange their precedence, control their actions, terminate their disputes, rule them as one flock, and that for fifteen centuries together?" ("See of Peter," p. 87).

IS CHRIST THE ROCK?

Does not the rock (Matt. xvi. 18) mean Christ?

The word *rock* refers to St. Peter, as many Protestant commentators of the passage have admitted, *v. g.*, Weiss, Keil, Mansel, Bloomfield, Marsh, Thompson, Alford, Rosenmuller, etc. Thompson, of Glasgow, in his *Monatesseron* says (p. 194): "Peter was the rock on which

Christ said his Church should be built. To this the connection and scope of the passage agree. There seems to be something forced in every other construction. . . . Protestants have betrayed unnecessary fears, and have therefore used all the hardihood of lawless criticism in their attempts to reason away the Catholic interpretation.''

Does not the use of the two different words, petros and petra, in Matt. xvi. 18 prove that Peter and rock are not identical?

This argument is obsolete to-day, for the study of Syriac in the past century has told us that in the vernacular of Palestine in our Lord's time Syriac was the language used, and in that version of the Scriptures (the Peshito) the same word is employed for Peter and rock, thus: ''Thou art *Kepha*, and upon this *Kepha* I will build My Church.'' Thus scholarship again robs the old-time controversialist of one of his pet arguments against the Primacy.

If Christ is the Supreme Head of the Church, what need is there of the Pope? Is it not derogatory to Christ to have a mere man at the head of His Church?

The will of Christ was to establish His Church as a visible society in the world, and, to prevent anarchy in doctrine and government, He chose a central authority on earth to represent His divine authority. God seldom acts directly, but uses human agencies as the ministers of His will. The Primacy is a question of fact to be learned from a study of Scripture and history.

The supremacy of the Popes is no more derogatory to Christ than the supremacy of the high-priest under the Old Law to the authority of God. A visible church needs a local government upon earth according to the divine plan. The authority of Christ can be vested in a man, to rule His Church, just as the truth and the grace of Christ can be given men through the ministry of human agents.

Is not Christ called the only foundation of the Church ? "For other foundation can no man lay than that is laid, which is Jesus Christ " (I. Cor. iii. 11).

Is not Christ called the rock, the stone, etc., in the Bible ? " This is the stone which was set at naught by the builders," etc. (Acts iv. 11); "And that rock was Christ " (I. Cor. x. 4).

Catholics do not claim that Peter is the head of the Church independently of Christ, which indeed would be blasphemy ; but that he is the visible head on earth, representing the chief and invisible Head, Christ Jesus in heaven. He is the rock whereon Christ, the Divine Builder, has built His Church, that from His divinely given strength the Church might ever be kept one, firm and strong. Christ, as the rock primarily, could make Peter rock also, even as Christ, as chief Shepherd (John x. 11), could make Peter shepherd of the flock after he had gone (John xxi. 15).

Fair-minded Protestant commentators have granted that the expression rock, or foundation, may be applied to either Christ or St. Peter, "since the two expressions are employed in two very different senses" (Bloomfield in Matt. xvi. 18).

Indeed, we find the word *foundation* applied even to the Apostles and the prophets in Eph. ii. 20, and surely they were not foundations in the same sense as Christ. The meaning of I. Cor. iii. 11 is plain : the Apostle declares that our Lord is the only one in whom our hope of salvation should rest, for "there is no other name under heaven given to man whereby we must be saved" (Acts iv. 12).

In Acts iv. 11 St. Peter tells the Jews that the Messias whom they rejected is now glorified, even as the rejected stone is afterwards given by the builders a prominent place in the building. How any of these texts contradict Matt. xvi. we fail to understand.

Are not all the Apostles equal? For we read in Eph. ii. 20 that the Church was built upon them all; "built upon the foundation of the Apostles and Prophets" (cf. Apoc. xxi. 14).

The Church is indeed built upon all the Apostles and Prophets, but not in the same manner, for surely the prophets were not teachers of Christ in the same sense as the Apostles. The United States is built upon the judiciary, legislature, and executive. Does that make all these three branches of the government similar in function, and prove that Mr. Roosevelt is not the President of our country?

If the Apostles knew that Peter was their head, why then did they dispute as to who was the greatest? (Luke xxii. 24).

Even suppose that before the descent of the Holy Spirit (Acts ii.) the Apostles were doubtful of the primacy of St. Peter; they were also ignorant of the passion and resurrection of the Saviour, although he had frequently prophesied it (Luke ix. 45; xviii. 34; xxiv. 25; Matt. xx. 17–19).

Our Lord could have ended the dispute at once by declaring that there would be no chief or "greatest" apostle in His kingdom, if that were the fact. On the contrary, He implies by His comparison that there will be a ruler among them, although his character should be child-like and humble, as distinct from the pagan princes of the time. I quote the Protestant version: "The kings of the gentiles exercise lordship over them: and they that exercise authority upon them are called benefactors. But ye shall not be so (*i.e.*, proud)'; but *he that is greatest among you*, let him be as the younger; and *he that is chief*, as he that doth serve" (Luke xxii. 25–26). He then, moreover, cites His own example—surely not to deny His headship, but to give them a divine example of humility. "I am among you as he that serveth" (v. 27), an allusion to his having washed their feet as a slave (John xiii. 5).

And finally, in verse 32, he actually promises that St. Peter shall be the chief Apostle to confirm the faith of the wavering brethren: "I have prayed for thee, that thy faith fail not; and thou, being once converted, confirm thy brethren."

Is not the fact that the Apostles sent St. Peter and St. John to confirm the Samaritans proof positive that he exercised] no supreme power over the other Apostles? (Acts viii. 14).

Not at all. "For although St. Luke mentions Peter and John, he sets Peter first; and in his record of what happened to Simon, John acts the second part, and it is Peter alone who

teaches, commands, judges, and condemns
with authority, as the head and supreme ruler ''
(*cf.* Acts viii. 19–23 ; Allies, '' St. Peter, His
Name and His Office,'' pp. 164-166).

Besides, Josephus tells us that in the reign
of Nero the Jews sent ten legates of their
princes, their high-priest, Ishmael, and another Jewish priest. We see, therefore, that
there is nothing incredible in two persons of
unequal rank being sent on a joint mission in
those times (Rivington, preface to Allies' '' St.
Peter,'' p. ix.)

**Did Peter act as Pope in the Council of Jeru-
salem ? (Acts xv.) If so, why did James preside,
and give the definitive sentence ?**

There is no proof that the Apostle James pre-
sided at the Council of Jerusalem, or that he decided any question whatsoever. The Greek
word *Krino*, '' I judge '' (xv. 19), or '' I am of
the opinion,'' does not imply an authoritative
decision. On the contrary, we notice that the
dispute over circumcision which was carried
on first in Antioch, and renewed again at the
Council, ceased when Peter arose, declared how
he had been chosen to announce the gospel to
the gentiles, and rebuked those who were insisting on the observances of the Old Law.
'' And all the multitude held their peace.''
Whoever rises to speak after this merely

confirms what St. Peter said by narrating the miracles wrought among the gentiles, as did St. Paul and Barnabas, or citing the prophets, and suggesting a practical remedy of settling the dispute, as did St. James.

Why is it that Paul makes no mention of the Pope when he speaks of the various offices in the Church ? (1. Cor. xii. 28, and Eph. iv. 11).

Because it is not the purpose of St. Paul to describe the hierarchy, but to show that as in the body there are different members, so in Christ's body, the Church, there are different offices—apostles, prophets, doctors, etc. You could not argue that because the Council of Trent declares the hierarchy to consist of bishops, priests, and deacons, without special mention of the Pope, it thereby denies his primacy. Besides, conditions were vastly different in Apostolic times, for the Catholic Church teaches that each Apostle was infallible with and under the Pope, while to-day the plenitude of Apostolic power of teaching and ruling resides only in the Bishop of Rome.

Did Paul acknowledge Peter as his superior when he " withstood him to the face " ? (Gal. ii. 11–14).

This rebuke of St. Peter by St. Paul cannot logically be brought forward as an argument

against the Primacy, unless it be first proved,
that it is always unlawful for an inferior to correct a superior. But this is not the teaching of
Christianity (Matt. xviii. 15). To reprehend
one's superior in defence of justice and of truth,
firmly though with due deference to his authority, may sometimes be an imperative duty.
There are several instances in the history of
the Church where holy men and women, like
St. Bernard, St. Thomas of Canterbury, and
St. Catherine of Siena, have rebuked Popes
while fully acknowledging their authority.

St. Alphonsus thus answers this objection
("Verità della Fede," p. iii. c. vii. 12) : "As
to the reprehension of St. Peter by St. Paul,
.   .   .   some, as St. Jerome (Com. in Gal. ii.
11), answer that this dispute was preconcerted
purposely to tranquillize the Jews; but others,
with St. Augustine (Epistle 82 n. 22), St. Cyprian (Ad. Quint., ep. 71), St. Gregory (Sup.
Ezech., Hom. 18), St. Thomas (2. 2. q. 33,
a. 4 ad 2), and St. Jerome himself (Adv.
Pelag., lib. i. 1), when he afterwards retracted,
say more commonly, and with greater probability, that these words were a real reprehension,
but that there was no question of doctrine involved; viz., as to whether, under the Evangelical law, the legal observances of the Jews
were to be still maintained. St. Peter was
well aware that these observances were to be

abolished.; nay more, before this—when St. Paul brought tidings of what the converted Jews were doing at Antioch, and how they would have the gentiles who believed to be circumcised—it was St. Peter who severely blamed such a pretension, saying : ' Now, therefore, why tempt you God, to put a yoke upon the necks of the disciples, which neither our fathers nor we have been able to bear ? ' (Acts xv. 10). But in this case the question was one only of a point of discipline and expedience ; that is, whether or not it was then fitting and expedient to wholly abolish the Mosaic Law. For though it was already dead, it had not yet become deadly to those who observed it (*cf.* Acts xvi. 3, where St. Paul has Timothy circumcised). . . . It was with good reason, however, that St. Paul afterwards blamed St. Peter, when, from fear of displeasing the Jewish converts, he separated from the gentiles, who did not observe the Mosaic Law : for at that time it was of more importance not to shock the gentile believers, who were many, than not to displease the Jewish converts, who were few in number, and ought to have had no reasonable grounds for scandal because the uncircumcised did not follow their customs." (Livius, " St. Peter, Bishop of Rome," pp. 334–348, who also cites Döllinger, " First Age of the Church," vol. i, pp. 79–105.)

THE POPES IN HISTORY.

Did not Pope Gregory the Great repudiate the title of Universal Bishop?

Pope Gregory tells us that he rejected the title because he took it to involve a claim of being the one only bishop (lib. v. epis. 21, ad Const. Aug.) When John the Faster, Patriarch of Constantinople, proudly called himself " Ecumenical Bishop," Gregory to rebuke him humbly called himself " the servant of the servants of God " (servus servorum Dei) —a title which has always been retained by his successors. He by no means denies his universal jurisdiction; for, with regard to Constantinople, he writes: " As to what they say of the Church of Constantinople, who doubts that it is subject to the Apostolic See? This is constantly owned by the most pious Emperor, and by our brother the Bishop of that city " (lib. ix. ep. 12). And again: " It is evident to all acquainted with the gospel, that by our Lord's words the care of the whole Church was committed to St. Peter, Apostle, and prince of all the Apostles " : John xxi. 17 ; Luke xxii. 32 ; Matt. xvi. 17–19 (lib. v. ep. xx.; Ryder, " Catholic Controversy.")

By what right did Alexander VI. divide the Spanish and Portuguese possessions in the New

World ? Was not that an unwarranted assumption of power ?

Alexander VI. merely did what international treaties or congresses do to-day ; that is, regulate the rights of different nations so as to avoid as far as possible the danger of war. At the date of the Bull " Inter Cætera " (May 4, 1493) all the European nations acknowledged Rome—the centre of Christendom—as the Supreme Court of international law. Relations between Spain and Portugal were strained at the time, so that war was imminent, threatening to prevent the peaceful explorations of the New World, and the preaching of the gospel to the heathen. The Bull did not, as some pretend, confer upon the two kings lands which the Pope owned or pretended to own, but only marked out the limits in which the two nations could operate without danger of conflict. As a matter of fact, by thus preventing war between the two countries, Alexander VI. helped the opening up of America (*Amer. Cath. Quarterly*, vol. iii. p. 338-340).

Was there not at one time (A. D. 855-857) a female Pope ?

No; this fable is rejected by Protestant and infidel scholars; *e. g.*, Blondel, Leibnitz, Gibbon, Bayle, Casaubon, Jurien, Basnage, Burnet, Cave, Gabler, Mosheim, Gieseler, Shröckl, Neander, etc. Indeed, as Bene-, dict III. (September 29, 853) immediately succeeded Leo IV. (July 17, 855), there was no interval left for the alleged two years' reign of the Popess Joan (Gibbon, "Decline and Fall," ch. xlix.) The subject is exhaustively treated by Döllinger, " Papal Fables," p. 1–45.

Did not the Popes forge a number of documents, now known as the False Decretals, to establish their monstrous claim of universal dominion ?

It has been conclusively proved, by both Catholic and Protestant critics, that the "*False Decretals*" did not originate in Rome, but in Western France, about A.D. 845–857. The forgeries in the collection were not compiled in the interests of the Popes at all, but directly to restrict the power of the metropolitans, and relieve the bishops from oppression by the secular power. This is admitted by Protestant scholars, as Splitter, Knust, Vasserschleben, Walter, and Moehler.

"In fact, there is not a single prerogative or privilege of Rome asserted in the False Decretals which was not generally recognized as the common law of the Christian Church. They changed nothing, altered nothing, added nothing ; at most they only put into convenient shape what was before less easy of access, and so helped to popularize a doctrine which was sometimes forgotten by local prelates, and to keep before their minds that dependence on the Holy See which is the central doctrine of Catholic ecclesiastical discipline " (Rev. R. F. Clarke, S.J., Historical Papers, p. 44, Catholic Truth Society publications). Catholic critics like Cardinal de Cusa, the Ballerini, Bellarmin, and Baronius proved long ago that these documents were forgeries. The Popes saw them disappear with perfect equanimity, for their power rested not on them, but on the words of Christ.

What became of the Papal succession at the time of the great Western Schism (A.D. 1378–1417).

Were there not at one time three men, each claiming to be the real Pope ?

How can you claim your Church was always one, when for forty years it was destroyed by the Western Schism ?

The Papal line was in no way broken by the great Western Schism, for there was always a true Pope; it seems historically most probable that Urban VI. was the validly elected Pope, April 9, 1378. So, after careful consideration, think many Catholic (Hefele, Papencordt, Hergenröther, Heinrich) and non-Catholic historians (Leo, Hinschius, Siebe-

king, Lindner, Gregorovius, Erler; *cf.* Pastor,
" History of the Popes," vol. i. p. 102). In that
case his successors during the schism, Boniface IX., Innocent VII., Gregory XII.,
formed the direct line of legitimate Popes, and
the others, Clement VII., Benedict XIII.,
Alexander V., John XXIII., were merely antipopes.

We must remember, too, "that the schism
was not a schism in the ordinary sense of
the term. For by schism is ordinarily meant
withdrawal of obedience from one who is known
to be the unquestionably legitimate Roman
Pontiff. It is quite possible and likely that
the authors of the mischief, whom we cannot
but identify with the cardinals who withdrew
from Urban after electing him, were schismatics in the true sense. But the name is
not truly applicable to the vast number
of prelates and Christian people who, amidst
so many conflicting testimonies, were utterly
unable to discover which was the true Pontiff.
They were not schismatics, because they acknowledged the Papal authority, did their best
to discover who was its true living incumbent,
and were prepared to submit at once when
the discovery was made.

"There was, moreover, *a true Pope all the
time*, for the fact that this truth was involved
in doubt did not make it less a truth; and

this true Pope was a true fountain of authority and a true centre of unity to all the world " (Rev. Sydney Smith, S.J., " The Great Schism of the West," Catholic Truth Society publications). The succession to the throne of England was not interrupted because at various times pretenders rose up to claim it.

In 1876 there was considerable doubt regarding the validity of the election of President Hayes. Suppose a Civil War arose on the matter between Democrats and Republicans. Both sides would agree that there was one President ; the only question would be which is the legitimate one. So with the Pope and anti-popes in the fifteenth century. All the Catholics of the time believed firmly that there was but one Pope ; the only question was, which was the legitimate one.

Catholics, of course, realize that this schism caused great harm to souls, and weakened in the hearts of many the true reverence for the Papal power which has ever been the mark of true Christianity. In a measure it prepared the way for the schism of the sixteenth century, whereby many lost for themselves and their descendants the pure gospel of Christ.

Still, the true succession went on through Martin V., the choice of the Council of Constance, and continues to this day unimpaired—

a proof to every true follower of Christ of the supernatural character of the bark of Peter, which has weathered many a storm by the power of Christ, the Son of God. (Alzog, vol. ii. p. 845, *et seq.;* Pastor, "History of the Popes," vol. i.; Smith, Catholic Truth Society publications; *American Catholic Quarterly*, A.D. 1891, p. 67.)

Does not the Primacy of the Pope interfere with the rights of individual bishops?

Not at all. The Pope does not absorb all episcopal authority.

Suppose Peter was primate, and Bishop of Rome, how do you prove that his authority has been transferred all down the centuries to [the Pope?

It is evident that the divine society established by Christ was to continue until the end, just as He established it; for He guaranteed its permanence by His own abiding presence and the Holy Spirit's (Matt. xxviii. 20; John xiv. 16, 26).

Peter, therefore, must ever abide in the Church as its firm foundation (Matt. xvi.), its perpetual confirmer of the faith (Luke xxii.), and its ruler and shepherd (John xxi.) Unless our Saviour provided for the succession in Peter's primatial office, His work would not have been

as well done as the work of the founders of
our Republic, who provided against anarchy
in the appointment of presidents to succeed
one another as long as the United States
would last. Surely the All-Wise Son of God
was wiser than statesmen and politicians.

No one outside the Bishop of Rome ever
claimed to be St. Peter's successor, whilst all
history is the witness of the universality of
his claim.

**Your Pope is Anti-Christ. Does not he wear
the number 666 in his belt—the mark of the
beast? (Rev. xiii. 18).**

My questioner has fallen far behind his intelligent Protestant brethren, who reject as
mere raving this old-time absurdity. Luther
was the first to set the fashion when he wrote
his pamphlet " Against the Execrable Bull of
Anti-Christ," in answer to the document that
condemned him. It was an argument to catch
the ignorant and unthinking multitude. So
our Saviour had said : " The disciple is not
above the Master, nor the servant above his
Lord. . . . If they have called the good
man of the house Beelzebub, how much more
them of his household? (Matt. x. 24, 25 ;
John xvi. 2; 3).

If the Pope is the successor of St. Peter, why

don't he imitate him in simplicity of life ?   Why
ape the pomp and luxury of worldly princes ?

The greater number of the Popes have been
remarkable for their holiness of life.   Surely
the private life of Pope Leo XIII. is full of
Apostolic simplicity.   As continually dealing
with temporal rulers, the Popes have followed
the customs of European princes.   For many
years indeed the Papal Court was recognized as
the Supreme Court of Christendom, and kings
and emperors were proud to do him homage.
Catholics, moreover, do not pretend to apologize for the failings of individual Popes.

**Is it not disgusting that your Pope claims to
be a temporal ruler ?   Did not the Saviour say :
" My Kingdom is not of this world " ?**

The temporal power of the Pope is necessary for the perfect freedom and independence
of the Holy See.   Once admit the doctrine of
the Primacy—that the Pope is the head of the
Universal Church—and it follows logically that
the Pope, to be free to teach and guide his
entire flock, ought not to be subject to any
authority outside himself.   If he be subject to
a prince, laws impairing his freedom of action
may be passed in the interests of the government
to which he is subject, and Catholics of the other
nations would naturally view with suspicion
letters of a Pope that might merely voice the

views of a foreign civil ruler. Even to-day, when the Pope is still independent because of his continued protest against the spoliation of 1870, although practically a prisoner in the Vatican, the Italian government has suppressed newspapers favoring the claims of the Holy See, and has forbidden a representative of the Pope to represent him at the Hague Conference. Napoleon's object in bringing Pius VII. to France was undoubtedly to make him a pliant tool of French interests in Europe. The sojourn of the Popes at Avignon in the fourteenth century, called the Babylonian Captivity (1309–1378), merited the protest of the Catholics of other nations, who demanded the return to Rome because of the predominant influence of France at the Papal Court.

The Pope, therefore, as ruler of Christ's Church must be independent from the very nature of his office, and this independence cannot be had to the full unless he possesses a territory—large or small, it matters not—which is entirely his own. Since the fifth century the Popes possessed political power in Rome, which finally developed into what were known as the Papal States. For centuries they held and exercised temporal power by a title better than that of any ruler of the world to-day.

In our own country we have a striking illustration of the principle on which we claim the temporal power of the Pope rests. The framers of our Constitution, to preserve the independence and free action of President and Congress, willed that a small territory called the District of Columbia should be free from any State authority, and directly dependent upon Congress. Although more numerous than the inhabitants of certain States, the citizens of the District have no representatives in Congress, and have no right to vote on national or even local issues. So in the Catholic Church: there has been for centuries a territory reserved to the Sovereign Pontiff, to preserve him independent of any temporal ruler, and insure his free and untrammelled relations with the nations of the world.

No wonder, then, that the Roman See has protested against the outrage and injustice, willed not by the Italian people but by a small body of Freemasons and anti-Christians, who now see Italy on the verge of national bankruptcy. "Qui mange du Pape en meurt"— "He who eats the Pope dies," said Thiers, as the present Italian government will one day learn. (*Amer. Cath. Quarterly*, Jan., 1892; 1886, p. 193; 1891, pp. 330, 569; Cardinal Manning, "The Temporal Power.")

What is the Catholic argument for Papal infallibility?

We have already seen that Christ established a divine, infallible authority to teach His gospel until the end of the world, just as He taught it.

Once this is admitted, it follows logically that the Supreme Head of this infallible Church must needs be infallible. For if St. Peter or his successor, speaking authoritatively to the Church, could teach false doctrine, then he would instantly cease to be the firm rock-foundation on which Christ built His Church, the gates of hell would prevail, error would be sanctioned by God in heaven (Matt. xvi. 18, 19), the prayer of Christ for Peter personally would be fruitless, for the faith of the brethren would not be strengthened (Luke xxii. 32), and the whole flock of Christ would be deprived of the true food of divine faith (John xxi. 15–17).

Does it not seem probable that if in these United States the framers of our Republic were wise enough to establish a Supreme Court to settle practically and finally all disputes regarding the Constitution, in the Church the All-Wise Son of God, foreseeing and prophesying that false teachers would arise ("For there will arise false Christs and false prophets," Mark xiii. 22), would have provided a Supreme Court to *infallibly* (else no man is bound to believe) decide every controversy about written or unwritten doctrine? What has the Protestant denial of one Pope brought about save the creating of many, and an anarchy of opinion destructive among millions of all supernatural religion whatsoever? (Lyons, "Christianity and Infallibility"; Schanz, "A Christian Apology," vol. iii. ch. xiv.)

Must Catholics believe that every utterance of the Pope is infallibly true?

By no means. The definition of the Vatican Council ("On the Church of Christ," ch. iv.) is as follows: "Therefore faithfully adhering to the traditions of the Christian faith, which has come down to us from the beginning, . . . we teach and define it to be a doctrine divinely revealed, that the Roman Pontiff when he speaks *ex cathedra*—that is, when he in the exercise of the office of pastor and doctor of all Christians, by virtue of his supreme apostolic authority, defines a doctrine regarding faith and morals to be held by the Universal Church, by the divine assistance promised him in Blessed Peter, possesses that infallibility with which the Divine Redeemer willed His Church to be endowed in the definition of a doctrine regarding faith or morals." The Pope, therefore, is infallible only:

1. When he speaks *ex cathedra—i.e.*, as supreme teacher of the Universal Church. He is not infallible as a private theologian, preacher or author, as local bishop, archbishop or primate, or as supreme legislator, judge or ruler.

2. When he *defines* a doctrine—when he gives an *absolutely final* decision.

3. When he treats of faith or morals, including the whole revealed Word of God, and all truths of philosophy and facts of history which are essential to the preservation, explanation, and defence of the content of revelation—*v. g.*, the existence of substance, the fact that St. Peter was Bishop of Rome, the interpretation of Holy Scripture and the writings of the true and false teachers of the gospel.

4. When he clearly manifests his intention to bind the Universal Church (*American Cath. Quarterly*, 1893, p. 677).

How can a man be infallible? Is that not a prerogative of God alone?

God alone is absolutely infallible, for He alone is Absolute Truth that can neither deceive nor be deceived. He can, however, for a certain purpose—for example, to maintain His Church in unity of faith—make the Pope the true mouthpiece of His gospel by divinely safeguarding him from error when he teaches the Universal Church. It is a question of fact to be learned from the witness of Scripture and history. ·

How can an intelligent man believe that the Pope is exempted from the sins common to humanity?

Catholics do not believe this. Infallibility has nothing whatever to do with the personal moral character of the Pope. He may commit sin as any other Catholic, and he is bound to use the same divine means of pardon, the sacrament of penance. There is absolutely no connection between the two ideas of *impeccability*, which means immunity from sin in keeping the moral law, and *infallibility*, or freedom from error in teaching the Church the doctrines of Christ.

Do Catholics hold that the Pope's utterances are inspired, like the Bible?

No. Inspiration implies a direct revelation of truth by the Holy Ghost, whereby God is truly the author of the written or spoken word.

Infallibility merely implies a divine assistance whereby the official teaching of the Pope is, under certain conditions, guaranteed from error.

"Some have thought that by the privilege of infallibility was intended a quality inherent in the person, whereby as an inspired man he could at any time, and on any subject, declare the truth. Infallibility is not a quality inherent in any person, but an assistance attached to an office ; and its operation . . . is not the discovery of new truths, but the guardianship of old ones. It is simply an assistance of the Spirit of Truth by whom Christianity was revealed, whereby the head of the Church is enabled to guard the original deposit of revelation, and faithfully declare it to all ages " (Manning, " Story of the Vatican Council," p. 183).

Does not your Pope pretend to make wrong right, by claiming the power of dispensation ?

The Pope makes no such claim. A dispensation is a relaxation of some law—*v. g.*, the law of fasting. A legislator has power not only to make laws, but for sufficient reason to free some from their observance. This holds good in all systems of law—*v. g.*, English licenses in mortmain. Papal dispensations—direct or delegated—are only granted for things which would not be wrong, were they not forbidden by the legislator ; they remove the prohibition, and in the particular instance the thing ceases to be wrong.

It is false to pretend, as my questioner does, that the Pope or any one can dispense from the eternal laws of God, or from essential moral duties, for these are beyond man's power to tamper with. For instance, when Henry VIII. demanded a dispensation to marry Ann Boleyn, or when Napoleon desired Pius VII. to grant a divorce to his son Jerome, the answer of both Pontiffs was that they had not the power to dispense from the law of God.

Luther, on the contrary, could dispense himself from his vows and marry a nun, although strangely enough the Lutheran lawyers of the time would not recognize his marriage ; and again, the Landgrave of Hesse found him quite willing to grant a special dispensation in favor of polygamy. But these are not Catholic principles.

If St. Peter was infallible, why did he deny the Saviour ?

Infallibility is in nowise connected with the personal errors, weakness, or sins of individual Popes, but is limited only to *ex cathedra* utterances intended for the whole Church. At any rate, the objection falls to the ground, for at the time of the denial St. Peter was not Pope, for he had not yet received the gift of Pentecost, which was necessary for the fulness of his powers.

Did not Pope Liberius subscribe to an Arian Creed ? How could a heretic be infallible ? Did he not condemn St. Athanasius as a heretic ?

It is by no means certain that Pope Liberius subscribed any Arian Creed, for the documents alleging this are of doubtful authenticity. Granting that he did, there is no certainty which one he signed. It by no means follows, therefore, that he was a heretic, for the first and third of the formulas could be understood in a Catholic sense, and were faulty because they did not expressly exclude Arianism, while Sozomen (book iv. c. 15) tells us that Liberius condemned the second, the evidently heretical one. As to the alleged anathema against St. Athanasius, Protestants grant that this letter is spurious (Smith and Wace, "Dictionary of Christian Biography," Athanasius 1, p. 192). The whole objection is not to the point, however, for all grant that if the Pope did subscribe any creed, he did so, as St. Athanasius tells us, under the fear of death. No act extorted by violence can be an *ex cathedra* act; and again, there is no evidence of his giving forth a decision on a point of faith with the express intention of making it binding upon the Universal Church. (*Dublin Review*, Oct., 1868, July, 1891 ; *Irish Eccl. Record*, April, May, June, 1888 ; *Amer. Cath. Quarterly*, vol. xix. p. 82, vol. viii., p. 529; L. Rivington, "Dependence," chap. iv.)

How could Pope Honorius be infallible when

he was condemned by the Sixth General Council
as a heretic ?

"Pope Honorius may be reproached with
having encouraged error indirectly by not proceeding against it with timely vigor; but it
cannot be said that he defined error, which
would alone tell against the dogma. . . .
A Pope is not infallible in proceedings such as
those of Honorius, who contributed uninten-
tionally to the increase of heresy by not issu-
ing decisions against it. His letters (to Ser-
gius) contain no decision, neither do they contain any false doctrine. No decision of his
was or could be condemned as false; otherwise
the Sixth Council would have contradicted itself, for it recognized that the Holy See had at
all times the privilege of teaching truth. He
was condemned for having rendered himself
morally responsible for the spread of heresy by
having neglected to publish decisions against
it; and in this sense alone was his condemnation confirmed by Leo II." (Hergenröther,
"Church and State," vol. i. p. 83).

Even granted that the Council condemned
him, his utterances were not *ex cathedra*, for in
no less than four passages he declares that he
has no intention of defining doctrine, and far
from imposing his teaching on the Universal
Church, it was not even heard of until after his
death. Writes Cardinal Newman : "The con-

demnation of Honorius by the Council in no
sense compromises the doctrine of Papal infallibility. At the most, it only decides that
Honorius in his own person was a heretic,
which is inconsistent with no Catholic doctrine." (" Difficulties of Anglicans," vol. ii. p.
317; Cardinal Manning, " Petri Privilegium,"
part iii. appendix vi.; Hettinger, " Supremacy
of the Apostolic See," ch. xvii. pp. 83–97;
Ryder, " Catholic Controversy " ; Hergenröther, " Anti-Janus," p. 82; Pennachi, " De Ho-
norii Causa in Conc. VI.," Rome, 1870; Fran-
zelin, " De Verbo Incarnato," thesis xl.; *Dublin Review*, July, 1868, Jan., 1869, April, 1870,
July, 1872.)

Is it reasonable to expect that God would choose
wicked men like Alexander VI. to be the mouthpiece of His revelation ?

It is reasonable to expect that the Vicars
of Christ, taken as a body, would be holy men,
and in point of fact we find this is the case.
Proportionately there have been fewer bad
Popes than bad Apostles. Still the individual
wickedness of a Pope would by no means interfere with his power of teaching infallibly, which
rests not on man but on the promise of God.
Did not Balaam (Num. xxii. 38) and Caiphas
(John xi. 49, 51), although wicked men, prophesy infallibly? Did not our Lord Himself

tell the Jews of His time that the personal unworthiness of the teachers of Israel in no way
interfered with their official teaching? (Matt.
xxiii. 2, 3). Would the decision of a judge of
the Supreme Court of the United States regarding some clause of the Constitution be
void because of his immoral private life?

**How could an infallible Pope order Joan of Arc
to be burnt as a witch, while to-day another
Pope is trying to make her a saint?**

Joan of Arc was never condemned as a witch
by any Pope. The court that condemned her
was composed of French and English ecclesiastics who were enemies of France, and enemies
of the Pope, as was evident two years later at
the Council of Basle. Joan died a good Catholic, receiving Holy Communion the very morning of her execution. Time and time again
during her mock trial had she appealed ''to
our Holy Father the Pope,'' but her unjust
judge, the unscrupulous Bishop of Beauvais,
refused her appeal. Within twenty-five years
after her death, Pope Calixtus III. declared
the nullity of the trial and the innocence of
Joan, and ordered a trial of rehabilitation,
which on July 7, 1456, declared her innocent
of all the charges against her.

**How in the face of history can you hold the
dogma of Papal infallibility when every one**

knows that two Popes, Paul V. and Urban VIII., officially declared the Copernican system held by the great astronomer Galileo to be false, heretical, and contrary to the Word of God ?

Does not his cruel treatment and the mistakes of two infallible Popes show your infallible Church's hatred of true science and progress? For every one to-day says that Galileo was right —even Catholics.

Before answering the several questions involved in this old shibboleth of controversy let us give a cursory glance at the facts in the case, as set forth in the records of the trial, published for the first time in 1877.

In the beginning of the seventeenth century the world of scientists and theologians, with some few exceptions, believed most firmly in the Ptolemaic system of astronomy, relying on the authority of Aristotle, the Scriptures, the Fathers of the Church, theologians, and certain scientific arguments.

Galileo, professor of mathematics at the University of Padua (1599–1610), and an astronomer of note, on a visit to Rome in 1611 vigorously attacked the Ptolemaic system of astronomy then in vogue, and declared the Copernican system, put forth tentatively by Copernicus in 1543, in his work "De Revolutionibus orbium cœlestium," as the only theory in accord with both faith and science.

A letter of his to Padre Castelli, a Benedictine, setting forth his views as already published in two works ("Discourse on Floating Bodies," 1612; "The Solar Spots," 1613), was sent to the Congregation of the Index by the Dominican Father Lorini, Feb. 15, 1615.

After a private discussion by a special committee, the two following propositions of Galileo were condemned:

1st. That the sun is the centre of the world and altogether immovable.

2d. The earth is not the centre of the world, nor immovable, but revolves of itself in diurnal motion.

The first proposition was declared "stupid and absurd in philosophy, and formally heretical, inasmuch as it expressly contradicted the words of Holy Scripture in many passages, according to the sense of the text and the common interpretation and opinion of the holy fathers and learned theologians."

The second "received the same censure in philosophy, and theologically was declared to be at least erroneous in faith."

Pope Paul V. then ordered Cardinal Bellarmin to summon Galileo before him, and ask him, under threat of imprisonment, utterly to renounce his theory and to cease teaching or defending it in any form. This Galileo consented to do.

The decree of the Roman Inquisition published March 5, 1616, declared the doctrine of Copernicus false and absolutely contrary to the Scriptures, removed from circulation the book of Copernicus, that of Astunica and others of the same school, until corrected. The text of this decree continued in all the editions of the Index—in full or in abstract—until suppressed by Benedict XIV. in 1757.

In 1622 Galileo wrote his "Saggiatore"—a thinly-veiled defence of the Copernican system—which he dedicated to Pope Urban VIII., and in 1632 his famous "Dialogo," which was an evident defiance of the old decree of the Inquisition.

The master of the Sacred Palace at Rome wrote the printers of Florence to suppress this work, and Galileo was cited before the Inquisition for trial. After considerable delay (Oct. 1, 1632–Feb. 13, 1633) Galileo arrived in Rome, and resided with Nicolini, the ambassador of the Duke of Tuscany. In the course of his trial, given out in the interests of the truth by the Holy See in 1877, and published by H. de l'Epinois, "Les pièces du procès de Galilée" (Paris, 1877), Von Gebler, "Les actes du procès de Galilée" (Stuttgart, 1877), and others, Galileo was asked: 1st, Did his book ("Dialogo") teach the Copernican theory condemned in 1616? and 2d, Did he hold that theory? The first question, after some hesitancy, was answered in the affirmative by Galileo ; with regard to the second, he declared that prior to 1616 he held that both theories were probably true, and that after 1616 he held merely the Ptolemaic.

Soon after, at the Dominican Convent, his condemnation was read by seven cardinals, and Galileo in their presence made abjuration on the Gospels of all false doctrine in general and of the Copernican system in particular.

The favorite piece of old controversy dating from 1761 ("*E pure si muove*—but it does move"), as well as the use of torture, is given the lie direct by the published records of the trial. Galileo's prison, moreover, was not the dark, terrible dungeon evolved out of the controversial imagination, but successively the palace of his friend, the Grand Duke of Tuscany, at Rome ; the palace of his friend, Archbishop Piccolomini, at Siena, and his own villa of Arcetri, near Florence.

The condemnation of Galileo has been brought forward ever since the Reformation as disproving the dogma of Papal infallibility ; but illogically and wrongly, as even fair-minded Protestants admit.

Thus, the astronomer Proctor ("Knowledge," vol. ix. p. 274) writes : "The Catholic doctrine on the subject [of Papal infallibility] is perfectly definite; and it is absolutely certain that the decision in regard to Galileo's teaching, shown now to have been unsound, does not in the slightest degree affect the doctrine of infallibility, either of the Pope or of the Church. . . . The decision was neither *ex cathedra* nor addressed to the whole Church; in not one single point does the case illustrate this doctrine of Papal infallibility as defined by the Vatican Council.''

Another Protestant, Karl Von Gebler, in his work '' Galileo Galilei and the Roman Curia,'' writes to the same effect: '' We grant that the two congregations of the Index and the Inquisition, with the two Popes who sanctioned and promulgated their decrees, were in error; but no one ever held that the decisions of the Roman congregations were in themselves infallible, even when approved by the Pope, unless specially set forth by the Pope with all the conditions required for an *ex cathedra* definition.''

This is the teaching of Catholic theologians of the seventeenth as well as of the twentieth century.

Thus, Caramuel in his '' Theologia Fundamentalis,'' published in Lyons, 1676, declared that if the Copernican system should one day prove true, ''it could never be said that the Church had been in error, as the doctrine of the double motion of the earth had never been condemned by an œcumenical council, nor by the Pope speaking *ex cathedrà*, but only by the tribunal of cardinals '' (cited by J. Bagshawe, '' The Church,'' p. 134).

So Tanquery in his ''Synopsis Theologiæ Dogmaticæ,'' published in New York, 1897, writes : '' We readily grant that these congregations were wrong in condemning Galileo, . . . and that the two Popes (Paul V. and Urban VIII.) erred, not only as private persons, but as the heads of these congregations, whose decrees were valueless unless approved by the Pope. But the decisions of the congregations, even when approved by the Supreme Pontiff, are not infallible, unless the Pope makes them his own, and promulgates them in his own name, with all the conditions required for an *ex cathedra* definition. This was not done in the present case, . . . nor can any theologian of repute be brought forward who declared these decrees to be infallible definitions '' (vol. i. p. 477).

The very insistence on the one case of Galileo out of 1900 years of history proves to all fair-minded non-Catholics the falsity of the accusation that the Church is opposed to science. For Galileo was honored by the greatest churchmen and scholars of his day for his scientific knowledge and discoveries. It was his bitter attacks on the defenders of the commonly received Ptolemaic system, and his appeal to the Scriptures as proof, that brought about his condemnation. We must put ourselves in the stand-point of the sixteenth, and not of the twentieth century, remembering that the scientific arguments adduced by Galileo by no means proved the Copernican system. Many facts that we possess to-day—*v.g.*, the phenomena of aberration, the depression of the earth at the poles, the variations of the pendulum according to latitude, etc.—were utterly unknown to Galileo and his contemporaries.

If Galileo's condemnation proves the Church's hostility to science, how is it that two centuries before that Nicholas Cusa, the first defender of the Copernican theory, was made Cardinal by Pope Nicholas V., and Bishop of Brixen, while Copernicus himself was made professor in the Pope's university at Rome in 1500, and given a life pension by Paul III.? Moreover the decrees against Galileo did not hinder in the least scientific advance in Italy; but at Rome, Florence, and Bologna we find Catholic names by the score illustrious in the history of scientific discovery. (Jaugey, "Diction. d'Apologétique," Galilée; H. de l'Epinois, "Les pièces du procès de Galilée," Paris, 1877, "La Question de Galilée," Paris, 1878; Von Gebler, "Les actes du procès de Galilée," Stuttgart, 1877; Berti, "Le procès de Galilée," Rome,

1878 ; Schanz, " Galileo Galilei et son procès," Wurzburg, 1878 ; Bouquard, " Galilée son procès, sa condemnation, et les Cong. Rom.," Paris, 1886 ; *Dublin Review*, July, 1838, October, 1865, April and July, 1871 ; *Catholic World*, January, 1869, October, 1887.)

How could one Pope (Clement XIV., 1773) suppress the Jesuits, and another (Pius VII., 1814) restore them, and yet both be infallible in their opposite decrees?

Infallibility does not belong to the Pope as supreme legislator or judge in matters of discipline, but only as supreme teacher in defining doctrine to be held by the Universal Church, as explained above. He is by no means infallible, therefore, either in suppressing a religious order or in restoring it, and so Catholics can answer that the Pope may in such cases have erred. (Alzog, vol. iii. 562–572, 683; *American Cath. Quarterly*, 1888, p. 696.)

Does not your dogma of infallibility give the Pope to-day the power he so arbitrarily exercised in the Middle Ages of deposing sovereigns, and absolving peoples from their allegiance?

The deposing power has nothing whatsoever to do with the dogma of infallibility. Pius IX. in a letter to the Roman Academy (July 20, 1871) fully answers this objection. " This

right," he says, " has without doubt been
exercised by the Supreme Pontiffs from time
to time in crucial circumstances; but it has
nothing to do with Papal infallibility, neither
does it flow therefrom, but from the authority
of the Pope. Moreover, the exercise of this
right in those ages of faith which regarded the
Pope as the Supreme Judge of Christendom,
and recognized the great advantages of his
tribunal in the great contests of peoples and
of sovereigns, was freely extended by public
jurisprudence and the common consent of nations to the most important interests of states
and of their rulers. But altogether different
are the conditions of the present time ; and
malice alone can confound things so diverse,
viz., the infallible judgment concerning the
truths of divine revelation with the right which
the Popes exercised in virtue of their authority when the common good demanded it."

We must be careful not to view the Middle
Ages with the eyes of the twentieth century.
Then Christendom was a society of Catholic
nations, acknowledging one only faith under
the supremacy of the Pope, the Vicar of Christ.
Everywhere in the public jurisprudence of the
time his right to depose sovereigns was acknowledged without question. He was made
supreme arbiter in the Ages of Faith, to safeguard the people against the tyranny of their

rulers. To say that the Popes exercised this power arbitrarily is to give the lie to history. On the contrary, the Popes only acted in virtue of the public law, and in cases where a ruler had violated his coronation oath, or set at naught all laws, both human and divine.

The action of the Popes may be justly compared to the impeachment of the President of the United States as laid down in the Constitution. Again, the same principle is voiced in the Declaration of Independence: " We, therefore, the representatives of the United States of America, in general council assembled, . . . do solemnly publish and declare that these united colonies, . . . *are absolved from all allegiance* to the British Crown, and that all political connection between them and the State of Great Britain is, and ought to be, totally dissolved."

Is it true that according to Catholic teaching the State ought to be subject to the Church ?

How can Catholics give this country an undivided allegiance when they are subject to a foreign power ?

If the law of the Pope should conflict with the laws of the United States, which would you obey ?

The Catholic doctrine on the relations of Church and State are thus set forth in Leo

XIII.'s Encyclical on the "Christian Constitution of States":

"The Almighty, therefore, has appointed the charge of the human race between two powers—the ecclesiastical and the civil; the one being set over divine, the other over human things. Each in its kind is supreme; each has fixed limits within which it is contained, which are defined by the nature and the special object of the province of each, so that there is, we may say, an orbit traced out within which the action of each is brought into play by its own native right; but inasmuch as each of these two powers has authority over the same subjects, and as it might come to pass that one and the same thing—related differently, but still remain one and the same thing—might belong to the jurisdiction and determination of both, therefore God, who foresees all things and who is the Author of these two powers, has marked out the course of each in right correlation of the other. For the powers that are, are ordained of God (Rome xiii. 1)." And further on he marks clearly the connection: "One of the two has for its proximate and chief object the well-being of this mortal life; the other, the everlasting joys of heaven. Whatever, therefore, in things human is of a sacred character, whatever belongs either of its own nature or by reason of the end to which it is referred, to the salvation of souls, or to the worship of God; is subject to the power and judgment of the Church. Whatever is to be ranged under the civil and political order is rightly subject to the civil authority. Jesus Christ has Himself given command that what is Cæsar's is to be rendered to Cæsar, and what belongs to God is to be rendered to God " (Luke xx. 25).

The Catholic Church teaches that no man's allegiance to the State is absolute and undivided, but must always be limited by conscience and the law of God.

Patriotism—love for country in all things not opposed to the law of God—is with the Catholic not a mere caprice or emotional feeling, but a positive religious duty, commanded by Jesus Christ and His Apostles (Luke xx. 25; Rome xiii. 1–4; I. Pet. ii. 13–15).

If the laws of the State go counter to Christianity, then of course the Catholic says with St. Peter, even though it mean death: "We ought to obey God rather than men" (Acts v. 29). Thus, frequently in the course of history loyalty to Christ meant disobedience to a State that taught anti-Christian principles, or exacted obedience to an iniquitous law, as the sacrifice to the gods of pagan Rome in the early days of the Church, the attempt in England in penal days to enforce attendance at

Protestant worship and to exact the denial of the Pope's supremacy in things spiritual, or the permission of divorce contrary to the Scriptures (Mark x. 2–12).

The Pope, as the universal Pontiff of the Christian Church, does not claim any right to interfere in purely temporal affairs, so that the A.P.A.'s denial of the loyalty of Catholics to their country because in the things of God they knew and believed that the Roman Pontiff was their head in spirituals, arose from ignorance of the very first principles of Catholicism.

For suppose—to take an impossible case—the Pope had commanded all the Catholic soldiers and sailors in the American army and navy not to fight for their country against Spain in the late Spanish-American War, they would on Catholic principles be perfectly justified in refusing compliance. When in the Middle Ages the Popes were temporal princes, we find Catholic princes and peoples making no scruple in opposing them on merely political lines, while fully acknowledging their supremacy in spirituals.

At the time of the Spanish Armada there was not the slightest question of the loyalty of English Catholics, even though they were being persecuted to the death.

As a matter of fact, the Catholics of these

United States have ever been ready to rally by
the thousands to their country's defence in time
of danger, from the American Revolution down
to the late war with Spain. It is good to recall the address of George Washington thank-
ing the Catholics of his day for their loyalty :
" I hope ever to see America among the foremost nations in examples of justice and liberality. And I presume that your fellow-citizens
will not forget the patriotic part which you
took in the accomplishment of their Revolution
and the establishment of their government, or
the important assistance they received from a
nation in which the Roman Catholic faith is
professed " (Sparks's Washington, vol. xii.;
Cardinal Newman's and Manning's answer to
Gladstone's " Vatican Decrees " ; Hergenröther, " Church and State " ; Archbishop Keane,
"Loyalty to Rome and Country " ; *American
Cath. Quarterly*, 1890, p. 509.

THE DOCTRINE OF JUSTIFICATION.

Does not St. Paul teach : " Therefore we conclude that a man is justified by faith without
the deeds of the law " ? (Rom. iii. 28).

" St. Paul here contends," writes Moehler,
" against the Jews of his own time, who obsti-
nately defended the eternal duration of the
Mosaic law, and asserted that, not needing a

Redeemer from sin, they became righteous and acceptable before God by that law alone. In opposition to this opinion, St. Paul lays down the maxim, that it is not by the works (deeds) of the law, *i.e.*, not by a life regulated by the Mosaic precepts, man is enabled to obtain the favor of Heaven; but only through faith in Christ, which has been imparted to us by God for wisdom, for sanctification, for righteousness, and for redemption. Unbelief in the Redeemer, and confidence in the fulfilment of the law performed, through natural power alone, on the one hand, and faith in the Redeemer and the justice to be conferred by God on the other (Rom. i. 17, x. 3; Phil. iii. 9)—these, and not faith in the Redeemer, and the good works emanating from its power, constitute the two points of opposition contemplated by the Apostle" ("Symbolism," ch. iii. sec. xxii. p. 165).

The Scriptures clearly show that man cannot be saved by faith alone, but by that living, vital faith that produces good works.

"If thou wilt enter into life, keep the commandments" (Matt. xix. 17).

"Seest thou that faith did co-operate with his works, and by works faith was made perfect? . . . Do you see that by works a man is justified, and not by faith only? . . . For even as the body without the spirit is dead,

so also faith without works is dead" (James
ii. 22–26).

"If I should have all faith, so that I could
remove mountains, and have not charity, I am
nothing" (I. Cor. xiii. 1, 2).

"Not every one who saith to me, 'Lord,
Lord,' shall enter into the kingdom of heaven,
but he that doth the will of my Father, who is
in heaven" (Matt. vii. 21).

When St. Paul declares, "Therefore being
justified by faith, we have peace with God
through our Lord Jesus Christ" (Rom. v. 1),
he plainly means, "For in Christ Jesus
neither circumcision availeth anything, nor
uncircumcision; but faith that worketh by
charity" (Gal. v. 6).

The old Protestant doctrine which attributes
to faith alone the power of saving has not the
slightest warrant in Scripture. "Love must
already vivify faith, before the Catholic Church
will say that through it man is truly pleasing
to God. Faith in love, and love in faith, justify; they form here an inseparable unity. This
justifying faith is not merely negative, but
positive withal; not merely a confidence that,
for Christ's sake, the forgiveness of sins will be
obtained, but a sanctified feeling, in itself agreeable to God. Charity is undoubtedly, according to Catholic doctrine, a fruit of faith. But
faith justifies *only when it has already* brought

forth this fruit" (Moehler's "Symbolism," ch. iii. sec. xix. pp. 146–7; *cf.* pp. 115–153).

What do you think of the doctrine of total depravity ?

It was the doctrine of Luther and Calvin that human nature, because of original sin, became essentially corrupt, so that men could neither think, speak, do, or love anything but evil. "Sin is not an act or a phenomenon of our nature," taught Luther; "it is our very nature, and our whole being itself." "All that you can do begins in sin, remains in sin; it may appear ever so good and pretty; you can do nothing but sin, act as you please."

And Calvin says : "There remains this indubitable truth which no artifice can shake, that the mind of man is so far alienated from God's justice that he violently conceives, desires, and strives after nothing that is not impious, fallacious, filthy, impure. His heart is so filled with poison, that it breathes forth nothing but stench." (*Cf.* Presbyterian Confession of Faith, 1827, Art. xi.; Anglican Articles, viii.; quoted by Hecker, "Aspirations of Nature," ch. xix., p. 142, 145, 146, etc.)

The Catholic Church in the Council of Trent condemned this dreadful doctrine of the Reformers, which made God the author of evil (Sess. vi., De Just., can. 5–7). She declares that man is made to the image and likeness of God, essentially good, with reason to know the truth and free will to choose the good, and that the fall left man's reason and free will essentially uninjured. The supernatural always builds upon the natural. If human nature were essentially corrupt man would be incapable of the supernatural (see "Aspirations of Nature," xxvi. xxvii.; Moehler's "Symbolism," ch. ii.)

Of course Protestants of to-day, as a rule, repudiate the teachings of Luther and Calvin regarding total depravity, and the sinfulness of good works. Indeed, thousands have by an inevitable reaction from this fearful doctrine come to deny altogether the fact of original sin, the necessity of faith, or the existence of a supernatural order. This is the Nemesis of error.

What is the Catholic doctrine of merit?

Do you teach that men merit heaven by their good works? How, then, is salvation absolutely free? "By grace are ye saved through faith; and that not of yourselves; it is the gift of God. Not of works, lest any man should boast" (Eph. ii. 8, 9).

The Council of Trent thus sets forth the Catholic teaching: "Eternal life is to be proposed to those who do good unto the end and hope in God, both *as a grace* mercifully promised to the children of God through Jesus Christ, and *as a reward* to be faithfully rendered to their good works and merits, in virtue of the promise of God. . . .

"For since Christ Jesus Himself constantly communicates His virtues to those who are justified, as the head to the members, and as the vine to the branches (John xv. 4) ;—which virtue always precedes, accompanies, and follows their good works, and without which they could be nowise agreeable to God and meritorious,—we must believe that nothing more is wanting to the justified, nor is there any reason why they should not be considered as having fully satisfied the divine law, as far as the condition of this life admits, by such works as are done in God, and truly merited the attainment of eternal life in due time, if they die in the state of grace" (Trent, De Just., Sess. vi. cap. xvi.)

Catholics believe that eternal life is indeed a free gift of God's mercy and love, won for us by Christ's death ; but God having promised it as a reward to those who love and serve Him, we can by performing good works through God's grace really merit the glory in heaven.

The Scriptures continually speak of God giving us eternal blessedness as a reward due to merit:

"Be glad and rejoice, for your reward is very great in heaven" (Matt. v. 12).

"There is no man that hath left home . . . who shall not receive . . . in the world to come life everlasting" (Luke xviii. 29, 30).

"God, who shall render to every man according to his works. To them indeed, who according to patience in good work seek glory, . . . eternal life" (Rom. ii. 6, 7).

"He that soweth in the spirit, of the spirit shall reap life everlasting. And in doing good let us not fail, for in due time we shall reap, not failing" (Gal. vi. 8, 9).

"I have fought a good fight. I have finished my course. I have kept the faith. As to the rest, there is laid up for me a crown of justice, which the Lord, the just Judge, will render to me in that day" (II. Tim. iv. 7, 8; *cf.* Matt. xxv. 34; I. Tim. vi. 18; Apoc. xiv. 12).

Protestants frequently believe that Catholics ascribe the merit of their good works to themselves and not to Jesus Christ, the Saviour. This is not the fact. Catholics believe that no natural act can merit eternal salvation; that we can do nothing for heaven without the merits of Jesus Christ, the one Mediator, and the grace of God won for us all by His redemption. "Our sufficiency is from God" (II. Cor. iii. 5). "Without Me you can do nothing" (John xv. 5). Every good work we do is the effect of the Holy Ghost, and our free will co-operating with Him. " By the grace of God I am what I am; and His grace in me hath not been void, but I have labored more abundantly than all they; yet not I, but the grace of God with me " (I. Cor. xv. 10). " As ink is required for the pen," says St. Thomas Aquinas, "so the grace of the Holy Ghost is necessary to inscribe the virtues in our souls."

What do Catholics mean by "works of super- erogation "? I hold that no matter what a man does, he still falls far short of his duty, accord- ing to the word of Christ: " When ye shall have done all those things which are commanded you, say : We are unprofitable servants " (Luke xvii. 10).

Works of supererogation are those not posi- tively commanded, but counselled by the law of Christ. Such, for example, are the three counsels of poverty, chastity, and obedience, freely embraced by those who wish more per- fectly to follow the Master (Matt. xix. 12– 21; I. Cor. vii. 25). Thus, the early Chris- tians were not obliged to sell their possessions and hand over the proceeds to the Apostles (Acts v. 4), but they did so out of love for Jesus Christ, who declared voluntary poverty to be a counsel of the perfect life (Matt. xix. 21).

" The consciousness of being in the possession of an all-sufficing, infinite power ever discloses the tenderer and nobler relations of man to God, and to his fellow-creatures ; so that the man sanctified in Christ, and filled with His spirit, ever feels himself superior to the law.   It is the nature of heaven-born love— which stands so far, so infinitely far, above the claims of the mere law, never to be content with its own doings, and ever to be more ingenious in its devices; so that Christians of this stamp not unfrequently appear to men of a lower grade of perfection as enthusiasts, men of heated fancy and distempered mind.   It is only in this way that remarkable doctrine can be satisfactorily explained, which certainly, like every other which hath for centuries existed in the world, and seriously engaged the human mind, is sure to rest on some deep foundation—the doctrine, namely, that there can be works which are more than sufficient (*opera supererogationis*)—a doctrine, the tenderness and delicacy whereof eluded, indeed, the perception of the Reformers ; for they could not even once rise above the idea that man could ever become free from immodesty, unjust wrath, avarice, and the rest " (Moehler, " Symbolism," ch. iii. sec. xxiii. p. 168).

Catholics know full well that the love of God essential for salvation is comprised in the words of the Saviour: "If thou wilt enter into life, keep the commandments" (Matt. xix. 17) ; that Christian humility demands of every one the recognition of his sins against God (I. John i. 8) ; that no good works of their own can ever merit the grace of justification, and the right to God's Kingdom, which come through Christ's passion and death upon the cross. But, on the other hand, the Scriptures clearly teach, and Christian antiquity is witness thereof, that there is an essential distinction between the commandments of God and the evangelical counsels, and that many saints by the following of poverty, chastity, and obedience, and the practice of heroic virtue, have obtained many graces and helps for their weaker brethren of the Communion of Saints. In this sense St. Paul could say: "Who now rejoice in my sufferings for you, and fill up those things that are wanting of the sufferings of Christ in my flesh for His body, which is the Church" (Col. i. 24).

PRAYER.

Is not prayer an asking God to change the laws of nature He Himself established ?

Is it not absurd to ask God to change His mind, when He knows what is best for us ?

St. Thomas Aquinas thus answers this difficulty (" Summa," 2a. 2ae. q. 83. a. 2) : "In proclaiming the utility of prayer, we are not to be understood as putting any restraint on human acts subject to Divine Providence, nor are we supposing any change in the ordinances of God. Divine Providence has determined in advance, not only the effects which are to be produced, but also their order and the causes which are to produce them. Among these causes are included human acts. Man, therefore, must do something, not indeed to change by his acts the arrangement of God, but to concur in producing certain effects in accordance with the divine dispensation. Just as it is with regard to physical causes, so it is too with regard to prayer. The aim of prayer is not to alter the designs of God, but to ask that we may obtain what God had determined to grant us by our prayers." (Card. Gibbons, " Our Christian Heritage," ch. ix.; *American Cath. Quarterly*, 1896, p. 491.)

Does not prayer encourage laziness and make people neglect doing what they should do themselves?

Not in the slightest. The intelligent Christian who prays earnestly for the cure of a sick friend does not neglect to employ a good physician also. The good priest who prays hard for the conversion of sinners does not neglect the personal visit and the word of advice, warning, encouragement, or threat. He knows that God wishes us to use every natural means at our disposal, but he knows also that God has given us the supernatural help of prayer. And so every nation has prayed, even though its religion or philosophy gave the lie , thereto; so deeply rooted in the human heart is the belief in a supernatural help vouchsafed man for the asking.

Our objector has in mind, undoubtedly, the superstitious fanaticism of the Dowieties, for example, who, contrary to Christian principles, neglect the use of remedies in curing diseases ; or perhaps the Christian Scientists, who speak of prayer, although their denial of a personal God makes the term a mockery.

Why tell God our needs when God knows them beforehand ?

The object of prayer is not to inform God of our necessities or of our inmost sentiments of love, praise, sorrow, or thanksgiving, for He, the Omniscient One, knows all the secrets of our hearts.

The Christian prays, however, to fulfil a duty written in the heart of man and insisted on constantly by the Son of God. The elemental principle of religion is the acknowledgment of God as our Creator, Lord, and Final

Destiny, and our utter dependence upon him. The revelation of Jesus Christ, unfolding to us so many new proofs of that Creator's love, makes this acknowledgment the more imperative.

The Son of God teaches us how to praise, bless, adore, thank, and crave pardon of God, and promises us favors through the invocation of His holy name: "If you ask the Father anything in my name, he will give it to you" (John xvi. 23).

Why do not Catholics pray as the heart dictates, instead of always repeating a certain number of set prayers?

Because our Lord taught us the beauty and efficacy of special prayers in that most perfect of all prayers, the Our Father (Luke xi. 1-4). The Catholic Church, teaching in His name and with His divine authority, has followed His example in sanctioning many other beautiful prayers, as the Hail Mary, the Creed, the Confiteor, the prayers of the Mass, the Angelus, the Rosary, etc., in order that the members of a universal society may have in the unity of common prayer a common bond of devotion to God and His saints.

Our objector must not forget, however, that besides vocal prayer, there exists in the Catholic Church the higher forms of mental and con-

templative prayer, in which great saints, like
St. Paul, St. Teresa, St. Catharine, excelled.
We recommend to his careful study some of
our elementary books on Christian Perfection,
which will open a new field of vision into the
spiritual life of Catholics. (*Cf.* Baker's "Holy
Wisdom," Lallemant's "Spiritual Doctrine,"
Hilton's "Scale of Perfection," St. Teresa's
Autobiography, à Kempis' "Following of
Christ," the works of St. John of the Cross, etc.)

**Is not a broken and a contrite heart a better
offering to God than a thousand repetitions of
prayer?**

**Did not Jesus rebuke repetitions in prayer,
saying: "Use not vain repetitions as the heathens do"? (Matt. vi. 7).**

Our questioner must distinguish between two
kinds of repetition. There is in the house
near me as I write a parrot who repeats by the
hour, with all the different changes of inflection
and without the slightest spark of intelligence,
"How do you do?" "Bad—bad—bad boy!"
"Hello, Polly!" "Good-by," etc. So it is
possible some people pray parrot-like without
thinking of God at all. This manner of praying our Lord rebukes when He said: "This
people honoreth Me with their lips, but their
heart is far from Me" (Matt. xv. 8; Is. xxix.
13).

But there is, on the other hand, the oft-repeated "I love you" of the mother speaking to the babe at her breast, which loses none of its force in the repeating, but rather intensifies the love of that mother's heart by outward expression. Such the repeated prayer to God of the devout soul—be it a prayer of praise, adoration, thanksgiving, petition, or sorrow for sin.

A contrite heart is essential to forgiveness, both for the Catholic who confesses his sins to an apostolic priesthood, vested with divine authority to pardon (John xx. 23), and the one, who, unable to confess, is bound to make a perfect act of love of God to obtain pardon. The voicing of that sorrow in heart-felt words, no matter how often repeated, is both rational and scriptural.

Our Lord never rebuked in the slightest degree repetitions of prayer. The text of old-time controversy—Matt. vi. 7—is mistranslated in the Protestant version. The literal original Greek is "speak not much," while the untrue Protestant paraphrase, "Use not vain repetitions," is read into the text by designing men who sought some scriptural basis for an attack upon the Church. On the contrary, Christ Himself exhorts us to repetition in prayer in the parable of the unjust judge (Luke xviii. 3-8) and the importunate friend (Luke xi.

5–8). In the Garden He repeats His prayer to the Father three times : " And He prayed a third time, saying the self-same words " (Matt. xxvi. 39, 42, 44). In heaven the angels never tire of repeating day and night " Holy, Holy, Holy, Lord God Almighty " (Is. vi. 3 ; Apoc. iv. 8). The repeated prayer of the blind man, " Son of David, have mercy upon me " (Matt. xx. 31 ; Mark x. 48 ; Luke xviii. 39), was answered by the gift of sight (*cf.* Ps. cxxxv.)

What, then, does our Lord condemn ? It is the much speaking, or the "long prayers," of the Pharisees (Matt. xxiii. 14 ; Mark xii. 40 ; Luke xx. 46, 47), not because of their mere length, but because of the motive of the Pharisees in praying : " For all their works they do to be seen of men " (Matt. xxiii. 5).

The hypocritical Pharisees prayed just as they gave alms and fasted (Matt. vi. 1–8 ; Mark xii. 38 ; Luke xxi. 1), to awaken public admiration. They prayed long, elaborately-composed prayers just as the heathens did, of whom St. Augustine wrote : " And truly all much speaking comes from the Gentiles, who give more attention to the elegant delivery of their prayers than to the cleansing of their souls."

Neither the heathens nor the Pharisees prayed silly " vain repetitions," as Protestants imagine, for these would never have been such a source of pride. Their extempore prayer was rather on the order of certain Protestant ministers to-day whose public prayers are really speeches for the congregation, affording an opportunity for the display of their literary ability. So a Unitarian convert, now a priest, told me that the prayer of the Unitarian minister in the church he attended in Boston years ago used to be elaborately prepared, and discussed afterwards by the people. "What a beautiful prayer! What a poor effort to-day! etc." This kind of praying, when it is merely of the lips and not from the heart, is what our Lord condemns. "True prayer," says St. Gregory, commenting on the text in question (Matt. vi. 7), "consists rather in the bitter groans of repentance than in the resounding periods of an oration" (J. F. Sheahan, "Vain Repetitions," Cathedral Library Association, New York).

Why are not all our prayers answered, when Christ said, "If you ask the Father anything in my name, He will give it to you"? (John xvi. 23).

What did you pray for?—temporal blessings? We have a right to ask God for health, success, fortune, and the like, according to our Lord's own words: "Give us this day our daily bread" (Matt. vi. 11), but He often refuses what we ask, because He knows it would keep us from His love here and His kingdom hereafter. If a sick bed brought us close to God, while health would make us forget Him ; if failure humiliated us and forced us to turn to God for comfort, while success would puff us up with self-sufficiency ; if poverty made us friends of the poor Christ, while riches would render us full of avarice, lust, and irreligion, then God, foreseeing all this, grants our petitions for these temporal favors by not giving us what we ask for. We in our ignorance. may not understand the reason why; God knows what is best for us all.

Did you pray for spiritual blessings for others, viz., the conversion of a friend or relative ? Your prayers were not unheeded, for God undoubtedly poured forth His grace in superabundant measure upon the soul you loved. There may be no outward sign of the efficacy of your prayer, but who knows the secret workings of God ? Undoubtedly man has the power to resist God's grace unto the end. He wants a free service and will compel no man to serve Him. But constant prayer has melted many a hard heart, as Christians know full well.

Have you prayed for yourself, "Forgive us our trespasses ; lead us not into temptation, but deliver us from evil," with humility, faith, love, and sorrow for sin? God never refuses such prayers.

Most important, too, is the manner in which you prayed. If, for instance, while your lips framed some careless, mechanical prayer, your heart was bent upon other things, could you expect God to answer you?

You would not dare to speak thus to a friend you loved dearly.

"This people honoreth me with their lips; but their heart is far from me" (Matt. xv. 8).

Again, our Lord taught us to pray with *humility*, realizing well our sins and unworthiness, and our utter dependence upon Him. Some people demand favors of God as a right, and blaspheme His holy Name for not answering at once. "The prayer of him that humbleth himself shall pierce the clouds" (Ecclus. xxxv. 21; *cf.* the parable of the Pharisee and the Publican, Luke xviii. 10–14).

Other conditions on which He insists are faith, confidence, and perseverance, by which, despite every difficulty, one continues to ask of God every needful grace of body and soul; consider the woman of Chanaan (Matt. xv. 22–28), the parable of the importunate friend (Luke xi. 5–8), the unjust judge (Luke xviii. 2–5; xi. 9–13).

Why don't Catholics finish the Lord's Prayer?
Why is our " Our Father " different from yours?

Catholics do finish the Lord's Prayer. They repeat it as the Saviour taught it, without any human additions. The words "for thine is the kingdom, and the power, and the glory for ever," in the King James version of Matt. vi. 13, are not found in the most ancient manuscripts of the New Testament, and were rejected by St. Jerome in the fourth century in his edition of the Vulgate, as they are rejected to-day by Protestant scholars ; *v. g.*, the Protestant revised version of 1881, the Greek text of Westcott and Hort, etc. The words in question are a marginal gloss interpolated by some copyist, who while writing had in mind those words of the Greek liturgy which are probably borrowed from a passage in the Old Testament.

In Luke xi. 2-4 the King James version omits the above gloss.

THE SACRAMENTS.

What do you mean by a sacrament?

A sacrament is a visible sign permanently instituted by Jesus Christ to signify and confer grace upon men. Three things are necessary for a sacrament: 1st, the sensible sign, as in Baptism the outward washing of the body with the invocation of the Blessed Trinity ; 2d.

the inward grace signified and conferred, as in Baptism, the cleansing of original sin and actual sin if it exists; and 3d, institution by Jesus Christ.

The chief reason of the sacraments is the will of Jesus Christ manifested in the gospels, and infallibly witnessed to by His Church. It is perfectly in accord with man's nature that sensible things should be made by God the stepping-stones to things supernatural. The whole idea of the Incarnation is "a redemption of the internal through the external" (George Tyrrell, S.J., "External Religion," ch. i. B. Herder, 1900), and the sacraments are merely the application to the individual soul of the fruits of the Incarnation. They are the seven precious channels of the blood and merits of the atonement, flowing from the cross upon the hearts of sinful men to wash away their sins, and give them the life of grace which Christ died to gain. They give the Church, a visible society, a visible bond of union, and visible witness, especially baptism and the Eucharist, to the oneness of her children in the faith and love of Christ. Practically speaking, they have helped religion wonderfully, for they give certain, concrete, and ready helps to uproot sin from the hearts of men, and to promote, as in the Blessed Sacrament, the highest love for and the closest union with Jesus Christ. (Humphrey, "The One Mediator"; Wilhelm–Scannell, "A Manual of Theology," vol. ii.; Hunter, "Outlines of Theology," vol. iii.)

Are not the sacraments mere signs or ceremonies to excite sentiments of faith and love in the heart; to mark off the Christian from the unbeliever?

No; the Council of Trent (Sess. vii.; can. 6–8) has defined that the sacraments are not merely external signs of grace, but actually confer of themselves (*ex opere operato*) the grace which they signify. The proof from Scripture is plain.

"He that believeth and is baptized shall be saved" (Mark xvi. 16).

"Unless a man be born again of water and the Holy Ghost, he cannot enter into the kingdom of God" (John iii. 5; Eph. v. 25, 26).

"Do penance and be baptized every one of you in the name of Jesus Christ for the remission of your sins, and you shall receive the gift of the Holy Ghost" (Acts ii. 38).

"They laid their hands upon them, and they received the Holy Ghost, and when Simon saw that by the imposition of the hands of the Apostles the Holy Ghost was given, etc." (Acts viii. 17–18. *Cf.* Acts xxii. 16; II. Tim. i. 6; Tit. iii. 5.)

If the sacraments were mere signs, would not the practice of infant baptism by the Church from the beginning, or by Protestants generally, be perfectly useless, as likewise the ancient custom of giving Confirmation and Holy Eucharist to children, as is still done in the East to-day. (For the Fathers, Wilhelm–Scannell, "A Manual of Catholic Theology," vol. ii. p. 363.)

Does not the teaching of your Church regarding the sacraments give to the mere performance of material rites a certain magical power ?

Not at all, for we do not believe that the sacraments act like magic to cleanse a soul from sin independently of the interior disposition of the one receiving them.

The Catholic Church demands : 1st. That a person be qualified to receive them ; for instance, an unbaptized person cannot receive the sacrament of penance, or one in good health cannot be given Extreme Unction. 2. That a person possess the necessary dispositions ; for example, a sinner who is not sorry for grievous sin from supernatural motives, or who refuses to promise not to offend God in future, cannot be pardoned in the Sacrament of Penance, and is guilty of the still greater sin of sacrilege by accepting absolution in that state of soul.

All the conditions being present, however, the sacraments do not merely signify the grace of God, but they effect the grace they signify, being channels of the grace of God, won for us by Christ's death upon the cross.

If, as your Church teaches, the efficacy of a sacrament depends on the intention of the minister, how can any one ever be certain of having received a sacrament?

We have a strong moral certainty which is practically absolute, for only an insane person would perform an action without the intention of performing it. And if perchance, through the malice or neglect of an individual, one were to be deprived of the benefit of a sacrament, God could give the grace independently thereof. (Rev. Sydney Smith, S.J., "Doctrine of Intention," Catholic Truth Society publications.)

Can any one administer the sacraments in your Church?

No; the Catholic Church believes, with St. Paul, in a ministry ordained by Christ for that purpose, and therefore limits the administration of the sacraments to those in holy orders, with the exception of baptism in cases of necessity, it being necessary for salvation— "So let a man think of us as the ministers of

Christ, and the dispensers of the mysteries of God " (I. Cor. iv. 1)—and that of matrimony, in which the parties themselves are the ministers of the sacrament, while none the less obligated to be married in the presence of their pastor.

Can a sinful man, or one who denies the Christian faith, be the minister of a valid sacrament?

Yes; for the minister acting merely as an instrument, the sacramental action derives its power and efficacy from the principal cause, God. So we read that Pope St. Stephen (A.D. 255–7) decided against St. Cyprian that the baptism conferred by heretics was valid, and that rebaptism was unlawful. Again, in the fifth century St. Augustine wrote against the Donatists, who declared that sinners could not validly baptize: "The sacrament of baptism is not dependent on the merit of those who administer it, but on Him of whom it is said, It is He who baptizes " (lib. iii. c. 4, De Baptismo; *cf.* Trent., Sess. vii. can. 12).

Two things are required in the minister of the sacrament: *attention*, for he must know what he is doing, and "the *intention* of doing what the Church does " (Trent., Sess. vii. can. 11). Thus, infidel and Jewish physicians in the hospitals of New York, who do not believe in the Catholic Church, know what a sacrament is, and believe that it is something sacred, have in cases of necessity validly baptized dying children, because they out of courtesy and respect to the wishes of Catholic priests have had the intention of performing an act held sacred by the Catholic Church.

How many sacraments are there ? We Protestants believe but two, Baptism and the Lord's Supper ?

The Catholic Church (Trent., Sess. vii. can. 1) defines that there are seven sacraments of the New Law, neither more nor less, while the doctrine of Protestants on this point is set forth in the XXV. Article of the Church of England : '' There are two sacraments ordained of Christ our Lord in the Gospel, *i. e.*, Baptism and the Supper of the Lord. Those five commonly called sacraments, *i. e.*, Confirmation, Penance, Orders, Matrimony, and the Extreme Unction, are not to be counted for sacraments of the Gospel,'' etc.

Before the Reformation it was universally maintained, by both East and West, that there were seven sacraments. Peter Lombard (lib. iv. dist. 2, Sentent.) in the twelfth century mentions them all, and the other Scholastics never question the fact. The Greeks, who discussed every possible point of variance with the Latins at the Council of Lyons (A.D. 1274) and of Florence (A.D. 1439) never doubted on this point. Indeed, the Patriarch of Constantinople, Jeremias (A.D. 1574–1581), when the German reformers sought to obtain recognition in the East, answered their appeal by expressly repudiating their new teaching, among which he mentions their doctrine of only two sacraments. That the Fathers of the Church never mention expressly the number need not surprise us, when we reflect that they never attempted to write systematic theologies. From an historical point of view, the agreement of the East and West on this matter is a sufficient proof that their doctrine was held for at least a thousand years before the Council of Trent; for what both teach surely dates from the beginning of the controversies between them. A belief as old as this is, on the argument of prescription, apostolic teaching. "Is it likely that so many and so great churches should have gone astray into one Faith? Never is there one result among many chances. The error of the churches would have taken different directions. Whatever is found to be one and the same among many persons is not an error but a tradition" (Tertullian, De Præscr., c. 28).

Did not your Church originate the seven sacraments?

By no means, for we believe that God alone is the author of grace, and only by His special appointment could material rites be made the channels of His grace to men. The Council of Trent teaches (Sess. vii. can. 1, De Sac.) that all the sacraments of the New Law were instituted by Christ. We do not hold, however, that the Saviour prescribed every detail of the ceremonies, words, and actions to be used in each sacrament, for as a matter of fact the custom of the Church on these points has varied at different times and in different places.

Is there any difference between Christian baptism and the baptism of John?

Yes; the difference defined by the Council of Trent (Sess. vii., De Bap., can. 1) was set forth expressly by John himself (Matt. iii. 11): "I indeed baptize you in water unto penance, but He that shall come after me is mightier than I. . . . He shall baptize you in the Holy Ghost and fire." The ceremony performed by John was not a sacrament at all, but aroused feelings of sorrow, which prepared the hearts of his hearers for the true sacrament of Christ, as we learn from Acts xix. 3-5.

Why do you not call the washing of the feet a sacrament? (John xiii. 4-10).

If we were to judge by the Bible only, we might fall into this error with the modern Dunkards, but the Catholic Christian has a divine, infallible interpreter of Scripture, the Church, which declares that there are but seven sacraments (Trent., Sess. vii. can. 1). The words of our Saviour are to be considered a counsel, not a commandment ; a ceremony of devotion, and not a sacrament, in this case.

Why do you hold that Baptism, Confirmation, and Holy Orders cannot be repeated?

Because they impress "a certain spiritual and indelible sign," as we learn from the definition of the Council of Trent (Sess. vii., De Sacr., can. 9), which voices the constant tradition of the Church, following the Scriptures (II. Cor. i. 21, 22 ; Eph. i. 13 ; iv. 30).

What is original sin ? Is it not unjust to hold us guilty for Adam's sin ?

"Original sin is distinguished from actual or personal sin in this : that actual or personal sin is the sin which we *personally with our own free will* commit, whilst original sin is that which our human nature committed *with the will of Adam*, in whom all our human nature was included, and with whom our human nature is united as a branch to a root, as a child to a parent, as men who partake with

Adam the same nature which we have derived from him, and as members of the same human family of which Adam was the head" (Faa di Bruno, "Catholic Belief," p. 28).

Our first parents were created in the grace and friendship of God, and endowed with great gifts of soul and body; namely, immortality, immense knowledge, perfect dominion over the passions, freedom from sickness, pain and labor, on condition of their not eating the fruit of the forbidden tree in the Garden of Eden. They disobeyed this easy commandment, and thus forfeited for themselves and their descendants sanctifying grace, all their supernatural gifts, and wounded and weakened even their natural powers.

"The supernatural end or destiny of man still held good. But he lost that original gift, the exercise of which was to enable him to attain it. He became as the eagle whose home and nest is on a peak of the Andes, and whom the trapper snares and maims, until his mighty pinions will carry him no more. . . . Henceforth man could do no work capable of meriting the life to come. Henceforth the life to come was out of his reach. . . . The child of God became a child of wrath. . . . Fallen man became the slave of the devil, to be tempted in life, to be punished after death. It was from such a state as this that man had to be saved " (Bishop Hedley, "Our Divine Saviour," Sermon iii.)

The doctrine of original sin is taught by St. Paul : " Wherefore, as by one man sin entered into this world, and by sin death, and so death passed upon all men in whom all have sinned " (Rom. v. 12).

It would indeed have been unjust had God imputed to us the personal sin of another, or deprived us of something due to human nature. But "it is not the sin of Adam inasmuch as that was personal which God imputes, but the necessary effect of his sin—that is, the deprivation, the rejection, as it were, of original justice, which Adam wilfully incurred as head of the whole human race, and which therefore we also, as united to Adam, have incurred. In this no vestige of injustice appears. Men do not thereby lose anything which their nature requires " (" Catholic Belief," p. 340). Sanctifying grace is God's free gift, which He can give or take away on conditions laid down by Himself alone. And though we are all to-day, through Adam's sin, born " children of wrath " (Eph. ii. 3), God in His infinite love gives every one ample opportunity of regaining the grace His only Son died on the cross to merit.

Does your Church hold that Baptism is abso-

lutely necessary for salvation? How can a merciful and just God allow little infants, who through no fault of theirs die unbaptized, to suffer for ever in hell fire?

The Catholic Church has defined (Trent., Sess. vii., De Bapt., can. 5) that baptism is necessary for salvation. The words of Christ are plain : " Unless a man (in the Greek *tis,* any one) be born again of water and the Holy Ghost, he cannot enter into the kingdom of God " (John iii. 5). He commands universal baptism (Matt. xxviii. 19), declaring : " He that believeth and is baptized shall be saved, but he that believeth not shall be condemned " (damned, in Protestant version ; Mark xvi. 16).

This necessity follows from the fact that all men are born " children of wrath " (Eph. ii. 3); that is, in original sin (Rom. v. 12), and need therefore the regeneration or new birth of which the Saviour speaks. This doctrine of the Church was clearly taught in the fourth century by the condemnation of the Pelagians, who denied the necessity of baptism for children.

This necessity is not strictly absolute, as we learn from Trent., Sess. vi., De Justif., can. 4, which declared that " since the promulgation of the Gospel there is no translation from the State of Old Adam to the State of Grace,

. . . without the laver of regeneration, or
the desire of it" (John iii. 5; Eph. v. 25, 26).

In cases of necessity, therefore, this baptism
of desire will suffice for salvation; and the perfect love of God (" He that loveth Me shall be
loved of My Father," John xiv. 21), and sorrow for sin, surely include the desire to fulfil
every command of Christ. Such is the teaching of St. Augustine (De Bapt., iv. 22), and
St. Ambrose in a sermon preached at Milan
on the death of the catechumen Valentinian II.

Martyrdom also, or baptism of blood, has
always been considered equivalent to baptism
of water, according to the words of Christ:
" Every one, therefore, that shall confess Me
before men, I will also confess him before My
Father who is in heaven " (Matt. x. 32). Even
unbaptized children, murdered out of hatred
for Jesus Christ, are considered saints by the
Church (see Feast of the Holy Innocents, Dec.
28). In the case of adults martyrdom must
be fully embraced, and from supernatural
motives alone. " He that shall lose his life for
Me, shall find it " (Matt. x. 39).

With regard to children who die unbaptized,
Catholics generally hold, against Calvin (Inst.,
lib. iii. ch. 23, sec. 7), that they do not suffer
any punishment. The most common teaching
on the matter is that they are indeed excluded
from heaven and the supernatural vision of

God, because they have not fulfilled the condition laid down by Christ (John iii. 5). This
privation, however, is not unjust on God's
part, for the glory of heaven is a free supernatural gift, not due to human nature; nor
does it imply suffering, for the little ones most
likely do not even know there is such a thing
as the Beatific Vision, and so know God and
rejoice in Him, as St. Thomas teaches, "by a
natural knowledge and love." We might compare them to adopted children on this earth
who, not knowing the fact of their real mother's
death, have never felt the pain of that privation.

**Is not Baptism a mere external ceremony of
initiation into the body of the Christian fellowship?**

No; this is a new doctrine of the Reformation, following logically from the doctrine of
justification by faith alone. The Catholic
Church teaches that "Baptism is a sacrament
which cleanses us from original sin, makes
us Christians, children of God, and heirs of
heaven" (Catechism of Third Plenary Council, lesson xii.) It is not a mere outward sign,
but a sign (washing of the body with the invocation of the Blessed Trinity) that of itself
signifies and confers grace, cleansing from
original sin as well as actual sin previously

committed, and imprinting on the soul a spiritual and indelible character.

Scripture with all Christian antiquity clearly expresses this notion of the sacrament of Baptism which effects our entrance into the Church of God.

" Unless a man be born again of water and the Holy Ghost, he cannot enter into the kingdom of God " (John iii. 5).

" He that believeth and is baptized shall be saved " (Mark xvi. 16).

" Going therefore, teach ye all nations, baptizing them in the name of the Father, and of the Son, and of the Holy Ghost." (Matt. xxviii. 19. *Cf.* Acts ii. 37–41, viii. 12, 16, 38, ix. 18, x. 48, xvi. 33, xviii. 8, xix. 5 ; I. Cor. i. 14, 16 ; Rom. vi. 3, 4 ; Col. ii. 12 ; I. Cor. xii. 13 ; Eph. iv. 5 ; Tit. iii. 4–7. For the Fathers see Waterworth, " Faith of Catholics," vol. ii. pp. 108–131.)

May we not understand baptism of water in a figurative sense ? Is not baptism of the Spirit sufficient ?

No, as the Church has declared (Trent., Sess. vii. can. 2). I remember on a non-Catholic mission in Jacksonville, Ill., meeting a man who assured me that the voice of the Holy Spirit had told him that he was sanctified by a spiritual baptism without any external washing of water. Of course it is as impossible to argue with such a one as with an insane man who believes himself the Emperor Napoleon.

Our Saviour clearly and emphatically declares water necessary (John iii. 5) : '' Unless a man be born again of water and the Holy Ghost '' ; and so he was understood by the Apostles (Acts viii. 27–39, x. 44–48, etc.), and ever since by the Universal Church. When, however, baptism of water is impossible because unknown, or water is unobtainable, it may be supplied by what is known as the baptism of blood or martyrdom, or the baptism of desire, which consists in the perfect sorrow which blots out sin.

Do you not read in the Scripture that many were baptized in the name of Jesus Christ? (Acts ii. 38, viii. 12–16, xix. 2–5).

Yes ; but it is plain that these words do not indicate a denial of baptism in the names of the Trinity, as laid down by Christ Himself (Matt. xxviii. 19), but rather a description of Christian baptism as opposed to John's baptism, or the various Jewish ablutions of the time. This is clear from Acts xix. 2–5.

Is it not unjust to impose the obligations of a church on children without their consent, and before they understand their import ?

Christ's baptism is not something to be accepted or rejected at will, but is an absolute necessity of salvation. No obligations, therefore, are imposed on the child, save those which he is bound to accept when he reaches the age of reason. We acquire our civil citizenship by the fact of our natural birth, without being questioned on the matter. Why not our divine citizenship, an infinitely greater good, by the fact of our supernatural birth in baptism. If some one left your child a large inheritance, would you demand that it be left in abeyance until your child was old enough to accept it or reject it? And behold baptism makes us heirs of the kingdom of God, our " eternal inheritance " (Heb. ix. 15).

Why do you rebaptize Protestants when they enter your Church ?

I know of a case of a minister of the gospel whom the priest required to be baptized again.

We do not rebaptize them, for baptism can be received only once. The conditional baptism that we often administer to converts, with the form " If thou art not baptized, I baptize thee, etc." is a safeguard made necessary because of the lax views and careless practice regarding baptism that generally prevail outside the Catholic Church.

Some, for instance, deny altogether its sacramental character ; others in baptizing a number at once sprinkle the water, and that so carelessly that · it merely touches the clothes of some ; and again, others use a different form than the one prescribed by our Lord (Matt. xxviii. 19).

I remember hearing of one case not long since when one minister immersed the subjects for baptism in a large tank near the pulpit, while another from a distance repeated the form '' I baptize thee in the name of the Lord Jesus.'' Unless, therefore, there is certainty about the validity of the former baptism, non-Catholics are baptized conditionally on entering the Catholic Church. If perchance the original baptism was validly performed, the subsequent ceremony is not a sacrament at all.

May I, a Protestant, be sponsor for a Catholic child at its baptism ?

No ; for it is evident that a non-Catholic sponsor would not be likely to provide for the Catholic bringing up of the child, if perchance the parents failed in their duty.

Again, no outsider has a right to participate in the sacraments of the Catholic Church.

I am a Baptist, and hold that nothing else but immersion is baptism. Was that not the practice of the primitive Christians ? Was not Christ the Lord baptized by immersion ?

Well, you are a good close-communion Baptist, I suppose; but you hold a new teaching that dates only from the seventeenth century. Catholics are fully aware that the early practice of the Church (*cf.* the baptism of Christ, Matt. iii. 16, Mark i. 10; that of the eunuch, Acts viii. 38, 39, and St. Paul's symbol of burial and resurrection, Rom. vi. 4, Col. ii. 12) was to immerse, and that this custom prevailed in both the East and West in the solemn administration of the sacrament till the end of the thirteenth century.

But, on the other hand, there is abundant evidence to prove that immersion was not the only mode, and that pouring on of water was considered equally valid. It is doubtful, to say the very least, whether the three thousand converts of St. Peter on Pentecost day (Acts ii. 41) were immersed, because of the scarcity of water in the city of Jerusalem (Robertson, "Biblical Researches in Palestine," vol. i. pages 479–516); or whether immersion was practised in the home of Cornelius (Acts x. 47, 48), or in the prison at Philippi (Acts xvi. 33). It is certain that invalids unable to leave their beds were not immersed, as St. Cyprian (A.D. 248) expressly declares when questioned as to the validity of clinical baptism. Quoting Ezech. xxxvi. 25 as a prophecy of Christian baptism, and Num. viii.

and xix., where reference is made to the Jewish sprinkling, he says: " Whence it is apparent that the sprinkling of water has like force with the saving washing " (Epis. lxix. 11–12). In the " Doctrine of the Apostles," a document written towards the close of the first century, reference is made to baptism by pouring (N. vii.)

Indeed, the positive necessity of baptism, which is plain from John iii. 5, proves conclusively that immersion, which is generally difficult and often impossible to practise, could not have been established as essential by the All-Wise Son of God. Must men in prison, the sick and the dying, the child just born, the Esquimaux in the bitter cold of the Arctic circle, or the Bedouin of the parched Syrian desert, where water is most scarce, each and all be immersed, or allowed to die without baptism?

So say many Baptists, who without a thought suffer infants and adults to die unbaptized, a criminal neglect against which the Catholic Church protests most emphatically.

If, again, immersion be the only valid mode, none are really baptized save those who have been immersed. It would follow then that over a hundred years after the Reformation unbaptized men (A.D. 1638) restored the Church, which had been entirely lost in the world, by giving to one another that which they did not possess themselves. If baptism had entirely perished, whence the right of any man to restore it on his own authority?

The Catholic Church, therefore, as the infallible interpreter of the Gospel of Jesus Christ, declares that all three ways of baptizing are equally valid, by immersion, by pouring, or by sprinkling. The present mode of pouring arose from the many inconveniences connected with immersion, frequent mention of which is made in the writings of the early Church Fathers.

But, as a necessary safeguard, Catholics are not permitted to use the form of sprinkling.

Does not the word Baptize always signify immersion in the original Greek?

By no means; it sometimes means in profane authors, and even in the Scripture, pouring or sprinkling (Num. xix. 12; Mark vii. 4). Referring to Mark vii. 4, a Protestant writer, Hodge (vol. iii. page 533, "System. Theol."), says: "To maintain that beds or couches were immersed, is a mere act of desperation. Baptism means here, as it does everywhere when used of a religious rite, symbolical purification by water, without the slightest reference to the mode in which that purification was effected" (See Kitto, "Bibl.

Encycl.,'' Baptism; McClintock and Strong, Cyclopædia).

Why do you baptize children in your Church, when the Scriptures plainly require faith and repentance? '' He that believeth and is baptized shall be saved '' (Mark xvi. 16). '' Repent (do penance) and be baptized '' (Acts ii. 38. See also Acts ii. 37–41, viii. 12–37, xvi. 14–31, xviii. 8, xix. 18).

It is evident that these passages of Holy Scripture refer to adults only.

The Apostles, preaching to adults, required faith in the gospel of Christ and repentance for all past sins as absolute conditions before administering baptism. So the Catholic Church to-day, in perfect accord with this Apostolic teaching, demands of all unbaptized adults who seek admittance to her fold faith in all the doctrines of Christ and repentance of all past sins.

The necessity of infant baptism rests,—

1st. On the fact of original sin. Every man because of Adam's sin is born into the world deprived of God's grace, and of the right of entrance into heaven. '' We were by nature children of wrath '' (Eph. ii. 3). '' Wherefore as by one man sin entered into this world, and by sin death; and so death passed upon all men, in whom all have sinned '' (Rom. v. 12).

2d. On the words of Jesus Christ, who expressly teaches the necessity of *every individual's* being cleansed from this sin and freed from this wrath by baptismal regeneration. ''Unless a man be born again of water and the Holy Ghost, he cannot enter into the kingdom of God'' (John iii. 5). The word for ''a man'' in the original Greek is *tis,* which means any one—man, woman, or child.

3d. On the constant practice of Christian tradition. Origen wrote in the third century : '' The Church received from the Apostles the tradition of baptizing even little ones'' (In Epis. ad Rom., lib. v. n. 9); and again : '' Whence is it that since the baptism of the Church is given for the remission of sins, baptism is, according to the observance of the Church, given even to little children? Because assuredly, if there were nothing in little children needing remission and pardon, the grace of baptism would be superfluous '' (Hom. viii. in Levit.) (For other patristic testimony see Waterworth, ''Faith of Catholics,'' vol. ii. pp. 108–131.)

It is probable that there were children in the households baptized by St. Paul (I. Cor. i. 16 ; Acts xvi. 15, 33), although there is no conclusive proof in the New Testament of the practice of infant baptism. In this matter many Protestants inconsistently violate their principle of the Bible only as a rule of faith, and follow the divine tradition of the Catholic Church.

Again, if a man must be justified by an act of faith in Jesus Christ, and an infant is incapable of such act, it follows logically on Protestant principles that children ought not to be baptized. So are they "tossed to and fro, and carried about with every wind of doctrine" (Eph. iv. 14)—Baptist against Methodist or Episcopalian. Denying the existence of a divine authority, how can they know the truth? In the meantime countless little ones die as they were born, "children of wrath."

What is meant by Baptism for the dead? (I. Cor. xv. 29).

No one knows with certainty what is meant by this obscure text of St. Paul. Many interpretations have been suggested, viz., that it refers to baptism administered over the tombs of the martyrs, or at the point of death, or some symbolic ceremony performed by the relations of a deceased catechumen.

CONFIRMATION.

Is there any proof in the Bible that Christ instituted Confirmation as a sacrament distinct from Baptism ?

Jesus Christ, the night before He died, promised to send the Holy Spirit (John xv. 26, xvi. 13; *cf.* vii. 39), which promise He fulfilled in the upper room at Jerusalem (Acts ii. 4). The sacrament of Confirmation, whereby through the imposition of the bishop's hands, anointing and prayer, baptized Christians receive the Holy Ghost in order to be confirmed in the faith, is clearly mentioned in Acts viii. 14–17. "Now when the Apostles who were in Jerusalem had heard that Samaria had received the word of God, they sent unto them Peter and John. Who, when they were come, prayed for them, that they might receive the Holy Ghost. For He was not as yet come upon any of them; but they were only baptized in the name of the Lord Jesus. Then they laid their hands upon them, and they received the Holy Ghost."

St. Paul administered this sacrament at Ephesus. "And when Paul had imposed his hands on them, the Holy Ghost came upon them, and they spoke with tongues and prophesied" (Acts xix. 6). In writing to the Corinthians he says: "He that confirmeth us with you in Christ, and that hath anointed us, is God; who also hath sealed us, and given the pledge of the Spirit in our hearts" (II. Cor. i. 21).

The Fathers of the Church frequently mention the sacrament of Confirmation ("Faith of Catholics," vol. ii. pp. 132–149). St. Cyprian, for example, commenting on Acts viii., says: "Because they had received the legitimate baptism, . . . what was wanting, that was done by Peter and John, that prayer being made for them, and hands imposed, the Holy Ghost should be invoked, and poured forth upon them. Which now also is done amongst us, so that they who are baptized in the Church are presented to the Bishops of the Church, and by our prayer and imposition of hands, they receive the Holy Ghost, and are perfected with the seal of the Lord" (Ep. 73).

The fact that those Oriental schismatic churches which separated from Rome in the fifth century still recognize Confirmation as a sacrament of Jesus Christ, is proof positive of its apostolic origin. The Catholic, however, has the divine, infallible witness of the Church of God (Trent., Sess. vii., De Conf., can. 1).

PENANCE.

Why does your Church distinguish between sins? Are they not all equal before God?

Sin is the conscious and voluntary transgression of the law of God, a direct violation and contempt of the moral order established by the Divine Will, and a turning from God, our Ultimate End, to find our satisfaction in creatures. In the Christian it implies, furthermore, contempt for our Lord and Master Jesus Christ.

Reason tells us that sins are not all of equal malice. The hurried mechanical prayer, or the quickly repented outburst of temper, are surely not on an equal plane with deliberate murder, adultery, or slander. Scripture is also witness to the distinction between *mortal* sins, which are deliberate and voluntary transgressions of a commandment gravely binding (such as Thou shalt not kill, Thou shalt not commit adultery), depriving the soul of God's friendship and causing the loss of eternal life ("Neither fornicators, nor idolaters, nor adulterers, nor drunkards shall possess the Kingdom of God," I. Cor. vi. 9, 10; "If thou wilt enter into life, keep the commandments," Matt. xix. 17), —and *venial* sins, which do not cause the spiritual death of the soul, although they imply neglect of the commandments of God. "In

many things we all offend" (James iii. 2) ;
"If we say that we have no sin, we deceive
ourselves" (I. John i. 8; Matt. xii. 36).

**Does not St. James teach that one sin is as bad
as another when he says : "Whosoever shall
keep the whole law, and yet offend in one point,
he is guilty of all "?** (James ii. 10).

Yes; but he is speaking of the comparative
guilt and malice of *mortal* sins, like murder
and adultery, as we learn from the verse following (James ii. 11).

**What is the sin against the Holy Ghost? Is
this the only unpardonable sin ?**

The sin against the Holy Ghost is generally thought to be the continued and wilful
resisting until death of the grace of God,
whether to embrace God's truth or to obey
God's commandments. It is not unpardonable, absolutely speaking, for God is always
ready to forgive the repentant sinner ; as a matter of fact, it is not pardoned, because the sinner deliberately refuses to co-operate with God's
grace, or to do what he knows is absolutely
necessary for salvation.

The case mentioned by our Saviour (Matt.
xii. 31, 32 ; Mark iii. 28-30 ; Luke xii. 10)
was the wilful rejection of the miracles Jesus
Christ had wrought in proof of His divine

mission, and the malicious ascribing of them to the power of Beelzebub, the prince of devils (Matt. xii. 24).

In our own day, those are guilty of the same sin who, knowing the Catholic Church to be the one, true Church of Jesus Christ, persistently refuse to enter it because of worldly interests, loss of property, friends, social or political position.

Where in the Bible is auricular confession taught ?

Why do Catholics have secret confession ?

Did Jesus ever tell us to confess our sins to a priest ?

Granted that the Apostles had the power to forgive sins, what proof is there that their power has been perpetuated ?

The Catholic confesses his sins to a priest because he knows that Jesus Christ commanded him to do so, by the institution of the Sacrament of Penance.

That the Saviour gave the power to pardon sin to His Apostles is clear from John xx. 21–23. "As the Father hath sent me, I also send you. When He had said this, He breathed on them, and He said to them : Receive ye the Holy Ghost. Whose sins you shall forgive, they are forgiven them ; and whose sins you shall retain, they are retained."

The Father had sent His only begotten Son into the world to redeem it from sin. Our Lord tells us Himself that His mission was to save sinners.

"For the Son of Man is come to save that which was lost" (Matt. xviii. 11).

"I was not sent but to the sheep that are lost of the house of Israel" (Matt. xv. 24).

"They that are in health need not a physician, but they that are ill, etc. For I am not come to call the just, but sinners" (Matt. ix. 12, 13, i. 21 ; I. Tim. i. 15).

He frequently pardoned sinners their offences : Magdalen (Luke vii. 47), the woman in adultery (John viii. 11), the thief on the Cross (Luke xxiii. 43), the man sick with the palsy (Matt. ix. 2). In the last instance He insists on this power of forgiveness as Son of Man, despite the objection of the scribes and their accusation of blasphemy (Matt. ix. 3), and performs a miracle to prove it. "But that you may know that the Son of Man hath power on earth to forgive sins (then said He to the man sick of the palsy), Arise, take up thy bed and go into thy house."

Remembering, then, that Christ was the Son of God ("All power is given to Me in heaven and in earth," Matt. xxviii. 18), and that His mission was the salvation of sinners, the meaning of His words is evident... As the Father hath sent Me to pardon sin, I also send you clothed with My divine authority to pardon sin in My Name. Receive the Holy Ghost, the Third Person of the Blessed Trinity, to whom is especially ascribed the sanctifying of the souls of men from sin ("the charity of God is poured forth in our hearts by the Holy Ghost, who is given to us") that you may give that spirit to repentant sinners. If you forgive a sinner, he is really forgiven by Me; if you refuse forgiveness, I will refuse also. " Whose sins you shall forgive, they are forgiven them; whose sins you shall retain, they are retained."

This ratifying of the Apostolic judgment in heaven is also declared by our Saviour on another occasion: " Whatsoever you shall bind upon earth, shall be bound also in heaven; and whatsoever you shall loose upon earth, shall be loosed also in heaven " (Matt. xviii. 18).

Did we not know the wonderful power of prejudice to read into the Scriptures its own views and theories, we could not understand how any believer in the word of God could deny that Jesus Christ gave to the Apostles the power of forgiving sins in His Name.

Indeed, the Scriptures are so clear that some have granted the Apostles had the power of pardoning sin, but they hold that the power died with them. But this is unreasonable. Useless indeed would have been so mighty a

power if its exercise were to be limited to the
sinners of the first century. No ; as long as
sin will last—that is, until the end of the world
—so long must this God-given remedy for sin
exist. The pardoning power was not an extraordinary gift, as the gift of tongues, prophecy,
or miracles (I. Cor. xii. 10), but the ordinary
and necessary power to continue Christ's work
for the salvation of souls. He came to teach,
and to pardon sin ; the Apostles are to teach and
to pardon sin for ever in His Name (Matt. xxviii.
20 ; John xx. 21–26). Every other way of obtaining forgiveness is now superseded by the
Apostolic priesthood, whose giving or denial of
absolution is by God's promise confirmed by
Himself in heaven.

How is this power to be exercised? Evidently this two-fold power of forgiving and retaining sin implies a judgment based on the
knowledge of each individual case. The Apostle or his successor must have reasons to forgive, viz., a supernatural sorrow on the sinner's
part for all grievous sins committed, with a
firm purpose to sin no more ; and reasons to
refuse forgiveness, namely, the lack of proper
dispositions of sorrow, shown, for example, by
refusal to restore ill-gotten goods, to pardon an
enemy, or to avoid the proximate occasions of
sin. This necessarily supposes full knowledge
of the state of the penitent's conscience, which

is possible only by personal acknowledgment, or confession., (Council of Trent, Sess. xiv. ch. 5.)

The Catholic interpretation of John xx. will, perhaps, be more clear to you by a comparison.

Suppose, to-day, that in a prison of the Philippines a number of prisoners convicted of various crimes under the Spanish rule were still confined, and that there was question of the justice or the exceeding severity of their sentences. President Roosevelt, informed of this, determines to send to Manila twelve commissioners with full powers to investigate the charges made. You hear him say in the White House to these twelve men : '' All necessary power in this case is given me by the people of these United States. As they have chosen me to represent them, so I have chosen you to act in my name and with my authority. I, as President, possess the pardoning power over crime. Receive your commission ; whose crimes you shall pardon, they are pardoned by me ; whose crimes you shall not pardon, they are not pardoned by me.''

What would honestly be your inference from these words? At once you would say : 1. That these twelve men had received from the President the power of pardoning ; 2. That they had sole and absolute control of the criminal cases in question, and that the power of all other judges immediately ceased on their appointment; 3. That their power could not be rightly exercised without a thorough investigation of each and every case; 4. That their authority would last until the last "guilty" or "not guilty" had been pronounced.

So the Apostolic commission supposes equally that: 1. That the twelve Apostles received from God the power of pardoning; 2. That the Jewish way of pardon was superseded by the Christian; 3. That the exercise of their power necessitates confession; 4. That their authority will last until the death of the last sinner.

Catholics, moreover, are not left to the varying, contradictory views of human private judgment, but have the divine, infallible witness of the Church of God (Trent., Sess. xiv.), which voices the constant Christian tradition from the beginning. (For the testimonies of the Fathers read "Faith of Catholics," vol. iii. pp. 36–113; "Manual of Catholic Theology," vol. ii. pp. 466–474.

One striking patristic argument is to compare the confession of sins in the spiritual life to the confession of one's bodily sickness to a physician. Says St. Basil: "The confession of sins follows the same rule as the manifestation of bodily infirmities. As men, therefore, do not disclose their bodily infirmities to every one, nor to a few at random, but to such as are skilful in the cure of them, so also ought the confession of sins to be made to those who are able to apply a remedy'' (Reg. Brev. 228).

The mind of the early Church is seen by the condemnation of the Novatians of Rome in the third century. They held that those who had fallen away during the persecution of Decius and who had offered sacrifice to idols could not be pardoned, whereas the Church then as always maintained that her power of pardoning extended to all repentant sinners without exception (Alzog, Church History, vol. i. p. 429 *et seq.*)

Indeed, when Christians reflect for a moment that the Saviour established the sacrament of baptism for the cleansing of original sin in which we had no personal share, ought they not naturally expect that He would have instituted the sacrament of penance for the cleansing of those mortal sins committed after baptism whereof we are personally guilty? If Christ Jesus gave us the certainty of admission into His friendship by baptism, is it not becoming His divine wisdom to give His people certainty of their return after having again become His enemies?

What degree of power do you priests claim in confession? Do you really pardon sin, or merely intercede with God for the sinner?

The Catholic priest pardons in the name of Christ, as his minister and ambassador.

"He hath placed in us the word of reconciliation. For Christ, therefore, we are ambassadors, God as it were exhorting by us. For Christ, we beseech you, be reconciled to God" (II. Cor. v. 20).

"Let a man so account of us as of the ministers of Christ, and the dispensers of the mysteries of God" (I. Cor. iv. 1).

Do priests ever refuse to forgive sins? If they do, what happens then?

A priest as Christ's ambassador of pardon cannot refuse forgiveness unless he perceives a lack of necessary dispositions of sorrow on the part of the penitent; for example, if the sinner refuse to make good an injury done, to avoid the proximate occasion of his sin, to accept the penance imposed, or to use the means of grace and perseverance in well-doing. The power given the Apostles was a two-fold power of forgiving or refusing forgiveness: "Whose sins you shall forgive, they are forgiven them; and whose sins you shall retain, they are retained" (John xx. 23). The denial of pardon by the priesthood means denial on the part of God, as the Saviour says clearly: "Whatsoever you shall bind upon earth, shall be bound also in heaven" (Matt. xviii. 18).

Is it not blasphemy to declare that a mere man can forgive my offences against God?

Catholics do not confess to any man indifferently, but only to a priest, whom St. Paul calls "the minister of Christ, and the dispenser (steward) of the mysteries of God" (I. Cor. iv. 1). The priest does not forgive as man, but as the representative and the ambassador of Jesus Christ. "For what I forgave, if I have forgiven anything, for your sakes have I done it, in the person of Christ" (II. Cor. ii. 10). "We are, therefore, ambassadors for Christ; God, as it were, exhorting by us. For Christ, we beseech you, be ye reconciled to God" (II. Cor. v. 20).

This indeed is the very objection urged against our Saviour when He forgave, as the Son of Man, the man sick of the palsy (Mark ii. 3–12). "Why," said the Jews, "does this man speak thus? He blasphemeth. Who can forgive sins but God only?" The enemies of Christ Jesus denied His divinity, and therefore His power of forgiving sins. The enemies of Christ's Church, denying its divinity to-day, logically must deny it the power to forgive sins, delegated it by Jesus Christ the day of His resurrection (John xx. 19–23).

Why not confess to God directly? Can God abrogate His power?

Because Jesus Christ taught us to go to God indirectly through the ministry which He established. Why does not a soldier report for duty directly to the . commanding general? Why does not a citizen pay his taxes directly to the governor of his State?

God does not abrogate His power, but delegates it to men who forgive in the name and with the authority of Jesus Christ, the Son of God. "For Christ, therefore, we are ambassadors" (*i. e.*, with delegated power: II. Cor. v. 20).

And do we not confess all the better to God when aided by His own ministry to do so sorrowfully and hopefully? Remember, too, that Catholics begin their confession by saying, "I confess to Almighty God and to you, Father."

Does not the confessional give the priest too much power? I object to outside interference with my private affairs.

The Catholic priest undoubtedly claims the right to lay down the moral law authoritatively in the sacrament of penance, and to enforce obedience thereto under penalty of the denial of absolution. His is the power to forgive sins in the name of Jesus Christ, and to advise, warn, encourage, and help souls in their daily struggle against sin and temptation. He has no right to pry into your private affairs, or to interfere in family matters; he has no right whatsoever to question you unless with regard to sin or the danger thereof.

Do you object to the interference of the state when, in the best interests of society, it enforces the law against criminals? Then you should not object to the Catholic priesthood when, in the best interests of the individual, it enforces the law of Christ against evil and the evil-doer.

How can a priest listen year after year to sins without his own mind becoming corrupted?

Because God gives His ministers great and special graces to keep their hearts pure, daily Mass and their own weekly confession being the chief. Because, again, the priest listens as another Christ, with sympathy and love for the repentant sinner, who is causing "more joy in heaven than the ninety-nine just that need not penance" (Luke xv. 7). The more he understands the malice of sin and the more he realizes its evil effects upon the sinner, the more he hates it as the great curse of the people of God. Does the judge on the bench or the physician in the sick-room become corrupted because both come in daily contact with sin and the effects of sin? No, the heart becomes corrupted only by consenting to personal temptation.

Is a priest always bound to keep secret what he hears in confession?

If a priest knew through confession the real murderer, and an innocent man was to hang for it, would not common justice demand that he tell it?

A priest is bound, even at the cost of life itself, never to betray in any way what he has heard in the secrecy of the confessional. Frequently priests have gone to prison rather than betray this trust, although most courts respect it on the mere basis of natural law. The confidence of millions of the Catholic people the world over and their frequent reception of the sacrament of Penance are ample proof that the Catholic priesthood has, through God's grace, been ever loyal to their trust.

One of the reasons why confession will never become the general practice in any Protestant church—for example, the Protestant Episcopal —lies in the fact that its ministers are not bound by any divine law to keep secret the sins confided to them, and fail to realize their responsibility.

The absolute secrecy of the seal of confession is also recognized by all the Oriental Christian sects, the Russian Church being the one exception because of its utter subserviency to the state.

Was not the practice of confession introduced by the IV. Council of Lateran in A. D. 1215?

By no means. This Council supposes the practice of confession everywhere existing, for it declares that "all the faithful, men and women, shall confess their sins, at least *once a year*, to a priest approved by the Church." The very fact of passing a law as to a detail of time, which was at once universally recognized as binding, proves conclusively that confession was universally practised. And we have witness after witness for this fact in the writings of the early Fathers (" Faith of Catholics," vol. iii. pp. 1-129).

Do you honestly think that such an institution, requiring of all Christians, from the Pope downwards, the humiliation of kneeling before a fellow-man to tell even the most hidden sins of the heart, could have been imposed on the Christian world so quietly and so easily that history says not a single word of any opposition thereto? Imagine to-day the Church of England attempting to compel all her church members to follow out as a binding obligation the views of the High-Church party on this point. Why, the pulpit and the press would re-echo the protest the world over.

Do you honestly think that if, as so many Protestants have declared, auricular confession is an invention of the Catholic priesthood, that popes, bishops, and priests who had the ability to invent such an institution, would not have

considered the terrible burden they were placing upon themselves? For, humanly speaking,
the hearing of confessions, although it has its
consoling side in the winning back of thousands of souls to God after lives of sin, is one
of the hardest trials in the priest's ministry.
To sit for hours—twelve sometimes in one day
—in fetid air, a close box, inhaling the bad
breaths of hundreds, and hearkening to the
sorrows and sins of men until the heart is sick
—this surely is not an occupation that any
human authority could devise, or any human
power compel men to submit to.

Remember, too, that it often means a hurried
drive of many miles in the most bitter weather,
in the blackest midnight, over almost impass-
able roads, to hear the confession of some poor
dying soul; or again, a visit to the hospital,
the pest-house, and the leper asylum; or again,
the going from soldier to soldier on the firing
line of a field of battle. A priest in Northern
Iowa told me not long since of many a drive of
fifty and seventy-five miles to hear the confession of the dying when the thermometer
registered twenty-five degrees below zero, in the
old days, thirty years ago, his parish embracing
then an area of some hundred miles or more of
Iowa and Minnesota. Will you tell me this is
of man's invention?

If, as you claim, you possess the Apostles' pardoning power, why not their power of working miracles?

Did not Jesus tell His Apostles to heal the sick as well as to pardon sin, and preach the gospel? Do you priests claim to heal diseases? "He gave them power against unclean spirits, to cast them out, and to heal all manner of sickness, and all manner of disease" (Matt. x. 1). "Heal the sick, cleanse the leper, raise the dead, cast out devils; freely you have received, freely give" (Matt. x. 8). Read also Luke ix. 2, x. 9; John xiv. 12.

Jesus Christ came to teach men the truth of God and by His death win for them God's grace and friendship, so that loving Him, and the brethren for His sake, they might save their souls. The Apostles were given for ever all things necessary to carry on this divine work of teaching and saving souls—*v. g.*, the power to teach (Matt. xxviii.; Mark xvi.), to baptize (*ibid.*), to pardon sin (John xx.), to offer sacrifice (Luke xxii.)

The Apostles were given for themselves, as an extraordinary gift, the power of winning by miracles countless Jews and pagans whom Christ knew would be won to His gospel in no other way.

Christ did not come to heal the bodies of men, but their souls; the Church of Christ is not a divine school of medicine or surgery, but a divine society to teach men the doctrines and commandments of the Son of God. The gift of healing is not at all necessary for this purpose.

Of course, there have been in the history of the Catholic Church many saintly men and women who have worked by the power of God wonderful works, as He promised (John xiv. 12); but that was a special, personal gift that thereby souls might be won to Christ, and not the ordinary prerogative of every Christian.

Again, God frequently works miracles through the ordinary administration of the Sacrament of Extreme Unction, which Christ established for the cure of the body as well as of the soul, and by the sacrifice of the Mass offered up by the priests of the New Law. But miracles are exceptional things, and are not a part of God's ordinary providential working.

The Catholic Church protests alike against the rationalistic denial of all miracles whatsoever despite the evidence, and the modern current superstitions of decadent Protestantism, which would declare every Christian a wonder-worker.

Does not confession weaken character?

Is not confession an incentive to sin by making forgiveness so easy?

Do not Catholics go to confession, and then commit the same sin over again?

On the contrary, we have already seen that certain conditions are absolutely required, before God will ratify the absolution of the confessor. Pardon is not granted, for instance, to the drunkard who has a mere natural sorrow because of his degradation and the poverty and shame of his wife and children; to the thief who has no intention of giving back the money he has stolen; to the impure man who will not avoid the proximate occasion of his sin; to the bitter, angry soul who refuses to forgive the offending brother, etc.

We know perfectly well that human nature is weak, and human passions strong; that the world of wicked men and women is full of temptations; that the flesh rebels against the Spirit (Rom. vii. 23), and the devil does his best to tempt us (I. Pet. v. 8). But if a Catholic yield to these temptations it is not in virtue of the sacrament he has received, but because he is false to the sacramental promise he made to God to sin no more.

We are willing also to grant that there have been abuses; that some Catholics go to their confession in a mechanical, perfunctory sort of a way, and do not realize the dignity and sacredness of this divine sacrament. But is there any good thing in the world that sinful man has not sometimes abused? The sacrament of matrimony, intended to sanctify and bless the pure union of man and woman, has often been made a mere tool for worldly advantage or a mere instrument of lust, as divorce statistics show. The sacrament of Baptism, established to initiate the Christian into the Church of God, has been used to serve an unbeliever's worldly aims. The Bible has been abused by every false prophet from the beginning, in imitation of Satan (Matt. iv. 6). The press, the pulpit, the theatre, the stock exchange, inventions, the arts—all these have been abused. Would you, then, abolish them altogether?

The history of the sacrament of Penance is proof positive of its being one of the greatest incentives to virtue the world knows of. Could it have survived during these nineteen hundred years if it were indeed an incentive to sin? Would millions of the most intelligent men and women still bend the knee? It is impossible to think so. The corruption of morals that everywhere followed the abolition of confession in the sixteenth century made many of the Reformers wish for its re-establishment. Voltaire wrote in the eighteenth century: "The enemies of the Roman Church, who have opposed so beneficial an institution, have taken from man the greatest restraint that can be put upon crime" ("Dict. Phil.," art. Catech. du Curé).

If confession were an incentive to sin, how is it that the most hardened sinners never go, and the best Catholics are seen frequently at the sacred tribunal? If it weakened character, how then do you account for its reformation of the habitual drunkard, its recall of the penitent Magdalen, and the comfort and peace it gives the condemned criminal? If it encouraged crime, why would Catholic fathers and mothers rejoice so much in seeing their boys and girls go frequently to confession, and be sad of heart when they begin to neglect this duty? If it made Catholics worse, how then do you explain the fact that Protestants often desire for their servants and employees Catholics who go regularly to confession?

The fact is evident. The sacrament of Penance is a guide to the doubting, a comfort to the afflicted, an encouragement to the weak, a warning to the young, a strong arm to the wavering, an adviser to the ignorant, a menace to the hardened sinner, a joy to the truly repentant; it is Jesus Christ speaking to the world: "Come to Me, all you that labor and are burdened, and I will refresh you" (Matt. xi. 28).

Why, sometimes non-Catholics, tormented by

the anguish of unconfessed sin, have desired to receive the sacrament, and finding this impossible, have craved the privilege of unburdening their conscience to the trusted Catholic priest.

What provision does the Catholic Church make for a Catholic who cannot reach a priest in order to confess?

How are non-Catholics forgiven their sins?

God does not require the impossible. A Catholic, therefore, in danger of death, and unable to obey the law of confession, is bound to make an act of perfect sorrow for all sins committed, namely, an act of sorrow from the highest supernatural motive—the love of God for Himself alone. A non-Catholic, who is invincibly ignorant of the Catholic Church, and the sacrament of Penance instituted by Christ, is pardoned in the same way.

Would not a confession to the one offended or wronged have a better moral effect upon the sinner than confessing to a priest? Would that not be a better proof of sorrow?

Catholics confess to the priesthood of Christ because they know the Sacrament of Penance to be a divine institution, and that obedience to Christ in this matter is evident proof of their sorrow and God's forgiveness.

Our questioner seems to forget that God is

offended when we injure our neighbor in thought, word, or deed, and He has prescribed clearly the way of pardon. Remember, too, that a Catholic who has grievously wronged his neighbor in character or property cannot be pardoned in the Sacrament of Penance, if he refuse to make good the injury done.

Again, there are certain sins against God, and against one's self, as unbelief, blasphemy, lust, in which our neighbor does not figure.

How can sin be pardoned by merely telling it?

It cannot be, according to the teaching of the Catholic Church. Judas was not pardoned, although he confessed his crime (Matt. xxvii. 4). Confession indeed is only one of the three parts of the sacrament of Penance, and by no means the most essential, the other two being contrition and satisfaction. Without contrition, or "sorrow and detestation of sin, with a firm purpose to sin no more" (Council of Trent), there is no forgiveness possible. The Catholic must have a true, intense sorrow for each and every mortal sin he has committed; the motive of his sorrow must be supernatural, resting not on the natural consequences of his sin, but on the fear of hell, the loss of heaven, or the love of God and Jesus Christ. He must hate and detest sin as the greatest evil in the world, and sincerely promise to avoid it.

and the occasions thereof for the future. He must be ready also to make good the past by repairing any injury he may have done his neighbor in his character or his property, and satisfy God in union with the infinite satisfaction of Jesus Christ by performing the penance enjoined by his confessor. Otherwise the mere confession or telling of sin is of no avail for pardon, the absolution of God's priest is null and void, and the penitent but adds the guilt of sacrilege to his original guilt.

Is not confession degrading and opposed to Christian manliness and independence ?

On the contrary, it is the noblest act of a true man and a true Christian to conquer his lower and sinful self by a heartfelt acknowledgment of sins committed. It is indeed humiliating, but true humility is no degradation, but a Christ-like virtue: " Learn of Me because I am meek, and humble of heart " (Matt. xi. 29); especially calculated to conquer the pride of sin. Suppose you had two boys, who had seriously violated your commands. One gives no hint of his disobedience, and the other cannot retire to rest that night until he has sobbed out everything. Would you consider this confession degrading? Nay, rather the common expression is " Own up and be a man." When a man convicted of murder confesses his crime, do you consider him less the man for that reason?

The best proof, however, is the fact that the noblest and most perfect types of men in the world are those seen frequently at the feet of a Catholic priest, crying out to God, as the publican in the Gospel: "O God, be merciful to me a sinner" (Luke xviii. 9–14). The Saviour indeed praised the humble publican who confessed, rather than the proud Pharisee who only boasted of his good deeds. "This man went down into his house justified rather than the other."

I have often heard that Catholics have to pay money for confession? Is this true?

You ought not to believe all that you hear; for, as the Scriptures say, "a faithful witness will not lie, but a deceitful witness uttereth a lie" (Prov. xiv. 5). I remember a Protestant in a country town once saying that he had heard the regular tax for confession was two dollars. I told him I had in one week heard upwards of eight hundred confessions ($1,600), which indeed would yield quite a comfortable income. No; it is not true, but a calumny due either to ignorance or malice. A Protestant gentleman in New York once told one of the Paulist Fathers that his servant had demanded money from him more than once to pay the priest in confession. "How then," says he, "can you deny the fact?" He never thought of the alternative, that the servant in question simply lied, as he could readily have found out had he inquired of her whereabouts. To demand money for confession would be the grievous sin of simony. The laws of the Church are most strict on this point, some bishops even threatening with suspension any confessor receiving money in the confessional due for ordinary debts because of the false impression this might give to non-Catholics.

Why not allow confession to be optional, as in our (Anglican) Church?

Because, if, as many High-Church Anglicans admit, according to the teaching of their prayer-book in the Communion Service, and the office for the Visitation of the Sick, Christ left the power of absolving from sins with His Church, then Christians by the very fact have no other way of obtaining forgiveness. Once an Apostolic body exists in the world whose pardon of sin on earth means pardon in heaven by God, and whose retention of sin means retention by God (John xx.), there is no more possibility of a Christian's being free to reject this sacrament than he is free to reject the sacrament of Baptism. The acceptance of the sacrament of Penance by the High-Church party rests merely on the Protestant principle of private judgment, which, exercised by other members of the same Church, rejects the doctrine as contrary to the Word of God.

Do Catholics believe in "conversion," or "change of heart"?

Conversion with Catholics means:

1st. The conversion from sin, whereby a man asks God pardon for his offences in the sacrament of Penance, and promises to sin no more; and 2d. The conversion from error, whereby a man renounces a false religion to embrace the one true Church of Jesus Christ.

Both conversions proceed from man's intellect and will, helped by God's grace to realize and to reject sin and error as hateful in God's sight.

Catholics do not find any warrant in reason or Christianity for the emotional conversion of a Protestant revival, or the superstitious expectancy of a sudden "change of heart," or "getting religion" which private judgment has begotten in simple souls, "tossed to and fro, and carried about with every wind of doctrine" (Eph. iv. 14). How frequently infidelity is born of the rational appreciation that revival religion cannot be of God.

I never could kneel down to a fellow-man and

tell my sins. That is asking too much of flesh and blood.

The true Christian should not ask, when there is question of a doctrine or commandment of Christ, Is this hard to believe or obey? but simply: Did Jesus Christ teach or command it?

If Jesus Christ established the sacrament of Penance, and commanded all Christians to henceforth obtain forgiveness of an Apostolic priesthood, who were to pardon until the end of the world in His name, the faithful soul should obey Him without question.

Remember, too, that the priest is prepared after many years of careful study and prayer for his divine ambassadorship. He has Christ's example and love for sinners set before him by men well versed in the spiritual life, so that a penitent can kneel before him with confidence. (For an idea of the Catholic priesthood, read Cardinal Manning's "Eternal Priesthood," and Cardinal Gibbons' "Ambassador of Christ.")

You find it difficult to kneel down to another man. Would you expect God to pardon you without the slightest suffering or mortification? Is not the sinner's pride to be cured by the exercise of the opposite virtue of humility? It is hard to acknowledge to a friend that we are in the wrong, but it is Christian.

We must not, however, exaggerate the difficulty of confession. The sacrament of Penance is indeed intolerably hard to the hardened Catholic sinner who does not desire to give up his wicked life, but it is full of joy and comfort to the repentant ones, who experience by it the blessing of the restored friendship of God. It seems very strange and trying to the non-Catholic who has never tasted of its divine sweetness, and yet converts soon learn to love it. "Father, it is not so hard after all"—so hundreds have said to me after the indefinable dread of their first confession was over.

INDULGENCES.

Why does the Catholic priest impose penances for sins already pardoned? Why do Catholics think they can atone for their sins by fasting, prayers, etc.? Do you believe that you can add to the all-sufficient atonement of Christ? When God forgives the sinner, does He not instantly free him from all deserved punishment at the same time, as in the case of the dying thief: "To-day shalt thou be with Me in Paradise" (Luke xxiii. 43)?

After confession, the penitent is asked to perform works of penance that he might better realize his guilt before God, and thereby pay the debt of temporal punishment still due to his forgiven sins. The Council of Trent declares

that these penances make the sinner more careful for the future, substitute for his vices the
contrary virtues, and prevent him from falling
into more grievous sins (Sess. xiv. ch. viii.)

Frequently the Scriptures declare that God
may forgive the repentant sinner—that is, free
him from the guilt of sin and its eternal punishment—without freeing him from temporal punishment. Thus in the case of Adam (Wisdom
x. 2; Gen. iii. 17–20), the rebellious Jews in
the desert (Num. xiv. 20–23), Moses (Num. xx.
12; Deut. xxxii. 51, 52), David (II. Kings xi.
xii. xxiv.), etc.

David, for example, having repented for his
murder and adultery, was forgiven by God, and
yet punished by the death of the child he loved.
"I have sinned against the Lord. . . . The
Lord also hath taken away thy sin; thou shalt
not die. Nevertheless, because thou hast given
occasion to the enemies of the Lord to blaspheme, for this thing the child that is born of
thee shall surely die" (II. Kings xii. 13, 14).

Is it not strange to find Bible Christians denying that the sinner may atone for the temporal punishment due his sins, when no doctrine is taught more clearly in the Scriptures?
(Jonas iii.; II. Paral. (Chron.) xxxiii. 12, 13;
Ecclus. iii. 33; Dan. iv. 24; Luke xi. 41).

Catholics do not believe that any man or all
men could ever satisfy for one grievous sin

against God. One alone, who was true God
and true man, Jesus Christ, satisfied for all the
sins of the world. He, according to Catholic
dogma, is the only Mediator ; " for there is one
God, and one Mediator of God and men, the
man Christ Jesus " (I. Tim. ii. 5). But we believe that by the help of God's grace, which
Jesus Christ died to gain, we can apply to ourselves the satisfaction of Jesus Christ, through
the sacraments of baptism and penance. This
in no way interferes with the infinite atonement
of God's only Son. "Neither is this satisfaction which we discharge for our sins so much
our own as not to be Jesus Christ's, for we who
can do nothing of ourselves as of ourselves,
can do all things with the co-operation of Him
who strengthens us. Thus man hath not
wherein to glory, but all our glorying is in
Christ ; in whom we live, in whom we merit, in
whom we satisfy " (Trent., Sess. xiv. ch. viii.)

As for the thief on the cross, it is not evident
that he went instantly to heaven ; for Catholics,
believing that Christ's soul immediately after
His death went down to Limbo, to announce
to the souls there detained the glad tidings of
the redemption (I. Pet. iii. 19), declare that
paradise in this passage does not mean heaven
at all. But granted that it did, a miracle
wrought by the Son of God as a sign of His
exceeding great mercy and love for sinners, is

not to be regarded as the general law of God's working, especially when the Scriptures in many other passages declare the contrary. Of course, Catholics believe that God may at any time remit the guilt of sin, and all the punishment due thereunto, just as he does always in baptism; but we say that is not the ordinary law of His providence, as taught by His holy Scriptures and His infallible Church.

How can your Church be God's Church, when it grants permission or an indulgence to commit sin?

This old fable of Protestant tradition still lingers in the mind of many Protestants, although it has been refuted time and time again. Many will remember how Cardinal Newman nailed the calumny with regard to the catalogue of sins fastened on the door of the Church of St. Gudule's, Brussels ("Present Position of Catholics," pp. 108–118). The catalogue, written in French, turned out after investigation to be the price paid, *not for sins but for the use of chairs*. And yet a Catholic lawyer had but lately to correct the same calumny repeated by a correspondent of a Chicago daily with regard to a South American bishop granting an indulgence to commit sin. So persistent is the unthinking or malicious disregarding of the eighth commandment.

Catholics know that an indulgence is in no sense whatever the remission of sin past, present, or future, nor does it do away with the eternal punishment due to sin. The most elemental concept of God renders it impossible to imagine Him giving a person permission to commit sin. If our objector would take the trouble to read any catechism of our Church he would find it clearly stated, that unless a Catholic is free from mortal sin and in God's grace and friendship, he cannot in the slightest degree gain an indulgence ("Baltimore Catechism," lesson xxi. questions 1 and 2).

An indulgence is the remission by the Church of the whole or part of the temporal punishment due to sin, valid before God because of the divine authority Christ gave His Church (Matt. xvi. 19, xviii. 18). It is gained only by one in a state of grace, in virtue of the application of the superabundant merits of Christ and His saints to all of the Communion of Saints.

Thus, in the first days of Christianity, the Church imposed upon repentant sinners severe public penances, such as exclusion from the church service, denial of the Eucharist, fasting on bread and water for a term of years, for the grievous crimes of murder, apostasy, surrendering the Bible to the pagan persecutors, and the like. We read, however, that frequently the bishops remitted, wholly or partially, these penitential works, if a penitent manifested extraordinary sorrow, if a persecution was imminent, if one of the martyrs about to die requested it, if the penitent was unable to undergo the penance because of bodily infirmities, or if death were imminent. This is essentially the Catholic doctrine of indulgences to-day.

From the eighth century this public penitential discipline was gradually done away with, until it disappeared in the thirteenth century. Penitents who manifested sincere sorrow were absolved before the penance enjoined was performed. The severe public penances were commuted into prayers, almsgiving to churches, monasteries, and hospitals, pilgrimages, taking the cross to free Christ's sepulchre from the Saracen (Council of Clermont, A. D. 1098, can. 2), making the Jubilee (A. D. 1300), etc.

This divine power exercised by the Catholic Church with regard to the temporal punishment decreed by divine law to the sinner, is somewhat akin to the power which every well-ordered state exercises for the common good of society, by remitting wholly or in part the punishment decreed by the civil law to the criminal. Thus our President, or governor, has in certain cases the right to grant a complete pardon to criminals by law condemned to life imprisonment. And in every prison we find the State remitting part of a criminal's sentence for good behavior.

Just as the State possesses the right to condemn or acquit the criminal, and to regulate in every way the punishment due his crime, so the Catholic Church possesses the divine right to pardon sin or retain it (John xx.), and to remit wholly or in part the punishment it deserves in the sight of God (Matt. xvi. 19, xviii. 18),—all according to the penitent's interior dispositions towards God. (Lepicier, "Indulgences"; Thurston, "The Holy Year"; Bellarmin, "De Indulgentiis"; Beringer, "Indulgences.")

Where in the Bible are indulgences mentioned?

Did not the doctrine of indulgences originate in the year 1200?

By what authority does your Church grant indulgences?

By the divine power that Jesus Christ gave to Peter and the Apostles in union with Him to free the repentant sinner from everything that hindered his entrance into heaven, namely, sin and the eternal and temporal punishment due to sin.

"Whatsoever thou shalt loose on earth, it shall be loosed also in heaven" (Matt. xvi. 19); "Whatsoever you shall loose on earth shall be loosed also in heaven" (Matt. xviii.

18) ; " Whose sins you shall forgive, they are forgiven them " (John xx. 23).

St. Paul exercised this power upon the incestuous Corinthian, whom he first excommunicated and then pardoned in the name of Christ after he had given proof of heartfelt sorrow. ''I indeed, absent in body, but present in spirit, have already judged . . . to deliver such a one to Satan for the destruction of the flesh,'' etc. (I. Cor. v. 3–5). '' So that, on the contrary, you should rather forgive him and comfort him, lest perhaps such a one be swallowed up with overmuch sorrow. . . . What I have pardoned, if I have pardoned anything, for your sakes I have done it in the person of Christ '' (II. Cor. ii. 6–10). Catholics believe that many members of the Church —for instance, virgins, martyrs, confessors, and countless saints—have performed penances far exceeding what was due their sins, and that their merits in union with the infinite merits of Jesus Christ form a spiritual treasury, which the Apostles and their successors can draw from to pay the debt of temporal punishment for all who belong to the Communion of Saints.

'' For as the body is one, and hath many members ; and all the members of the body, whereas they are many, yet are one body, so also is Christ ; . . . and if one member suffer anything, all the members suffer with it ; or if one member glory, all the members rejoice with it'' (I. Cor. xii. 12–26).

To me indulgences are destructive of true religion, by freeing one from the necessity of repentance (Luke xiii. 5).

Do not indulgences make Catholics trust too much in externals, set prayers, visiting churches, processions, etc.?

Why should not a man suffer all the punishment due his sins?

Inasmuch as indulges necessarily suppose on a sinner's part heartfelt, sorrowful confession of all his grievous sins, and his restoration to God's grace and friendship, they cannot help fostering true love of Jesus Christ.

By what right does a man judge his neighbor guilty of externalism, or Pharisaism, when he prays to God, fasts in obedience to Christ's word and the law of His Church, or visits Jesus Christ really present on the Catholic altar?

A true Christian, realizing the infinite malice of sin and God's offended justice, is thankful not only for Christ's institution of the sacrament of Penance for the pardon of grievous sin and the remission of the eternal punishment it deserves, but also for that extra-sacramental remission of the temporal punishment which, according to the Scriptures, may remain even after the eternal punishment is remitted.

I have frequently met non-Catholics who in one breath found fault with the dogma of indulgences as not allowing full scope to God's justice, and in the next not scrupling at all to declare eternal punishment incompatible with God's mercy. Is not this straining at a gnat and swallowing a camel? (Matt. xxiii. 24).

Indulgences, as a matter of fact, are great helps to true devotion, for they foster the spirit of prayer, encourage almsgiving in the name of Christ (Luke xi. 41, xii. 33; Matt. vi. 2), cause Catholics to meditate upon the Passion and death of Christ through whose infinite merits they avail, insist on the reception of those wonderful helps to God's love and friendship, the sacraments of penance and the Eucharist, bring vividly before men the dogma of the Communion of Saints, etc.

Were not indulgences sold by the Catholic Church at the time of the Reformation?

Are not pardons bought for money in your Church?

I have heard it said that in South America absolution can be had beforehand for the most outrageous crime, if one will only pay the price required.

" It is utterly false to' assert that it has ever
been held in the Catholic Church that the
perpetration of crime could be indulged for any
sum of money. Neither for sins committed,
nor sins to come, has money ever been taken as
an equivalent; for one no more than the other.
On the other hand, it is quite true that the injury done to the Church, when it happens to
be visited with a censure (which is not a common case), has certainly sometimes been com-
pensated by the performance of some good
work, and in the number of such works alms-
deeds and religious offerings are included "
(Newman, " Present Position of Catholics,"
Lecture iii. p. 13).

We have stated elsewhere that the ordinary
Protestant notion of an indulgence being a
pardon for sin is absolutely false, although to
our shame be it said we find this calumny
voiced by some of the teachers paid by the
state to instruct our children in our high and
normal schools. The sacrament of Penance is
alone concerned with the pardon of sin, and in
that sacrament no money is or can be paid.
An indulgence has to do merely with the remission of the temporal punishment of the sinner already pardoned by the sacrament of Penance, and can never be purchased.

When a non-Catholic remembers that a
heartfelt supernatural sorrow for all grievous

sin, with a firm purpose to offend God no more, is an absolute prerequisite for gaining an indulgence, how, believing in the Scriptures, can he find fault with the Catholic Church for promising the remission of temporal punishment as a reward for good works—among which is almsgiving in the name of Christ—performed by those in God's grace and friendship.

Christ told us that the giving of a cup of cold water in His name would not be without a reward (Mark ix. 40). How then can a Christian find fault with Pope Leo X., who in the sixteenth century, by his apostolic power granted, as many Popes and Bishops for hundreds of years had done before him, *not the pardon of sin*, but the remission of temporal punishment due to those repentant sinners who would give an alms towards the building of one of the greatest temples ever erected in honor of Jesus Christ. Pope Leo, the Vicar of Jesus Christ, had the same right as Moses in the Old Law, who in God's name demanded from the Jews offerings of gold, silver, brass, precious stones, oil, spices, for the tabernacle.

The Catholic Church has never denied that abuses have existed; that over-zeal led some preachers of indulgences to go beyond the teaching of the Church, or engage in some personal trafficking. What thing holy or sacred in the world but the avarice of men can put a price on it? Women have sold their honor for money, fathers have sold their daughters in marriage, respectable Christians have trafficked in human flesh without blushing, men have betrayed their country for a price, legislatures, judges, jurors, voters have been frequently bought up. What then? Would you abolish the jury-system or the ballot, or condemn matrimony, because of the evils of avarice incident thereto?

Various Popes, from Gregory VII. in the eleventh century to Leo X. in the sixteenth, and many councils (2d Lateran, A. D. 1139; 1st Lyons, A.D. 1245; Vienne, A.D. 1311, and Trent, A.D. 1545–1563) have condemned these abuses. The Council of Trent (Sess. xxv.): '' Being desirous that the abuses which have crept in, and by occasion of which the excellent name of indulgences is blasphemed by heretics, be amended and corrected, ordains . . . that *all evil gains* for the obtaining thereof—whence a most prolific cause of abuses among the Christian people has been derived—*be wholly abolished.*''

If Luther had merely protested against these abuses as was his right, he would only have been following in the footsteps of Popes, Bishops, and Councils. But to deny the dogma because of these abuses, is about as sensible as

to advocate free love because of the sad abuses
of the marriage bond so prevalent to-day. That
he was most oblivious to the nature, conditions, and effects of indulgences his ninety-
five propositions give ample proof, even if we
did not have his own word for it.

The statement frequently made that Tetzel
promised indulgences without requiring contrition is absolutely without proof, and his supposed ignorance of the true Catholic doctrine
is amply refuted by his answer to Luther " On
Indulgences and Grace," and his defence of
one hundred and six theses against Luther on
the occasion of his taking his licentiate in theology at the University of Frankfort, A.D. 1517.
(" Tetzel und Luther," Gröne.)

**Does not an indulgence of one hundred days
mean that, by certain prayers recited by the sinner, one hundred days of his punishment in purgatory are taken off? How do you know what
happens in the other world ?**

Not at all; for the Church does not pretend
to know how much of Purgatory God remits by
a partial indulgence of so many days, years,
etc.

Historically, the phrase arose in reference to
the canonical penances of the early Church
which were imposed for certain fixed periods.
Catholics believe that by the gaining of what
is called " an indulgence of one hundred days,"

the repentant sinner does as much toward the remission of the temporal punishment due by God to his sins as was done in former times by the performance of one hundred days of public penance.

This historical formula is still retained to remind the Christians of to-day how strongly the early Church realized the malice of offences against God, that they the more readily might do the little required of them in atonement for their sins.

How can indulgences avail for the dead whose dispositions cannot be known? .

The Catholic Church does not claim to directly apply the infinite merits of Jesus Christ and the superabundant merits of His saints to the souls in Purgatory, over whom she has no jurisdiction. She can only offer these merits to God by way of suffrage, and leave the application entirely to His good pleasure. Thus, a Catholic may gain a plenary indulgence and offer it up for a particular soul in Purgatory ; but God is not pledged to apply it, and it by no means follows that this soul is at once ushered into the presence of God. This seems, however, to be the ordinary Protestant notion, although it was expressly condemned by the Church in the Council of Vienne, A.D. 1311.

Cannot God apply the infinite satisfactions of Jesus Christ without the means of indulgences ?

God can, if He so will, remit the guilt of sin, and both its eternal and temporal punishment 'directly and immediately. But the ordinary way He established in His Church is the sacrament of Penance for the guilt of sin and the eternal punishment, and indulgences for the remission of the temporal punishment.

What do you mean by a Jubilee ?

The Jubilee (Lev. xxv.), or Holy Year, is an institution originating with Pope Boniface VIII. in the year 1300. It consists of a universal plenary indulgence, or remission of all temporal punishments, to those who, "truly penitent and having confessed and communicated, shall piously visit the Basilicas of the Blessed Peter and Paul, St. John Lateran, and St. Mary Major" (Bull of Leo XIII., Properante ad exitum, 1899). The *extended* Jubilee, which dates from the time of Alexander VI., grants the same privilege to the Catholics of the world who are unable to visit Rome. (For a complete history of the Jubilee see Herbert Thurston, S.J., "The Holy Year of Jubilee." Herder, 1900.)

THE HOLY EUCHARIST.

How can you believe that the wafer given in Communion is Christ the Lord?

We believe •it on the words of Jesus Christ, the Son of God, who promised to give us His flesh to eat and His blood to drink, at the lakeside of Galilee (John vi. 48–69), and who fulfilled that promise at the Last Supper (Matt. xxvi. 26-28 ; Mark xiv. 22–24 ; Luke xxii. 19, 20 ; I. Cor. xi. 23–25). We have also the divine infallible testimony of the Catholic Church He established. "The Holy Synod (the Council of Trent) teacheth . .. . that in the august sacrament of the Holy Eucharist, after the consecration of the bread and wine, our Lord Jesus Christ, true God and man, is truly, really, and substantially contained under the appearances of those visible signs" (Sess. xiii. ch. i. ; Wiseman's "Lectures on the Real Presence " ; Faber, "The Blessed Sacrament" ; Dalgairns, "The Holy Communion ").

What do you mean by transubstantiation ?

Is it not a new teaching of the Council of Trent ?

The Council of Trent says (Sess. xiii. ch. iv.) "that by the consecration of the bread and wine a change is wrought of the bread's whole substance into the substance of Christ our Lord's Body, and of the wine's whole substance into the substance of His Blood, which change has been by the Holy Catholic Church suitably and properly called Transubstantiation.''

By the *substance* of bread we mean its very essence, that internal, invisible something which, itself devoid of color, shape, weight, taste, etc., supports the qualities or accidents which are perceived by the senses.

Transubstantiation, therefore, means that when Jesus Christ, at the Last Supper, pronounced the words '' This is My Body ; this is My Blood,'' the Son of God by His omnipotent power transubstantiated, or changed, the substance of the bread and wine into His living flesh ; so that no bread or wine whatsoever remained, but Himself—Body, Blood, Soul, and Divinity, under their appearances. So in like manner, every day at Mass, the priest, acting in the Name of Christ, pronounces the same words, and God effects the same change.

This is by no means a new teaching, but the clear, obvious interpretation of the words of the Saviour (Matt. xxvi. 26, etc.) When Christ took bread into His hands He did not say '' This is a figure of My Body,'' '' In this bread is My Body eaten by faith,'' '' In, with, or under this is My Body,'' as he ought to have said if our Lutheran or other Protestant brethren are right, but merely, *This is My Body.* What He held could not be bread and His Body at the same time; and as there was no change in the appearances of bread, the change must have taken place in the invisible substance—that is, by transubstantiation.

The doctrine of the early Fathers may be studied in "Faith of Catholics," vol. ii. pp. 191-374; "Manual of Theology," Wilhelm-Scannell, pp. 417, 418. They clearly taught transubstantiation, although the word itself is not older than the eleventh century. A word often becomes the test of orthodoxy, as *omōousios* against the Arians, or *theoticos* against the Nestorians. I give one testimony of the fourth century, St. Cyril of Jerusalem: "What seems bread is not bread, though it seems so to the taste, but Christ's Body; what seems wine is not wine, even though the taste will have it so, but Christ's Blood" (Catech. iv. 9).

The fact that the Council of Trent first defined the way in which Christ was present in the Eucharist, no more makes this a new teaching than the several definitions regarding the Incarnation and Trinity in the early Church, which defined these dogmas more clearly as various errors of Arianism, Nestorianism, Macedonianism, etc., arose concerning them.

Ought not the sixth chapter of St. John's Gospel to be interpreted figuratively ?

Does not the phrase "to eat the flesh" signify to believe in the doctrine of Christ?

Let us consider the whole passage, John vi. 48–70 :

"I am the Bread of Life. Your fathers did eat manna in the desert, and are dead. This is the bread which cometh down from heaven; that if any man eat of it he may not die. I am the living bread which came down from heaven. If any man eat of this bread he shall live for ever; and the bread that I will give is My flesh for the life of the world. The Jews, therefore, strove among themselves, saying : How can this man give us His flesh to eat ? Then Jesus said to them : Amen, amen, I say unto you : Except you eat the flesh of the Son of Man, and drink His Blood, you shall not have life in you. He that eateth My flesh and drinketh My Blood, hath everlasting life, and I will raise him up in the last day. For My flesh is meat indeed; and My Blood is drink indeed. He that eateth My flesh and drinketh My Blood abideth in Me and I in him. As the living Father hath sent Me, and I live by the Father: so he that eateth Me, the same also shall live by Me. This is the bread that came down from heaven. Not as your fathers did eat manna, and are dead. He that eateth this bread shall live for ever. These things He said, teaching in the synagogue in Capharnaum. Many therefore of His disciples hearing it, said: This saying is hard, and who can hear it? But Jesus knowing in Himself, that His disciples murmured at this, said to them: Doth this scandalize you? If then you shall see the Son of Man ascend up where He was before? It is the Spirit that quickeneth; the flesh profiteth nothing; the words that I have spoken to you are spirit and life. But there are some of you that believe not. . . . After this many of His disciples went back, and walked no more with Him. Then Jesus said to the twelve: Will you also go away? And Simon Peter answered Him: Lord, to whom shall we go? Thou hast the words of eternal life. And we have believed, and have known, that Thou art the Christ the Son of God."

This question is fully answered by Cardinal Wiseman in his lectures on the Real Presence (Lectures i.–iv.) His arguments are as follows:

1. "I assert, therefore, that if we accurately consider the phraseology of this portion of the chapter (from verse 48 to the end), according to the only manner in which it could possibly be understood by the Jews whom Christ addressed, we must conclude that they would necessarily infer a change of topic in it, and be convinced that the doctrine now delivered was of a real

eating of the flesh and drinking of the blood of Him who addressed them " (p. 69, Lecture ii.)

2. In every language, ancient or modern, a figure of speech has a definite meaning. If, for instance, I call a man a fox, I refer to his cunning ; if a lion, to his bravery, and the like. We cannot use figures of speech arbitrarily, and give them at will a new meaning, merely to meet the demands of controversy. "If I dis-cover," argues Cardinal Wiseman, "that among the persons whom Jesus addressed, it (that is, the phrase *to eat flesh*) did bear a figurative signification besides its literal sense, then I must conclude that those persons could only select between that *established figurative sense* and the literal import of the words" (p. 77). . . . "Now I do assert that whether we examine (*a*) the phraseology of the Bible (Ps. xxvi. 2, Job. xix. 22, Mich. iii. 3, Ec-cles. iv. 5, Gal. v. 15), (*b*) the ordinary lan-guage of the people who still inhabit the same country, and have inherited the same ideas (*i. e.*, the Arabs), or (*c*), in fine, the very language in which our Saviour addressed the Jews (Syro-Chaldaic), we shall find the ex-pression *to eat the flesh* of a person signifying invariably, when used metaphorically, *to at-tempt to do him some serious injury, prin-cipally by calumny or false accusation*. Such, therefore, was the only figurative meaning

which the phrase could present to the audience at Capharnaum '' (p. 80 ; *cf.* pp. 80–91).

3. As no one would ever imagine that Christ could promise eternal life on condition of our calumniating Him, there remains but one possible sense of the words—the literal.   '' The ideas of *drinking blood* and *eating human flesh* presented something so frightful to a Jew, that we cannot allow our Saviour, if a sincere ' teacher, to have used them as images, for consoling and cheering doctrines ; nor in fact to have used them at all, under any other circumstances than an absolute necessity of recurring to them, as the most literal method of representing his doctrines '' (p. 106).

The Old Law expressly forbade the drinking of blood (Gen. ix. 4 ; Lev. iii. 17, vii. 26, xix. 26 ; Deut. xii. 16, xv. 23), so that the Jews ever regarded it as a heinous crime (Lev. xvii. 10 ; I. Kings xiv. 33 ; Ezech. xxxiii. 25 ; Judith xi. 10–12) ; it is frequently mentioned as the most dreadful curse of God upon His enemies (Wisdom xi. 7 ; Isa. xlix. 26 ; Apoc. xvi. 6 ; Jer. xix. 8, 9. Lecture iii. pp. 104–110).

4. It is clear that the Jews understood our Saviour's words literally, for they question the possibility of their eating His flesh : '' How *can* this man give us His flesh to eat '' (verse 53). Were they right or wrong ? To determine this, Cardinal Wiseman lays down two

rules gathered from the constant practice of Jesus Christ in teaching His doctrine to the people.

" Whenever our Lord's hearers found difficulties, or raised objections to His words, from taking them in their literal sense, when He intended them to be taken figuratively, His constant practice was to explain them instantly in a figurative manner, even though no great error could result from their being misunderstood " (pp. 116, 117). For example :

"Jesus answered and said to him (Nicodemus) : Amen, Amen, I say to thee, unless a man be born again, he cannot see the kingdom of God. Nicodemus saith to Him : How can a man be born when he is old? " Jesus at once explains His meaning : "Amen, Amen, I say to thee, unless a man be born again of water and the Holy Ghost, he cannot enter into the kingdom of God " (John iii. 3–5). And again : " It is easier for a camel to pass through the eye of a needle, than for a rich man to enter into the kingdom of heaven ? " The disciples believe that He means no rich man can be saved : " Who then can be saved? " Jesus at once corrects this false impression, saying: " With man this is impossible, but with God all things are possible " (Matt. xix. 24–26. Compare also Matt. xvi. 6–12 ; John iv. 32–34 ; John xi. 11–14, viii. 21–23, 32–34, 39–44).

"When His words were rightly understood in their literal sense, and by that correct interpretation gave rise to murmurs or objections, it was His custom to stand to His words and repeat again the very sentiment which had given the offence." Thus:

(a) Jesus "said to the man sick of the palsy : Be of good heart, Son; thy sins are forgiven thee." The Scribes, understanding the words aright, object, "saying within themselves : He blasphemeth." Our Saviour then reiterates His teaching : "Whether it is easier to say, Thy sins are forgiven thee; or to say, Arise and walk ? But that you may know that the Son of man hath power on earth to forgive sins," etc. (Matt. ix. 2–7). (b) "Abraham your father rejoiced that he might see my day : he saw it, and was glad." The Jews understood Him to claim to have lived in Abraham's time. "Thou art not yet fifty years old, and hast Thou seen Abraham ?" Jesus reiterates clearly the self-same teaching : "Amen, amen, I say to you, before Abraham was made, I am" (John viii. 56–58).

If we now consider the words in John vi., we see that our Lord repeats the teaching of verse 52 in the six following verses, declaring that to eat His flesh and to drink His blood is a precept, a pledge of everlasting life, a true eating and drinking, a means of intimate union with

.Himself, a proof of supernatural life, and an earnest of immortality (vv. 54–59). (Lecture iii. pp. 112–127.)

5. Another strong argument for our Lord's literal meaning is the following:

(*a*) Verse 54—"Amen, amen, I say to you, except you eat the flesh of the Son of Man and drink His blood, you shall not have life in you"—expresses a precept, in the strongest possible way, both negative and positive (compare with Mark xvi. 16: "He that believeth and is baptized shall be saved: but he that believeth not shall be condemned"). Understood figuratively, this precept would be utterly unintelligible to His Jewish hearers. (*b*) The distinction made by our Saviour between eating His body and drinking His blood is without any real significance unless He is speaking of the Real Presence; for to partake of the blood of Christ by faith adds nothing to the idea of partaking of His body. (*c*) The "Amen, Amen" (v. 54) of our Saviour is evidently intended as a strong emphatic statement, which in the Protestant interpretation would betoken insincerity on His part. (*d*) In verse 56, Jesus assures the Jews that His flesh is truly meat and His blood is truly drink. We cannot imagine Him making such an answer, if they were wrong in understanding Him literally. (*e*) His reply, instead of removing their previous difficulties, confirmed them, for we read: "Many therefore of His disciples, hearing it, said: This saying is hard"—*i.e.*, harsh or revolting, and who can hear it; that is, who can bear to listen to it? These words are utterly without meaning if we accept ,the Protestant idea of an eating by faith. (*f*) Seeing that the disciples objected still, He appeals to the striking miracle of His future ascension (vv. 62, 63) as proof positive of His words, even as He appealed to His second coming as proof of His divinity before the High-Priest at His trial (Matt. xxvi. 63, 64). (*g*) Is it probable that if He did not wish His words to be taken literally He would have allowed the unbelieving disciples to depart without explaining His meaning? For we read: "After this many of His disciples went back, and walked no more with Him" (v. 67).

(6) Finally His words to the twelve, "Will you also go away?" and St. Peter's answer: "Lord, to whom shall we go? Thou hast the words of eternal life" (vv. 68, 69), clearly prove that they really understood Him literally, and that they accepted without question His teaching on His word as the Son of God, although they did not comprehend the mystery (Lecture iv. pp. 154–155).

A careful study of all these arguments, together with the fact that the figurative interpretation is a modern one of the sixteenth century, ought to convince any earnest, prayerful student of the Sacred Scriptures that our Lord spoke of a real eating and drinking of His Body and Blood in His sermon at the synagogue at Capharnaum.

Does not Jesus plainly indicate that He speaks in figure by the words: "It is the Spirit that quickeneth: the flesh profiteth nothing; the words that I speak to you, they are spirit and they are life" (John vi. 64).

Cardinal Wiseman (Lecture iv. pp. 175–177) thus answers this commonplace of controversy, although most learned Protestant commentators agree with us in rejecting the interpretation of our questioner (as, Kuinoel, Bloomfield, Schleusner, Horne, Koppe, Sartorius, Storr, Schmid, Roller).

1. There is not a single instance in the Old or New Testament in which the word *flesh* is used to denote the literal sense of words. Yet this is necessary, if by the word *spirit* their figurative or spiritual signification is here denoted.

2. "If by the *flesh* we are to understand the material flesh of Christ, by the spirit we must understand *His* spirit. If so, in what way does the phrase explain that the foregoing words are to be taken figuratively?"

3. " The terms *flesh* and *spirit*, when opposed to each other in the New Testament, have a definite meaning which never varies." . . . Then, citing as examples Rom. viii. 1–14, the cardinal continues : " From this passage, were others wanting, it would be clear that the *flesh* signifies the corrupted dispositions and weak thoughts of human nature; and *the spirit* means the sentiment of man as elevated and ennobled by grace. . . . Christ's words then are, spirit and life ; . . . in other words, such as the mere man cannot receive, but which require a strong power of grace to make them acceptable. (Compare Gal. v. 13– 26 ; I. Pet. iv. 6 ; Matt. xxvi. 41 ; John iii. 6 ; Rom. vii. 5, 6, 25 ; I. Cor. v. 5 ; II. Cor. vii. 1 ; Gal. iii. 3, iv. 29 ; I. Pet. iii. 18, etc.)

Ought not the words of Christ at the Last Supper (Matt. xxvi. 28) be understood in a figurative sense ?

But carefully consider them :

Matt. xxvi. 26–28 : " And whilst they were at supper, Jesus took bread and blessed and broke, and gave to His disciples, and said : Take ye and eat, *This is My Body*. And taking the chalice He gave thanks, and gave to them, saying : Drink ye all of this, For *this is My Blood* of the New Testament, which shall be shed for many unto the remission of sins."

Mark xiv. 22–24 : "And whilst they were eating, Jesus took bread ; and blessing, broke, and gave to them and said : Take ye, *This is My Body*. And having taken the chalice, giving thanks, He gave it to them. And they all drank of it. And He said to them : *This is My Blood* of the New Testament, which shall be shed for many."

Luke xxii. 19–20 : "And taking bread, He gave thanks and brake, and gave to them, saying : *This is My Body*, which is given for you. Do this for a commemoration of Me. In like manner the chalice also after He had supped, saying : *This is the Chalice, the New Testament in My Blood*, which shall be shed for you."

I. Cor. xi. 23–25 : "The Lord Jesus . . . took bread, and giving thanks, broke and said : Take ye and eat : *This is My Body*, which shall be delivered for you ; this do for the commemoration of Me. In like manner also the Chalice, after He had supped, saying : *This Chalice is the New Testament in My Blood ;* this do ye, as often as you shall drink, for the commemoration of Me." (*Cf.* Lecture v., On the Real Presence, p. 189 *et seq.*)

St. Cyril answered this objection in the fourth century : "Since Christ Himself affirms thus of the bread, *This is My Body*, who is so daring as to doubt it ? And since He affirms, *This is My Blood*, who will deny that it is His

Blood? At Cana of Galilee He, by an act of His will, turned water into wine, which resembles blood; and is He not then to be credited when He changes wine into Blood? Therefore, full of certainty, let us receive the Body and Blood of Christ; for, under the form of bread, is given to thee His Body, and under the form of wine His Blood" (Catech. Mystagog., 4, 1, 2).

The words of St. Luke are most clear (xxii. 19, 20): This is My Body now given for you—that is, the very Body that was to be offered on the cross; this is My Blood now shed for you—that is, the very blood that was to flow from His Sacred Heart. When, therefore, a Protestant interprets these simple words of our Saviour, "This is My Body—this is My Blood," to mean this is a figure or symbol of My Body and Blood, He must show some valid reason for denying the Lord's statement of the Catholic Doctrine of the Real Presence.

That was no time to speak in misleading figures of speech, for our Lord was making His Last Testament, and instituting a sacrament and a sacrifice which would last until His second coming (Luke xxii. 19; I. Cor. xi. 26). Would He, the Infinite Wisdom, and the Lover of souls, use words which were calculated to deceive the greater number of His people for all time, and lead them into the idolatry He came expressly to abolish ? Shall Christians hesitate between the " black or white spirit " that told the figurative meaning to Ulrich Zwingli in a dream, and the constant voice of Eastern and Western Christendom from the beginning ?

The literal interpretation of the words of Christ is also plainly taught a second time by St. Paul : " The Chalice of Benediction which we bless, is it not the communion of the Blood of Christ ? And the bread which we break, is it not the partaking of the Body of the Lord ? " (I. Cor. x. 16).

The word " partaking " used several times in the following verses (18, 20, 21) refers to a real sharing in the sacrifices of the pagans ; why then, in verse 16, should it not refer to a real partaking of the Body of the Lord ?

I. Cor. xi. 27–29 is even more explicit : " Therefore, whosoever shall eat this bread, or drink the chalice of the Lord unworthily, shall be guilty of the Body and of the Blood of the Lord. But let a man prove himself; and so let Him eat of that bread, and drink of the chalice. For he that eateth and drinketh unworthily, eateth and drinketh judgment to himself, not discerning the Body of the Lord."

" Plain and simple reason," says Cardinal Wiseman, " seems to tell us that the presence of Christ's Body' is necessary for an offence committed against it. A man cannot be ' guilty of majesty,' unless the majesty exists in the object against which his crime is committed. In like manner, an offender against the Blessed Eucharist cannot be described as guilty of Christ's Body and Blood if these be not in the sacrament" (Lectures on the Eucharist, pp. 318, 319).

Again, if Christ is not really present, how can the Apostle denounce the unprepared communicant as guilty of grievous sin for "not discerning the Body of the Lord?"

Does not the word "to be" frequently mean to represent? Why not in the words of Christ at the Last Supper? "The seven good kine are seven years" (Gen. xli. 26), "The ten horns . . . are the ten kings" (Dan. vii. 24), "The field is the world" (Matt. xiii. 38), "That rock was Christ" (I. Cor. x. 4), "The seven stars are the angels of the seven churches" (Rev. i. 20), "These (they) are the two covenants" (Gal. iv. 24.)

1. The passages above cited are by no means parallel to the words of the institution of the Eucharist: This is My Body ; This is My Blood.

2. If there are some few passages of Holy Writ where *to be* means *to represent*, there are thousands of others where the verb *to be* is to be taken literally.

3. According to this argument, the words of

St. John (i. 1) "The Word was God" should mean "the word *represented* God"—*a reductio ad absurdum* evident to any Protestant Bible student who believes in the Divinity of Christ.

4. These texts are not parallel passages, for they all refer to the *explanation of a symbol*, and not to the *institution* of one. It is not the recurrence of the same word but of the same thing that constitutes a parallelism.

The context clearly shows that in the cases cited there is question of a vision, a parable, an allegory, or a metaphor : Gen. xli. 25 : "the *dream* of Pharao is one," etc. Dan. vii. 15 : "the *visions* of my head troubled me." Matt. xiii. 36 : "Declare unto us the *parable* of the tares." I. Cor. x. 4 : "They drank of the *spiritual* rock." Apoc. i. 20 : "The *mystery*," *i. e.*, allegory or symbol, "of the seven stars." Gal. iv. 24 : "Which things are an *allegory*."

5. All these texts differ in point of construction from "This is My Body." In each a definite subject is said to be something else, and as we know that two material objects cannot be identical, we are obliged to look for a figurative meaning (Wiseman's Lectures on the Real Presence, Lecture v. pp. 206–222).

Does not the verb "to be" mean to represent, in this text, "It is the Lord's passover"? (Exod. xii. 11).

Not at all, although "the black or white spirit" told Ulrich Zwingli in a dream that this text alone was conclusive against a literal interpretation of "This is My Body." The original reads : "the passover to the Lord"; that is, a sacred thing to the Lord. This is proven conclusively by verse 27 of the same chapter : "this is to the Lord the sacrifice of the passover." Here the paschal feast is spoken of not as any emblem of the Lord's passover, but as its sacrifice; and the thing so spoken of is said *to be* sacred to the Lord. The verb which expresses this idea must necessarily be taken in its own strict sense. In the other passage, therefore, in which the same thing is spoken of, and the same construction employed, we must conclude that the word has the same meaning; this *is* the paschal feast sacred to the Lord (Wiseman, Lecture v. p. 235). It is interesting to note that the original does not contain the words *to be* at all.

Does not Christ say of Himself figuratively : "I am the door" (John x. 9), "I am the true vine" (John xv. 1)? Might He not therefore call the Eucharist His body only in figure?

The texts are by no means parallel, for: 1. *To be* here does not mean to represent, for our Lord did not intend to make Himself the symbol or figure of material objects. He evidently meant by the two comparisons to show that He resembled a door inasmuch as all must have access to the Father through Him,—"By Me, if any man enter in, he shall be saved,"—or that He was like a vine to which they by grace were united as branches (John xv. 1–6). The context in both cases makes our Lord's figurative meaning perfectly evident. 2. The fact again of identity being predicated of two different objects (Christ and a door, Christ and a vine) forbids any one thinking for a moment of a literal interpretation (Lecture v. pp. 222–225).

Is not the doctrine of the Real Presence impossible? How can the Eternal God be contained in the wafer Catholics receive?

The Blessed Eucharist is a dogma full of mystery, but it involves no contradiction or absurdity, and is no more impossible than any other of the mysteries of Christianity.

If God can create the universe out of nothing, why cannot He change the substance of bread and wine into the substance of the Body and Blood of Jesus Christ?

Jesus Christ, the Son of God, taught this doctrine, and "with God all things are possible" (Matt. xix. 26).

The true follower of Christ does not ask "how," with the unbelieving Jew (John vi. 53), but says with the Apostle Peter, who did not comprehend the mystery of the Real Presence, but accepted it on the divine word of the Saviour: "'Thou hast the words of eternal life. And we have believed and known that Thou art the Christ, the Son of God" (John vi. 69, 70).

The Apostles who had witnessed the transubstantiation of water into wine at the marriage feast of Cana in Galilee (John ii. 1–11), the feeding of the five thousand with five barley loaves and two fishes (John vi. 1–14), and the many other miracles wrought by the Son of God, never questioned His power to change bread and wine into His Body and Blood. So Catholics believe this dogma on the words of the Son of God, and ask not to fathom a mystery of God.

Transubstantiation has an analogy in nature, imperfect though it may be. For is not the human body, which changes entirely every few years, made up of the food we have assimilated? Does not at least a part of this food become body and blood? Why believe in this gradual, mysterious change that God works in us continually, and deny Him the power of instantly changing food into His Body and Blood (J. S. Vaughan, "Thoughts for all Times," pp. 140–142; Wiseman, Lectures on the Real Presence, Lecture vi.)

Does not the dogma of the Real Presence directly contradict the evidence of my senses? They declare that what I see and taste is merely bread and wine.

Not in the slightest degree. "All that we can see, touch, or taste are the accidents (appearances), but they have not been changed, or in any way affected. There is no miracle, therefore, in the fact that when we look at a consecrated host we do not see the substance of Christ's Body. The miracle would be if we did. All that we see after the consecration is just precisely what we saw before the consecration, viz., the accidents of bread. And our senses are not deceived, for the things we see are really there, viz., the accidents of bread—the invisible substance alone having departed" (J. S. Vaughan, "Thoughts for all Times," p. 139).

Our objector must remember that the senses judge only of appearances, and therefore often cause a man to make false inferences of fact. The rational mind corrects these when reason, science, or revelation declares them false. Consider, for example, the sense of sight. It will not prove the Copernican theory, but rather tell us that the sun rises in the east and sets in the west; it will not perceive the myriads of animalculæ in a glass of water unless aided by the microscope; it will not distinguish the difference between two pieces of iron—the one magnetized and the other not; it could not perceive the divinity of our Lord, but declared, in the mouth of the unbelieving Jew, "Is not this the Carpenter's Son?" (Matt. xiii. 55).

If, then, Jesus Christ declares that the substance underlying the appearance of bread in the consecrated host is His Body and Blood, we accept His testimony without question, for we know He is the infallible God.

How can Christ be at the right hand of the Father, and on earth at the same time?

How can the Body of Christ be in so many places at the same time?

Does not the Saviour expressly deny His Real Presence among the people to-day? "For ye have the poor with you always, . . . but Me ye have not always" (Mark xiv. 7).

"The whole question," writes Father Dalgairns, "resolves itself into this: Can a body be unextended? Who will say that God cannot take from a body the property of extension? What contradiction is there in it? Is it not easy for us to conceive substance without extension? If you take to pieces the idea of substance, we shall find that it is quite independent of quantity, on which extension depends; for the smallest grain of gold is as really and substantially gold as all the precious metal contained in the whole universe.

"Again, quantity is a sensible thing which is seen by the eye and felt by the touch; but as for substance, it is revealed to us by the mind alone. Let God but only reduce a body to the state of pure substance, and it ceases at once to be extended without ceasing to be a body. It is by extension that a body becomes subject to the laws of space; take extension away, and it partakes at once of some of the prerogatives of spirit.

"This then is what God has done to the Body of Jesus in the Blessed Sacrament. It has ceased to be extended, and all at once it is freed from the fetters which bound it to place. It is not so much that it is in many places at once as that it is no longer under the ordinary laws of space at all. It pervades the Host like a spirit. It uses indeed the locality formerly occupied by the bread, in order to fix itself into a definite place; but it only comes into the domain of space indirectly, through the species (the appearances of bread and wine), as the soul only enters into its present relations with space through the body. Who will say that this involves contradiction or that it is beyond the power of omnipotence?" (Dalgairns, "The Holy Communion," pp. 33, 34).

We find this multiplication of the sacramental presence of Christ foreshadowed in the miracle of the multiplication of the loaves and fishes in the desert (John vi. 13). Who can explain how five barley loaves would suffice to satisfy the hunger of five thousand, or how each loaf could have been at one and the same time in the hands of several persons? (*Cf.* J. S. Vaughan, "Thoughts for all Times," pp. 142–146).

It is indeed a wonderful mystery that Jesus Christ should be really present on thousands of altars the world over; but the Christian does not deny a fact merely because it is mysterious. Mystery is often the law for the finite intelligence in things human; much more, therefore, in divine things. We know little indeed of substance, or of glorified bodies, although the Apostle tells us that our own will possess new and wonderful qualities (I. Cor. xv. 42–44). Who can explain how the glorified Body of the Risen Christ passed through the stone of the Sepulchre (Mark xv. 46), or through the closed door of the upper room in Jerusalem? (John xx. 26). Who can explain how the human soul is really and wholly present in every part of the human body?—a fact of philosophy admitted even by the pagan Aristotle.

The text cited above clearly refers to His natural visible presence among the disciples during His earthly ministry. It in no way contradicts the fact of His sacramental presence in the Eucharist. He also says: "I am

with you all days, even to the consummation
of the world" (Matt. xxviii. 20).

**Do not many Episcopalians in this country and
in England believe in transubstantiation as much
as you Catholics do?**

Yes; but they believe it on the Protestant principle of private judgment, and being deprived
of valid orders, their ministers have no power
whatsoever to change the bread and wine into
Christ the Lord's body. Their Church is hopelessly divided on this point, having no divine
authority to teach the Gospel, and indeed in its
official capacity declares "transubstantiation,
or the change of the substance of bread and
wine in the supper of the Lord, cannot be
proved from Holy Writ; but is repugnant to
the plain words of Scripture, overthroweth the
nature of a sacrament, and hath given occasion
to many* superstitions" (Art. XXVIII.)

Dr. Ryle, the Protestant Bishop of Liver-
pool, wrote in his Visitation Charge, Novem-
ber, 1893, regarding "the real divisions" on
this point of doctrine: "One section of our
clergy, and probably the majority, maintains
that the Lord's Supper is a sacrifice ; another,
and probably the minority, maintains with
equal firmness that it is not, and should only
be called a sacrament. One maintains that the
communion table is an altar, and should al-

ways be treated as such. Another maintains that it is only the Holy Table.

"One maintains that the minister at the Lord's Supper is a sacrificing priest. Another maintains that he is only an officiating presbyter, though called a priest, and that there is no authority for sacerdotalism in the New Testament or the prayer-book.

"One maintains that there is a real objective presence of Christ's body and blood under the form of the consecrated bread and wine. The other maintains that there is no real presence whatsoever except in the heart of believing communicants."

Can a Church powerless to teach infallibly on so vital a dogma claim to witness divinely to the Gospel of Christ? Can a Church which cannot answer with certainty when questioned by eager, earnest souls, pretend to be God's Church? High-Churchmen believe firmly in the Real Presence on the Catholic altar. If they find all the Eastern Christians, all Roman Catholics, and many of their own Church declare unanimously that they are kneeling in adoration to a mere piece of bread, should they not investigate most thoroughly into the reasons why? (*American Cath. Quarterly*, A.D. 1899, p. 137.) •

Why do you deny the cup to the laity?

Why do you deprive the people of half the Lord's Supper ?

Why don't Catholics give the Communion as it was given in Apostolic times ?

How can your Church change a divinely appointed Sacrament ?

Did not Jesus command us, saying : " Drink ye all of it " ? (Matt. xxvi. 27).

The Catholic Church teaches that the reception of Communion under the form ot wine is not absolutely necessary, for she has ever believed "that as much is contained under either species as under both ; for Christ, whole and entire, exists under the species of bread, and under each (divided) particle of that species ; and whole under the species of wine, and under its (separated) parts " (Trent, Sess. xiii. c. 3). The Eucharist is the living Christ; and as a living body is not without its blood, or living blood without a body, so Christ is received whole and entire under either form of bread and wine.

It is natural enough that Protestants who deny the Real Presence of Jesus Christ in the Eucharist, and believe that the sacrament consists merely in· the eating bread and drinking wine in memory of the Saviour—a partaking by faith—should insist on receiving both bread and wine. But Catholics having the Christ— Body, Blood, Soul, and Divinity—beneath the appearances, regard it as a matter of discipline which of them is to be received in Holy Communion.

The Scriptures show us the Saviour promising the same reward to Communion under one kind as under both. To quote the Council of Trent: "He who said: Except you eat the flesh of the Son of Man and drink His Blood, you shall not have life in you (John vi. 54), has likewise said: If any man eat of it he may not die (vi. 50). And He who has said: He that eateth My flesh and drinketh My Blood hath everlasting life (vi. 55), has also said: The bread that I will give is My flesh, for the life of the world (vi. 52). And lastly, He who has said: He that eateth My flesh and drinketh My blood, abideth in Me and I in him (vi. 59), has nevertheless said: He who eateth this bread shall live for ever (vi. 59)" (Sess. xxi. ch. i.)

Frequently, too, the receiving of Communion under the form of bread is mentioned in the Scriptures: "They were persevering in the doctrine of the Apostles, and in the communication of the breaking of bread, and in prayers" (Acts ii. 42); "Whosoever shall eat this bread *or* drink the chalice of the Lord unworthily, shall be guilty of the body *and* blood of the Lord" (I. Cor. xi. 27; Acts xx. 7; Luke xxiv. 30, 31).

In this passage in the King James' Protestant version the word *and* is substituted for *or* without any warrant save the need of controversy, although the late revised version corrects the text in accordance with the original Greek and the Catholic English version.

The words "drink ye all of it" (Matt. xxvi. 27) were addressed, not to the faithful in general but to the Apostles who alone were present. "And they (the Apostles) all drank of it" (Mark xiv. 23). The Eucharist is not only a sacrament but a sacrifice ("do this for a commemoration of Me," Luke xxii. 19), and the sacrifice requires that the Victim, Jesus Christ, be at least mystically immolated, and His precious Blood shed in a mystical way. This is the reason why the Body and Blood of the Saviour, although inseparably united, are produced at Mass by a two-fold consecration—"This is My Body," "This is My Blood"—and under both forms. It was also required to complete the sacrifice that the Apostles and their successors, the priests of the New Law, should partake of the sacrifice under both forms. When, however, priests do not celebrate Mass, as when receiving the Viaticum in illness, they receive just as the laity, under the form of bread alone.

Moreover, any one versed in Church history knows that the practice of the Church has varied at different periods, according to circumstances. The Fathers of the Church tell us that the anchorites of the desert, travellers going on long journeys, people in their homes before their morning meal, and others in danger of death, as well as the martyrs in the prisons, received under the form of bread alone, whilst infants received under the form of wine alone.

In the fifth century Pope Gelasius (A.D. 492) commanded the laity to receive under both forms, to deter from Communion the Manicheans, who heretically considered wine evil in itself. The law commanding the laity to receive under the form of bread dates from the Council of Constance (A.D. 1414), and was directed against the heretical Hussites, who declared the use of the cup absolutely necessary. Custom, however, had long before this done away with Communion under the form of wine, for the reasons set forth in the catechism of the Council of Trent (Part ii. ch. 14, n. 64), viz., the scarcity of pure wine in certain places, the danger of spilling the consecrated species, the repugnance of some, etc. (Milner, "The End of Religious Controversy," Letter xxxix.; "Faith of Catholics," vol. ii.)

What would happen to the Sacrament if your

church was destroyed by fire? Is it not blasphemy to assert that Christ's sacred Body is digested by one of His followers?

Catholics believe that Christ's Body is now a glorified Body, and therefore incapable of suffering or change. Christ remains under the appearances of bread and wine no longer than these material appearances remain; once they cease because of digestion, or from any other cause, the presence of Christ ceases also.

Why do Catholics place one knee on the floor before entering the pew?

Catholics genuflect on entering and leaving the Church as a mark of love and adoration to Jesus Christ, the Son of God, who is really present upon the Catholic altar.

Why do Catholics fast before receiving Communion?

Out of honor and respect to Jesus Christ, whom they are going to receive. This was the practice of the primitive Christians, as we learn from Tertullian in the second century (Ad Uxorem, ii. 5).

What is meant by Benediction of the Blessed Sacrament?

Benediction is the blessing of the people by Jesus Christ, really present in the Blessed Sacrament.

After the candles are lighted upon the altar, the priest takes the Host consecrated at Mass out of the tabernacle, and places It in a stand of gold or silver called the monstrance or ostensorium, which remains upon the altar, or upon an elevated throne where it may be seen by all the people, who kneel and adore the Saviour.

The priest then puts incense into the thurible, and waves it three times in the direction of the Blessed Sacrament, as a symbol of the people's prayer. "Let My prayer be directed as incense in Thy sight" (Ps. cxl. 2). The choir or the people sing special hymns in honor of Jesus Christ, usually "O Salutaris Hostia" (O Saving Host) and the "Tantum Ergo" (Down in adoration falling).

Then placing over his shoulders a long silk scarf, called the humeral veil, the priest takes up the monstrance, and with it makes the sign of the cross over the people; and thus the Eucharistic Christ blesses the people.

There is no more beautiful or impressive ceremony in the Catholic Church, as many non-Catholics who have witnessed it have testified. After the Benediction the consecrated Host is again placed in the tabernacle, whilst the choir sings the cxvi. Psalm: "O praise the Lord, all ye nations," or the hymn "Holy God, we praise Thy Name."

THE MASS.

What do you mean by the Mass?

"The Mass, according to Catholic doctrine, is a commemoration of the sacrifice of the Cross, for as often as we celebrate it, we show the death of the Lord until He come (I. Cor. xi. 26). At the same time, it is not a bare commemoration of that other sacrifice, since it is also itself a true sacrifice in the strict sense of the term. It is a true sacrifice because it has all the essentials of a true sacrifice : its Priest, Jesus Christ, using the ministry of an earthly representative ; its Victim, Jesus Christ, truly present under the appearances of bread and wine ; its sacrificial offering, the mystic rite of consecration. And it commemorates the sacrifice of the Cross, because whilst its Priest is the Priest of Calvary, its Victim the Victim of Calvary, and its mode of offering a mystic representation of the blood-shedding of Calvary, the end also for which it is offered is to carry on the work of Calvary, by pleading for the application of the merits consummated on the Cross to the souls of men " (Vindication of the Bull on Anglican Orders, by the Bishops of England, p. 12).

What is the difference between a High Mass and a Low Mass?

They are essentially the same, and differ

only in the external ceremonies, which are more numerous and solemn in the former. A Solemn High Mass implies the presence of a deacon and subdeacon to assist the priest.

Did not Christ do away with sacrifices altogether in founding a new religion? What proof, indeed, is there in the Scriptures that He established a new one, which you call the Mass?

Among all nations and peoples from the beginning (Gen. iv.), Mohammedans and Protestants alone excepted, sacrifice, or the offering to God of the visible things of His creation in token of His supreme dominion and of our utter dependence upon Him, has been the chief external act of religion.

· In the Old Law, God answered this natural instinct of the human heart by giving to the Jewish people clear and explicit details of the various sacrifices, known as holocausts, or burnt-offerings; eucharistic, or thank-offerings (Exod. xxix.); impetratory, or peace-offerings (Lev. xxiv. 5–9), and propitiatory, or sin-offerings (Num. xxviii. 15).

We know from the Epistle to the Hebrews that these sacrifices were indeed only temporary, and types of the great sacrifice of Christianity. The priesthood of the Old Law foreshadowed the High-Priest Christ Jesus (Heb. viii.); the Jewish sacrifices, unable of themselves to take away sin (Heb. x. 4), pointed to the Sacrifice of Calvary, where "Christ being come, an High-Priest of the good things to come, . . . by His own blood . . . obtained eternal redemption" (Heb. ix. 11, 12).

This sacrifice, whereby man was redeemed, could not be repeated (Heb. x. 14), but the Catholic Church teaches that the Mass is this identical sacrifice, applying daily on the altars of the world the infinite merits of Jesus Christ to individual souls.

The prophet Malachi foretold a new sacrifice in place of the Jewish sacrifices, which was to be offered up among all the nations of the earth: "I have no pleasure in you (the priests), saith the Lord of hosts, and I will not receive a gift of your hand. For from the rising of the sun even to the going down, My name is great among the Gentiles ; and in every place there is a sacrifice, and there is offered to my name a clean oblation ; for My Name is great among the Gentiles, saith the Lord of hosts" (Mal. i. 10, 11).

Again, St. Paul (Heb. vii. 17) calls Jesus Christ a priest for ever according to the order of Melchisedech (Gen. xiv. 18), as distinguished from the order of Aaron. The unbloody sacrifice of Melchisedech—bread and wine—typifies therefore, as a type the reality, the sacrifice that Jesus Christ instituted at the Last Supper.

The sacrifice of the Mass was instituted at the Last Supper, where, as we read in Luke xxii. 20, Mark xiv. 24, Matt. xxvi. 28, our Lord declares that His blood contained at that moment in the chalice "*is shed* for the remission of sins," as the blood of victims in the Old Law was offered to the Lord for a sin-offering (Num. xxviii. 15). This shedding of the blood of Christ, physically upon the Cross, is in the sacrifice of the Mass mystical, and consists in the representation of Christ's death by the separate consecration of the Body and the Blood of Christ, although both are really inseparably united.

St. Paul, warning the Corinthians (I. Cor. x. 14–21) against taking part in the idolatrous worship around them, makes a comparison between the Corinthian pagan sacrificial altar and the "table" (altar) of the Christians. Again, he declares eating the flesh of a victim makes the pagan a sharer in the sacrificial offerings, and that therefore a Christian who, at the table (altar) of the Lord, receives Jesus Christ ("the Body of the Lord" and "the Blood of Christ"), ought not to eat victims sacrificed to idols. If there were no Eucharistic sacrifice of which the Christians partook, the argument of the Apostle would be utterly without meaning.

One other reference to the Mass is made by

St. Luke, when he tells us that the Christians of Antioch "were *ministering* to the Lord" (Acts xiii. 2). The word *ministering* here used always refers to sacrifice (Heb. ix. 21, x. 11), and has ever been the Greek equivalent (liturgy) for the Latin Missa (Mass). (For the testimonies of the Fathers, see "Faith of Catholics," vol. ii. p. 385–505; Wm. Humphrey, S.J., "The One Mediator"; Daniel Rock, D.D., "Hierurgia," vol. i.; Wilhelm–Scannell, "Manual of Catholic Theology," vol. ii. p. 431–463; O'Brien, "History of the Mass.")

Is not the sacrifice of Jesus on the Cross perfect and all-sufficient? St. Paul says: "By one oblation He hath perfected for ever them that are sanctified" (Heb. x. 14), and "we are sanctified by the oblation of the body of Jesus Christ once" (Heb. x. 10).

Catholics hold that the infinite merits and efficacy of the sacrifice of the Cross cannot be increased by any new sacrifice. The Mass is not a new sacrifice, but the continuation of the bloody sacrifice of the Cross applied in an unbloody manner to the souls of individual Christians, announcing daily "the death of the Lord until He come" (I. Cor. xi. 26), in fulfilment of the command of Christ: "Do this for a commemoration of me" (Luke xxii. 19). Was it fair to translate the Greek word "*ephapax*" in

the Protestant authorized version (Heb. x. 10)
"*once for all,*" whereas in all other passages
where the word occurs it is translated merely
by the word "*once*"? (Rom. vi. 10; I. Cor.
xv. 6; Heb. ix. 12, etc.)

Catholics denounce the irrational and incredible doctrine of the Atonement held by the
Reformers, that no matter how wicked a man
might be, he might still rest content with the
thought that Christ has made full atonement for
all his sins, which was imputed to the sinner
without any co-operation on his part. We believe the merits of Christ were indeed infinite,
but they must in some way be applied to the
sinner. They afford the means of salvation;
but a sinner must freely, through the sacraments and the Mass which apply that atonement, make them through God's grace his own.

**How can you be sure that Masses take souls out
of Purgatory? Do you know the secrets of God?**

We do not pretend to know how far God applies the infinite merits of the sacrifice of the
Mass to either the living or the dead. We
know, however, its propitiatory character by
the infallible witness of the Church (Trent.,
Sess. xxii. can. 3), which voices the teaching
of all the ancient liturgies, and of the Fathers.
"By Apostolic laws," says St. Chrysostom
(A.D. 398), "it is determined that in the vener-

able mysteries commemoration of the dead be made" (In Phil. Hom., 3, n. 4).

Why must Catholics go to church every Sunday under penalty of sin ? Our churches are not so exacting.

Because it is one of the laws of their Church, who as the divine, infallible teacher of the revelation of Jesus Christ alone dares command men with authority, to show at least this much homage to Jesus Christ present on her altars at the sacrifice of Calvary. I remember being asked once by a Congregational minister in Connecticut the secret of our large church attendance compared to the average small attendance in the Protestant churches throughout the country. "Jesus Christ really present," was my answer, "with the conviction that the Church, His living, divine voice, has power to command even as He, under penalty of damnation." When men disclaim all notion of infallibility for their church, and teach merely views, opinions, and speculations about the gospel of Christ, religious faith becomes daily more and more vague and shadowy, and its obligations soon vanish entirely.

What prayers does the priest say at Mass?

The chief prayers of the Mass are : the Forty-second Psalm, "Judge me, O Lord "; the Con_

fiteor, or confession of sins; the Introit, consisting generally of a verse of a psalm from the old
Itala version of the Scriptures; the Kyrie Elei-
son, or Lord have mercy on us (Matt. xx. 30;
Luke xvii. 13); the Gloria in Excelsis, or the
angels' song of joy at the birth of Christ (Luke
ii. 13, 14); the Dominus Vobiscum, the Lord be
with you (Ruth ii. 4; Luke i. 28; II. Tim. iv.
22); the Collects or Prayers, some of which are
over thirteen hundred years old; the Epistle
and Gospel, read from the earliest times, as the
Jews used to read Moses and the prophets in
the synagogue (Acts xiii. 15); the Credo, or
Nicene Creed; the Offertory, so-called for the
offerings formerly made by the people of bread
and wine for the sacrifice; the Preface, or the
introduction to the most solemn part of the
Mass, called the Canon; the Sanctus (Isaias vi.
3; Apoc. iv. 8; Matt. xxi. 9); the memento, or
special prayer for the living; the consecration,
This is My Body; this is My Blood (Matt.
xxvi. 26); the memento for the dead; the Pater
Noster, or Our Father (Matt. vi. 9); the Agnus
Dei (John i. 29); the Communion, the Blessing,
the Last Gospel—generally John i. 1–14.

The prayers of the liturgy breathe the simple
sweetness of the Word of God and of the early
Fathers, who prayed with hearts full of love for
Jesus Christ. No non-Catholic can read them
once and not perceive their wondrous beauty and

devotion. Indeed, a study of these prayers has made more than one earnest soul realize how false the spirit of the Reformation that could stigmatize them as "blasphemous fables and dangerous deceits" (Rev. John O'Brien, "A History of the Mass"). Most of the beautiful prayers in the Episcopal prayer-book, so much admired and loved, are merely translations of the old Catholic prayers.

Why do you charge for Masses? Is not this the sin of Simon Magus? (Acts viii. 18–24).

Why do you exact a fixed sum of money to get people out of Purgatory? Should not salvation be free to all?

Is not the money-payment for the so-called release of souls from Purgatory a human invention for filthy lucre, without the slightest warrant in the word of God?

Do you think it just that a rich man, simply because he has bequeathed money for Masses, should be liberated sooner from Purgatory than the poor man who leaves nothing, and has no wealthy friends to give money to the priest? Why have different prices for High and Low Mass?

We do not charge for Masses. The sin of Simon Magus consisted in his endeavoring to purchase the apostolic gift of miracles. Simony in every form—that is, the buying and selling of benefices, bishoprics, and abbacies, traffic in Masses, etc.—has ever been denounced as a grievous sin by the Catholic Church, and severest measures possible taken to guard against it (*cf.* Alzog, "Universal Church Hist.," vol. ii. pp. 160, 327, 369, 487). Her words to the simoniacal are the words of the first Pope, St. Peter: "Keep thy money to thyself, to perish with thee, because thou hast thought that the gift of God may be purchased with money. . . . Thy heart is not right in the sight of God. Do penance, therefore, for thy wickedness" (Acts viii. 20–23).

The *honoraria*, or stipends, for Masses are not the purchase-price of the Holy Sacrifice, but offerings or donations made by the people, in a spirit of love for the Church, to provide for the support of the clergy. The custom of making this donation dates from the twelfth century, for prior to this the people made at the offering of the Mass donations of all those things required for the carrying on of divine service, viz., bread, wine, oil, incense, etc.

The Church allows the priest to receive money for only one Mass a day; and if more Masses are asked for than he can say, he is bound to have them said by other priests— generally in poor districts where no offerings are made. As for the variation in stipends for a Requiem High Mass, we must take into account the expense incurred for the extra services of organist, choir, etc.

Of course abuses have occurred and will occur, for "the desire of money is a root of all evil" (I. Tim. vi. 10), as the Apostle tells us. The logical mind, however, will always ascribe these abuses to the sins of the individual, and not to the Church, which is most zealous to do away with them.

The religious duty of supporting the clergy is clearly set forth in the Old and New Testament, and the Catholic Church commands her children to do so by a special precept. In the Old Law the Jews set aside one-tenth of their flocks for their priests : "Of all the tithes of oxen and sheep and goats that pass under the shepherd's rod, every tenth that cometh shall be sanctified to the Lord" (Lev. xxvii. 32; Gen. xxviii. 22). Again, God ordered the people to make certain specified donations to the priests when they exercised their ministry. Thus, women after child-birth offered the priest "a lamb for a holocaust, and a young pigeon, or a turtle, for sin" (Lev. xii. 6); or if too poor, like the Blessed Virgin (Luke ii. 24), two turtle doves, or two young pigeons, . . . "and the priest shall pray for her" (Lev. xii. 8).

In the New Testament St. Paul expressly teaches the same duty : "Know you not, that they who work in the holy place, eat the things that are of the holy place ; and that they who serve at the altar, partake with the altar. So also the Lord, ordained that they who preach the gospel should live by the gospel '' (I. Cor. ix. 13, 14).

The custom, therefore, of making donations to the priesthood is sanctioned by God Himself. Why, even non-Catholics, on the occasion of a marriage or baptism, give a donation to their ministers. Do they consider this simony ? Why, in all fairness, is it right for the minister to accept his marriage fee, and yet wrong for a priest to receive a stipend for a Mass? The principle involved is identical in both cases.

As a matter of fact, it is the poor, and not the rich, who, as a general rule, contribute most generously to the support of the Church and the priesthood in our country. As for the objection about praying souls out of purgatory, one which I have frequently met with on missions to non-Catholics, I would say that the Catholic Church claims no jurisdiction over souls in the other world, and professes absolute ignorance regarding God's particular application of the infinite merits of the passion and death of His Son to the souls in purgatory. All Masses and prayers for the dead are applied ''by way of suffrage ''—that is, are dependent on God's secret mercy and will, who in His infinite justice may apply to another soul altogether the Masses said for a certain individual.

Non-Catholics generally think that five hundred Masses have five hundred times the efficacy of one. This is not the case. The value of each Mass is infinite, but we never know with perfect certainty whether or not God has applied it to the individual soul for whom it has been offered, although we do know He answers all our prayers.

Non-Catholics also forget that thousands of Masses and prayers are offered up yearly for all the souls in purgatory, and that in every Mass a special prayer is said by the priest for all the faithful departed: "To these, O Lord, and to all who rest in Christ, grant, we pray Thee, a place of refreshment, light, and peace. Through the same Christ our Lord. Amen" (Memento for the dead). There is no danger that God will allow any soul to suffer more than it deserves, or that one's poverty will make a soul less pleasing in God's sight. Besides, thousands of Masses are said yearly by priests for individuals too poor to make any donation whatsoever.

Why do you carry on your services in a tongue not known by the people? Why not say Mass in the language of the congregation?

Why do priests preach in Latin ? Why do you·
deliver so many of your sermons in Latin? Is it
to keep the people in ignorance ?

Sermons are never preached to the people in
Latin, but always in their own tongue. As to
the words of the Mass and other official services,
we do not consider the use of the Latin language essential, for in the East the use of the
vernacular is permitted. The Latin language,
however, is the official language of the Catholic
Church in her liturgy, councils, etc., for many
reasons :

1st. Historically, it bears witness to the origin of the faith of Western Christendom, Rome,
the converter of the nations—for instance,
France, Belgium, Spain, Portugal, England,
Ireland, Scotland, Germany, Hungary, Poland.
The Catholic Church, founded by Jesus Christ,
when the Roman Empire was supreme, naturally adopted in her liturgy the language of
the people, and her missionaries kept the language of Rome in the divine service even when
they had to preach in the vernacular. Protestant churches, born in modern times, adopted
as a consequence the modern languages.

2d. Again, Latin being a dead language, is
free from all those changes inevitable to modern
tongues. In these latter, words are continually
becoming obsolete, and so change in meaning
as to become unintelligible and ridiculous to the

ears of succeeding generations. Latin, therefore, preserves the dignity of the liturgy and
the perfect exactness of the dogmatic decrees of
Councils, so necessary in a perennial, unchangeable Church.

3d. A Universal Church, moreover, should
have a universal language. It is the same
principle that made business men some years
ago endeavor to establish Volupük as a common means of communication, or medical men
of late discuss the advisability of adopting some
common language in their congresses. Did any
one ever object, for example, to French as the
language of diplomacy? Latin allows the
Catholic people to feel at home everywhere in
the universal bond of a common language at
their Sunday Mass, and enables the Catholic
bishops of the world to correspond easily with
the Roman See, and discuss matters of dogma
and discipline in the councils of the Universal
Church.

4th. In the Jewish synagogue the services
were conducted in Hebrew even after it had
ceased to be ~~the~~ language of the people, who
lost it at the time of the Captivity (II. Esdras viii.
13). And so in the East to-day the Melchites
say Mass in Greek and the Syrians in Syriac,
although Arabic is the language of the people.

Indeed, there is no reason for fault-finding,
for remember that in those parts of the service

that we have in common with Protestants, namely, preaching, public prayers, and hymn-singing, we use the language of the people. But the Mass with us is more of an action than a prayer—an act of sacrifice which the priest offers up in the name of Christ for the people.

The people are, therefore, perfectly free to follow their own special devotion in the manner of hearing Mass, either meditating on the passion and death of Jesus Christ, or, if they so desire, following the prayers of the liturgy in the translations to be found in their prayer-books. It would indeed be practically impossible in some of our large churches for the priest to be understood, even if he did celebrate Mass in English, and as a matter of fact the liturgical laws of the Church command that certain prayers be read, for sake of greater reverence, in a very low voice. There is no more necessity for the people of our day understanding what the priest says than of old when Jewish priests prayed alone in the Tabernacle at the hour of sacrifice (Luke i. 9, 10).

I have frequently wondered why so many otherwise well-informed non-Catholics imagined that we preached in Latin to our congregations. Aside from ignorance arising from deliberate calumny in the past, I know of no way to account for this save that some Protestants attending a Catholic burial service have mistaken the

Latin liturgical prayers read by the priest over the body of the deceased for a sermon to the people.

Does not St. Paul condemn your use of Latin when he says: " Yet in the church I had rather speak five words with my understanding, that by my voice I might teach others also, than ten thousand words in an unknown tongue " ? (I. Cor. xiv. 19).

No ; St. Paul is not speaking of the liturgy of the Church at all, but is condemning those Christians at Corinth who, instead of teaching the people, were merely making an ostentatious display of their miraculous gift of tongues— praying and preaching words unintelligible to their hearers without an interpreter. In the Catholic Church all the sermons, instructions, and private prayers are in the language of the people.

Why did the Protestant translators of this chapter add the word " unknown " in verses 2, 4, 13, 14, 19, and 27, and omit this same word in verses 18 and 39, where the use of unknown tongues is approved ?   The same phrase occurs in the Greek original: " I thank my God I speak with (unknown) tongues more than ye all."   " Wherefore, brethren, .   .   . forbid not to speak with (unknown) tongues " (vv. 18 and 39).

Why, again, were the Irish people, in the reign of Queen Elizabeth, compelled by statute to be present at the reading of the English liturgy, which they did not understand, if Protestants were so zealous for having service celebrated in the language of the people? (P. Heylin, ''Hist. of Reformation,'' p. 128).

ORDERS.

May not any one who is filled with the Apostolic spirit preach the Gospels of Christ without going through a ceremony of so-called ordination?

No, for the Scriptures expressly declare there must be a divine commission to teach: ''Neither doth any man take the honor to himself, but he that is called by God, as Aaron was'' (Heb. v. 4); and again, '' How can they preach unless they be sent'' (Rom. x. 15; *cf.* Matt. xxviii. 19).

Our Lord instituted the Christian priesthood when he gave his Apostles and their successors the power to offer up the sacrifice of the Mass (Matt. xxvi. 26–28; I. Cor. xi. 23–25), and to forgive and retain sins (John xx. 23). This power was to be handed down by the sacrament of Orders (Trent., Sess. xxiii. can. 2), spoken of by the Apostle: ''Neglect not the grace which was given thee by prophecy, with impo-

sition of the hands of the priesthood " (I. Tim.
iv. 14); "I admonish thee that thou stir up the
grace of God, which is in thee by the imposition of my hands " (II. Tim. i. 6). We have
here a special sacrament : the external sign,
namely, the imposition of hands and prayer, the
grace conferred thereby, and the institution by
Christ (*cf.* Acts vi. 6; xiii. 2, 3; xiv. 22; I.
Tim. v. 22; Tit. i. 5).

**Is there the slightest evidence of episcopacy
in the primitive Church? Were not bishop and
presbyter synonymous terms?**

It is undoubtedly true that in the New Testament the words Bishop (Episcopos) and Priest
(Presbuteros) were applied without distinction
to the same person (Acts xx. 17, 28; Tit. i.
5-7), but it by no means follows from this that
they had the same office and dignity. The
Bishops, for instance, of the third century were
often called presbyteri, although their superi-
ority over priests was everywhere acknowledged. The distinction is mentioned by Clement of Rome (A. D. 101), and most clearly and
distinctly brought out in the letter of Ignatius
Martyr (A. D. 105-117). Even St. Jerome,
who is often adduced to the contrary, says
clearly : "What, except ordination, can a
bishop do that a priest cannot do?" (Epis.
101). There is no evidence in all history of a

priest having the power to ordain. Indeed, at the second Council of Alexandria, under Hosius (A. D. 324), all the ordinations of Colluthus, an Alexandrine priest, were declared null and void. This power, too, is clear from St. Paul, who advises the Bishops Timothy and Titus to "ordain priests in every city" (Tit. i. 5), and " not to impose hands lightly on any man " (I. Tim. v. 22 ; Alzog, vol. i. pp. 198–204).

Why do Catholics call their priests "father," when Christ says : "Call no man father upon the earth; for one is your Father, which is in heaven"? (Matt. xxiii. 9).

If this passage is to be taken universally, it would be wrong to call our parents father, or our teachers master. Our Lord merely meant to rebuke the pride of the Scribes and Pharisees, who gloried in the salutation of Rabbi, father, etc.

The word "Father" is given by Catholics to their priests from their sense of his spiritual relationship to them, and is fully sanctioned by Holy Scripture. St. Paul says : "For if you have ten thousand instructors in Christ, yet not many fathers. For in Christ Jesus, by the gospel, I have begotten you " (I. Cor. iv. 15). Again, he calls Timothy "his beloved son" (I. Tim. i. 2), and St. John calls the early Christians "little children" (I. John ii. 18).

RELIGIOUS COMMUNITIES.

Can we not serve God by serving mankind, thus following Christ's example? Why then the life of the recluse and the cloistered orders?

What is the good of religious communities? Is there any mention of them in the Bible? Are they essential to Christianity? Is it not unmanly to subject one's will to another under vow? Is not a life of perpetual chastity impossible? Is it not the duty of good men and women to stay in the world and make it better by their good example? Did not Christ say: "Let your light so shine," etc.? (Matt. v. 16).

There is no mention of our religious orders in the Bible, any more than there is mention of hospitals, foundling asylums, homes for the aged, or pest-houses for the leper. But the ideal that prompts their organization is there— the example and teaching of the poor, obedient, heroic Jesus Christ, the Son of God, and of the early Christians. Religious orders of this or that special kind could all be suppressed to-morrow, and the Catholic Church would still exist in her dogmas, her morality, her discipline, her sacraments, and her divine infallible authority. But they are the natural fruit and flower of the tree of God's planting. They are the answer to that craving of the human heart for association in the perfect following of Christ. The com-

mandments are for all under penalty of damnation; the counsels of Christ are very different,
and are for those who out of the generosity of
their hearts desire to follow Him in the freedom
of the way of perfection (Matt. v. 48).

The New Testament gives us clearly the essence of the religious community—the love of
God and the brethren for His sake. The privileged ones remember Christ's promise to be
present in a special way to those that prayed in
common (Matt. xviii. 20); they realize that
self-denial and mortification are the true marks
of perfect discipleship (Matt. xvi. 24); they
practise poverty, because Christ "being rich
became poor for our sakes" (Matt. viii. 20),
while he told the young man of the Gospel:
"If thou will be perfect, go sell what thou hast,
and give to the poor, . . . and come follow
me" (Matt. xix. 21); they observe chastity,
because the virgin Christ was born of a virgin
Mother, and praised virginity as the perfect life
of the few. "He that can take it, let him take
it" (Matt. xix. 12); they subject their will to
another, because Jesus Christ came to do the
will of His heavenly Father even unto the death
of the cross, and was obedient unto Joseph and
his mother Mary (John iv. 34; Phil. ii. 8;
Luke ii. 51).

Why should any one object to men and
women banding together to serve God and the

brethren ? If in religious communities men can conquer more easily the temptations of pride, avarice, and lust, pray with greater fervor, follow out the counsels of the Saviour more perfectly, and yet withal help the world by the greatest possible service of prayer, as in contemplative orders, or by the extraordinary charity and zeal in the active orders, why should men grudge them this liberty of association, which is not denied to the man of business or politics, whose only God is too often self?

Is chastity impossible? This question proceeds only from the lips of those whose hearts are full of sin and passion, and know no higher ideal than that of carnal lust. It is an insult to the wives, sisters, and mothers of thousands.

Is obedience unmanly and degrading? The Scriptures do not consider the obedience of a child to its parent or a wife to her husband degrading (Eph. v. 22, vi. 1). No one calls the obedience of a soldier to the commands of his officer unmanly. Why should subjection to another out of love of God and in the things of God be evil, when subjection to another out of self-interest and in the things of this life of business, politics, etc., is considered good ?

But, you object, men should not thus withdraw from society ; they should take their share of the burden. History is the witness how no-

bly and well the religious communities of men
and women have served their fellow-men. Is
there a man outside the Catholic Church whose
charity for all has been more fruitful in good
works than St. Vincent de Paul's? In the
Middle Ages who but the monks were the patrons of literature, the arts and the sciences, the
cultivators of the soil, the educators of the ignorant? Indeed, we have only to look around
us to-day, and we must needs bear testimony to
the wonderful work done by such devoted
women as the Sisters of Charity, the Little
Sisters of the Poor, the Sisters of the Good
Shepherd, and the Sisters of Mercy. How
many Protestants have written and spoken in
their praise? "Father," said one to me lately,
"I don't know much about your Church, but I
do know for a certainty that the good sisters of
your Church are the best nurses in the world."
Another: "Father, I saw the Sisters of Charity
in the Civil War serving equally the Blue and
the Gray, and serving me on what I thought
my death-bed. I desire to join the Church,
feeling convinced that the Church that inspires
such devotion must needs be the Church of
Christ." A third: "I intend to send my girls
away to school; and though a non-Catholic, I
feel the good influence of the sisters of your
Church is something no money can buy." And
so witness on witness can be appealed to—Prot-

estant, Jew, and infidel alike—concerning the
zeal, charity, and devotion of these women,
who freely dedicate their lives to the service of
the neighbor. The light of their good works
does indeed shine forth before all men, so "that
men give glory to our Father in Heaven."

But why bind one's self to such a life by a
vow? The answer is simply this : that men and
women have the same right and liberty in
things divine as in things human. Is it a
blessed thing to swear loyalty to a woman in
the pure bond of marriage, and a curse to swear
loyalty to Christ Jesus in the pure bond of a supernatural espousal? The world may not understand, but that is rather due to its spirit
being alien to Christ, for " the sensual man perceiveth not those things that are of the Spirit of
God ; for it is foolishness to him, and he cannot
understand, because it is spiritually examined "
(I. Cor. ii. 14).

"I can understand," says another, "the
charitable work done by the Apostolic men and
women in your Church ; but what is the good
of contemplative orders?" To a busy, utilita-
rian, and materialistic age it does indeed seem
strange that men should retire from the world
merely to pray. But to the Christian, who
knows the value and efficacy of prayer, as witnessed to in the Old and New Testaments,
there is no difficulty. He realizes the great

lack of prayer in the world. He knows that these contemplative orders make atonement for the sins of many, ask God's mercy upon His people, and give Him the glory, the praise, and the honor denied by those who will not serve, like Satan of old. The efficacy of such prayers will not be known until the day of Judgment.

In conclusion, let men divest themselves of their prejudices, and study the history of the saints of the religious orders, as is being done to-day by many outside the Catholic Church, and all his objections will disappear like mists before the rising sun. One does not learn the beauties of the landscape from a blind man, or the blessings of a country's institutions from one who has proven traitor to it. So fair-minded men should not listen to the false and impure utterances of a wicked priest who has been false to his Church, or an outcast woman, who, in return for the charity of the sisters who rescued her from the streets, poses impudently to a curious world as an "escaped nun" and calumniates for a price the Church that helped her in her need.

Were not the monks of the Middle Ages an idle, ignorant, and immoral set of men ?

Sometimes, indeed, in the course of history we read of monasteries that relaxed their ancient discipline, and became a scandal to the

Church of God. But, as the Protestant historian Maitland says: "It appears to be the testimony of history that the monks and the clergy, whether bad or good in themselves, were in all times and places better than other people" (Preface to "The Dark Ages," p. 8). Again, he speaks of monasteries "as a quiet and religious refuge for helpless infancy and old age, a shelter of respectable sympathy for the orphan maiden and the desolate widow; as central points whence agriculture was to spread over bleak hills and barren downs and marshy plains, and deal bread to millions perishing with hunger and its pestilential train; as repositories of the learning which then was, and well-springs of the learning which was to be; as nurseries of art and science, giving the stimulus, the means, and the reward to invention, and aggregating around them every head that could devise and every hand that could execute; as the nucleus of the city, which in after days of pride should crown its palaces and bulwarks with the towering cross of its cathedral. This, I think, no man can deny" (S. R. Maitland, "The Dark Ages," p. 2).

Listen to another Protestant testimony (Cutts, "Scenes and Characters of the Middle Ages," p. 9): "Their general character was, and continued throughout the Middle Ages to be, that of wealthy and learned bodies; influential from their broad possessions, but still more influential from the fact that nearly all the literature and art and science of the period was to be found in their body. They were good landlords to their tenants, good cultivators of their demesnes; great patrons of architecture and sculpture and painting; educators of the people in their schools; healers of the sick in their hospitals; great alms-givers to the poor; freely hospitable to travellers; they continued regular and constant in their religious services; but in housing, clothing, and diet they lived the life of temperate gentlemen rather than of self-denying ascetics. Doubtless, as we have said, in some monasteries there were evil men, whose vices brought disgrace upon their calling; and there were some monasteries in which weak or wicked rulers had allowed the evil to prevail."

No one at all conversant with the Middle Ages can deny that the monasteries were the centres of the intellectual life of the age; that their buildings, farms, libraries, prove that every moment of the day was busily employed according to strict rule; that the universal respect in which the monks were held by their contemporaries witnesses to their high moral and religious character.

Did not Henry VIII. dissolve the monasteries in his time because of their gross immorality?

No, he suppressed six hundred monasteries in a few years (1536–1547) that he might confiscate their property. No one who knows history can accuse this wretch of a king, whose whole life is marked with lust and murder, of any zeal for religion or morality (Dom Gasquet, "Henry VIII. and the English Monasteries"; Cobbett, "History of the Reformation ").

Were not recalcitrant nuns walled up alive in the Middle Ages?

"To any one who honestly looks into the matter it will be clear that no statutes of any religious order have yet been brought forward which prescribe such punishment, that no contemporary records speak of its infliction, that no attempt is made to give details of person or time, that the few traditions that speak of the discovery of walled-up remains crumble away the moment they are examined, that the growth of the tradition itself can be abundantly accounted for, that the few historians or antiquaries of repute, whether Catholic or Protestant, who have looked into the matter, either avowedly disbelieve the calumny or studiously refrain from repeating it " (Rev. H. Thurston, S.J., "The Myth of the Walled-up Nun," Catholic Truth Society Publications. *Cf.* "The Immuring of Nuns," by same author).

Are women detained in nunneries against their will? Why are not convents open to public inspection ?

Because they are private dwellings. Would you want your home open to every stranger, good or bad? They can always be visited by the Bishop of the diocese, or any one who takes the proper means to be introduced there. The objection seems based on that false notion which is so prevalent among non-Catholics, that only weak-minded women under stress of some strong emotion, as disappointed love, fanaticism, great sorrow, and the like, take the vows that bind them willy-nilly in a bondage worse than death. Much of the evil that has been suggested originates from apostate priests, or abandoned women who have been under the care of the good sisters for a time, and repay their benefactors by calumniating them for money. How different the facts to one who investigates at first hand. Many of the noblest women in the world have freely given up all that the world holds dear, friends, ambition, wealth, social position, to serve God in poverty, chastity, and obedience in the silence of the cloister, or to minister to the wants of the sick, the aged, and the poor.

Why cannot women preach the Gospel as well as men ?

It has ever been the tradition of the Catholic Church that women, however high their office as wives and mothers, were incapable of ordination, according to the teaching of St. Paul: "Let women keep silence in the churches, for it is not permitted them to speak; but to be subject, as also the law saith. It is a shame for women to speak in the church" (I. Cor. xiv. 34, 35). "Let the women learn in silence, with all subjection. But I suffer not a woman to teach nor to use authority over the man, but to be in silence" (I. Tim. ii. 11, 12).

Tertullian in the third century reproaches the heretics of his time for their denial of this custom. "The very women of these heretics," he writes, "how wanton they are! For they are bold enough to teach, to dispute, to enact exorcisms, to undertake cures, it may be even to baptize" (De Præsc. xli.)

ANGLICAN ORDERS.

What is the attitude of your Church regarding Anglican Orders?

Why do Catholics deny the validity of the ordinations in the Episcopal Church?

Pope Leo XIII., after a careful study of the question, declared, in the Bull *Apostolicæ Curæ*, September 13, 1896, the invalidity of Anglican orders: "Wherefore, strictly adhering in this matter to the decrees of the Pontiffs our predecessors, and confirming them most fully, and, as it were, renewing them by our authority, of our own motion and certain knowledge, we pronounce and declare that ordinations carried out according to the Anglican rite have been, and are, absolutely null and utterly void.''

The two reasons for this condemnation were: 1st, the *defect of form in the rite used*, viz., the Edwardine Ordinal; 2d, *the defect of intention in the minister*. Pope Leo says: '' From (the Anglican rite) has been deliberately removed whatever sets forth the dignity and office of the priesthood in the Catholic rite. That form consequently cannot be considered apt or sufficient for the sacrament which omits what it ought essentially to signify. The same holds good of Episcopal consecration. As the sacrament of Order, and the true priesthood of Christ, were eliminated from the Anglican rite, and hence the priesthood is in nowise conferred truly and validly in the Episcopal consecration of the same rite, for the like reason, therefore, the episcopate can in nowise be truly and validly conferred by it; and this the more so because among the first duties of the episcopate is that of ordaining ministers for the Holy Eucharist and sacrifice.''

It is historically certain that Cranmer and his followers, who drew up the Edwardine Ordinal

of 1550, which was used at the consecration of
the first Protestant archbishop, Parker, December 17, 1559, did not believe in a sacrificing
priesthood, but held that bishops and priests
became such by the mere appointment of the
crown. "In the New Testament," said Cranmer, "he that is appointed to be a bishop or a
priest *needeth no consecration* by the Scriptures,
for *election or appointment thereto is sufficient*"
(Burnet, "History of the Reformation," vol. i.
p. 201. *Cf.* Green, "History of the English
People," vol. ii. p. 234; London, 1880. For
Barlow's opinion read Burnet, *ibid.*, and Col-
lier's "Ecclesiastical History," vol. iv. p. 381).
Their views are clearly set forth in the Thirty-
nine Articles, which declared that orders
"would not be counted for a sacrament of the
gospel" (Article XXV.), and the Mass "a
blasphemous fable" (Article XXXI.)

The new Protestant ordinal omitted all the
anointings, the delivery of the vestments, and,
although retaining the imposition of hands as a
mere ceremony to signify the candidate's appointment, it purposely omitted those essential
words of the sacramental form which indicated
the sacrificial character of the priesthood. The
defective form ran as follows: "Take the Holy
Ghost, and remember that thou stir up the
grace of God which is in thee by the imposition
of hands, for God hath not given us the spirit

of fear, but of power and love and soberness.''
The Catholic argues that these men, who
denied the sacrament of orders, and declared
the essential power of the priesthood to be a
blasphemous fable and a dangerous deceit,
could not have intended to ordain priests in
the Catholic sense of the word.

Says Pope Leo XIII.: ''The Church does
not judge about the mind or intention in so far
as it is something by its nature internal; but in
so far as it is manifested externally, she is
bound to judge concerning it. When any one
has rightly and seriously made use of the due
form and the matter requisite for affecting or
conferring the sacrament, he is considered by
the very fact to do what the Church does. On
this principle rests the doctrine that a sacrament is truly conferred by the ministry of one
who is a heretic or unbaptized, provided the
Catholic rite be employed. On the other hand,
if the rite be changed with the manifest intention of introducing another rite not approved
by the Church, and of rejecting what the
Church does, and what by the institution of
Christ belongs to the nature of the sacrament,
then it is clear that not only is the necessary intention wanting to the sacrament, but that the
intention is adverse to and destructive of the
sacrament.''

Moreover, historically speaking, it is not certain that Barlow, the consecrator of Parker, was ever consecrated. (On this point read Canon Estcourt, "The Question of Anglican Ordinations," pp. 60 *et seq.*; Arthur Hutton, "Anglican Orders," p. 303; Bellasis, "Was Barlow a Bishop?")

The Catholic Church has never wavered in her attitude. From the days of Queen Mary she has always denied the existence of Anglican orders, by ordaining those ministers who wished on their conversion to enter the ranks of her apostolic priesthood (Gallwey, "Ritualism," two volumes, Catholic Truth Society Publications; Sydney Smith, "Reasons for Rejecting Anglican Orders"; "Rome's Witness against Anglican Orders"; Articles on the Bull Apostolicæ Curæ in *American Catholic Quarterly, Dublin Review, Ecclesiastical Review, London Tablet*, etc.)

CELIBACY.

Where in the Bible are priests forbidden to marry?

Why is it that Catholic priests do not marry?

Because celibacy is one of the disciplinary laws of the Western Church, which every one who is ordained subdeacon vows to observe for life. While not a dogma of the Catholic Church, it is an obligatory law, imposed with a view to the dignity and duties of the priesthood.

Jesus Christ, himself a Virgin born of a virgin Mother, commends the state of virginity most highly (Matt. xix. 11–13) : " All men take not this word, but they to whom it is given. For there are eunuchs, who were born so from their mother's womb ; and there are eunuchs, who were made so by men ; and there are eunuchs, who 'have made themselves eunuchs for the kingdom of heaven. He that can take, let him take it." The Pharisees had questioned our Lord as to the lawfulness of divorce. Our Lord tells them that the Mosaic bill of divorce had been granted "by reason of the hardness of their hearts " (*ibid.*), contrary to the original law of marriage, which was the indissoluble union of one man with one woman. " What therefore God hath joined together, let no man put asunder" (*ibid.*) ; " From the beginning it was not so " (*ibid.*) This doctrine seemed so hard that his hearers replied that celibacy would be preferable to such a lasting bond of marriage. " If the case of a man with his wife be so, it is not expedient to marry " (*ibid.*) Christ answers that some are celibates from natural defect, others from being made so by men, while a third class freely chooses this state of life for the kingdom of heaven (*ibid.*) It is not a commandment for all, but a counsel for

the few : " All men take not this word, but
they to whom it is given " (*ibid.*) Evidently
our Lord expressly praises celibacy when voluntarily undertaken for His service.

.The teaching of St. Paul is exactly the same
(I. Cor. vii.) The Apostle himself led a life of
celibacy and recommended it, as Christ had
done, to those who felt called thereto : " I say,
to the unmarried and to the widows : It is good
for them if they so continue even as I. But if
they do not contain themselves, let them
marry " (vv. 8, 9). He declares, moreover,
that there was no commandment of the Lord
either to marry or to lead a life of celibacy ;
both were the free choice of the Christian.
" Concerning virgins, I have no commandment
of the Lord " (*ibid.*) ; " Art thou bound to a
wife ? Seek not to be loosed. Art thou loosed
from a wife ? Seek not a wife. But, if thou
take a wife, thou hast not sinned ; and if a virgin marry, she hath not sinned " (vv. 27, 28).
However, he expressly declares that the state
of celibacy is a higher state than the state of
marriage : " Therefore both he that giveth his
virgin in marriage, doth well ; and he that giveth her not, doth better " (*ibid.*) Why, then,
in face of the explicit example and teaching of
Jesus Christ and His great Apostle Paul, can
men question the excellence of the virgin life,
and deny certain privileged souls the right of

following more closely in the footsteps of the Master?

St. Paul, again, gives us the practical reason why the priesthood of Christ practises celibacy : "He that is without a wife, is solicitous for the things that belong to the Lord, how he may please God. But he that is with a wife, is solicitous for the things of the world, how he may please his wife, and he is divided" (vv. 32, 33). The Catholic Church realizes well that better work can be done for God's people by a celibate clergy than by a married clergy. The married minister must needs divide his time, work, and money between his flock and family. He is hampered in his ministry by many household cares; he must provide for his wife and children; look after the education of his boys and girls, settle them in life, etc. So evident is this, especially when a married minister is living in a poor country district, or goes abroad on foreign missions, that some Protestants have advocated celibacy in these cases. A Presbyterian said not long since to me: "I do not care about men settled in big cities, like Calcutta or Pekin, with beautiful homes and comfortable salaries from America or England. But I've met some zealous men returning from a hard mission, with a pale-faced wife and sickly children, who instead of helping him, were only a burden on his ministry."

We must remember also the vast difference between the duties of the Protestant minister and the Catholic priest. As a rule, the minister preaches but one or two sermons a week, looks after the Sunday-school, and some few societies of men and women, and visits his flock, or certain portions thereof, from time to time. The Catholic priest, over and above his preaching, Sunday-school, societies and the like, is the servant of the people—at their beck and call every hour of the day and night. He must spend many a long hour in the confessional, bearing his people's burden of sin and sorrow; he must venture out in the cold and rain and snow, no matter what the distance or the danger, to administer the last sacraments to the dying; he must instruct his people in the dogmas of faith, and be ready at all times to answer the questions of outsiders, seeking for the light; he must advise, correct, and warn, when there is question of the gospel of Christ, and he cares for no man when duty is to be done. He is freer to face danger, because he never need question the effect of his actions on the affections, health, interests, or opinions of wife and family. How often has the world seen him speaking the word of comfort to the sick in the small-pox hospital, as in Philadelphia to-day; hearing the confession of the dying soldier on the firing-line, as American priests in the late war with Spain; going from house to house in the city of the plague, and burying the dead with his own hands, as the sons of St. Vincent de Paul did in France in the seventeenth century.

Again, the people would not as a rule trust their secrets to a married clergy. "I believe in confession," said a High-Church Episcopalian once to me, "just as much as you do. But I could not go to my minister." "Why?" "He might tell his wife." Not that we question the honor of such men, but their whole trend and tendency veto practically their ever receiving the confidence of any great number of their flock. The Catholic priest hears the confessions of thousands. Often, on our Catholic missions, we hear eight and nine hundred confessions in one week.

We know also of ministers who to support their families are obliged to engage in secular business during the week. Surely the soldier of Christ should be free from this. "No man, being a soldier to God, entangleth himself with secular business" (II. Tim. ii. 4). Indeed, a Catholic priest, with all the work that usually devolves upon him, would find it impossible. Imagine, too, an hereditary caste, formed in the Church of God, handing down property from father to son, and enriching relatives, to the great harm of the Church of God. Something like this is the actual condition in the Russian Church, resulting from a married clergy.

Is it not wrong for your Church to impose the impossible and intolerable burden of celibacy upon the clergy?

How can a celibate clergy be chaste? Is not celibacy against nature?

These objections date from Martin Luther, whose sermon on the universal obligation of marriage would not bear repetition in any Christian pulpit of the world ·to-day. He followed out most exactly his own teaching by attempting to marry a nun, who broke her enclosure before breaking her vows.

Celibacy is not impossible, for the grace of God is given abundantly to his priests to keep them pure. Would you say that all the unmarried find it impossible to be chaste? Are your own unmarried children, sisters, widowed cousins, maiden aunts, and bachelor uncles impure? Are all husbands who for certain reasons are separated from their wives for a long period, bound to commit adultery? The objection is a libel on the pure character of thousands, clerical and lay, and proceeds from hearts full of lust, who judge that others are even as they. Celibacy is not an intolerable burden, for it is voluntarily chosen by men and women who are old enough to know what they are doing, and who feel freer thereby to serve God and the brethren.

Men have declared it against nature. Would you then forthwith compel every one to get married, whether he will or no? If so unnatural, why is it that virginity has been admired and practised all down the centuries, even among the pagans? Judæa, Greece, Rome, Gaul, Peru, all bear witness to the fact that chastity is not unnatural.

Many have pointed to the scandals that have arisen from time to time. Will any man dare say that the married clergy—whether Greek, Russian, or Protestant—have been freer of scandals than the Catholic priesthood? Will you abolish marriage because thousands of men and women have broken their marriage vows? Voltaire, no lover of Christianity or the clergy, was forced to write: "The life of secular men has always been more vicious than that of priests; but the disorders of the latter have always been more remarkable, from their contrast with the rule." And Dean Maitland: "In fact, it appears to be the testimony of history, that the monks and clergy . . . were in all times and places better than other people" ("The Dark Ages," preface, p. 8, John Hodges, 1889).

Did not celibacy originate in the desire of Pope

Gregory VII. to secure a greater control over the clergy?

No; celibacy originated by Christ's appointment, and flows naturally out of the Christian sense of the dignity of the priesthood; and voluntarily entered upon in Apostolic times, it became the law for the Western Church in the beginning of the fourth century. Pope Gregory VII. in the Roman synod of 1074 merely revived the old laws, and enforced their observance under the severest penalties.

I think priests ought to marry, because the husband and father develops a finer and kindlier nature, and gathers experiences which enable him to teach religion with greater force than the unmarried.

It is rather strange, in view of law-court statistics, to declare that the husband and father *necessarily* develops a finer and kindlier nature. What kindlier man than the good old parish priest, loved by all—old and young, rich and poor, cultured and uncultured?

Again, whose experience is wider and more varied than the priest, who is trusted as no other living man with the secrets of all in the sacred tribunal of the sacrament of penance? To say that a priest ought to marry the better to understand how to teach men well, is about as sensible as to tell a physician to taste his

every medicine in order to prescribe correctly
for his patients.

Does not God say in the first chapter of Genesis
"increase and multiply"? (Gen. i. 28).

Yes; but this is said as a general blessing on
the race, and by no means implies that a man
or woman who chooses to remain unmarried
thereby breaks a commandment of God.

Did not St. Paul say that he was married?
"Have we not power to carry about a woman
a sister, as well as the rest of the Apostles and
the brethren of the Lord, and Cephas?" (I. Cor.
ix. 5).

The Apostle expressly states that he was not
married (I. Cor. vii. 8). The above text by no
means refers to a wife, but, as St. Jerome explains (Contra Jovinian, i. 14), refers to the
holy women who, according to Jewish custom,
adopted by Christ himself, followed their religious master about, and ministered to his wants
(Matt. xxvii. 55). ("Was St. Paul married?"
American Catholic Quarterly, 1890, p. 697.)

Was not St. Peter a married man?

He undoubtedly was, yet tradition declares
that he did not live with his wife after the
divine call (Jerome, Ep. 48 ad Pammachium);
the words of St. Peter to Christ are plain:

"Behold we have left all things and have followed thee." What matters it, however, whether he were married or not? We have undoubtedly the example and the teaching of the Saviour and St. Paul as ample warrant for the discipline of Western Christendom in this matter.

Why don't priests marry, when St. Paul says: "To avoid fornication, let every man have his own wife?" (I. Cor. vii. 2).

The Apostle is not urging the unmarried to marry, as our questioner seems to imagine, for in this very chapter he extols virginity as a counsel of Christ and a higher state of life (*ibid.*) besides urging his own example (*ibid.*), the better to serve God (*ibid.*)

On the contrary, he is exhorting (vv. 2–11) those already married to fulfil the duties of their state of life in all purity, to hate adultery, to shun divorce, polygamy, etc.

Does not the Scriptures say: "It is better to marry than to burn"? (I. Cor. vii. 9).

Undoubtedly; but these words of the Apostle in no way imply a general prohibition against celibacy. The Apostle is addressing the unmarried, whom he advises to remain so, if they feel called, as he was, to follow Christ in the virgin life, and desire thereby to be freer in

their work for the brethren. " I say to the unmarried, and to the widow : it is good for them
if they so continue even as I " (vv. 8–33).

If, on the contrary, men and women are living unmarried, the better to satisfy their lusts,
and subject to carnal thoughts and desires (to
burn), he urges them to marry. " But if they
cannot contain themselves, let them marry.
For it is better to marry than to be burned (to
burn)."

So in like manner to-day the Catholic priest
advises a higher grade of souls to follow out
our Lord's counsel of virginity (" All men take
not this word, but they to whom it is given,"
Matt. xix. 11), but he warns all others to
marry and not to take upon themselves the vow
of virginity, whether in the priesthood or the
cloister.

**Do not the Scriptures teach that " it behooveth
a bishop to be the husband of one wife " ? (I.
Tim. iii. 2 ; *cf.* Tit. i. 6 ; I. Tim. iii. 12).**

Until the fourth century (Council of Elvira,
305 ; Arles, 314 ; and Ancyra, 314) there was
no strict law enforcing celibacy, and therefore
many married men received orders. The texts
in question show not that all deacons and
bishops should be married men—St. Paul himself was not—but that no one would be considered fit for ordination who had been twice

married. Any one conversant with the writings of the early Church Fathers is fully aware of their horror of second marriages. Indeed, the same law against ordaining a widower who has been twice married exists in the Church to this day, as proof positive of the ancient Christian interpretation of this text of Holy Scripture.

Does not St. Paul reckon "forbidding to marry" as one of the doctrines of the devil? (I. Tim. iv. 3).

St. Paul is denouncing the early Ebionite, Marcionite, and Manichean heretics who condemned marriage as evil in itself, and proceeding from an evil principle. The Catholic Church has always considered matrimony one of the seven sacraments of Jesus Christ, and therefore holy in itself and in all its relations.

Does not St. Paul say that "marriage is honorable in all"? (Heb. xiii. 4).

Undoubtedly: but this by no means implies a command that all should marry. He is addressing married people, and is urging them to be true to their vows; "for," he adds, "fornicators and adulterers God will judge" (Heb. xiii. 4). He elsewhere explicitly declares that marriage is not honorable when entered into contrary to the law of God or of God's Church, as in the marriage of the inces-

tuous Corinthian (I. Cor. v. 1–5), and of the consecrated widows (I. Tim. v. 11, 12). Marriage
is not honorable for the man or woman who has
voluntarily vowed celibacy, as Martin Luther
had done.

Every student of history knows that the
Catholic Church has ever been the defender
and guardian of the honor or dignity of the
marriage bond. Leo XIII., in his encyclical
Arcanum, says: "It must be allowed that the
Catholic Church has been of the highest service
to the well-being of all peoples by her constant
defence of the sanctity and perpetuity of marriage.

"She deserves no small thanks for openly
protesting against the civil laws which offended
so grievously in this matter a century ago; for
striking with anathema the Protestant heresy
concerning divorce and putting away; condemning in many ways the dissolution of marriage common among the Greeks; for declaring
null and void all marriages entered into on condition of future dissolution; and, lastly, for rejecting, even in the early ages, the imperial
laws in favor of divorce and putting away.
And when the Roman Pontiffs withstood the
most potent princes, who sought with threats
to obtain the Church's approval of their
divorces, they fought not only for the safety
of religion, but even of that of civilization."

Why are priests allowed to marry in the East?

Because the Easterns follow the legislation of the Synod of Ancyra, 314 A. D., which gave permission to deacons to marry after ordination, provided they had obtained the permission of their bishops. Celibacy is a question of discipline, not of dogma, so that the Eastern churches that are united to Rome—for instance, the Maronites—are still permitted a married clergy.

The evident intellectual and moral inferiority of the Eastern compared with the Western Church proves conclusively the wisdom of the West in enforcing celibacy. Father Gagarin, S.J., in his book "Le Clergé Russe," gives such a picture of the degradation of the married Russian clergy, and its utter lack of influence over the people, that no one for an instant would desire to introduce such a state of affairs into the vigorous, strong clergy of Western Christendom.

MATRIMONY.

Why will not the Catholic Church allow divorce?

Is it not cruel to force a woman to live until the end with a drunkard or an adulterer?

Did not Christ expressly permit divorce in case of adultery? "Whosoever shall put away his wife, except it be for fornication, and shall marry another, committeth adultery; and who so marrieth her which is put away, doth commit adultery" (Matt. xix. 9).

The absolute prohibition of divorce from the marriage bond, with the right to marry another, rests on the express words of Jesus Christ and His Apostle St. Paul (Trent., Sess. xxiv. can. 7). The words of our Saviour are: "What therefore God hath joined together, let not man put asunder. . . . And He saith to them: Whosoever shall put away his wife and marry another, committeth adultery against her." "And if the wife shall put away her husband, and be married to another, she committeth adultery" (Mark x. 9–12). "Every one that putteth away his wife, and marrieth another, committeth adultery; and he that marrieth her that is put away from her husband, committeth adultery" (Luke xvi. 18).

St. Paul, commenting on these words of our Saviour, says:

"But to them that are married, not I, but the Lord commandeth, that the wife depart not from her husband. And if she depart, that she remain unmarried, or be reconciled to her husband" (I. Cor. vii. 10, 11). "A woman is bound by the law as long as her husband liveth, but if her husband die, she is at liberty; let her marry to whom she will, only in the Lord" (*ibid*. 39). " For the woman that hath an husband, whilst her husband liveth is bound to the law. But if her husband be dead, she is loosed from the law of her husband. Therefore, whilst her husband liveth, she shall be called an adulteress, if she be with another man; but if her husband be dead, she is delivered from the law of her husband, so that she is not an adulteress if she be with another man " (Rom. vii. 2, 3).

Words could not more clearly express the absolute prohibition of divorce with right to marry again. Nothing but death can dissolve the marriage bond, which the Saviour now restores to its primitive unity and indissolubility, abrogating for ever the Mosaic bill of divorce. To remarry during the life-time of wife or husband is clearly termed adultery by Christ and the Apostle.

There are two other texts in St. Matthew's gospel which are frequently cited as granting the right of divorce in case of adultery; but a candid study of these passages will prove that our Saviour does not contradict his clear teaching elsewhere. "But I say to you, that whosoever shall put away his wife, excepting for the cause of fornication, maketh her to commit adultery; and he that shall marry her that is put away, committeth adultery " (Matt. v. 32). It is clear from these words that no exception is made, for—1st. Our Lord is not speaking of a man putting away his wife *to marry another*, which He expressly forbade as a violation of the sixth commandment, in Mark x. 11: "Whosoever shall put away his wife, *and marry another*, committeth adultery"; and in Luke xvi. 18: "Every one that putteth away his wife, and marrieth another, committeth adultery." 2d. He clearly indicates that the marriage tie is indissoluble, for otherwise how could he call the remarriage of the repudiated woman adultery? "He that shall marry her that is put away, committeth adultery" (Matt. v. 32).

The other alleged exception is Matt. xix. 9: "And I say to you that whosoever shall put away his wife, except it be for fornication, and shall marry another, committeth adultery; and he that shall marry her that is put away committeth adultery."

The argument of the defenders of divorce is: Whoever puts away his wife, except for adultery, and remarries, is an adulterer. Therefore, whoever puts "away his wife" for adultery, and remarries, is not an adulterer. The Catholic answers: Why cannot the conditional clause refer to the words that precede rather than to those that follow it? Every one must admit that it is at least doubtful whether the exception for adultery refers to the right of separa-

tion only or the right to remarry. The Catholic
settles the doubt by having recourse to the
other clear passages of St. Mark, St. Luke, and
St. Paul, and concludes with them that a man
cannot remarry during the life-time of his wife
without becoming an adulterer.

The sense of Matt. xix. 9, then, is : Whosoever shall put away his wife, which shall not
be lawful except for fornication, and shall
marry another, etc. That this is not a forced
interpretation is clear from the context. Our
Lord is restoring marriage to its primitive
purity ("in the beginning it was not so," *ibid.*
8) ; He is abrogating the Mosaic bill of divorce,
and elevating marriage to the dignity of a
Christian sacrament, which no human authority can nullify. "What therefore God
hath joined together, let no man put asunder."

It is ever a law of Scripture interpretation
that an obscure text should always be explained in the light of clear and explicit passages. All doubt on the matter is settled for
the Catholic by the divine, infallible witness of
the Church of God (Trent., Sess. xxiv. can. 7),
which voices the constant tradition of the
Church, and declares the text in question to refer only to separation from bed and board.

Even non-Catholics, who do not regard marriage as a sacrament, have admired the Catholic
Church for her firm stand in this matter ; espe-

cially in our age and country, where all are beginning to realize that the excessive laxity of
our divorce legislation is a menace to the public
good. When, in the sixteenth century, the
Reformers doctrinally denied the sacramental
character of marriage, and in their exercise of religious authority granted divorces contrary to
the law of Christ, they prepared the way for the
modern disregard of the marriage tie which is
somewhat akin to the notions prevalent among
the pagans in the first centuries of the Roman
Empire.

We know that often in particular cases this
law is hard in its application, although in the
Catholic Church, for adultery, cruelty, and the
like, separation from bed and board is granted,
without, however, the liberty of marrying again.
It is indeed hard to say to a young woman who
has contracted an unhappy marriage, that she
can never marry again as long as her husband
lives. But the law of Christ is clear. And,
moreover, history is the witness that the individual ought to yield to the higher interests of
religion and society, which are materially in-
jured by the permission of divorce.

**Does not St. Paul allow divorce? (I. Cor. vii.
12–15).**

St. Paul is not speaking of the sacramental
marriage between Christians at all.

He says (I. Cor. vii. 15) : "If any brother have a wife that believeth not, and she consent to dwell with him, let him not put her away. And if any woman have a husband that believeth not, and he consent to dwell with her, let her not put away her husband. . . . But if the unbeliever depart, let him depart. For a brother or sister is not under servitude in such cases. But God hath called us in peace."

The Catholic Church teaches that even by the law of nature marriage is commonly indissoluble ; but God can dissolve it, as He did under the Old Law. The only instance under the New Law of the dissolution of the bond of *natural* marriage is the one here mentioned by St. Paul, known as the Pauline privilege. If in a marriage between a Christian and one not baptized the unbeliever refuses to live with the Christian, or is willing to do so but strives to pervert or tempt the Christian to mortal sin, the latter, after having fulfilled certain conditions laid down by the Church law, is free to marry again. But it must be borne in mind that this refers exclusively to a marriage contracted between unbaptized persons, one of whom afterwards becomes a baptized Christian. It then lies with the party remaining unbaptized as to whether or not the marriage shall be made perpetual.

Granted that your Church *theoretically* forbids divorce, does not its system of dispensations *practically* admit of many exceptions? I know personally of divorced Catholics.

No; as a matter of fact we challenge any one to point out one divorce ever granted under the sanction of the Church after the consummation of a valid marriage. The firm stand of the Popes in this matter is evidenced in the protest against divorce by Nicholas I. against Lothair, by Urban II. and Paschal II. against Philip II. of France, by Celestine III. and Innocent III. against Philip II. of France, by Clement VII. and Paul III. against Henry VIII., and, lastly, by Pius VII. against Napoleon I. (*cf.* Leo XIII., Encyclical *Arcanum*).

As guardian of the Sacraments, she claims the right to make laws affecting their administration and reception. Thus she claims exclusive control over the sacrament of marriage, and besides the divine impediments, over which she has no power, she, for the good of society, has established other impediments, some *diriment*, which render an attempted marriage invalid, and others *impeding*, which, while not affecting the validity of the marriage, render the contracting parties guilty of grievous sin. Thus, a marriage of first cousins without a dispensation would be invalid; whereas the marriage of a Catholic to a baptized Protestant before a minister would be valid, yet the Catholic party would thereby commit grievous sin, involving recourse to the Bishop for pardon.

By the same power wherewith she makes these laws, the Church, for the good of the individual or for society, claims the right to dispense therefrom. One can readily conceive that in some instances the impediment would be a source of harm rather than of good.

Whenever, therefore, you have met Catholics who seem to have married again after a divorce, one of two things is certain: 1st, Either they are Catholics living outside the pale of their Church; or, 2d, Their first marriage, which seemed valid in the eyes of the world, was invalid from the beginning because of one of the diriment impediments of the Church or of God.

Many outsiders realize the wisdom of the Catholic Church in her impediment laws. Governor Rollins, of New Hampshire, declared, about a year ago, that in a certain town of Maine, because of marriages between close relations, there was an imbecile in nearly every family (*Sacred Heart Review*, Jan. 6, 1900, p. 4).

Did not the Pope grant a divorce to the Emperor Napoleon? And again in the case of his son Jerome?

No, the Pope did not grant a divorce in either case.

1st. Napoleon was married to Josephine de Beauharnais, March 9, 1796, by a civil ceremony only. On December 1, 1804, the day preceding the coronation of Napoleon, Josephine mentioned this fact to Pius VII., who had shared the common belief that she had been married according to the laws of the Church. Napoleon, who desired to be free to contract another marriage in hopes of an heir to the throne of France, was greatly displeased at this disclosure. Yet he hoped still to leave a loophole in the religious marriage ceremony, which was performed on the eve of the coronation by Cardinal Fesch, by purposely incurring the impediment of clandestinity which required the presence of the parish priest and two witnesses. The Pontiff, however, granted to the cardinal the necessary dispensation from this impediment, so that the marriage was valid. Thus, Prince Jerome Napoleon in 1887 (" Napoleon and his Detractors ") wrote: " Napoleon and Josephine, who had been only civilly married in the time of the Directory, were united religiously by Cardinal Fesch, in order to satisfy the scruples of Josephine, on the evening preceding the consecration, and in the presence of Talleyrand and Berthier, in the chapel of the Tuileries. I know this from the traditions of my family." The tribunal which declared the nullity of this marriage, therefore, acted on false testimony which denied the religious marriage, and exercised an authority it did not possess, for the Pope is the proper judge in such cases. The Pope had nothing whatsoever to do with the case. It never was brought before him.

2d. As for the marriage of Jerome Bonaparte with Miss Patterson in 1803, performed by Bishop Carroll of Baltimore, it was annulled in France by a civil decree March 21, 1805. The Pope, far from recognizing this, pronounced in a letter to the emperor that the marriage of his brother Jerome was perfectly valid according to the laws of the Catholic Church. (Parsons, "Studies in Church History," vol. v. ch. ii.)

What proof have you that Luther sanctioned bigamy?

His permission to the Landgrave, Philip of Hesse, to take a second wife during the lifetime of the first, and his published writings, afford ample proof.

Philip of Hesse, a great friend of the Reformation, applied in 1539 to Luther for authority to marry an additional wife, bigamy being punishable at that time with death by the German law. In his letter he cites the example of the Old Law prophets, declares bigamy not forbidden by the Old Law and the New, and personally declares it impossible for him to be pure with only one wife. The Landgrave had in mind a published sermon of Luther, 1527, in which he said : "It is not forbidden that a man should have more than one wife. I could not forbid it to-day. But I would not advise it." (*Cf.* Luther's complete works, vol. xxxiii. p. 322 *et seq.*) This permission was granted on condition that it be kept secret (De Wette, Luther's Letters, etc., vol. v. pp. 237 *et seq.*), and Philip was married March 4, 1540, to Margaret Von Sala by Melander, himself a minister with three wives living (Janssen, "History of the German People," vol. iii. p. 408). When the matter became public, Luther, on the principle that the end justifies the means, declared it lawful to deny the fact of the marriage. "What would it matter if, for the sake of greater good and of the Christian Church, one were to tell a big lie?" (Janssen, iii. 432). On this question read, "Luther: An Historical Portrait," J. Verres, ch. xxi. p. 312-329.

MIXED MARRIAGES.

Why is the Catholic Church so bitterly opposed to the marriage of Catholics with Protestants ?

If you consider it wrong, why do you grant a dispensation for money ?

What does your Church require of me—a Protestant—if I marry a Catholic girl ? Must I be baptized and join your Church ?

Can a Catholic and Protestant be married first by a priest, and afterwards by a minister to please the husband's Protestant parents ?

Why is not the marriage celebrated in the church ?

The Catholic Church has always disapproved of mixed marriages, because : 1st. The Catholic party is in great danger of losing the faith. How frequently a strong-minded unbeliever, who daily ridicules all that a Christian woman holds dear, or a bigoted Protestant, who only manifests his hatred of the Catholic religion after marriage, is the cause of the apostasy of a weak-minded, indevout, and ill-instructed woman. In a non-Catholic environment, as in the Southern States, many such souls have drifted away from the Church. 2d. The possibility of the children being reared non-Catholics. How often the Catholic party dies, and the non-Catholic marries again, bringing up all the children in an alien faith. Moreover, the example of an unbelieving, indifferentist, or Catholic-hating parent will have a pernicious influence upon the children, unless counteracted in strong measure by the other parent, the Church and the school. Add to this the fact that many men refuse to allow their children to be baptized in the Catholic faith, despite their written promise to that effect. 3d. The unhappiness that often follows in the train of such marriages. The non-Catholic, too, may at any time secure a divorce and remarry, while the Catholic cannot do so without grievous sin. 4th. The essentially distinct moral principles regarding the marriage relations held by Protestants generally and Catholics, with regard to divorce, abortion, the limiting of the family.

The Catholic Church grants a dispensation from the ecclesiastical law forbidding mixed marriages, because she hopes in certain particular cases that these evils may be obviated. She lays down three conditions: 1st. Both parties must promise that all the children be reared in the Catholic faith. 2d. The non-Catholic must promise not to interfere in any way with the religious life of the Catholic. 3d. The Catholic must promise to do everything possible —by prayer, good example, and persuasion— to bring the non-Catholic to the true faith.

Dispensations are never granted for anything which is absolutely wrong or sinful, or against the divine law. They cannot be bought, but the stipends paid are simply fines imposed only on those who can readily pay them for the exception to the ordinary law of the Church. The money obtained in this way is devoted to the support of religion and to charitable purposes ; the poor are granted dispensations gratis.

The general law in this country—it is different abroad—which forbids the celebration of such marriages in the church, the blessing of the parties and the ring, is witness of the Church's disapproval.

If the Catholic party consents to a first or a second marriage by a minister, he is guilty of a public denial of the faith, and is cut off from all share in the sacraments of the Church. To take part in a false worship is regarded as practical apostasy. Indeed, this manner of proceeding is irrational. For if the Protestant regards the first marriage binding, why then go through a meaningless ceremony; if invalid by his refusing to give consent, is it honest to deceive the priest, who would be bound to refuse acting as witness to a mock marriage?

In countries where the civil law refuses to recognize the Catholic marriage as legal, the parties are allowed to go through the formality of a so-called *civil* marriage before a state official to insure their civil privileges. This enforced appearance before the magistrate, however, has no religious significance whatsoever.

Does the Catholic Church regard the marriage of Protestants valid, or can a Protestant be divorced and marry again on entering your Church?

Two baptized Protestants (for instance, a Methodist and a Lutheran), who are married without being subject to any of the diriment impediments of the Church, are as validly married as two Catholics, for they receive the sacrament of matrimony, which binds until death. The Catholic Church has no power to dispense in the divine law, which absolutely prohibits divorce.

Do you recognize as valid a marriage performed by a Protestant minister or justice of the peace ?

Yes, if otherwise valid—that is, if no diriment impediment exists—for the minister of the sacrament is not the priest or minister, but the contracting parties themselves. If, however, a Catholic is married before any one but a priest, he is guilty of the grievous sins of disobedience, scandal, and practical denial of the faith, so that the Church has severely legislated against this, excommunicating the guilty party and refusing absolution until recourse has been had to the Bishop of the diocese.

The good Catholic will always be married by the priest, whose duty it is to safeguard his people from contracting illicit or invalid marriages.

Frequently, too, a Catholic who is married before a minister or justice contracts an invalid marriage, because the non-Catholic had never been baptized.

Why are Catholics forbidden to marry in Lent?

The Council of Trent (Sess. xxiv., De Reform., c. 10) forbade the public solemnization of marriage—that, is with a nuptial Mass, etc.—in Lent and Advent, because these are times of fasting and penance. Private marriages are not forbidden, although the Catholic people are strongly advised to observe the spirit of the Church's law by marrying outside the penitential season.

EXTREME UNCTION.

Why do priests anoint Catholics with oil when they are dying? Does not the text of James v. 14, 15 refer merely to the miraculous powers for healing in the early Church? (I. Cor. xii. 9, 28, 30).

Because it is a sacrament instituted by Jesus Christ whereby, according to the Scripture, the sick being anointed with oil, in danger of death, and prayed over, receive, if necessary, the remission of sins, the strengthening of the soul, and, if it be God's will, the restoration of health. "Is any man sick among you, let him bring in the priests of the Church, and let them pray over him, anointing him with oil in the name of the Lord; and the prayer of faith shall save the sick man, and the Lord shall raise him up; and

if he be in sins, they shall be forgiven him"
(James v. 14, 15).

We have here all the essentials of a sacrament, the outward sign—that is, the anointing
with oil and prayer—the inward grace, in the
saving and raising up of the sick man, and the
forgiveness of sins. Although there is no mention of the *institution* of the sacrament in the
Bible, the Apostolic practice is proof positive,
together with the Church's infallible witness
(Trent, Sess. xiv., De Ext. Unc.), of its institution by the Saviour. How indeed, in virtue of
the clear words of St. James, can Bible Protestants entirely reject this sacrament?

The passage in St. James does not refer
merely to the gift of healing, which many who
were not priests possessed, but to a sacrament
which not only performed cures in certain cases,
but also *forgave sin* through the ministry of the
priesthood alone. Only Jesus Christ could give
to an anointing with oil the power of remitting
sins; the gift of healing was by no means coin-
cident with the power of pardoning. (For the
Fathers *cf.* "Faith of Catholics," vol. iii. pp.
206–210.)

THE BLESSED VIRGIN AND THE SAINTS.

What justification is there for your adoration of the Virgin?

Do Catholics adore the Virgin Mary?

No; Catholics adore God alone. They love and honor Mary as the Mother of God and the greatest of His saints, but they know she is only a creature, and that therefore to adore her would be idolatry. "We adore no saints," wrote St. Epiphanius in the fourth century. ". . . Let Mary, then, be *honored*, but the Father, Son, and Holy Ghost alone be *adored*" (Adv. Collyrid, 1. xxix.)

This accusation of idolatry, met even to-day so frequently in small country towns, although rarely in our large cities, where non-Catholics have more opportunity of unlearning the lies of the Reformation, was in the beginning a deliberately dishonest charge, the better to cloak the robbery of the riches of the churches and monasteries in England and on the Continent. It is rather interesting, in view of the modern High-Church party movement in the Church of England, to read its Second Homily "against the peril of idolatry and the worshipping of images," and to think of the eight hundred years of so-called idolatry which preceded the pretended Reformation. Misrepresentation, calumny, pulpit declamation, forged catechisms, mistranslations of the sacred text (Col. iii. 5, Eph. v. 5, II. Cor. vi. 16, I. John v. 21, I. Cor. x. 7), and of the word *"invocare"* used by the Council of Trent,—these were the means employed to keep alive the stupid charge of idolatry, which many sincere Protestants to-day confess they are heartily ashamed of. (Northcote, "Mary in the Gospels"; Nicolas, "The Virgin Mary"; Newman, "Anglican Difficulties," vol. ii.; Livius, "The Blessed Virgin in the Fathers"; Petilalot, "The Virgin Mother.")

Does your Church believe the Virgin Mary to be like God, everywhere present ?

Not at all; omnipresence is an attribute of God alone. We learn from the Scriptures that the saints of God know what happens here on earth, and offer our prayers to God. They most likely see our actions and hear our prayers in God and through God, whom they see face to face (I. Cor. xiii. 12). *How* they know, matters but little to the Christian. The power of the Blessed Virgin or the saints to answer our prayers no more implies omnipresence than my power to accede to the request of a friend three thousand miles away implies my presence in that place. When Eliseus saw the ambush prepared for the king of Israel, was he necessarily in Syria at the time? (IV. Kings vi. 9).

By no means. So God can reveal our prayers to His mother and the saints in heaven as readily as He can. give His revelations to His saints on earth.

Can a human being be the mother of the eternal God ?

Why do you call the Virgin Mary the mother of. God ?

Because she is the mother of the divine person, Jesus Christ, who is true God and true man. "And whence is this to me, that the mother of my Lord should come to me?" (Luke i. 43 ; *cf.* i. 35). "His Son, who was made to Him of the seed of David, according to the flesh " (Rom. i. 3). "God sent His Son, made of a woman " (Gal. iv. 4).

Many Protestants, unaware of the true doctrine of the Incarnation, call the Blessed Virgin the mother of Jesus, and not the mother of God, as though our Saviour existed in a twofold personality—human and divine. The Catholic doctrine, however, is that the Second Person of the Blessed Trinity, in His divine nature eternally begotten of the Father, took to Himself from the womb of His Virgin Mother a human nature of the same substance as hers ; and therefore the mother of that divine person, Jesus Christ, the God-man, is in very truth the mother of God.

As our mothers are not called the mothers of our bodies, but simply our mothers, because the soul which is directly created by God is united with the body in one human personality, so the Blessed Virgin is not called the mother of Jesus —that is, of the human nature alone—but simply the mother of God, because the divine nature which is eternally begotten of the Father is united with the human nature in one divine personality.

Strange indeed, too, I have met Episcopalians who in one breath admitted the authority of the first six General Councils, and yet in the next denied the divine maternity which was expressly declared by the Third Ecumenical Council of Ephesus, in 431, against the Nestorians. Strange, again, that the followers of Luther and Calvin seem unaware of the fact that both of these reformers never questioned Mary's claim to be called the Mother of God. (Luther, "Deutsche Schriften," vol. xlv. p. 250; Calvin, "Com. sur l'har. Evang., p. 20.)

Why do you pay so much honor to the Blessed Virgin, when she was only an ordinary woman on earth?

The Blessed Virgin was not an ordinary woman. Would the Father, having the choice of countless millions, create an ordinary woman to be the mother of His only begotten Son? It is preposterous even to imagine it. On the contrary, she is the most extraordinary of women, before whom the greatest saints of the Old Law and the New, pale as do the stars at the rising of the sun.

We honor her as the masterpiece of God—whom God honored, indeed, above all creatures in her divine maternity. An ordinary woman? Why the prophet Isaias tells of her (Isa. vii. 14) coming ; the court of heaven sends an embassy to her (Luke i. 26) and to her spouse Joseph (Matt. i. 20); the Angel Gabriel salutes her with the words " Hail, full of grace, the Lord is with thee ; blessed art thou among women" (Luke i. 28); her cousin St. Elizabeth greets her, " Blessed art thou among women, ' and blessed is the fruit of thy womb. And whence is this to me, that the mother of my Lord should come to me ? " (*ib.*, 43); and Mary herself prophesies truly : " Behold from henceforth all generations shall call me blessed " (*ib.*, 48). Are not we therefore, who daily fulfil this prophecy, stamped thereby as belonging to the generations of God's people? Must we not love her who was close to Christ from Bethlehem to Golgotha? Must we not love the Virgin Mother of God, immaculately conceived and sinless, who shows the world what human nature is capable of through the grace of God, who teaches men the dignity of motherhood

and the purity of virginity, which the pagans
of those days had forgotten? I could never
understand why Protestants seem so jealous of
the love we have for the sweet Mother of God.
I never could understand how men hoped to ex-
tol the Christ by belittling the mother He loved
so dearly. Every true child resents bitterly the
slightest disrespect to a beloved mother. Is
Christ, the Son of God, an exception to the law
He himself planted in the hearts of men?

God could no more be jealous of the love we
have for Mary, the masterpiece of His creation,
than an artist jealous of the picture he painted,
or an author jealous of the book he had
written.

**Do not the terms applied to the Virgin in
Catholic prayer-books border on blasphemy?
She is sometimes called "the only hope of
Christians," "the mother of grace," etc.? One
prayer says: "Mary, command thy Son!"**

We readily grant that some expressions in
Catholic prayer-books or books of devotion are
literally inexact and exaggerated; but there is
no semblance of blasphemy, for every Catholic
knows perfectly their true sense. We must in
all honesty carefully distinguish the language
of devotion from the language of dogma. To
the unprejudiced the exaggeration, if there be
any, will always be manifest, and the accuracy

of dogma may be easily obtained by consulting a catechism or a manual of theology.

Often the impassioned words characteristic of the Italian or Spaniard may be distasteful to the colder and less imaginative Englishman or American. The expressions of an ardent lover to his sweetheart may not all be literally true, for warmth of feeling often begets exaggeration in language. But who would cavil thereat, and ask the lover always to speak in cold, matter-of-fact terms? Must there be no warmth in the expression of our love of the saints of God?

Speaking of these expressions of devotion, Ruskin says that they "are rather poetical effusions than serious prayers; the utterances of imaginative enthusiasm rather than reasonable conviction. And as such, they are rather to be condemned as illusory and fictitious than as idolatrous; nor even as such condemned altogether, for strong love and faith are often the roots of them, and the errors of affection are better than the accuracies of apathy" ("The Stones of Venice," vol. ii. p. 390, appendix 10). We read in the Scripture (Josue x. 14) of "the Lord obeying the voice of a man." Now, this does not mean a real obedience, but God's readiness to hear the prayer of Josue.

To say that Mary commands God is heretical doctrine (decree of the Roman Inquisition, Feb. 28, 1875). If the expression is used, it merely implies that out of His great love for His mother, Jesus Christ is ever ready to hear her prayer. Every country has its peculiar idioms, which a foreigner must master; so the Church has her idioms, which non-Catholics should learn before they find fault. (Newman, "Anglican Difficulties," vol. ii. pp. 89–117; Ganss, "Mariolatry," Ave Maria Press.)

Does not the Catholic devotion to Mary as a matter of fact detract from the worship due to Christ?

On the contrary, it is an historical fact that the Catholic Church, which has always cherished a great love for the Mother of Christ, has ever been the great defender of the divinity of Jesus Christ, her Son. Outside her fold, thousands of nominally Christian ministers and people deny the divinity of the Son of God, because, among other reasons, their forefathers lost the true sense of the unique dignity of that Son's Blessed Mother.

"If we look through Europe," writes Cardinal Newman, "we shall find, on the whole, that just those nations and countries have lost their faith in the divinity of Christ who have given up devotion to His Mother, and that those, on the other hand, who had been foremost in her honor, have retained their orthodoxy. Contrast, for instance, the Calvinists with the Greeks, or France with the North of Germany, or the Protestant and Catholic communions in Ireland" ("Difficulties of Anglicans," vol. ii. p. 92).

All prayer to Mary indeed is virtually and ultimately prayer to God. Love of her, by its very nature, carries us to the love of God, whose masterpiece she is. Strangers at times have entered our churches and been scandalized at what they deemed an excessive manifestation of devotion on the part of our people, who were praying devoutly before some statue of the Blessed Virgin. They forget, however, that on the altar is Jesus Christ really present, and that during Mass in the early morning those same devout souls have knelt in adoration to Him alone. Catholics ever make an infinite difference between their love for the Son and the Mother, realizing perfectly that all her graces and privileges are from Him. If some words or expressions of our devotional writings seem to contradict this, let the objector remember that it is unreasonable to insist that a devotional tract be couched in the accuracy of dogma. Love never expresses itself in the exact language of a mathematical formula.

Did not the adoration of the Virgin in the Middle Ages tend to encourage harmful superstition, by overshadowing entirely the mediatorship of Christ?

There has never been any adoration of the Virgin in the Catholic Church. In the fourth century the heresy of the Collyridians, who paid her divine honors, was expressly condemned by the Fathers of the time; for instance, St. Epiphanius (Adv. Collyridians). The love and reverence for the Mother of God which characterized the ages of faith helped greatly to keep the doctrine of the Incarnation free from all taint of heresy, and also in the days of chivalry begot a spirit of respect for woman, which could not but be beneficial in its influence on the fierce manners of the period.

This many Protestants and unbelievers, free from controversial bias, have been forced to admit. "The world," writes the rationalist Lecky, "is governed by ideals, and seldom or never has there been one which has exercised a more salutary influence than the mediæval conception of the Virgin" ("Rationalism in Europe," ch. iii. p. 234). . . . "There is, I think, little doubt that the Catholic reverence for the Virgin has done much to elevate and purify the ideal woman, and to soften the manners of men" ("History of European Morals," vol. ii. p. 389).

The Middle Ages had too perfect a knowledge of the unique mediatorship of Jesus Christ, who alone "gave himself a redemption for all" (I. Tim. ii. 6), ever to put a creature in the

place of God. Instead of encouraging superstition, the Catholic love for Mary has ever
been "productive of true holiness of life and
purity of character" (Ruskin, "Fors Clavi-
gera," letter 41), by holding up her example
for imitation and showing what human nature
is capable of by the grace of God.

**Is not the high place the Virgin holds in your
Church due to the exaggerations of the mediæval
mind ?**

No, the true dignity of Mary was appreciated
from the beginning by all Christians who knew
her as the Mother of God. For the witness of
the early Fathers, and the catacomb frescoes
and paintings, consult: Newman's "Letter to
Pusey"; Livius, "The Blessed Virgin in the
Fathers"; Shahan, "The Blessed Virgin in
the Catacombs."

**Did not Christ speak harshly to Mary, when
He said (John ii. 4), "Woman, what have I to do
with thee ? "**

The milder Catholic version is also the more
accurate one: "Woman, what is it to thee and
to me?" How could men imagine for a moment that the sweet Saviour of men could ever
speak rudely to His own mother? Do we respect any son who treats the mother who bore
him with disrespect? The title "woman" in
the East is one of the greatest reverence, as we

learn from its frequent use by our Lord himself (Matt. xv. 28; Luke xiii. 12; John iv. 21, viii. 10, xix. 26, xx. 13, 15).

Would He, for instance, speak harshly to His mother when commending her to the care of His beloved disciple, John: "Woman, behold thy son"? (John xix. 26). So, many Protestant scholars, French, Alford, Edersheim, and others, admit to-day that the old controversial use of this passage, to prove Christ's harshness to His mother, arose merely from ignorance. Thus, Dr. Westcott, commenting on this text, says: "In the word *woman* there is not the least tinge of reproof or severity. The address is that of courteous respect, even tenderness."

The phrase "what is it to me and to thee" cannot convey any rebuke, for He immediately afterwards works the miracle she requests (Ganss, "Mariolatry"; *American Cath. Quarterly*, 1895, p. 399).

Did not Christ evidently make little of His mother when, at the cry of the woman in the crowd calling Mary blessed, He said: "Yea, rather, blessed are they that hear the word of God and keep it"? (Luke xi. 28).

By no means. For "if in Christ's '*yea, rather*' He be supposed to deprecate His mother's cultus, He must no less be supposed to deprecate His own; for the woman in the crowd 'primarily extolled Him, and His mother only for His sake'' (Ryder, ''Catholic Controversy,'' p. 107).

Does not Luke viii. 20, 21, clearly show that Christ showed no special honor to Mary ? (Matt. xii. 46–50).

I quote the commentary of St. Ambrose: '' He did not mean to reject the attentions of His mother; for He Himself commands, Let whosoever dishonors father or mother, die the death; but He acknowledges Himself obliged rather to attend to the mysteries of His Father than to indulge maternal affection. His mother is not disowned here, *as some heretics insidiously pretend;* even from the cross He acknowledges her '' (John xix. 26, 27).

It shows a very imperfect grasp of the infinite perfection of the All-Perfect Son of God, to imagine for an instant that He could show the slightest disrespect to His own most blessed mother. What greater honor than to have been subject to her for thirty years in the seclusion of the home at Nazareth? (*American Cath. Quarterly,* 1894, p. 712.)

Why do you pray to the Virgin Mary, when the Bible says nothing about it ?

Is not the intercession of Christ all-sufficient? '' We have an advocate with the Father, Jesus Christ the righteous '' (I. John ii. 1). Did not

the Saviour say: "No man cometh to the
Father, but by Me?" (John xiv. 6); and again,
"Come unto Me, all ye that labor"? (Matt.
xi. 28).

Why call her mediator, when the Bible says
that Christ is the only Mediator? (I. Tim. ii. 5).

The fact of intercessory prayer—the power
and desire of the Saints to help us—is evidenced
in both the Old Testament and the New
(Gen. xviii.; Exod. xvii.; Job xlii.; Tob. xii.
12; Zach. i. 12; Rom. xv. 30; Eph. vi. 18;
I. Thess. v. 25; James v. 16).

Our Lord's intercession is unique; as the
Divine Incarnate Word He is, as the Apostle
tells us (I. Tim. ii. 5), the one Mediator of justice. The mediatorship of the Saints is of
grace and prayer, helping us through the Mediatorship of Jesus Christ.

Among the saints, the Blessed Virgin because of her supereminent dignity as Mother
of God holds the first place; and because of her
intimate association with her Son in the redemption of mankind, her power with Him is
naturally the greatest.

Catholics believe that no one can come to the
Father save through Jesus Christ; and the
Council of Trent declares anathema upon all
those who deny His unique Mediatorship.
Catholics answer His appeal "Come unto Me"
more than non-Catholics in the close union of

Holy Communion, whereby "they abide in Him and He in them" (John vi. 57).

The Blessed Virgin no more interferes with our access to Christ than the pipe which carries water from the reservoir prevents that water entering into our houses. She merely unites her most powerful prayers to our weak petitions, and the heart of her Son is moved to answer, even as a stern judge might hearken to the appeal of a criminal's mother to soften the sentence against her boy. Her power is thus described by Cardinal Newman:

"Her presence is above, not on earth; her office is external, not within us; . . . her power is indirect. It is her prayers that avail, and they are effectual by the *fiat* of Him who is our all in all. Nor does she hear us by any innate power, or by any personal gift; but by His manifestation to her of the prayers which we make to her. When Moses was on the Mount, the Almighty told him of the idolatry of his people at the foot of it, in order that he might intercede for them; and thus it is the Divine Presence which is the intermediating Power by which we reach her, and she reaches us" (Letter to Dr. Pusey, p. 89).

Do you mean by the Immaculate Conception that the Virgin Mary had no father?

Does not the Bible teach: "As in Adam *all* die"? (I. Cor. xv. 22).

Did Catholics believe this doctrine prior to 1854?

What shadow of truth is there for this teaching?

We do not believe that the Blessed Virgin was conceived by the Holy Ghost like her Divine Son (Luke i. 35), but, on the contrary, that she was conceived and born as the other children of Adam, of human parents, the saintly Joachim and Anne.

Many rationalistic or "liberal" Protestants refuse to accept this dogma because they reject, with the unbeliever, the dogma of original sin. The orthodox Protestant, moreover, finds a difficulty because of his erroneous idea of original sin. Says Cardinal Newman on this point:

" Our doctrine of original sin is not the same as the Protestant doctrine. Original sin with us cannot be called sin, in the mere ordinary sense of the word sin; it is a term denoting Adam's sin as transferred to us, or the state to which Adam's sin reduces his children; but by Protestants it seems to be understood as sin, in much the same sense as actual sin. We, with the Fathers, think of it as something negative— Protestants as something positive. Protestants hold that it is a disease, a radical change of nature, an active poison internally corrupting the soul, infecting its primary elements, and disorganizing it; and they fancy that we ascribe a different nature from ours to the Blessed Virgin, different from that of her parents, and from that of fallen Adam.

"We hold nothing of the kind; we consider that in Adam she died, as others; that she was included, together with the whole race, in Adam's sentence; that she incurred his debt as we do; but that, for the sake of Him who was to redeem her and us upon the cross, to her the debt was remitted by anticipation; on her the sentence was not carried out, except indeed as regards her natural death, for she died when her time came, as others.

"All this we teach, but we deny that she had original sin; for by original sin we mean, as I have already said, something negative, viz., this only, the deprivation of that supernatural, unmerited grace which Adam and Eve had on their first formation—deprivation and the consequences of deprivation.

"Mary could not merit, any more than they, the restoration of that grace: but it was restored to her by God's free bounty from and at the very first moment of her existence, and thereby, in fact, she never came under the original curse, which consisted in the loss of it" ("Difficulties of Anglicans," vol. ii. pp. 48–49).

The Bull *Ineffabilis* of Pius IX., December, 1854, declares "that the doctrine which holds that the Blessed Virgin Mary, at the very first instance of her conception, by a singular grace and privilege of the Omnipotent God, in virtue of the merits of Jesus Christ, the Saviour of mankind, was preserved free from all stain of original sin, has been revealed by God, and therefore should firmly and constantly be believed by all the faithful.''

It is false to call this a new teaching, for the feast of the Immaculate Conception had been celebrated since the seventh century, and the Fathers of the first five centuries either imply her absolute sinlessness, or set it forth in express terms. Thus St. Ephrem, in a passage of his *Carmina Nisibena*, first discovered and published in 1866 : '' Verily indeed Thou and Thy Mother, alone are you, in being in every respect altogether beautiful. For in Thee, Lord, is no spot, nor any stain in Thy Mother '' (Livius, '' Blessed Virgin in the Fathers,'' p. 232). This dogma was not defined until the year 1854, but definition does not create a dogma, but puts it for ever out of the domain of controversy, as giving a divine, infallible witness to its truth.

The Scriptures also, viewed in the clear light of patristic interpretation which ever regards Mary as the second Eve, declare the enmity between Mary and Satan absolute and lasting: '''I will put enmities between thee and the woman, and thy seed and her seed ; she shall crush thy head" (Gen. iii. 15. *Cf. loc. cit.*, pp. 35-59). The words of the Angel Gabriel, "Hail, full of grace," are true in their fullest absolute sense only if we believe the Blessed Virgin to have been immaculately conceived.

Why do Catholics claim that the Virgin Mary never committed sin, when the Bible says : " If we say that we have no sin we deceive ourselves, and the truth is not in us " ? (I. John i. 8).

Because the Catholic Church, the infallible interpreter of Holy Scripture, declares that she was kept sinless her life long by a special favor of God (Council of Trent, Sess. vi. c. 23). This was the doctrine of the early Church, as one may read in Father Livius' " The Blessed Virgin in the Fathers of the First Six Centuries," ch. iv. pp. 229–245.

To quote St. Augustine : " Now, with the exception of the Holy Virgin Mary, touching whom, out of respect to our Lord, when we are on the subject of sins, I have no mind to entertain the question," etc. (De nat. et grat., c. 41). Cardinal Newman discusses some passages of the Fathers which are cited to the contrary in vol. ii. of " Difficulties of Anglicans," pp. 128-152.

Even some Protestant writers (Dietlein, " Evangelisches Ave Maria," p. 3) have granted that, in view of her unique and supereminent dignity as Mother of God, the Blessed Virgin should be exempt from the slightest stain of sin.

The text in question should no more prevent our believing in Mary's sinlessness, than the text "who only hath immortality" (I. Tim. vi. 16) prevents our believing in the immortality of angels and of men.

How can you claim that Mary was always a virgin, when the Scriptures speak so frequently of the "brethren of the Lord"? (Matt. xii. 46-50; Matt. xiii. 55-56; Mark iii. 31-35, vi. 3; Luke viii. 19-21; John ii. 12, vii. 3-10; Acts i. 14).

The word *brother* is used in the Hebrew and in all languages in a general sense, and therefore by no means necessarily implies children of the same parent. In the Old Testament it is applied to any relation, viz., nephew (Gen. xiv. 16, xiii. 8, xii. 5), uncle (Gen. xxix. 15), husband (Cant. iv. 9), one of the same tribe (II. Kings xix. 12), of the same people (Ex. ii. 21), an ally (Amos i. 9), any friend (II. Kings i. 26), one of the same office (III. Kings ix. 13).

To determine, therefore, the meaning of the word in the gospel texts, we must trust that most generally received tradition, handed down by St. Jerome and St. Augustine, which is, that the father of James was Alpheus (Cleophas) and his mother Mary, sister of the Blessed Virgin, and his brothers Jude, Joseph, and Simon; the "brethren" of the Lord were therefore the first cousins of Jesus. (Compare Matt. xxvii. 56, 61, xxviii. 1; Mark xv. 40, 47, xvi. 1; and John xix. 25.)

The early Church held most firmly to the perpetual virginity of the Blessed Virgin, as we learn from the condemnation of Helvidius, Jovinian, and other heretics of the fourth century by the synods of Rome (A. D. 381) and Capua (A. D. 392). The Council of Lateran in A. D. 649 finally voiced the infallible witness of the Catholic Church, so that the Catholic is not left to the mere conjecture of private opinion. Indeed, Luther, Calvin, Zwingli, and Beza among the Reformers, besides many Protestant writers to-day, deny as emphatically as any Catholic that the Blessed Virgin had any other children. (*Cf.* Lange, Alexander, Grotius, Lightfoot, Westcott, Bloomfield, Trench, Bright, Kuinoel, Koster, and Mill, quoted by Rev. Henry G. Ganss, "Mariolatry," p. 38; Fouard, "Life of Christ," vol. i., appendix v.; P. Corluy, "Les Frères de N. S. Jesus Christ"; Jaugey, Dict. Apol., 1303–1308.)

Our Lord, dying on the cross, commended His mother to the care of His beloved disciple, St. John (John xix. 26, 27). He would not have done this if she had children of her own.

Does not St. Matthew say: "And knew her not till she brought forth her first born son"? (i. 25). And yet you claim that she had no other children!

The word "first born" by no means implies other children, for the law regarding the first born (Exod. xxxiv. 19, 20) was binding at once, whether there were other children or not. Again, we find Machir, the only son of Manasses, called the first born (Josue xvii. 1). The words "not till" mean, not till then nor after; as, for example, Gen. viii. 6, 7: "Noe, opening the window of the ark, sent forth a raven, which went forth and did not return, till the waters were dried up upon the earth"—*i.e.*, never returned.

What proof is there of Mary's ascension into heaven?

Catholics believe that this doctrine accords with the supereminent dignity of the Mother of God, whose body her Divine Son would not allow to see corruption; and the fact of the feast of the Assumption having been celebrated since the sixth century, and the general belief of Catholics the world over to-day, render the denial of this teaching rash, although it has not yet been defined as a dogma of faith. (Wilhelm-Scannell, "Manual of Theology," vol. ii. p. 218 *et seq.*)

Why do uneducated people count beads?

Does not the counting prevent real prayer?

Why ten prayers to the Virgin and only one to God?

. Why do you make the people repeat mechanical prayers on the Rosary without any warrant in the Bible?

The Rosary is a simple method of prayer, consisting of the repetition of the Our Father and ten Hail Marys, five or fifteen times. It is not for the uneducated alone, being used with profit by all classes.

It was originally, a devotion of the faithful in the Middle Ages, who, unable to read the psalter, used to recite the Our Father and Hail Mary instead of each psalm, while the monks chanted the divine office in choir. The same custom is also recorded of St. Paul, the first hermit, in the fourth century. It owes its present form to the Dominicans of the thirteenth century, and is to-day one of the chief devotions of Catholics.

Its fifteen mysteries—the Annunciation, the Visitation, the Nativity, the Presentation, the Finding in the Temple, the Agony, the Scourging, the Crowning with Thorns, the Carrying of the Cross, the Crucifixion, the Resurrection, the Ascension, the Descent of the Holy Ghost, the Assumption, and the Coronation of the Blessed Virgin—present a beautiful summary of the gospels to the devout meditation of loving souls.

It is natural that in a devotion especially hers, the major portion of the prayers should be addressed directly to the Blessed Virgin. Catholics know full well that in honoring the Mother of God they necessarily honor God, whose masterpiece she is.

It is absurd to imagine that in reciting the Rosary we are counting prayers. Indeed, the very arrangement of the beads prevents our counting the number of Aves we say. Instead of preventing real prayer, the Rosary on the contrary helps greatly to concentrate our attention, as even Protestants (Episcopalians) who have practised this devotion for a long time have acknowledged to me. Many a simple soul reciting the Rosary before the altar of God will put to the blush many a speech-prayer of the proud pharisee. As for Bible warrant, the Our Father and half of the Hail Mary are taken from the Holy Scriptures (Matt. vi. 9–13 ; Luke i. 28), while the repetition of these prayers so much objected to by non-Catholics rests on the word and example of the Saviour (Luke xi. 5–8, xviii. 3–10 ; Matt. xxvi. 44 ; *cf.* Ps. cxxxv. ; Matt. xx. 31).

What constitutes a saint in your Church ?

A saint is one whose extraordinary holiness

of life and heroic virtues have attracted the notice of the Universal Church, and who after the most exact scrutiny into every detail of his life, writings, etc., has been placed on the approved list of God's chosen followers. Except in the case of martyrs, their holiness must be proved conclusively by evident miracles before they are canonized. Of course there are many men and women who live and die unknown to the world, but whose lives are just as holy in God's sight.

Why do you give honor to the saints, when it all belongs to God?

Why do Catholics worship and adore the saints?

Catholics do not adore the saints; they adore God alone. They venerate and love the saints as the special friends of Jesus Christ. Just as the state honors and respects its great men, and holds up to the imitation of the citizens their love of country, so the Church of God honors its heroes, and holds up to the faithful the ideal of their love of God. The word "worship" in the question is ambiguous, for in the English language it by no means is synonymous with adoration. It may be applied either to the supreme divine worship of the one God *(latria)*, or the infinitely inferior respect and veneration of the saints of God *dulia* (or *hyperdulia*). In the old Protestant marriage service, for instance,

the phrase " with my body I thee worship " by
no means signified a divine adoration. Nor,
again, does the term " your worship " or " wor-
shipful sir " applied to the judge on the bench
necessarily give him the divine honor paid to
the old Roman emperors.

Strange, indeed, that despite the fact of the
constant protest of Catholics for nearly four
hundred years, and despite the acknowledgment of Protestant misrepresentation frequently
made by Protestants everywhere, this old calumny should still be voiced by the ignorant. To
learn the Catholic doctrine one has merely to
read a Catholic catechism, which refutes this
calumny, as of old it was refuted by St. Augustine. He says: "We venerate the martyrs
with that veneration of love and fellowship
which, even in this life, we honor the holy servants of God, whose hearts we feel are ready to
endure a similar suffering for the truth of the
Gospel. But we honor them the more devoutly
because they are safe, having conquered in the
strife. . . . But with that worship which
in Greek is called *latria* (adoration), . . .
we neither worship them, nor teach men to worship any but the one God." (Cont. Faust.
Man., lxx. n. xxi. For the Fathers, see
" Faith of Catholics," vol. iii. p. 318–409.
Cf. Gen. xix.; Num. xxii. 31; John v. 4;
Apoc. xxii. 8.)

Is every Catholic bound to pray continually to the saints?

Why not go directly to Christ—the one Mediator? (I. Tim. ii. 5).

What proof is there that the saints know our needs?

How do you know that they really intercede for us?

Does not your teaching make the saints practically omnipotent?

The teaching of the Catholic Church on the invocation and intercession of the saints is clearly set forth by the Council of Trent (Sess. xxv.): "It is good and useful suppliantly to invoke them, and to have recourse to their prayers, aid, and help for obtaining benefits of God, through His Son, Jesus Christ, our Lord, who alone is our Redeemer and Saviour."

The fact of intercessory prayer, the veneration and the mediation of the angels and saints, is evident to any student of the Scriptures:

Gen. xix. 1: "And seeing them (the two angels), he rose up and went to meet them; and worshipped prostrate to the ground."

Gen. xlviii. 16: "The angel that delivereth me from all evils, bless these boys."

Zach. i. 12: "O Lord of hosts, how long wilt thou not have mercy on Jerusalem, etc."

Matt. xviii. 10: "Their angels always see the face of My Father who is in heaven."

Apoc. v. 8: "Golden vials full of odors, which are the prayers of saints."

Apoc. viii. 3, 4: "That he should offer of the prayers of all saints upon the golden altar, . . . and the smoke of the incense of the prayers of the saints ascended up before God."

The Scriptures, moreover, tell us that the prayers of a saint on this earth avail much (James v. 16), and give us many an example of the efficacy of intercessory prayer, as the prayer of Abraham (Gen. xviii.), of Moses (Exod. xvii.), of Job (xlii.), the brethren for St. Paul (Rom. xv. 30; Eph. vi. 18, 19; I. Thess. v. 25). According to the ordinary Protestant notion this intercessory prayer was useless. Why not go to God directly? or in the new law, why not go to Christ directly?

Catholics ask, is it reasonable to suppose that nearness to the throne of God destroys this power of intercession? Is it to be expected that in the joy of God's presence the saints will forget their brethren upon earth, who are still fighting the good fight? Nay, rather their love for us must become more intense with the greater realization of the joys of God's kingdom, and their prayers be multiplied as their power becomes greater with God.

I have met many Protestants who imagine that after death the saints have no further knowledge of what happens upon earth. They fail to grasp the essential doctrine of the Communion of Saints, although they may recite the words of the Apostles' Creed. Scripture plainly declares that the angels in heaven know our actions upon earth (Tob. xii. 12´; I. Cor. iv. 9 ; Matt. xviii. 10), and even our very thoughts (Luke xv. 10). Why, then, deny the same knowledge to the saints?—especially as our Lord declares that the children of the resurrection shall be as "the angels of God in heaven " (Matt. xxii. 30 ; Luke xx. 36).

How do they know? continues the objector. Scripture tells us the fact, not the mode of their knowledge. The common Catholic teaching is that they know all things conducive to their happiness in the face-to-face vision of God (I. John iii. 2 ; I. Cor. xiii. 12).

The intercession of Jesus Christ is unique and totally distinct from the mediatorship of the saints, His followers. He is the one Mediator of justice in virtue of His redemption, according to the Apostle : " There is one Mediator of God and men—the man Christ Jesus, who gave Himself a redemption for all " (I. Tim. ii. 5, 6). The mediation of the just upon earth and the saints in heaven is not of justice but of grace, and efficacious only in union with His mediation.

There is no possibility of disunion between Christ, the Head of the mystical body, and the saints as members thereof. Their mediation, therefore, being in a true sense His own, by no means derogates from His honor or glory, but on the contrary redounds thereunto.

The early Church understood this doctrine well, as we can read on every page of the early Fathers. The veneration of the saints and martyrs was universal, countless miracles of their intercession are recorded, and the love of the early Christians shown by the honor paid to their tombs, relics, images, and pictures. (For many testimonies see "Faith of Catholics," vol. iii. pp. 318–409; Rev. Thomas Livius, "The Blessed Virgin in the Fathers," chs. vii. viii., pp. 278 *et seq.*) St. Ignatius, in the second century, writes to the Trallians: "My spirit be your expiation, not now only but when I shall have attained to God" (13). St. Cyprian, in the third century, writing to Pope Cornelius, says: "If one of us shall, by the speediness of the divine dispensation, depart hence the first, let our love continue in the presence of the Lord; let not prayer for our brethren and sisters cease in the presence of the mercy of the Father" (Ep. ad Cornel. 57, Pat. Lat., tom. iii. p. 836).

The principle of intercession presents no difficulty in things human; why, then, in things divine? If I desire a favor of President Roosevelt, I may ask him directly, or do so indirectly through some of his personal friends. Will he take it as an insult if I approach him indirectly? The request must come ultimately to him. So in the supernatural order. If I desire a favor of God, I may ask Him directly if I choose, or indirectly through His friends, the saints of God, as we are taught by the Scriptures and all Christian antiquity. The request must ultimately come to God, who alone can grant it. How absurd to think Him insulted if His loved ones add their prayers to ours.

The saints' intercessory power by no means implies omnipotence, for they have no power of themselves to grant us what we ask, but can merely plead to God on our behalf.

Has not the age of miracles passed for ever? Did it not cease with the death of the Apostles?

No, the age of miracles will last until the end of time. Christ foretold (Mark xvi. 17, 18) the miraculous power of His saints: "And these signs shall follow them that believe. In My Name, they shall cast out devils; they shall speak with new tongues; they shall take up serpents; and if they shall drink any deadly thing, it shall not hurt them; they shall lay their hands upon the sick, and they shall recover." And John xiv. 12: "He that believeth in Me, the works that I do he also shall do; and greater than these shall he do."

We grant that they are not so numerous to-day as in the first days of the Church, when they were specially meant to aid the spread of Christianity (St. Aug., De Civitate Dei, c. vii.), but no unprejudiced man can read the testimony for miracles in the lives of saints canonized by the Holy See, or performed, for instance, at Lourdes in France, without seeing at once that God's arm is not shortened, but that He still works His wonders as in Apostolic times. ("Medical, Testimony to the Miracles of Lourdes," vol. xvi., Catholic Truth Society Publications; Henri Laserre, "Miracles at Lourdes"; *American Cath. Quarterly*, 1876, p. 337; 1898, p. 382.)

Do Catholics have to believe all the miracles recorded in the lives of the saints?

By no means. They are historical facts, which depend on human and fallible testimony, which may be false, and therefore is to be weighed carefully as any other testimony. Many things related in the old lives of the saints are undoubtedly legends. Thus, Lingard, the Catholic historian, after speaking of many undoubted miracles in the Anglo-Saxon Church, admits "there are also many which must shrink from the frown of criticism; some which may have been the effect of accident or imagination; some that are more calculated to

excite the smile than the wonder of the readers;
and some which . . . depend on the distant testimony of writers not remarkable for
sagacity or discrimination" ("Antiquities of
the Anglo-Saxon Church," ch. xii. n. 6).
The Catholic Church, however, is most careful
in her acceptance of miracles, as we can see by
the rules laid down by Benedict XIV. in his
treatise on "The Canonization of Saints."
Evidence that critics have considered convincing has, as a matter of fact, been rejected
by the Congregation of Rites at Rome.

Catholics are not more credulous than other
people, but they protest against that modern
irrational prejudice which, denying the possibility of miracles, refuses to consider testimony for them, no matter how strong or overwhelming.

**Do not Catholics adore images and pray to
them ?**

No, Catholics do not. The Council of Trent
(Sess. xxv.) declares "that the images of
Christ, of the Virgin Mother of God, and of the
other saints, are to be had and kept especially
in churches, and that due honor and veneration
are to be given them; not that any divinity or
virtue is believed to be in them, on account of
which they are to be worshipped, or that anything is to be asked of them, or that trust is to

be reposed in images, as was done of old by
the Gentiles, who placed their hope in idols;
but because the honor which is shown them is
referred to the prototypes which these images
represent; in such wise that by the images
which we kiss, and before which we uncover
the head, and prostrate ourselves, we adore
Christ, and we venerate the saints whose simili-
tude they bear.''

**Does not God absolutely forbid us to make any
graven images or bow down to them ? (Ex. xx.
5). Yet you Catholics bow to statues, the cruci-
fix, etc.**

God prohibits here and elsewhere in Scripture the making of idols (*pesel*) and worshipping them. '' Thou shalt not make to thyself a
graven thing. . . . Thou shalt not adore
them nor serve them '' (Ex. xx. 4, 5). This is
evident from the context, for God gives the reason of the prohibition : '' I am the Lord thy God,
mighty, jealous,'' etc.; that is to say, One who
wants the undivided love of His people, and is
jealous of strange gods or idols representing
them. If the text meant an absolute and perpetual prohibition, we would have God prohibit-
ing here what He commands elsewhere. For God
Himself expressly ordered images to be made
and used for religious purposes, viz.: the golden
cherubim (Ex. xxv. 18), the brazen serpent

(Num. xxi. 8; John iii. 14), and "divers figures and carvings" in the Temple of Solomon
(III. Kings vi. 29-35). The Ark of Covenant,
for example, received the same veneration that
Catholics pay to images: "And Josue . . .
fell flat on the ground before the ark of the
Lord until the evening" (Josue vii. 6; II. Kings
vi.) Logically, if the commandment refer not
to the idolatrous worship of images, but absolutely "to the making of any graven thing"
whatsoever, Protestants ought to destroy all the
statues of our great men and burn all the por-
traits of their relatives and friends. The Israel-
ite prostrating himself before the king, the Englishman saluting the throne, the American soldier saluting the flag—all should fall under the
ban of this peculiar command of God.

We can readily understand that the Jewish
discipline on this matter was most strict, because of their proneness to imitate the idolatry
of the pagans amongst whom they lived. The
same difficulty met the early Christians whose
great struggle was directed against the idol-
worship of the pagans. And yet the catacombs
reveal to us clearly by the many paintings,
gilded glasses, etc., that have come down to us
—representing various scenes in the life of
Christ, His Mother, the Apostles and other
saints of the Old Law and the New—that the
mind of the early Christians was identical with

that of Catholics to-day. For the witness of Christian antiquity read "Faith of Catholics," vol. iii. pp. 303–318.

The wanton destruction of crucifixes, statues, and paintings that marked the beginning of the Reformation in Germany, Scotland, and England, deplored by many non-Catholics the world over, was merely a revival of the old Iconoclastic heresy condemned in 787 by the Second Council of Nice. Strange, indeed, that the statues and pictures of kings, queens, and Reformation "saints" soon filled the vacant niches and walls of the old churches! Error is never consistent.

Did not Catholics suppress the second commandment, in order to get over its prohibition against graven images?

Why are the ten commandments divided differently by Protestants and Catholics?

Catholics have never suppressed the second commandment. They have abridged at times the first commandment in catechisms intended for children, but in that they have the example of the Holy Spirit (IV. Kings xvii. 35), who does exactly the same thing.

The Scriptures tell us that there were ten commandments, but do not indicate how they were divided. The Protestant division follows rather Ex. xx. 1–17, while the Catholic follows

Deut. v. 6–21. The Catholic division is the older and the more logical. We hold that desire for another man's wife and desire for another man's property are two essentially distinct crimes, and therefore merit two separate commandments, the ninth and tenth. On the other hand, the first commandment. insists on the virtue of religion and forbids all sins 'against that virtue, the chief of which is idolatry. Logically, therefore, the Protestant second commandment has no reason of being, and was born of the exigency of controversy to justify the early Reformers.

The Catholic division (St. Augustine, Clement of Alexandria, St. Jerome) is to be found in the works of John Huss and Martin Luther. (Opera Huss, Norimbergiæ, 1558, p. 30; Catechism of Dr. Martin Luther for Parsons, etc. ; Appendix to Luther's German Bible; Alcuin, De Decem Verbis Legis, Opera, vol. i. p. 340; the Council of Lambeth, A. D. 1281 ; the Synod of Exeter, A. D. 1287, and books of devotion written for the English people, as "The Festival," Rouen, 1499, the "Pilgrimage of Perfeceyon, A. D. 1531, "Dives et Pauper," 1496, the catechisms of Erasmus and of Cranmer, 1548, etc., all follow the Catholic division.)

It is true indeed that some Jewish and Christian writers of the first centuries, viz., Philo, Josephus, Origen, Ambrose, Procopius, and

Rupertus, followed the Protestant division, but they did not forbid the veneration of images like the latter, but regarded the first commandment as forbidding the interior act of idolatry, and the second the external act. It is not until 1552 that we find the decalogue divided in the Book of Common Prayer as Protestants divide it to-day. ("The Use of Holy Images," Rev. L. Meurin, S.J., 1866, Bombay.)

What good are statues and pictures ? Can we not pray to God without them ?

Undoubtedly a man could pray to God alone on a barren island, or wrecked on a spar of a sunken ship, or in the dark cell of a prison, without the help of painting or of statue. But we must take man as he generally is. We could respect the heroes of our country without raising statues to them in the national capital; we could commune in spirit with our friends without the need of the photograph on our walls; a mother could sigh over the babe she lost without taking in her hands the little trinkets of the dead dear one; but it is not the way of human nature.

The Catholic Church claims to answer every need of the human heart. She uses every possible means to unite her children to God. It is an undoubted fact that statues and pictures of the saints are great helps to devotion. They are the books of the illiterate, who thus learn easily the story of the gospels; they adorn our churches, which are the home of Jesus Christ, with masterpieces of art still the envy of those who believe not; they bring vividly before all the lives of Christ and his saints, and incite us to imitate them.

The newspapers and magazines of our day know well the power of illustration to help the imagination; the theatre speaks to-day of the thousands it spends on scenic display; in processions on holidays floats are carried throughout our cities with statues representing the various handicrafts. Can you therefore object to our rational, traditional, and Scriptural custom?

Is it not superstition to venerate relics, viz.: the bones of a dead man or woman?

What warrant is there for such practice in the Scriptures?

The reverence paid by Catholics to the relics of the saints is by no means superstitious. On the contrary, it is an act of religion and the teaching of the Christian Church from the beginning "that the holy bodies of holy martyrs, and of others now living with Christ, . . . are to be venerated by the faithful, through which (bodies) many benefits are bestowed by God on men" (Council of Trent, Sess. xxv.) St. Jerome in the fourth century wrote a book against the heretic Vigilantius, who called the Christians of the time who venerated the relics of the martyrs "cinder-worshippers and idolaters" (*cinerarii et idolatræ*). In writing on the matter to the priest Riparius he says : " We worship not, we adore not, I do not say relics only, but not even the sun and moon, not angels, not archangels, not the cherubim, not the seraphim, . . . lest we serve the creature, rather than the Creator. But we honor the relics of the martyrs, that we may adore Him whose martyrs they are. We honor the servants, that the honor given to the servants may redound to the Lord," etc. (Ep. c. ix. ad Riparium). For other testimonies of the veneration of relics in the early Church from the second to the fifth century see "Faith of Catholics," vol. iii. pp. 235–303.

Scripture speaks plainly of astonishing miracles wrought by means of material objects belonging to the saints, viz. : the mantle of Elias divided the waters of the Jordan (IV. Kings ii. 8–14), the rod of Moses performed wonders at the court of Pharao (Ex. vii. 10 *et seq.*), the bones of the prophet Eliseus raised a dead man to life (IV. Kings xiii. 21), the hem of our Lord's garment cured the woman sick twelve years with the issue of blood (Matt. ix. 20, 21, xiv. 36), the handkerchiefs and aprons which had touched the body of St. Paul cured diseases and drove out wicked spirits (Acts xix. 12), the shadow of St. Peter healed multitudes that were "sick, and troubled with unclean spirits" (Acts v. 15, 16).

The same spirit has actuated Christians from the beginning zealously to gather up and venerate the relics of the saints of God, that prompts a mother to save carefully and love dearly a lock of her dead baby's hair, or that prompts us Americans to keep with great reverence the chair and the pen of the signers of the Declaration of Independence at Philadelphia, the sword of Washington at Mount Vernon, the home of Jefferson Davis at Richmond with its several rooms devoted to the relics dear to the several Southern States. The Church of God claims the same privilege to show her love and reverence for her heroes.

Remember that Catholics do not believe that relics have any secret power strictly of themselves, but they know that God has often granted special favors and blessings through their instrumentality. There is no divinity in them, but God uses them in the same way that he uses men to do his will.

Are there not many relics going about that are not genuine?

What proof have you in any particular instance that you are not being deceived?

There are undoubtedly, through ignorance and fraud, some spurious relics (Letter of January, 1881, by Cardinal-Vicar of Rome to all Bishops warning against spurious relics), and indeed we do not claim absolute certainty in this matter. No Catholic, indeed, is bound to believe any relic genuine unless he has satisfactory evidence to the fact. The Council of Trent ordered bishops to take special pains in this regard, and the Congregation of Indulgences and Relics at Rome has done its best to prevent false relics being offered to the veneration of the faithful, requiring always a special document of authentication. Suppose, however, the relic to be false, the saint would still be honored by us; for we pray not to a bit of bone, but to the saint to whom it is supposed to belong.

What historical proof is there that the Cross on which the Saviour died was really discovered ?

Are there not enough relics of the true Cross in existence to make hundreds of the original?

This is an utterly false statement of fact. M. Rohault de Fleury in 1870 refuted this calumny, and his work has been summarized by Rev. James Bellord in one of the Catholic Truth Society pamphlets. Estimating the size of the cross at 15 feet for the upright, 7½ feet for the cross-beam, 7½ inches for the breadth and 6 inches for the thickness, it would follow that it contained $6\frac{5}{8}$ cubic feet of timber, or about 11,448 cubic inches. All the relics in the world fall far below this amount. In all his long and arduous researches M. de Fleury, so far from finding enough relics of this kind to make three hundred "true crosses," cou d only discover, including 370 cubic inches of notable relics that no longer exist, enough of the sacred wood to make up a bulk of about $\frac{2}{8}$ of a cubic foot. (*Cf. The Month*, March, 1882, vol. xliv. p. 358.)

As to the finding of the Cross, Cardinal Newman, while yet a Protestant, discussed this fact in his essay on the miracles of Early Ecclesiastical History, ch. v. sect. v. pp. 286–326.

What is the good of pilgrimages to certain places when God is everywhere?

Undoubtedly God is everywhere, but some places are especially chosen by Him to show forth His power, goodness, and mercy, and are therefore naturally dear to those who love Him. When visited in the right spirit and not out of curiosity ("Following of Christ," Book IV. ch. l.), they cannot fail to arouse sentiments of true devotion. How many thousands of Christians have felt their hearts burn with love for the Saviour, how many non-Christians have learned for the first time the mystery of the Cross, as they visited the different cities of the

Holy Land, once blessed by the presence of Jesus Christ. Every country, too, has had its shrines of the saints of God, viz.: Rome, Tours, Lourdes, St. Albans, Compostella, etc., where good souls have prayed with greater fervor and great sinners have done penance for their sins. As early as the eighth century pilgrimages, especially to the Holy Land and to the tomb of the Apostles in Rome, were made a substitute for the severe canonical penances (Lepicier, Indulgences). In the Old Testament also we read of Elcana and Anna going every year to pray at Silo (I. Kings i. 1, 3), and the Jews used to go every year to the Temple at Jerusalem, a custom which our Lord Himself observed (Luke ii. 41). It is the teaching of the Scriptures that prayer has special efficacy in certain places (III. Kings viii. 29). In fine, it answers a need in human nature. All people have a special love and veneration for the relics, houses, and tombs of their great men. No one objects to the thousands who yearly visit the tomb of Washington at Mount Vernon, or of Napoleon at Paris; no one finds fault with those who make pilgrimages to the houses of Longfellow and Lowell in Cambridge, or of Hawthorne in Salem. Why, then, be so illogical as to deny Catholics the right to visit the shrines and tombs of Christ and the heroes of Christ's Church, the Saints of God?

THE HEREAFTER.

How do you know that a man is judged immediately after his death? If so, of what use then is the judgment on the last day?

The fact of the particular judgment at the hour of death, although not defined by the Catholic Church, is a logical inference from the teaching of Scripture and tradition from the beginning, that the eternal lot of every soul is determined at death. "And it came to pass that the beggar died, and was carried by the angels into Abraham's bosom. And the rich man also died; and he was buried in hell" (Luke xvi. 22). Such also is the teaching of the Council of Florence (A. D. 1438-45). It is probable too that the Epistle to the Hebrews mentions this doctrine: "It is appointed unto men once to die, and after this the judgment" (Heb. ix. 27).

The dogma of the General Judgment at the end of the world is clearly set forth by the Saviour in Matt. xxv. 31-46 (*cf.* II. Cor. v. 10; Apoc. xx. 12), and is embodied in the Apostles', the Nicene, and the Athanasian Creeds. Its purpose is to manifest to the world the wisdom of the divine plan, to vindicate the offended majesty of Christ, and to show forth the glory of the just and the shame of the reprobate.

What, and where is Limbo?

Limbo is the place where the souls of the just, who died before the death of Jesus Christ, were detained. It was distinct from Purgatory, inasmuch as the souls there did not suffer, although they did not enjoy the Beatific Vision. It is mentioned several times in the New Testament: for instance, "Abraham's bosom" (Luke xvi. 22), "Paradise" (Luke xxiii. 43), and "the prison" (I. Pet. iii. 19). The Apostles' Creed calls it hell (a term sometimes used to mean any place not Heaven); "He descended into hell," for Christ after His death on the cross went to announce to the souls of Limbo the glad tidings of their redemption. "In which also coming, He preached to those spirits that were in prison" (I. Pet. iii. 19).

RESURRECTION OF THE BODY.

How is it possible that we shall all rise again with the same bodies that we had upon earth?

The Catholic Church teaches (IV. Lateran Council) that all men "will rise again with their own bodies which they now bear about with them" (Apostles', Nicene, and Athanasian Creeds).

This doctrine of the resurrection of the body, and its reuniting with the soul at the day of Judgment, cannot be proved from reason, but is the clear teaching of the Scriptures. The doctrine of the Jews is plain from Dan. xii. 2; II. Mach. vii. 9; John xi. 24. Our Lord expressly taught it against the Sadducees of His time, who denied it (Matt. xxii. 30; Luke xx. 37. *Cf.* John v. 28, vi. 39, xi. 25; Luke xiv. 14), and St. Paul mentions it frequently, especially I. Cor. xv. 12. (*Cf.* Acts xvii. 18, 31, 32, xxiii. 6, xxiv. 15, xxvi. 8; Rom. viii. 11; I. Cor. vi. 14; II. Cor. iv. 14; Phil. iii. 21; I. Thess. iv. 12–16; II. Tim. ii. 11; Heb. vi. 2).

It is undoubtedly the teaching of Revelation that we shall all rise again with the *same* bodies (I. Cor. xv. 53; Rom. viii. 11); but how far this identity is to be kept, we do not know. We can only give the answer of St. Paul to the objectors of his day, when he asked them to explain how it was that God made the wheat spring up from the dying of the seed. "Senseless man, that which thou sowest is not quickened, except it die first. . . . But God giveth it a body as He will; and to every seed its proper body" (I. Cor. xv. 36, 38).

What does your Church teach regarding the millennium? (Rev. xx. 4, 5).

The Church has defined nothing whatsoever on this subject. The reign of Christ for one thousand years (Apoc. xx. 1–10), with the two

resurrections of the just and the wicked, held
in the early Church by some few writers, is
contrary to the Scriptures, which speak only of
the two-fold coming of Christ; the first as the
Babe of Bethlehem (Luke i.), and the second
as the Judge of the living and the dead (Matt.
xxiv. 27, xxv.) The Apocalypse is one of the
most obscure portions of Holy Writ, and no
one pretends to be able to interpret it with
any certainty.

**Where in the Bible is the word " Purgatory "
found ?**

The word Purgatory is not found in the
Bible; but what does that prove ? Many other
terms, *v.g.*, the Trinity, the Incarnation—sacred
to every orthodox Protestant as well as Catholic—are likewise not in Holy Writ. The doctrine of Purgatory is in the Bible.

**What is the teaching of your Church with re-
gard to Purgatory, and on what authority does
it rest ?**

The Catholic Church teaches " that there is
a Purgatory, and that the souls there detained
are helped by the suffrages of the faithful, but
chiefly by the acceptable sacrifice of the altar "
(Trent, Sess. xxv.)

The strongest argument for the existence of

Purgatory and the practice of praying for the dead is the universal and constant witness of divine tradition as voiced in the writings of the Fathers (see " Faith of Catholics," vol. iii. pp. 139–205), in the ancient Liturgies of both East and West, in the inscriptions in the catacombs of Rome (Northcote, " The Roman Catacombs," ch. vii.), and in the Councils of Florence (A. D. 1438–45) and Trent (1545–63). Thus, Tertullian writes (about 204 A. D.) : " We make, on one day every year, oblations for the dead, as for their birthdays " (De Corona, n. 3).

The evidence of Scripture (II. Mach. xii. 43–46) shows the belief of the Jews in a middle state where the dead can profit by the good works (sacrifices) and prayers of the living : " And making a gathering, (Judas Machabeus) sent twelve thousand drachms of silver to Jerusalem for sacrifice to be offered for the sins of the dead. . . . It is therefore a holy and wholesome thought to pray for the dead, that they may be loosed from sins." The historical value of this book of Scripture cannot be denied by those who reject it as canonical, for we have even to this day the witness of the orthodox Jewish prayer-book to the fact of such prayers. Its inspiration rests on the same authority as Genesis and the Apocalypse,—the divine witness of the infallible Church of God. If the doctrine of Purgatory were an innovation of the

Pharisees, surely it would have fallen under the condemnation of the Saviour, for there can be no doubt that in His day it was, as it is now, a Jewish belief.

There are, moreover, proofs of the doctrine in the New Testament, as we learn from the interpretation of the Fathers of the early Church, viz., Matt. xii. 32, in which Christ speaks of slight sins being forgiven in the world to come; I. Cor. iii. 13-15, in which St. Paul mentions "the fire which shall try every man's work, and through which he himself shall be saved"; I. Pet. iii. 18-20, in which St. Peter tells how our Saviour preached the fact of His redemption to "those spirits that were in prison" (*cf.* Matt. v. 26).

It is indeed strange how, in the face of this overwhelming testimony, the early Reformers dared deny the doctrine. They believed that nothing defiled could enter heaven, and that "the eyes of God were too pure to look upon iniquity" (Apoc. xxi. 27; Habacuc i. 3). What, then, was to become of the millions of souls who were not perfectly pure from sin at the hour of death? The denial of Purgatory implies either the cruel doctrine that the greater number of even devout Christians are lost, which in the reaction to-day outside the Catholic Church accounts in some degree for the common denial of eternal punishment; or the

unwarranted and unproved assumption that
God by "some sudden, magical change" puri-
fies the soul at the instant of death. (Möhler,
"Symbolism," Book I. ch. iii. sec. xxiii.;
Oxenham, "Eschatology," ch. i. pp. 26-40.)

How logically is doctrine interwoven with
doctrine in the clear, consistent gospel of Jesus
Christ, so that a denial of one central dogma
means the overthrow of all. Luther's new theory of justification by faith alone, led him to
deny the fact of temporal punishment, the distinction between mortal and venial sin, the efficacy of indulgences, the existence of Purgatory, and the usefulness of prayers for the dead.

The doctrine of Purgatory follows clearly
from the doctrine that some die with the burden
of venial sins on their souls, or with the temporal punishment due to forgiven sin still un-
paid. How few souls are fit to be ushered into
the awful presence of God! Are there not
many slight sins in our life-time that we never
even ask pardon for? And, again, do you believe that a perfectly just God would grant
heaven immediately to the death-bed penitent
who had not the time to satisfy for all his sins,
or to pay to the last farthing the debt of temporal punishment?

Indeed, Protestants have admitted to me that
they have felt instinctively that some of their own
relatives were neither wicked enough to deserve

hell nor good enough to deserve heaven at the
hour of death, and that despite their doctrinal
denial, they had prayed for them. One Lutheran woman lately, in Baltimore, told me that
for years she had thus gone to the grave of one
she loved, and prayed there as earnestly as any
Catholic.

Even the pagan philosopher Plato distinguished between *curable* and *incurable* offences
to be punished hereafter,—the one for a time,
the other for ever. He writes in his Gorgias,
"But those that are benefited, at the same time
that they suffer punishment both from gods
and men, are such as have been guilty of curable offences; their benefit, however, both here
and in Hades, accrues to them through means
of pain and torments; for it is not possible to
be freed from injustice in any other way"
(Cary's translation, vol. i. p. 230, n. 171).

Many non-Catholics to-day are, therefore,
coming to realize how irrational and unchristian was the Reformation rejection of this most
consoling doctrine. Mallock writes: "It is
becoming fast recognized on all sides that it
(Purgatory) is the only doctrine that can bring
a belief in future rewards and punishments into
anything like accordance with our notions of
what is just and reasonable. So far from its
being a superfluous superstition, it is seen to be
just what is demanded at once by reason and

morality ; and a belief in it to be not an intellectual assent only, but a partial harmonizing of the whole moral ideal " ("Is Life Worth Living?" ch. xi. p. 290).

Did not Christ say to the good thief : "Verily, I say unto thee, to-day shalt thou be with me in paradise "? (Luke xxiii. 43).

Catholics, believing that Christ's soul immediately after His death went down to limbo to preach deliverance to the souls of the just there detained (I. Pet. iii. 19), declare that paradise in the above text does not refer to heaven at all, but to limbo.

But at any rate, the fact that Christ, in view of the dying thief's suffering and sorrow, remitted unto him all the punishment due to his sins, does not prove that Purgatory does not exist. For Catholics believe that God may at any time remit the guilt of sin and all the punishment due thereto, just as he always does in the sacrament of baptism ; but this is not His ordinary law, as taught by His divinely infallible Church.

How does the Church or the priest know when a person has been delivered from Purgatory ?

The Catholic Church does not pretend to know anything about the duration of the sufferings of Purgatory, save that God, who is infinite justice, will render to every one the punishment he deserves. "Thou shalt not go out from thence till thou repay the last farthing" (Matt. v. 26).

Is it just that God should pardon men, and punish them afterwards in Purgatory? Does not Scripture say: "Blessed are the dead which die in the Lord"? (Rev. xiv. 13).

This question has been answered above, where we gave several instances in Scripture of God pardoning the guilt of sin yet inflicting temporal punishment for it afterwards. We hold that the dead in Purgatory are blessed, for they are certain ultimately to see the face of God.

HEAVEN.

Is heaven a place, or a state of the soul?
What do we really know about heaven?

Heaven is both a *place* of everlasting happiness, and a *state of the soul* perfectly happy in the presence of God. (Matt. iii. 16; Acts vii. 55; Wisdom v. 16; Matt. xxv. 46; Matt. xviii. 10; I. Cor. xiii. 12; I. John iii. 2).

In it there will be none of the evils of this world, *v. g.*, hunger, thirst, labor, sorrow, sin, or death (Ps. v. 6, liv. 7; Isa. xxv. 8; Job iii. 17; John xvi. 20; Apoc. vii. 16, xxi. 4, 27, xxii. 5).

Its joys are beyond the power of the intellect to conceive: "Eye hath not seen, nor ear heard, neither hath it entered into the heart of man, what things God hath prepared for them that love Him " (I. Cor. ii. 9. *Cf.* Ps. xxxv. 9; Isa. lxiv. 4).

No one can enter heaven unless he be free from sin and the penalty due thereunto, " Nothing defiled can enter heaven " (Apoc. xxi. 27); and each soul there is rewarded according to his merits (Luke xix. 16; John xiv. 2 ; I. Cor. xv. 41 ; II. Cor. ix. 6).

Will we know our own relatives and friends in heaven ?

Undoubtedly, for the love of the brethren will be intensified and strengthened in the knowledge and love of God which comes of the Beatific Vision. Seeing God face to face (I. Cor. xiii. 12) as He is (I. John iii. 2), we must needs know and love all the citizens of God's Kingdom ; the love of the brethren is the necessary consequence of the love of God. The unity for which Christ prayed will then be perfectly realized : "that they all may be one, as thou Father in Me, and I in Thee ; that they also may be one in us " (John xvii. 21).

What is the meaning of the words : " Heaven and earth shall pass away, but my word shall not pass away " ? (Mark xiii. 31).

I never could understand why this question was asked so frequently, save perhaps for one reason, that the unthinking questioner imagined that the word " heaven " referred to God's kingdom hereafter, whereas it refers to the stars and planets of the material heavens.

The meaning of the Saviour is evident. He declares that all created things are uncertain and perishable, but that His word is certain and eternal. If, then, He, the Son of God, prophesy the fall of Jerusalem and His second " coming with great power and glory," His word must be accepted as true.

HELL.

Do you believe in a personal devil ?

Why does God not destroy the devil, if He is omnipotent ?

Why did God create Satan ?

No believer in the Scriptures can deny the existence of a personal devil. Throughout the Old and New Testament there is mention of Satan, Belial, Beelzebub (Luke x. 17; II. Cor. vi. 15; Matt. xii. 24), a wicked (I. John ii. 13), proud (I. Tim. iii. 6), powerful (Eph. ii. 2, vi. 12), cruel (Luke viii. 29, ix. 39; I Pet. v. 8), deceitful (Gen. iii. 4; II. Cor. xi. 14; Eph. vi. 11; II. Thess. ii. 9) Spirit, who tempted our first

parents in the Garden of Eden (Gen. iii. 1),
David (I. Paral. xxi. 1), Job (ii. 7), Judas
(Luke xxii. 3), our Saviour (Matt. iv. 10), and
tempts all men to his own eternal ruin of hell.
(I. Pet. v. 8; Matt. xxv. 41; Luke x. 18. *Cf.*
Matt. xii. 24; Luke xxii. 31; John viii. 44,
xiv. 30; II. Cor. iv. 4, xi. 3.)

God did not create the devil. Out of His
infinite goodness He created an angel, Lucifer,
the head of the angelic host, to serve Him
freely and love Him for ever. By refusing to
pay God the service and worship due Him,
Lucifer was cast into hell to become the leader
of the evil spirits.

Why did not God give him another trial?
We simply do not know. Why does God allow
him to exist? Because in His infinite wisdom
He made Lucifer an immortal spirit, and despite
his power to tempt men, God gives to every
man sufficient grace to resist. "God will not
suffer you to be tempted above that which you
are able" (I. Cor. x. 13). We might ask a
further question: Why does God allow any
wicked men to exist on this earth to tempt souls
to hell? It is part of the insoluble mystery of
evil. God is not unjust, for to all He gives free
will and grace sufficient for the gaining of eternal happiness.

Do you believe in progression after death? I

believe that ultimately all mankind will be saved ?

It was the doctrine of the first Universalists (Relly and Murray, circ. A. D. 1770) that the elect go directly to heaven at death, and the non-elect are purified by fire till the day of Judgment, when they too will be ultimately saved. Some knew the interval of time to be exactly forty-four thousand years! Later teachers (Ballou, 1790) denied all future punishment. Many Anglicans (Stanley, Maurice, Farrar, etc.) cherish a hope in the future salvation of all mankind (Farrar's "Eternal Hope —Mercy and Judgment ").

The Catholic Church declares that probation ends at death, and that there is no other chance hereafter for the repentance of the sinner dying in grievous sin. His sentence will be, "Depart from me, you cursed, into everlasting fire" (Matt. xxv. 41).

To suppose that hereafter the hardened sinner will repent, is to assume without warrant that punishment always causes repentance. But even in this world obstinate criminals become worse when they do not accept their punishment as the just due of their misdeeds. A prisoner who was nearing the end of a twenty years' sentence once told me, when I asked him was he sorry for the crime he committed: "No, and I will be revenged on society when I am

free." On what principle, then, can any one
claim that punishment hereafter will inevitably
work the conversion of the obdurate sinner?

**What must Catholics believe regarding eternal
punishment?**

What proof is there of eternal punishment?

The Catholic dogma declares there is a Hell,
or state of eternal punishment. Thus we read
in the Athanasian Creed: "And they that
have done good shall go into life everlasting,
and they that have done evil, into everlasting
fire." The proof of the doctrine is found in the
many clear texts of the Scriptures, and the constant witness of the Church of God from the
beginning. Again and again the Scriptures
expressly declare that the pains of hell are eternal, that the fire will not be extinguished, that
the worm (of remorse) will not die, that the
wicked shall never enter the kingdom of God,
etc. "Depart from me, you cursed, into everlasting fire." (Matt. xxv. 41). "Their worm
dieth not, and the fire is not extinguished.
. . . It is better for thee to enter into life
maimed, than having two hands to go into hell,
into unquenchable fire" (Mark ix. 44, 45).
"He that shall blaspheme against the Holy
Ghost shall never have forgiveness, but shall
be guilty of an everlasting sin" (Mark iii. 29).
"Neither fornicators, nor idolaters, nor adul-

terers . . . shall possess the kingdom of God" (I. Cor. vi. 9, 10). " Who shall suffer eternal punishment in destruction from the face of the Lord " (II. Thess. i. 9). " To whom the storm of darkness is reserved for ever " (Jude 13).

No forced interpretation of the word *aionios (eternal)* can gainsay the clear sense of the sacred text. " If Christ had intended to teach the doctrine of eternal punishment, could He possibly have taught it in plainer or more direct terms ? If He did not intend to teach it, could He possibly have chosen language more certain *à priori* to mislead, as the unbroken experience of eighteen centuries proves *à posteriori* that it always has misled the immense multitude of His disciples " (Oxenham, " Catholic Eschatology," ch. iv. p. 102).

Reason cannot demonstrate the dogma of eternal punishment, but it can show that this teaching of Revelation cannot be gainsaid by reason. The whole question of evil is one of the most obscure and difficult for the human mind ; yet the Catholic Church, while declaring that its perfect solution is for the world to come, has the best answer to all the objections of unbelief.

Men have sometimes asserted that eternal punishment was a doctrine evolved by Christianity the better to control the ignorant multitude. How, then, do they account for the Hell, or Tartarus, of Plato and of Virgil? (Abbé Meric, "L'Autre Vie," Paris, 1880; Oxenham, "Catholic Eschatology," London, 1876; "That Unknown Country," Article by Rev. A. F. Hewit, Springfield, Mass., 1889, pp. 459–474; Carle, "Du dogme catholique sur l'enfer," 1842; Shedd, Prot., "The Doctrine of Eternal Punishment"; *Dublin Review*, Jan., 1881.)

How can an infinitely good, merciful God condemn the creatures He loves to everlasting torments?

It is common with unbelievers to throw dust in the eyes of the ignorant by presenting one side of a question and ignoring the other, forgetting that Christianity is one great harmonious system of the Revelation of God. One moment the argument runs: " God is too good to punish His creatures for all eternity "; the next moment, to deny His providence, the same man will argue: " The world is too full of misery and wretchedness to be the creation of an All–Good Creator." God is too good—or God is too evil; it all depends on whether the objector would deny hell or providence. Is this honest? We must remember, too, that it is only the weakness of our intellects which makes us separate the attributes of God, which by their nature are one and identical.

Without any knowledge of Christian principles, it would seem at first sight that infinite goodness and mercy are incompatible with eternal punishment. Granting that after all explanations the element of mystery must remain when finite man considers the infinite counsels of God ("How incomprehensible are His judgments, and how unsearchable His ways," Rom. xi. 33), still, reason has an answer.

You have not considered, on the other hand, that the denial of eternal punishment cannot be reconciled with the justice of God.

Will you tell me that a just God, who is the Lawgiver and Lord of men, can give His kingdom to one guilty of unrepented murder, adultery, seduction, avarice, or drunkenness? That a just God can give eternal happiness to one who has all his life long despised and set at naught His mercy, and who has died obstinate in evil?

Man is not a mere automaton, nor a mere animal of sense and instinct, nor an independent, self-ruling being, but a creature created after God's image and likeness, with intellect to know the good and free will to choose it,—with sufficient grace always to know God's revelation, and to do God's will. If such a being deliberately abuse these gifts and graces, refusing to acknowledge his dependence on God his Creator and Lawgiver, freely choosing mere creatures in place of his God, and die insolently refusing to fulfil his destiny,—can God do aught to this adorer of self than to leave him to his choice for all eternity? Why, the un-repentant sinner would be as out of place in heaven as a tramp amid the luxury of an Inau-guration ball. A son has rebelled against a Father; a friend turned traitor against a Friend; a creature against a Creator—and yet forsooth Jesus Christ, the God of all justice, must say to the rebel creature that still hates Him : " Come, ye blessed of my Father, possess you the king-dom " (Matt. xxv. 34). This is only thought-less sentimentality, which, having lost alto-gether the conviction of the malice of sin, re-fuses to see God's justice in punishing the sinner.

How could a loving God create some of His creatures for eternal damnation ?

John Calvin in the sixteenth century taught that God created some men for eternal perdition, but this has never been the teaching of the Catholic Church. It was natural that men who mistook this cruel God for the God of the Chris-tians rejected Christianity altogether.

The Council of Trent condemned most strongly this doctrine of predestination, by declaring that God sincerely wills to save those who are not of the number of the predestined. (On

Justification, Sess. vi. can. 17. *Cf.* Matt. xxiii. 27; John iii. 16.) Indeed, the doctrine of the Catholic Church is that God sincerely wills all men to be saved, as is evident from the Scriptures : '' He is the propitiation for our sins ; and not for ours only, but also for those of the whole world '' (I. John ii. 2) ; '' Behold Him who taketh away the sin of the world '' (John i. 29) ; '' And Christ died for all '' (II. Cor. v. 15) ; '' God our Saviour who will have all men to be saved, and to come to the knowledge of the truth '' (I. Tim. ii. 4).

It is undoubtedly true that God foreknows the eternal loss of the unrepentant sinner. Why, then, continues our questioner, did He create such a one ?

There is a great mystery involved herein, yet it is wrong to accuse God of this evil ; He is not the author of any evil. God is the Eternal present ; with Him there is no past, there is no future. He is the All-Knowing One, or He ceases to be God. He knows the event, therefore, because it occurs ; but it does not occur because God knows it. His foreknowledge in no way affects our freedom of will.

We are created by God with intellect to know the good, and free will to choose it. Moral creatures, therefore, with a conscience within us judging knowingly the right and the wrong, we are responsible for the wrong freely chosen.

If we die in sin, we choose the wrong for all eternity; and having had the sufficient grace of. God to the last, we are guilty of our own damning. We cannot lay the responsibility of it upon Him. This is common sense. This is the teaching of the Church of God.

I do not comprehend it, you tell me. Do you expect to comprehend the mysteries of the Infinite God? Like one who, looking at the reverse side of a beautiful tapestry, sees only the mere unmeaning medley of numberless slipped stitches and knots, so we from our world point of view understand not the grand plan of God. One day from His view-point we shall behold the beauty of the design unintelligible to us now.

In things human, we readily see how foreknowledge does not imply the causing of the thing foreknown. I warn a poor swimmer not to venture in an angry sea, for I am certain he will drown if he attempt it. Am I responsible for his death because he went counter to my bidding?

God warns a soul he loves not to venture in the sea of grievous sin, for He is certain that if he persist therein he will perish for life everlasting. Is God responsible for the sinner's eternal death, because freely and deliberately he refused to obey the bidding of his Lord and Master?

But you will tell me the comparison is faulty. You could not help your stubborn friend, but

God could help the sinner by giving him more grace, so that he must needs repent. Why does He not do it? No one can answer this question. The distribution of God's graces is an incomprehensible mystery. We know, however, that God has given the sinner sufficient grace to save him, and that if he is lost he used his free will to resist grace, and so fell short of his eternal destiny. God could give enough grace to insure this man's salvation, but you cannot call Him unjust because He does not. The sinner has chosen sin freely, and God leaves him his choice for ever.

Suppose for an instant that God could not create a soul whom He foresaw would be lost by the abuse of free will and grace. It would follow then that every one, by the very fact of creation, and without any effort on their part, would be infallibly certain of heaven.

If this were the case, man, who is created with the free will to choose either good or evil, could give himself up to the full satisfaction of every evil desire and passion, feeling confident that God must one day give him eternal happiness. What becomes then of the distinction between good and evil? What sanction would there be to the moral law?

Indeed, the foreknowledge of eternal ruin of the sinner brings out—paradoxical as it may seem—the goodness of God, who deigned to give to certain ones the gift of existence, even though He knew they would abuse this gift.

But you may object further, why did God give men this perilous gift of free will?

God, in His infinite goodness, created men to His image and likeness, to be one with Him in love for all eternity. To love God, we must know Him and serve Him, and that freely. As a circle implies a centre, so man's dignity implies the freedom of choice. How absurd, then, to call God cruel if I abuse His most precious gift of free will to my eternal ruin.

What is the Catholic teaching regarding the torments of hell ?

How can God take delight for ever in the agony of his creatures ?

Archbishop Kenrick, in his Dogmatic Theology (Tract x. ch. 3), says : " Of the kinds of punishments which the condemned undergo, the Church has put forth no definition. No one has satisfactorily explained what punishments are designated by the name of fire in the Scriptures. It is sufficient to regard the suffering as proceeding from the condition in which sinners are placed as being remote from the kingdom of heaven. It is not necessary to conceive of God positively inflicting pain."

No, hell is made by man himself. Eternal damnation is not, as Calvin taught, an arbitrary infliction of an eternally predestined decree, nor a satisfaction of a revengeful deity, as unbelievers love to call it. The essential punishment of hell is the abandonment by God of the sinner to himself and his formed habits of sin. After years of helping grace, God has at last withdrawn from a man the graces he persistently rejected, and thus he dies in his sins.

Many reject the doctrine of eternal punishment because they believe the Catholic dogma implies God and His saints gloating over the sufferings of the damned, tormented by countless demons armed with many instruments of torture; nothing but a fathomless abyss of impenetrable darkness and unimaginable stench, where snakes, and griffins, and worms, and blue-tongued flames encircle and entwine the writhing bodies of the lost—a Hell of the imagination only, evolved in bad taste out of the fertile brain of some exaggerated preacher, or from too literal an interpretation of highly figurative passages of Scripture. But the language of poetry should not be confounded with the gospel of Jesus Christ.

The chief punishment of Hell is the loss of the vision of God, and all that this entails. The Church has defined nothing further, although the common teaching, based on many passages of the Scriptures (Matt. xiii. 42 ; Luke xvi. 24 ; Heb. x. 27 ; Apoc. xx. 9, etc.), is that

The description is correct

there will also be a sensible suffering caused by fire.

Is it not unjust to punish a few years of sin with an eternity of punishment?

The comparison should not be made between a few years of sin, on the one hand, and an eternity of punishment, on the other, but rather between a sinner eternally obstinate in unrepented sin and a God eternally holy, whose eyes are too pure to look on iniquity (Hab. i. 13).

A man that realizes the immeasurable malice of sin, and the infinite holiness of God, will not question the justice of eternal punishment, especially when he reflects that it is of the sinner's own choosing.

You do not pronounce society unjust when it inflicts the death-penalty—the greatest possible —upon the murderer. Indeed, human justice never considers the *duration* of a crime as the measure of the duration of the penalty to be inflicted.

I could never be happy in heaven if I thought that any one I loved, *i. e.*, my child, was suffering in hell. Can a man be happy in heaven with his wife and children in hell?

This is equivalent to saying: I could not be happy in heaven if I were unhappy for all eternity in heaven. We fully appreciate the extremes of human affection in this life. We have known mothers loving to the last the most cruel, unnatural sons; wives faithful to the most heartless, drunken husbands, and friends true to the most ungrateful wretches in the world. But there always is the hope in these loving hearts that one day—it may be years hence—their love shall be returned. It is worth waiting for.

But the hate in the soul of the sinful one in hell is everlasting. Can we love what God does not want us to love, because totally unworthy? An illustration will make this clear. You have a strong affection for your mother and for a friend you have known and loved from boyhood. Your friend calumniates the mother that bore you, to her great sorrow and unhappiness. The greater love you bear your mother compels you to abandon your friend.

So likewise in the life to come, you will see things as they are from the view-point of God. You will only love what He loves. If, indeed, there were anything in Hell or on earth that would interfere with the everlasting happiness of heaven, God would divert your soul from considering it. Make the comparison. God and your unrepentant child in Hell are in a relation similar to your mother and your false friend. The higher love leads you instantly to abandon the one who died "having trodden under foot the Son of God, . . . and having offered an affront to the Spirit of grace '' (Heb. x. 29).

Is not every man punished enough in this life ? I believe that the sinner has his hell here.

Would not a limited punishment hereafter suffice ?

'' It is not true . . . that the culprit experiences already in this life chastisement enough for his faults. Gnawing remorse indeed torments him ; the infirmities produced by his irregularities grow on him, and the disastrous consequences of his perverse conduct weigh him down ; but neither is he wanting in means to blunt the sharp sting of his conscience ; neither is he devoid of artifices to neutralize the evil effects of his revels, nor short of resources to come clear out of the false positions in which his excesses have involved him '' (J. Balmés, '' Letters to a Sceptic,'' iii.)

Our Lord plainly taught that the sinner might be fairly well content in this life. '' Woe to you (wicked) that are rich; for you have your consolation '' (Luke vi. 24); and in the parable of Dives and Lazarus (Luke xvi. 19–30), '' Son, remember that thou didst receive good things in thy life-time, and Lazarus evil things ; but now he is comforted, and thou art tormented.''

It is unreasonable to suppose that a punishment hereafter of limited duration would answer just as well. Taking men as they are, we know that only the threat of an eternity of punishment would be a sufficient curb to their evil passions and desires in this life, and therefore a means of their repentance. A sinner could brave God with impunity; he could set at naught the whole moral law when it went counter to his present, sensible enjoyment, if he knew that after a certain term of punishment—be it ten, one hundred, or one thousand years—he were to enjoy an eternity of happiness. Hell would cease instantly to be the sanction of the moral order; it would become a Purgatory, inspiring little or no terror to the heart of the average man. Every man knows that there is no probation in the life to come, and that he is responsible to God for the life he has lived on earth.

Is it conceivable in reason that God should consign the great majority of the human race to eternal perdition?

The Catholic Church never advanced such a doctrine. Some individual writers—Catholic and Protestant—have done so, but it is the part. of wisdom not to mistake the private speculations of a few concerning the unfathomable secrets of God for the teachings of Christianity.

Is it just that the entire pagan world—more than two-thirds of the race—should be damned to eternal hell-fire?

The Reformers held such a teaching as the logical consequence of their false notion of original sin, but the Catholic Church never did. With Luther, Calvin, and others the virtues of the heathen were vices deserving of damnation (Möhler's Symbolism, Book I. ch. ii. sec. vii.), and consequently there was no possibility of their salvation. The Catholic Church condemns strongly these false and cruel teachings, and holds most firmly that no one, pagan or Christian, will ever be eternally punished hereafter who has not with full knowledge and deliberate consent turned his back upon God, and died in mortal sin.

Is not the fear of hell a low, unworthy motive on which to base our moral life?

We are willing to grant that it is not the highest motive, which is sorrow for sin and service of God out of pure love for Himself alone. But all men are not saints, nor are all striving after perfection. This pretended contempt for the motive of fear is without basis in reason or the Word of God.

"The fear of the Lord," says Holy Writ, "is the beginning of wisdom" (Prov. ix. 10). Those that do not fear God will never love Him.

So in the Old Law God continually appeals to this motive (Ps. xxxiii. 10, lxv. 16, cxiii. 11; Eccl. v. 6; Dan. vi. 26), and Jesus Christ is equally explicit: "rather fear Him that can destroy both soul and body in Hell" (Matt. x. 28. *Cf.* Matt. iii. 7).

In this life men value the motive of fear, as is evident from the punishments in every law code of the world. The same men who deny it as a motive in the moral order will often tremble before the bar of public opinion when voiced in the denunciation of the public press, or will, again, at the hour of death dread the prospect of facing the God they strove vainly in life to deny.

Is not the doctrine of eternal punishment repugnant to the spirit of the age?

Yes, undoubtedly, if by "the spirit of the age" you mean the spirit of modern unbelief which denies the existence of a personal God as the Creator, Lord, or Final End of all creatures; which is jealous of the supernatural, intolerant of dogma, sceptical of grace, contemptuous of the Word of God; independent of tradition, loving self-indulgence, judging all things by merely natural standards; which has, in fine, lost all idea of responsibility to God, and all sense of sin and its immeasurable malice.

It is the tendency also of human legislation

to lessen the penalty for crime. No nation—and rightly too—would tolerate for a moment to-day the fearful dungeons and tortures of a few hundred years ago. Many indeed inveigh most strongly against the justice of capital punishment, while others falsely regard all criminal penalties as merely corrective.

But the eternal law of God does not change with the varying laws of men. Hell exists because of the free, deliberate refusal of the rational creature to fulfil the destiny for which he was created.

To the true Christian of any age the only question can be : Is the doctrine of eternal punishment true? And reason, Scripture, and the infallible witness of the living voice of God's true Church say that it is.

END.

TABLE OF CONTENTS.

GENERAL INDEX.

INDEX OF AUTHORS.

Printed in Great Britain
by Amazon